# CHINA'S AGRICULTURAL DEVELOPMENT

# The Chinese Economy Series

This series examines the immense importance of China within the global economy. Books in the series view the Chinese economy in many ways, such as: a transition economy; a bridge between the developing and developed nations; a vital member of the WTO; and even as a potential rival to the US.

Providing readers with high quality monographs and edited volumes by authors from East and West, this series is a truly global forum on one of the world's key economies.

*Series Editors*

Aimin Chen, Indiana State University, USA
Shunfeng Song, University of Nevada-Reno, USA

*Recent Titles in the Series*

**China's Rural Economy after WTO**
Edited by Shunfeng Song and Aimin Chen
ISBN 0 7546 4695 5

**Chinese Youth in Transition**
Edited by Jieying Xi, Yunxiao Sun and Jing Jian Xiao
ISBN 0 7546 4369 7

**Grains in China**
Edited by Zhang-Yue Zhou and Wei-Ming Tian
ISBN 0 7546 4280 1

**Critical Issues in China's Growth and Development**
Edited by Yum K. Kwan and Eden S.H. Yu
ISBN 0 7546 4270 4

**Urban Transformation in China**
Edited by Aimin Chen, Gordon G. Liu and Kevin H. Zhang
ISBN 0 7546 3312 8

**Urbanization and Social Welfare in China**
Edited by Aimin Chen, Gordon G. Liu and Kevin H. Zhang
ISBN 0 7546 3313 6

# China's Agricultural Development
## Challenges and Prospects


*Edited by*
XIAO-YUAN DONG
*University of Winnipeg, Canada*

SHUNFENG SONG
*University of Nevada, USA*

XIAOBO ZHANG
*International Food Policy Research Institute, USA*



Routledge
Taylor & Francis Group
LONDON AND NEW YORK

First published 2006 by Ashgate Publishing

Published 2016 by Routledge
2 Park Square, Milton Park, Abingdon, Oxon, OX14 4RN
711 Third Avenue, New York, NY 10017, USA

*Routledge is an imprint of the Taylor & Francis Group, an informa business*



**British Library Cataloguing in Publication Data**
China's agricultural development : challenges and
prospects. - (The Chinese economy series)
1.Rural development - China - Sociological aspects -
Congresses 2.Rural-urban migration - China - Congresses
3.Rural women - China - Social conditions - Congresses
4.Rural development - Government policy - China -
Congresses 5.Income distribution - China - Congresses
6.China - Rural conditions - Congresses 7.China - Economic
conditions - 1976-2000 - Congresses 8.China - Economic
conditions - 2000- - Congresses
I.Dong, Xiao-yuan II.Song, Shunfeng III.Zhang, Xiaobo
307.1'412'0951

**Library of Congress Cataloging-in-Publication Data**
China's agricultural development : challenges and prospects / edited by Xiao-yuan Dong, Shunfeng Song, and Xiaobo Zhang.
p. cm. -- (The Chinese economy series)
Includes index.
ISBN 0-7546-4696-3
1. China--Rural conditions. 2. Agriculture and state--China. 3. Agriculture--Economic aspects--China. 4. Agricultural productivity--China. I. Dong, Xiao-yuan. II. Song, Shunfeng. III. Zhang, Xiaobo. IV. Series.
HD2097.C4624 2006
338.10951--dc22

2006003897

ISBN 13: 978-0-7546-4696-9 (hbk)

# Contents

# List of Figures

# List of Tables

# List of Contributors

**Xiwen Chen** Deputy Director of the Central Finance and Economics Leading Group, and Professor of Agricultural Economics, People's University, China.

**Zhuo Chen** Post–doctoral Scholar, Chicago Center of Excellence in Health Promotion Economics, University of Chicago, USA.

**Xiao-yuan Dong** Professor of Economics, University of Winnipeg, Canada.

**Wen Du** Assistant vice-president, Enterprise Risk Assessment Department, Countrywide Financial Corporation, USA. P.E., econometrics

**Shenggen Fan** Senior Research Fellow, the International Food Policy Research Institute, USA.

**Robert W. Fogel** 1993 Nobel Laureate of Economics and Professor of Economics, University of Chicago, USA.

**Guangwen He** Professor of Economics, China Agriculture University, China.

**Nico Heerink** Beijing Office coordinator and research fellow, International Food Policy Research Institute, China office, Beijing, China.

**Chia-Chu Hou** Emeritus Professor of Economics, Soochow University, Taiwan, China.

**Jack W. Hou** Professor of Economics, California State University, Long beach, USA.

**Jikun Huang** Director of Center for Chinese Agricultural Policy, Institute of Geographical Sciences and Natural Resource Research, and Chinese Academy of Sciences, China.

**Wallace E. Huffman** Charles F. Curtiss Distinguished Professor of Agriculture, Professor of Economics, Iowa State University, USA.

**Arie Kuyvenhoven** Professor of Development Economics, Wageningen University, The Netherlands.

**Justin Yifu Lin** Professor of Economics and Director of the China Center for Economic Research , Peking University, China.

**Wencong Lu** Professor of Economics, Center for Agricultural and Rural Development, Zhejiang University, China.

**Qingsen Mao** Ph.D. candidate of Agricultural and Resource Economics, University of Tokyo, Japan.

**Futian Qu** Professor and Dean, College of Land Management, Nanjing Agricultural University, China.

**Scott Rozelle** Professor of Agricultural and Resource Economics, University of California, Davis, USA.

**Shunfeng Song** Professor of Economics, University of Nevada, Reno, USA.

**Shuhao Tan** Lecturer and searcher, Nanjing Agricultural University, China and Wageningen University, The Netherlands.

**Holly H. Wang** Associate Professor of Agricultural Economics, Washington State University, USA.

**Guanzhong James Wen** Associate Professor of Economics, Trinity College, Hartford, USA.

**Weiyong Yang** Lecturer, Robert Shuman University of Strabourg, France.

**Xiaobo Zhang** Senior Research Fellow, the International Food Policy Research Institute, USA.

# Part 1
# Overview of the Challenges and Options

## Chapter 1

# China's Agricultural Development: Challenges and Prospects

Xiao-yuan Dong
Shunfeng Song
Xiaobo Zhang

Given its size and importance, the agricultural economy of China commands considerable attention of development scholars and policymakers. Home to 800 million rural residents, the transformation of China's agricultural sector is necessary to achieve the country's goal of building a stable and productive society. China's performance in the agricultural sector would not only affect the world's food and agricultural markets but also have a profound impact on the global war on poverty.

Over the past twenty-five years, China has achieved remarkable growth in its agricultural and rural industries and has made significant progress in alleviating poverty. Since 1978, China's GDP has grown at an average rate of 9.4 per cent per year—its agricultural production at 5.2 per cent and its rural industry at 31 per cent. As a result, the number of people the rural population living below the official poverty line has declined from 40.6 per cent to less than 5 per cent. Despite the progress, however, China's rural sector still faces tremendous challenges. Agricultural productivity remains low, and the growth of rural income has lagged behind that of urban income. Consequently, the progress in poverty reduction has been stalled since the mid-1990s

With China's accession into the World Trade Organization, farmers face fierce competition from cheap imports, making them more vulnerable to economic uncertainty and risk. The problems concerning rural development—termed in the Chinese media as "san-nong-wenti," which means issues concerning agriculture, rural residents, and rural areas—have become a major subject of academic research and policy discussions in China and abroad in recent years.

This book explores the challenges relating to development that face the agricultural sector, evaluates the potential for meeting these challenges, and discusses policy measures to maintain a strong agricultural economy. Most of the articles in this book are selected from the papers presented at the three-day international symposium, "China's Rural Economy: Problems and Strategies," which was organized by the Chinese Economists Society in Hangzhou, China and began on June 25, 2004. At this conference, the participants discussed a wide range of pressing issues concerning China's rural development. The book collects the papers that focus on the issues concerning agricultural production and farming income.

The book is divided into three parts. The first part, "Overview of the Challenges and Option," identifies the main obstacles to rural development and suggests policies and actions to overcome them. The second part, "The Performance and Potentials of China's Agriculture," empirically assesses the performance and potential of China's agricultural production and explores the factors that affect agricultural productivity, and the third and final part, "Agricultural Risk Management," analyzes the impact of risk and uncertainty on farm production and evaluates the performance of emerging market mechanisms for risk management. The content of each section is briefly reviewed below.

Part 1 begins with the chapter contributed by Robert Fogel, the 1993 Nobel Laureate in Economics. In it, the author reviews the trends of economic growth in South and Southeast Asia over the past five decades. He rejects the pessimistic views on the sustainability of rapid growth achieved by the countries in this region and predicts that growth will continue at a high rate in Southeast Asia for at least another generation. Sustained growth at a high level is possible because these countries have great potential in raising their labor force participation rates, shifting their resources from low to high productivity sectors, increasing the average education level of their labor forces, and improving the quality of output through technological innovation.

Chapter 3 then follows with Justin Lin Yifu's "Several Strategic and Political Thoughts on Promoting Rural Development." In this chapter, the author examines the nature of the rural "san nong wenti" in China and discusses what policy measures should be taken to address it. According to the author, the essence of the so-called "san-nong-wenti" is the slow growth of farmer income and the growing disparity between rural and urban areas. He contends that policy measures aiming narrowly at boosting agricultural production, such as the provision of farm subsidies, cannot effectively raise the income of farmers in the long run and that in order to increase their income in a sustained, effective manner, measures must be taken to accelerate the reallocation of laborers from the agricultural to the non-agricultural sector, develop an integrated nationwide farm products market, advance agricultural technological progress, and integrate the Chinese economy into the global market.

In Chapter 4, Chen Xiwen identifies five critical issues confronting China's rural economy. These include: the difficulty to raise the income of farmers; the instability of grain production; the growing disputes over farmland requisition; the inadequate public investment in education and health; and the lack of advocacy organizations for rural residents. The author analyzes the causes and subsequent consequences of these problems and makes several policy suggestions. Like Lin, Chen argues that it is pivotal to transfer farmers to the non-agricultural sector. He also stresses the importance of increasing public investment in education and health in rural areas, accelerating the pace of land tenure reforms, and promoting grassroots democracy in rural villages.

Chapter 5 is contributed by Scott Rozelle, Jikun Huang, and Keijiro Otsuka. In it, the authors analyze the sustainability of China's dramatic transformation from an agricultural to an industrial society. In their view, financial resources are needed to facilitate rural-to-urban migration and invest in the education of children from rural households so that future generations will enjoy greater benefits and opportunities. This is crucial because when rural households are optimistic about their children's futures, they are less likely to revolt or cause some other type of instability. The authors also review the development of China's land rental and commodity markets as well as the trends in agricultural productivity and rural income. While being optimistic over the future prospect of China's agricultural growth, they contend that to sustain the growth in agricultural productivity, it is imperative to establish an adroit fiscal regime and informed local governance in the rural communities. Technological changes in agriculture must also be accelerated.

In Chapter 6, Shenggen Fan explores the opportunities and challenges that China's entry into the WTO has brought to the rural economy in the country's western regions. The author shows that in the western regions, issues, such as farmer incomes, poverty, spatial inequality, and rural-to-urban employment, seem bleak. Increased global integration offers western farmers an opportunity to catch up with the rest of the country by producing more high value-added crops or switching to non-agricultural employment. To create an enabling policy environment, the central government must increase its investment in the education, infrastructure, and available technology in west China, correct its urban-biased policies, and take measures to protect the western region's pristine natural environment.

Part 1 concludes with Chapter 7, contributed by Chia-Chu Hou and Jack W. Hou. The authors analyze how China's agricultural economy may benefit from the Farmers' Association in Taiwan. They argue that this type of rural organization, which is "for the farmers, of the farmers, by the farmers," may be particularly helpful for developing markets and promoting technological changes in China's western regions. As a collective, farmers will have more purchasing power and better access to loans from which they may gain essential farming supplies, such as pesticides, fertilizers, tractors, and plows. With increased incentives—grants, for example, rather than subsidies—and state guidance and encouragement, farmers can become profit-seeking entrepreneurs, and research institutions will be able to innovate and develop crops more suitable to the western provinces. Farmers associations can also help retain local savings for the development of west China. While illustrating the usefulness of learning from Taiwan's experience, the authors acknowledge that Mainland China should not blindly copy Taiwan's agricultural reform experience because of their inherent differences in terrain, climate, and size.

The second part of this book begins with Chapter 8 in which Shenggen Fan and Xiaobo Zhang use a new approach to analyze the growth of China's agricultural productivity. They argue that the conventional method, which estimates the total agricultural output with constant prices, may generate biased results when relative prices of agricultural products change dramatically. To correct such a bias, Fan and Zhang adopt a rolling-weight approach. Their study reveals that while the reform period witnessed decent growth rates in production and productivity, the official reports have underestimated the total input used and have consequently overstated the total output growth. Thus, regional inequality may be greater than originally believed, and reforms may not have been as effective as official statistics have illustrated for the less-developed regions.

In Chapter 9, Zhuo Chen and Wallace E. Huffman examine technical efficiency in agricultural production and its spatial features using data derived from a survey that covers more than 2,000 counties. Using a stochastic production frontier model, the authors illustrate the critical importance of improving agricultural efficiency and productivity for China's farmers to compete in the world market. As China is rapidly integrated into the global economy, spatial studies of efficiency are increasingly important in evaluating and understanding China's agricultural economy. Regional protectionism has prevented neighboring counties from benefiting from the spillover effects of technological changes and has also led to monopolization, corruption, and trade conflicts among the localities.

In Chapter 10, Tan Shuhao and his co-authors draw attention to measures which may help farmers use their land resources more efficiently. Following the adoption of the household responsibility system, farmland has become more fragmented. Using household survey data, the authors evaluate the effects of land fragmentation on the technical efficiency of rice producers in the southeast region of China. They find that the average plot size has a significantly positive effect on the technical efficiency of rice production. The results suggest that with existing technology, a sizeable gain in productivity can still be obtained through land consolidation.

The remaining two chapters of Part 2 analyze the ability of China's grain production to meet the country's growing demand for food and discuss the desirability of China's grain self-sufficiency policy. In Chapter 11, Wencong Lu estimates China's production and consumption of rice, wheat, and corn around 2010 using a general agricultural region equilibrium model. The results project that China's grain production will recover from its decline, which occurred in the late-1990s. While the predicted rate of grain self-sufficiency may fall below the official target, it should remain high by international standards. In addition, the gap between the demand and the supply of food in east and south China is expected to widen during the projection period. Lu argues that a sustained recovery in China's grain sector requires that the domestic grain market become more competitive and integrated with the global market.

In Chapter 12, James Wen addresses the concerns about China's grain security by using a new forecast method. Instead of analyzing the trends in excess demand, the author focuses on the question of whether or not China's grain production can meet the demand when the population reaches its peak level. Corroborating with the optimistic assessment by Wencong Lu, the results of this analysis indicate that

China is able to maintain high rates of grain self-sufficiency even when the demand for grain is at its maximum. The author argues that China should make the income of farmers—rather than grain security—the first priority and continue encouraging farmers to produce crops according to the regional comparative advantages.

The papers in the final part of this book focus on the issues concerning risk and uncertainty in the rural sector. In Chapter 13, Qingsen Mao studies the effect of agricultural income risks on the acreage decisions of farmers by estimating their supply response. He looks at the mixed-cropping systems of soybean and corn production using data covering eleven major soybean-producing provinces from 1986 to 2002. While the farmers' response to risk is found to be modest, the study shows that price fluctuations have brought about considerable risks to soybean and corn production.

In Chapter 14, Weiyong Yang studies the trends of farm diversification from grain production to commercial crops and the major forces driving this trend using a data set that covers twenty-nine Chinese provinces between 1986 and 2001. The results show that the diversification decisions made by farmers are jointly determined by relative prices of crops, risks, such as climatic hazards and price variability, the degree of openness to international markets, and the development of market mechanisms.

As risks and uncertainties become major determinants of agricultural production and the well-being of rural households, insurance markets have assumed an increasingly prominent role in risk management within the post-reform rural economy. In Chapter 15, Holly Wang and Guangwen He provide an empirical analysis of the demand for different types of insurance in rural China, such as healthcare, life, and crop production and marketing. The results show that the demand for insurance products is primarily determined by the education level of a household's decision maker, the number of children in the family, and the location. They also find that the need for insurance often exceeds demand by a large margin and that needs vary among the different types of insurance. The authors attribute the gap between the need and demand for insurance to high prices and the unavailability, or inconvenience, of insurance services.

Part 3 concludes with an empirical study of China's emerging future agricultural commodity market. Wen Du and Holly Wang analyze the future prices in the China Zhengzhou Commodity Exchange (CZCE) for the maturing wheat contract in May for 2000 through 2002 using three time-series models. The results show that the movement of future CZCE wheat prices resembles the general pattern of future commodity prices around the world. Hence, future wheat in the CZCE provide an effective channel for Chinese farmers to hedge price risks and insure profits in addition to helping the formation of a rational market expectation of price in both the short and long runs.

In summary, this book provides an updated, comprehensive overview of China's agricultural economy. It has analyzed the nature of "san-nong-wenti" as well as the pivotal role of agricultural growth in the overall development of the rural sector and examined the performance of China's agriculture in terms of regional development strategies and grain security policies. This book also sheds light on the emerging market for risk and uncertainty in China's rural sector. A policy consensus has emerged from the analyses of this book: to meet developmental challenges, policy efforts must improve the quality of rural China's human resources and infrastructure, promote technological innovations as well as production efficiency, and help market development. The success of China's drive toward modernization depends on maintaining a healthy agricultural economy.

**Acknowledgements**

We thank all the participants of the international symposium, "China's Rural Economy: Problems and Strategies," for contributing their quality research. We are grateful to the Zhejiang University, the Ford Foundation, and the International Development Research Centre, Canada for their financial support. We appreciate many referees for their constructive comments and suggestions, and finally, we acknowledge Qingmiao Hu, Caren Roblin, Kelly Wilkin, Cindy Zhao, and Zishi Zhao for their helpful research and editorial assistance in preparing this volume for publication.

# Introduction

Chapter 2

# High Performing Asian Economies: Retrospect and Prospect

Robert W. Fogel

In 1945, the idea of high performing Asian economies was not in the mind of American or European economists. In the United States economists worried about the problems created by the demobilization of 20 million people (half from military ranks and half from war industries) and their integration into the civilian labor force. There were widespread fears that America might slide into a severe new depression. In Europe the central issues turned around the Allied occupation of German and Italy and the restoration of the war-devastated economies. In Asia the central issues were the demilitarization of Japan and the restoration of the nations that had been occupied by Japan. On the horizon were problems related to the dismantling of the colonial empires of Britain, France, and other European powers.

Several events between 1945 and 1950 set the stage for the political economy of the remainder of the twentieth century. One was the outbreak of the cold war and the strategy of containing the expansionist ambitions of the Soviet Union. Another was the rapid recovery of Western Europe and the transformation of West Germany into an ally in the anti-communist coalition. A third was the communist victory in the Chinese civil war that followed the defeat of Japan. Still another important event was the partition of India into independent Hindu and Muslim nations. There was also the emergence of newly independent governments throughout South and Southeast Asia[1] that were each struggling to find its road to rapid economic growth.

As Table 2.1 shows, the countries of South and Southeast Asia were at different economic levels in 1950, at the beginning of this quest. Japan, an occupied nation, had suffered severe reversals in fortune and had slipped to a level of per capita income characteristic of a low-middle-income economy. Even the more prosperous Asian nations shown in Table 2.1 had a per capita income that was less than a quarter of that in the United States. In contrast, the war-ravaged economies of Europe were by 1950 already on their way to a quarter century of unprecedented economic growth that would raise standards of living, health, and life expectancy for ordinary people to levels that few would have predicted (Crafts and Toniolo,

[1] As used in this paper, the term "Southeast Asia" applies to the first group of eight nations in Table 2.2.

1996). Thus, the stage was set for intense debates among economists and policymakers about the way to deal with global disparities. Among the points at issue were the virtues of centralized and decentralized planning and whether international trade was a handmaiden of domestic economic growth or an obstacle to it.

It is also worth noting that by current standards the United States of 1950 was not a rich country, although it would have been classified at the top of the World Bank's category of "upper-middle-income" nations. France and the United Kingdom would also have fallen into the upper-middle-income category, but Germany and Italy would have been in the lower-middle income category, much closer to the more prosperous Asian nations than to the United States.

**Table 2.1 A comparison of the per capita income of 15 nations in 1950 (International dollars of 1990)**

| | |
|---|---|
| China | 439[1] |
| Hong Kong | 2,218[2] |
| Indonesia | 840[2] |
| Korea (South) | 770[2] |
| Malaysia | 1,559[2] |
| Singapore | 2,219[2] |
| Taiwan | 936[2] |
| Thailand | 817[2] |
| India | 619[1] |
| Japan | 1,926[2] |
| France | 5,270[3] |
| Germany | 3,881[2] |
| Italy | 3,502[2] |
| United Kingdom | 6,907[3] |
| United States | 9,561[3] |

*Notes*: Rank by World Bank standards of 1990:
1. Low-income.
2. Lower-middle income.
3. Upper-middle income.

*Source*: Maddison 2001.

During the 1950s and 1960s economists were particularly interested in the relative progress of India and China. The political leadership of both countries was heavily influenced by the Soviet model of centralized planning. Both countries developed successive 5-year plans for economic growth of their countries. These plans sought rapid economic growth by placing special emphasis on the rapid development of heavy industry. Both taxed rural areas to subsidize cities and urban industries.

However, India sought to achieve its objectives under a political democracy, in which some industries would have government backing but the bulk of economic production and distribution would be left to the private sector. It also embarked on a protectionist policy aimed at promoting infant industries. New financial institutions were set up that placed the supply of capital largely under the control of the government, which directed investment into sectors given prominence by the plan. The first 5-year plan, which ran from 1951–1956, was successful in meeting its goals and private enterprise expanded. As indicated by Table 2.2, the annual rate of growth in per capita income during the plan was in the neighborhood of 2 percent. However, annual net investment was in the neighborhood of just 6 or 7 percent (Pepelases, Mears and Adelman, 1961; Malenbaum, 1959 and 1982).

**Table 2.2 Average annual percentage rate of growth in per capita income, 10 HPAEs compared with 5 rich nations, by quinquennia, 1950-2002**

| | 1950-55 | 1955-60 | 1960-65 | 1965-70 | 1970-75 | 1975-80 | 1980-85 | 1985-90 | 1990-95 | 1995-2002 |
|---|---|---|---|---|---|---|---|---|---|---|
| China | 5.5 | 3.2 | 1.0 | 2.1 | 2.2 | 5.1 | 9.1 | 6.2 | 11.1 | 7.1 |
| Hong Kong | 3.5 | 3.5 | 9.0 | 3.4 | 4.2 | 8.9 | 4.0 | 6.7 | 3.1 | 1.4 |
| Indonesia | 3.3 | 0.7 | -0.6 | 3.8 | 4.7 | 5.9 | 3.9 | 5.1 | 5.8 | 0.4 |
| Korea (South) | 6.5 | 1.0 | 3.2 | 8.6 | 10.1 | 5.4 | 6.5 | 7.8 | 6.4 | 3.9 |
| Malaysia | -1.3 | 0.9 | 3.4 | 2.9 | 5.0 | 6.2 | 3.2 | 3.1 | 6.9 | 1.9 |
| Singapore | 1.2 | -0.4 | 2.9 | 10.7 | 7.7 | 8.2 | 2.2 | 6.2 | 5.9 | 2.5 |
| Taiwan[1] | 6.0 | 3.7 | 6.6 | 7.7 | 6.0 | 8.3 | 6.7 | 3.9 | 5.6 | 3.9 |
| Thailand | 3.0 | 2.7 | 3.9 | 5.3 | 2.9 | 5.6 | 3.7 | 8.4 | 7.6 | 0.6 |
| India | 1.8 | 2.2 | 0.5 | 2.4 | 0.7 | 0.7 | 3.3 | 4.2 | 3.2 | 3.7 |
| Japan | 7.0 | 7.5 | 8.3 | 10.4 | 3.2 | 3.5 | 2.6 | 4.3 | 1.2 | 0.8 |
| France | 3.7 | 3.6 | 4.4 | 4.5 | 2.6 | 2.6 | 1.4 | 2.7 | 0.7 | 1.8 |
| Germany | 8.3 | 5.8 | 3.6 | 3.4 | 2.1 | 3.3 | 1.3 | 2.9 | 1.8 | 1.2 |
| Italy | 6.0 | 4.8 | 5.1 | 5.0 | 2.1 | 5.8 | 1.8 | 3.0 | 1.1 | 1.5 |
| United Kingdom | 2.5 | 2.0 | 2.4 | 2.0 | 1.9 | 2.1 | 1.8 | 3.1 | 1.3 | 2.1 |
| United States | 2.7 | 0.8 | 3.4 | 2.3 | 1.6 | 2.6 | 2.1 | 2.3 | 1.2 | 1.9 |

*Notes:* 1. 1950–1995: Maddison 2001; 1995–2002: Asian Development Bank 2003a and 2003b.

*Sources*: 1950–1975: Maddison 2001; 1975–2002: World Bank, World Development Indicators Online.

See *http://www.worldbank.org/data/wdi2004/index.htm.*

By the early 1960s, the Indian economy began to stumble. Not all of the problems were due to errors by policymakers. Some problems arose from border clashes with Pakistan and China. Some of the food shortages were due to droughts. But the main pressure on the food supply was due to explosive growth of population as mortality rates fell sharply. As a result of the successful public health measures undertaken during the 1950s and 1960s, such killer diseases as cholera, malaria, and smallpox were brought under control, helping life expectancy at birth to rise from 32 to 51 years between 1950 and 1968 (Chandrasekhar, 1968). Moreover, growth of per capita income also raised the demand for food, putting upward pressure on food prices that pinched both the urban and rural poor. Government efforts at land reform may actually have increased rural inequality (Mellor et al. 1968; Blyn, 1971). Attempts at government controlled industrialization thwarted private investment and promoted uncompetitive enterprises (Shenoy, 1968; Sklaeiwitz, 1966 and 1971; Healy, 1972; cf. Bhagwati and Chakravarty, 1969). As a result, Indian growth slipped badly during the first half of the 1960s (see Table 2.2).

Although India and China were the cases most frequently discussed by economists, attention was also paid to other nations in Southeast Asia. During the 1960s, there was considerable pessimism about Indonesia's future. Although there was a spurt of economic growth immediately after independence, during which the nation recovered from the setbacks associated with the Japanese occupation, the economy stagnated between 1955 and 1965, a period long enough to make economists wonder if Indonesia could overcome its problems (Mears, 1961). Beginning with the mid-1960s, however, the country began vigorous growth that lasted for three decades (see Table 2.2). Malaysia and Singapore also stagnated during the decade of the 1950s, contributing to the sense among some Western economists that adverse institutional factors might thwart their development. But in these countries fortunes changed decisively in the 1960s.

Table 2.2 shows that eight Southeast Asian nations all grew vigorously from 1965 on, and that several of them (China, Hong Kong, Taiwan and Thailand) had vigorous economic growth throughout the second half of the twentieth century. Indeed, their growth rates far exceeded the previous growth rates of the industrialized countries. Few American or European economists anticipated growth rates that would double, triple or quadruple the long-term rates of the industrial leaders between 1820 and 1950.

The most startling change of fortunes was in Japan. With outbreak of the Korean War, United Nations forces placed large orders with Japan, greatly stimulating its industrial growth. Even after the end of fighting, Japan's economy benefited from large orders for the build-up of the U.S. military establishment in the Pacific region. The Japanese export boom powered the dramatic rise in the Japanese economy. In one industry after another, including scientific instruments, cameras, sewing machines, and shipbuilding, Japanese firms displayed their command of the latest technology. During the 1960s, Japan moved from the production of under a half million cars to the world's second largest supplier, displacing Germany and France, among others. The rise of auto production helped promote the expansion of steel and moved the country toward world preeminence in that basic product (Allen, 1972). As Table 2.2 shows, from 1950 through 1970, the growth of Japanese per capita income exceeded that of all the other high performing economies. In the space of two decades Japanese per capita income increased by more than fivefold, a feat that had required more than a century for the nations that led the industrial revolution (Kuznets, 1971; Maddison, 1995). Although the growth of Japanese per capita income slowed after 1970, it still increased by about 40 percent between 1970 and 1980, making it the second largest economy in the world, bigger than France and the UK combined (Maddison, 1995).

During the late 1960s and early 1970s, many analysts became alarmed at what appeared to be the unchecked growth of population in Asia. It was widely predicted that such growth would not only swamp the capacity of South and Southeast Asia to feed itself, but would also smother the tenuous economic growth of the region. In the 1950s, many demographers had predicted that population growth would moderate, because a decline in fertility would soon follow the decline in the death rate, which had caused the Asian population explosion. That view was called the theory of the demographic transition. But fertility rates remained high through the end of the 1960s, causing some demographers to declare that the theory of the demographic transition was dead (Coale, 1975).

At it turned out, that gloomy forecast was incorrect. As Table 2.3 shows, between 1970 and 1980, total fertility rates fell sharply in all Southeast Asian nations. Today all of these nations, except for Malaysia and Indonesia have total fertility rates below reproduction. Indeed, fertility rates in most of these nations are below the fertility rates of three of the five rich nations shown in Table 2.3.

The forecast that Southeast Asia would be unable to feed itself because of the unbridled growth of population also turned out be erroneous. Table 2.4 shows the food situation throughout South and Southeast Asia in 1961. Per capita consumption of calories in China, even after the famine, was at or below the level of consumption in England and France toward the end of the eighteenth century. The same desperate situation prevailed in India, Thailand, and Korea. By 2000 the food situation had changed dramatically. Despite the erroneous agricultural policies that precipitated the famine of 1960-1961, and again slowed agriculture during the "Cultural Revolution" of 1966–1967, China's progress in agriculture between 1962 and 2000 has been remarkable (Clark, 1976). China not only found a way to feed itself, but did so well enough to increase its average daily consumption of calories by 73 percent, despite the near doubling of its population (cf. Lin, 1998).

**Table 2.3 Secular trends in total fertility rates**

| | 1950 | 1960 | 1970 | 1980 | 1990 | 2002 |
|---|---|---|---|---|---|---|
| China | 6.24 | 5.93 | 4.76 | 2.68[1] | 2.10 | 1.88 |
| Hong Kong | 4.43 | 4.97[3] | 3.49 | 2.06 | 1.27 | 0.96 |
| Indonesia | 5.49 | 5.42 | 5.10 | 4.10 | 3.04 | 2.32 |
| Korea (South) | 5.18 | 5.60 | 5.24 | 4.02 | 1.77 | 1.45 |
| Malaysia | 6.83 | 6.72 | 5.15 | 3.91 | 3.77 | 2.85 |
| Singapore | 6.41 | 5.43[4] | 3.10 | 1.74 | 1.87 | 1.37 |
| Taiwan | — | 5.79 | 4.00 | 2.51 | 2.27 | 1.3 |
| Thailand | 6.62 | 6.42 | 5.01 | 3.52 | | 1.80 |
| | | | | | | |
| India | 5.97 | 5.81 | 5.43 | 4.75 | 3.80 | 2.92 |
| Japan | 3.30[2] | 2.01 | 2.07 | 1.74 | 1.54 | 1.33 |
| | | | | | | |
| France | 2.86[2] | 2.80[3] | 2.48 | 1.95 | 1.78 | 1.88 |
| Germany (West) | 2.10 | 2.41 | 2.01 | 1.46 | 1.45 | 1.35 |
| Italy | 2.40[2] | 2.42[3] | 2.38 | 1.64 | 1.26 | 1.25 |
| United Kingdom | 2.18 | 2.82 | 2.45 | 1.89 | 1.83 | 1.66 |
| United States | 3.08 | 3.65 | 2.47 | 1.84 | 2.08 | 2.10 |

*Notes*: 1: 1981; 2: 1951; 3: 1961; 4: 1962.
*Sources*: Keyfitz and Flieger 1990; Population Reference Bureau
(see *http://www.prb.org/datafind/datafinder.htm*);
World Bank, World Development Indicators Online
(see *http://www.worldbank.org/data/wdi2004/index.htm*).

Although not as dramatic, there were also substantial gains in caloric consumption in the rest of South and Southeast Asia, ranging from 12 to 68 percent. Another point worth noting is the improvement in the quality of the diet, as indicated by the increase in the proportion of nutrients coming from animals. In China the rise was from under 4 to over 19 percent of total caloric consumption. Only Indonesia and India still have levels of the consumption of animal products that hark back to eighteenth-century conditions in England and France. Still another problem is the unequal distribution of food in many of the nations of South and Southeast Asia. In these countries, the proportion of low birth weights is still high, which implies the early onset of chronic disabilities at middle and late ages, a problem that will contribute to the high cost of medical care for the elderly in future years (Barker, 1998; Doblhammer and Vaupel 2001, Fogel, 2003 and 2004).

So far, I have focused on what has been accomplished in Southeast Asia to date, an accomplishment that has been hailed widely as an economic miracle. What about the future? Has the economic miracle run out of steam, as some analysts believe, or is there room for vigorous growth until 2030 and beyond? I believe that growth rates will continue at high levels in Southeast Asia for at least another generation. My forecast rests on three factors.

First, labor force participation rates will probably increase beyond current levels in most HPAEs. Both economic and demographic factors suggest that LFPR could rise to 60 percent or more. China is already near that level, so change in its LFPR will probably contribute little to its growth. However, given the large differences in labor productivity within sectors (see Table 2.5), shifts of labor from agriculture to services and industry and a small increase in the LFPR could account for 30 percent of the Chinese growth rate. In other words, labor productivity in China has to grow within sectors by about 5 percent per annum to produce a total growth rate in per capita income of 7 percent. Intersectoral shifts and increases in LFPR are also likely to account for between a fifth and a third of the total growth of per capita income in other Southeast Asian economies.

Second, further increases in the education level of the labor force should add to labor productivity and economic growth. Table 2.6 shows gross enrollment ratios in 1980 and 1997 in primary, secondary, and tertiary schools. At the primary level most of the HPAEs have reached the educational levels of the rich countries. With the exception of South Korea, however, the HPAEs are still a quarter to a half below the enrollment levels in secondary schools attained by rich nations. The biggest gap is at the tertiary level where, except for South Korea, enrollment rates are generally less than a fifth of the U.S. level. Closing the educational gap will improve the quality of the labor force in the HPAEs, and will also permit them to move to the frontier of technological innovation. The growth in the number of highly trained professionals will not only speed up technological catch-up in the HPAEs, but will also increase the global pace of technological change. The greater the number of scientists trying to advance the frontier of knowledge in stem cell research, nanotechnology, genetic engineering, and information technology, the more rapid the advance in science and technology is likely to be.

**Table 2.4 Trends in caloric consumption**

| | In calories per capita per day | | Percentage increase | Percentage of calories from animals | |
|---|---|---|---|---|---|
| | 1961 | 2000 | | 1961 | 2000 |
| China | 1725[1] | 2979 | 72.7 | 3.8 | 19.4 |
| Hong Kong | | | | | |
| Indonesia | 1727 | 2913 | 68.7 | 2.9 | 4.1 |
| Korea (South) | 2147 | 3093 | 44.1 | 2.7 | 15.0 |
| Malaysia | 2401 | 2917 | 21.5 | 10.5 | 17.8 |
| Singapore | | | | | |
| Taiwan | | | | | |
| Thailand | 1938 | 2459 | 26.8 | 8.8 | 11.7 |
| India | 2073 | 2489 | 20.1 | 5.5 | 7.9 |
| Japan | 2468 | 2753 | 11.5 | 9.6 | 20.5 |
| France | 3194 | 3597 | 12.6 | 31.7 | 37.7 |
| Germany | 2889 | 3505 | 21.3 | 32.7 | 30.0 |
| Italy | 2914 | 3663 | 25.7 | 15.5 | 25.5 |
| United Kingdom | 3240 | 3312 | 2.2 | 38.8 | 30.1 |
| United States | 2883 | 3814 | 32.3 | 35.1 | 27.4 |
| World | 2255 | 2805 | 24.4 | | |

*Note*: 1: 1962.
*Source*: FAOSTAT nutritional data, 2004 (*http://apps.fao.org/default.jsp*), using the "Food Balance Sheets" data collection.

**Table 2.5 Labor productivity by sector**

| | Distribution of the Labor Force in 2000 | | | Value Added per Worker in 2000 in PPP Dollars 1995 | | |
|---|---|---|---|---|---|---|
| | A | I | S | A | I | S |
| China | 50 | 22 | 28 | 448 | 3,205 | 1,534 |
| Hong Kong | 0 | 20 | 79 | -- | -- | -- |
| Indonesia | 45 | 17 | 37 | 747 | 4,550 | 1,025 |
| Korea | 11 | 28 | 61 | 13,758 | 41,492 | 21,164 |
| Malaysia | 18 | 32 | 50 | 6,894 | 15,625 | 9,800 |
| Singapore | 0 | 34 | 65 | -- | 55,852 | 53,307 |
| Thailand | 49 | 19 | 32 | 847 | 10,241 | 6864 |

*Notes*: A: agriculture; I: industry; S: services.
*Sources*: World Bank, World Development Indicators Online (see *http://www.worldbank.org/data/wdi2004/index.htm*); China Statistical Yearbook 2003.

**Table 2.6 Gross enrollment ratios**

| | Primary School | | Secondary School | | Tertiary School | | Age for compulsory attendance |
|---|---|---|---|---|---|---|---|
| | 1980 | 1997 | 1980 | 1997 | 1980 | 1997 | |
| China | 113 | 123 | 46 | 70 | 2 | 6 | 7–15 |
| Hong Kong | 107 | 94 | 64 | 73 | 10 | 22 | |
| Indonesia | 107 | 113 | 20 | 56 | 4 | 11 | 7–15 |
| Korea (South) | 110 | 94 | 78 | 102 | 15 | 68 | 6–15 |
| Malaysia | 94 | 101 | 48 | 64 | 4 | 12 | |
| Singapore | | | | | | | |
| Taiwan | | | | | | | |
| Thailand | 99 | 87 | 35 | 58 | 5 | 21 | 6–14 |
| | | | | | | | |
| India | 83 | 100 | 30 | 49 | 5 | 7 | 6–14 |
| Japan | 101 | 101 | 93 | 103 | 31 | 41 | 6–15 |
| | | | | | | | |
| France | 111 | 105 | 85 | 111 | 25 | 51 | 6–16 |
| Germany | — | 104 | — | 104 | 27 | 47 | 6–18 |
| Italy | 103 | 101 | 72 | 95 | 27 | 47 | 6–14 |
| United Kingdom | 104 | 116 | 83 | 129 | 19 | 52 | 5–16 |
| United States | 99 | 102 | 91 | 97 | 56 | 81 | 6–16 |

*Note*: 1. Gross enrollment ratios are equal to the total enrollment of all ages in the school level divided by the population of the specific ages that correspond to the specific age groups that correspond to the school level. Ratios may exceed 100 because of the students outside the relevant age range.
*Source*: National Center for Education Statistics 2002.

Third, as HPAEs become rich, and as labor becomes concentrated in the service sector, errors in the measurement of national income become increasingly severe. Economists in the United States have identified this problem. It is now clear that many of the numbers I have presented for the United States badly underestimate U.S. economic growth because they do not take into account improvements in the quality of output, especially in such services as education and health-care. Children in secondary schools are taught more today than post-graduate college students used to be taught a generation ago, let alone two generations ago.

Even more dramatic are the improvements in health care. A century and a half ago, people in their late thirties and early forties were more afflicted by chronic disabilities than people in their late sixties and early seventies are today. Not only has the average age of onset of disabilities been delayed by a decade or so, but once they appear, there are now numerous effective interventions. Hernias that used to be permanent and exceedingly painful conditions, afflicting one out of every four males, can now be repaired by a surgical procedure that in the U.S. requires hospitalization for only 23 hours. Other areas where medical interventions have been highly effective include genito-urinary conditions, control of hypertension and reduction in the incidence of stroke, replacement of knee and hip joints, curing of cataracts, and chemotherapies that reduce the incidence of osteoporosis and heart disease (Fogel, 2004).

Yet most of these great advances in health care and education are overlooked in accounts of Gross Domestic Product (GDP), because the values of these sectors are measured by inputs instead of by output. An hour of a doctor's time is considered no more effective today than an hour of a doctor's time was half a century ago, before the age of antibiotics and modern surgery. It has recently been estimated that improvements in health care, if properly measured, are at least twice the cost of health care, but such calculations have not yet made their way into the GDP accounts (Cutler and McClellan, 2001; Murphy and Topel, 2003; Nordhaus, 2003). In the case of the United States, my own rough estimates indicate that allowance for such factors as the increase in leisure time, the improvement in the quality of health care, and the improvements in the quality of education would come close to doubling the U.S. annual growth rate of per capita income over the past century (from 2.0 to 3.6 percent per annum).

What is the implication of these statistics for the understanding of change in standards of living for the typical American? If we use the conventional measure of growth, the real income of the typical American in 2000 was seven times greater than it was in 1900. However, if the adjusted measure is used, Americans in 2000 had real incomes that are 34 times greater than in 1900. In other words, 80 percent of the goods and services that Americans enjoy today are outside of the measured economy.

I close with a final question. Suppose HPAEs are able to grow at 6 or 7 percent per capita per annum for another generation. Does that mean that technological leadership will pass from the West to Southeast Asia? My answer is, not necessarily. Since new technologies in the information, biomedical, genetic engineering, and energy production industries are driven by the level of basic scientific knowledge, the key issue is not only the speed with which the HPAEs will be able to develop a large cadre of advanced scientists. It also turns on how rapidly these scientists can discover the most promising uncharted frontiers of scientific research.

The American experience shows that scaling such heights is not an easy task. The United States began the process of rivaling Western Europe in natural science when it began establishing post-graduate research programs in the U.S., beginning about 1875. During the next quarter century it sent some of its most promising young scientists to Europe to study with the great masters in Germany, France, and Great Britain. That policy yielded some successes, as indicated by the occasional Nobel prizes awarded to Americans. Yet in such fields as physics and chemistry, the Europeans remained dominant down to the outbreak of World War II. It was not until some of the European master-scientists emigrated to the United States, chased out of Europe by the Nazis, that the U.S. was able to gain the scientific dominance that it achieved during the second half of the twentieth century.

The conclusion I draw from that experience is that scientific training is still an artisanal craft that requires not just a few years of contact between the masters and students, but decades of patient interaction. It is not, of course, precluded that the HPAEs will do better than the U.S. did. Perhaps the old masters in the West will become too narrow in the range of issues they are willing to entertain and create new openings for younger minds. In any case, it will be interesting to see how the race for scientific excellence unfolds in the new millennium.

## References

Allen, G.C., *A short economic history of modern Japan*, 3rd edn (London: Allen & Unwin, 1972).

Asian Development Bank, *Asian development 2003 statistical appendix* (Oxford: Oxford University Press, 2003a).

———, *Key indicators 2003*, vol.34, (Manila: Asian Development Bank, 2003b).

Barker, D.J.P., *Mothers, babies, and health in later life*. (Edinburgh: Churchill Livingstone, 1998).

Bhagwati, J. and Chakravarty, S., 'Contributions to Indian economic analysis: A survey', *American Economic Review* 59, 4 (suppl.) (1969): 1–73.

Blyn, G., Review of *Developing rural India: Plan and practice*, by John W. Mellor, Thomas F. Weaver, Uma J. Lele, and Sheldon R. Simon. *Economic Development and Cultural Change* 19, (1971): 334–337.

Chandrasekhar, S., 'How India is tackling her population problem', *Foreign Affairs* 47 (1968): 138–150.

*China Statistical Yearbook 2003* (Beijing: China Statistics Press, 2003).

Clark, C., 'Economic development in communist China', *Journal of Political Economy* 84 (1976): 239–264.

Coale, A.J., 'The demographic transition', In *The population debate: Dimensions and perspectives. Papers of the World Population Conference, Bucharest, 1974*, (New York: United Nations, 1975), pp.347-355.

Crafts, N.F.R. and Toniolo, G., *Economic growth in Europe since 1945* (Cambridge: Cambridge University Press, 1996).

Cutler, D.M. and McClellan, M., 'Is technological change in medicine worth it'? *Health Affairs* 20, 5 (2001): 11–29.

Gabriele, D. and Vaupel, J.W., 'Life span depends on month of birth', *Proceedings of the National Academy of Sciences*, USA 98 (2001): 2934–2939.

Fogel, R.W., 'Forecasting the demand for health care in OECD nations and China'. *Contemporary Economic Policy* 21 (2003): 1–10.

———,*The escape from hunger and premature death, 1700–2100: Europe, America, and the Third World* (New York: Cambridge University Press, 2004).

Ghosh, A., 'India: Drifting toward chaos', *Wall Street Journal*(1971).

Healy, D.T., 'Development policy: New thinking about an interpretation', *Journal of Economic Literature* 10 (1972): 757–797.

Keyfitz, N. and Flieger, W., *World population growth and aging: Demographic trends in the twentieth century* (Chicago: University of Chicago Press, 1990).
Kuznets, S., *Economic growth of nations: Total output and production structure* (Chicago: University of Chicago Press, 1971).
Lin, J.Y., 'How did China feed itself in the past? How will China feed itself in the future' (Second Distinguished Economist Lecture presented, Centro Internacional Mejoramiento de Maiz y Trigo, Mèxico, D. F., Mexico, 9 January, 1998).
Maddison, A., *Monitoring the world economy* (Paris: OECD, 1995).
———, *The world economy: A millennial perspective* (Paris and Washington, DC: Organisation for Economic Cooperation and Development, 2001).
Malenbaum, W., 'India and China: Contrasts in development performance', *American Economic Review* 49 (1959): 284–309.
———, 'Modern economic growth in India and China: The comparison revisited, 1950–1980', *Economic Development and Cultural Change* 31 (1982): 45–84.
Mears, L.A., Indonesia. In Pepelases, Mears, and Adelman (1961), pp .418–467.
Mellor, J.W., Weaver, T.F., Lele, U.J. and Simon, S.R., *Developing rural India: Plan and practice* (Ithaca, NY: Cornell University Press, 1968).
Murphy, K.M. and Topel, R.H., 'The economic value of medical research', In *Measuring the gains from medical research: An economic approach,* ed. Kevin M. Murphy and Robert H. Topel (Chicago: University of Chicago Press, 2003).
National Center for Education Statistics, Digest of education statistics, 2002, Chapter 6, International comparisons of education, table 2.394. Available online at http://www.nces.ed.gov/programs/digest/d02/tables/dt394.aps.
Nordhaus, W.D., 'The health of nations: The contribution of improved health to living standards', In *Measuring the gains from medical research: An economic approach,* ed. Kevin M. Murphy and Robert H. Topel. (Chicago: University of Chicago Press, 2003).
Pepelases, A., Mears, L.A. and Adelman. I., *Economic development: Analysis and Case Studies* (New York: Harper and Brothers, 1961).
Shenoy, B.R., 'India: "Planning" for economic disaster', *Wall Street Journal*, 23 May 1968.
Sklaeiwitz, N., 'India's food plight', *Wall Street Journal*, 7 June 1966.

Chapter 3

# Several Strategic and Political Thoughts on Boosting Rural Development*

Justin Yifu Lin

## 1 Introduction

In the six years after Household Responsibility System reform in 1978, China had achieved fast development in agriculture. From 1978 to 1984, the grain production stepped up onto a new stage and has established what is later called the equilibrium between the supply and demand for grain. At the same time, the income of farmers increased rapidly, and the gap between urban and rural areas greatly narrowed. The situation was great. As our country has always attached an importance to grain production, the settlement of the grain problem made the government feel much more at ease. The government directed the market-oriented reform to take place in the cities in 1985, and our economy has since experienced fast economic growth for more than 20 consecutive years. Statistics show that from 1978 to 2003, our gross domestic product (GDP) had an average growth rate of 9.4 percent, which was the fastest growth rate in the world at that time—an achievement beyond anyone's expectations.

At the beginning of the reform in 1978, Deng Xiaoping put forward his goal to quadruple China's GDP in 20 years, suggesting an average annual growth rate of 7 percent, but we had attained 9.4 percent. Our foreign trade had also grown considerably during this period. Between 1978 and 2003, the annual growth rate of our foreign trade was 6 percent, which is 41 times that of 25 years ago, and China's foreign trade volume had risen from 31st to 3rd in worldwide ranking. This reform, which began in the countryside, has tremendously changed the Chinese economy. Recently, however, rural problems—especially the so-called *san-nong wenti* or *san-nong* problems—have received widespread attention both in China and internationally. As for the *san-nong* problems, we usually say, "the rural areas are so poor, farmers so toilsome, and agriculture so dangerous." This has drawn significant attention from various levels of government, including central. For example, the 16th National Congress put forward the goal of building a *xiaokang* (well-off) society. When talking about this goal, President Hu Jintao said that both the

* This article is based on a talk given at the annual Chinese Economists Society conference in June 2004, Hangzhou, China and translated by Qingting Hu at Peking Univeristy.

difficulty and emphasis of realizing this goal lie in the countryside, and he called for the whole Party to treat rural work as the most important task. The No. 1 document—issued jointly by the central government and Agricultural Department—is also about how to solve *san-nong* problems.

## 2 The Essence of the *San-nong* Problems: The Income of Farmers

In order to solve *san-nong* problems, it is necessary to revisit the sentence "the countryside is so poor, farmers so toilsome, and agriculture so dangerous" and to find out the key issue at stake. In my opinion, the sentence might not have accurately depicted our present rural problems.

As for agricultural production, it is no big problem, at least so far. From the Household Responsibility System at the beginning of the reform in 1978 through 1984, there appeared what Professor Zhou Qiren from Peking University called the fast growth of agricultural production, an unconventionally rapid growth at an average of 7.7 percent every year. In 1985, our reform entered the cities. Over the course of the next 18 years, the growth of agricultural production still reached 5.8 percent—measured by fixed price. Even from 1998 through 2003—when the *san-nong* problems were believed to be grave—the growth rate was still at 4.5 percent.

In agricultural and developmental economies, if a nation's agricultural production grows 1 percent faster than the population over the long-term--or if agricultural production maintains a 3 percent growth rate—then the nation's agriculture is normal. After 1998, the growth rate of agricultural production maintained 4.5 percent, while our natural population growth rate was only 0.8 percent. In other words, our agricultural growth rate has been 3.7 percent higher than the population growth rate. Therefore, we can then say that our agricultural production is reliable.

In regard to the *san-nong* problems, the problem lies in the so-called "the countryside is so poor, farmer so toilsome." The fact that "the countryside is so poor" reflects the ever-widening income gap between urban and rural workers. Presently, urban residents receive a higher income of 8,000 *yuan*, which equals about $1,000—still significantly lower than the income level of many other countries. Therefore, the core of the *san-nong* problems is still the income of farmers. The so-called "farmers so toilsome" means that a farmer's burden is heavy. We know that in areas where farmers are heavily burdened, their income grows rather slowly. In Zhejiang and Jiangsu provinces, where the income of farmers grows rapidly, no such heavy burden problems exist. Hence, the key to the *san-nong* problems is the slow income growth for farmers.

Statistics confirm the problem: from 1978 to 1984—thanks to the implementation of the Household Responsibility System, the rise of farmer enthusiasm, the increase of agricultural production, and the government's price rise, farmer income grew rapidly at an average of 16.4 percent every year, while the per capita income for city residents grew only 8 percent annually. The income of farmers grew twice as fast as the income of city residents. Although from 1985 to 2003, the situation was reversed. During these 18 years, the net income growth rate of rural residents was 4.3 percent per capita. From 1998 to 2003—the five years when the *san-nong* problems attracted the most attention—the income of rural residents only grew at an average of 3.9 percent, while the average disposable per capita income growth rate for urban residents is 8.7 percent.

Because of the relatively stagnant growth of income, the starting-to-narrow gap between urban and rural areas at the initial stage of the reform has been enlarging gradually, and today the gap is wider than ever before. For example, statistics show the urban-to-rural income ratio was 2.6:1 in 1978, 1.8:1 in 1984, back to 2.6:1 in 1992, and 3.2:1 in 2003, and it would be incomplete if we merely compared the rural net income with the urban disposable income. As we know, there are many welfare facilities, such as elementary education, medical care, and housing that are only accessible to city and not rural residents. If the welfare is taken into consideration, the real gap may exceed 6:1, which would be the highest in the world.

## 3 The Present Opinions on Solving the Problem of Farmer Income

The core of the *san-nong* problem is the slow growth of farmer income; the key to solving the problem is to increase this income. To increase a farmer's income is one of the key issues of the Agricultural and Development economies as well as China's agricultural policy. The traditional method and policy guidelines indicate to first increase agricultural production and help farmers yield more products and income. The World Bank, Asia Development Bank and the Chinese government have done this in the past. To increase production is: first, to invest more heavily in agricultural production and its relevant fields—the renovation of major rivers being one example; second, to boost the scientific level and increase per unit production, and; third, to adjust the structure of the agricultural industry, transforming low value-added agricultural products into those of high value-added.

There are many experiments in these areas being conducted either in China or abroad.

What we found was that when the experiments were first attempted—either to reorganize infrastructures, advance science and technology, or improve agricultural industrialization, it was indeed good for them. However, when the entire community began to benefit from these policies used in the experiment, we found that while production still increased, the income of farmers did not necessarily improve with it.

The problem stems mainly from the characteristics of the farm products themselves. First of all, farm products have very low-income elasticity. When the income of city residents grows, the demand of these residents for farm products increases only slightly. In addition, the price elasticity of farm products is low. An increase in production would lead to a drop in price, and a decrease would be followed by a price hike. All of the above-mentioned policies, however, are aimed at increasing production. As a basic strategy to enhance production, these policies are beneficial to increase supply and improve alimentation, but to improve income—particularly after a full-scale implementation of the policies—their potential effects are rather limited.

Because production increase is not a long-term solution for increasing farmer income, many have recently begun to consult relevant international experiences, proposing to give direct subsidies to farmers. In China, this argument is well-supported for the following two reasons: (1) developed countries all provide direct subsidies to their farmers, and since highly developed countries are taking measures to protect their farmers, China should too; and (2) before 1978, we supplemented industry with agriculture, meaning that the surplus from rural production was diverted to the cities to support industry through various institutional arrangements. We should now supplement agriculture with industry, meaning that urban industry should give back to agriculture, but something may be wrong with this point of view. Even if China's central government participates, I still have some reservations.

Only when the rate of subsidies exceeds the rate of income increases will the urban-rural gap narrow, but in reality, China cannot afford to do that. In developed countries, the rural population is quite small. Examples would be 2 percent in the United States, 3 percent in France—a major agricultural country in Europe—and 4 percent in Japan. The government cannot narrow the urban-rural gap by subsidizing farmers until the rural population in China reduces substantially. In 2003, rural residents still made up 59.4 percent of China's total population. Under these circumstances, providing price allowances would be a token of the government's concern about farmers with no real significance made in narrowing the gap.

Professor Johnson from the University of Chicago has done many theoretical analyses and practical demonstrations on this point. He points out that subsidies—no matter to price or income—would lead to a price increase for factors of small-supply elasticity, like land, while making no significant change in the wages of laborers. In other words, big landlords will benefit substantially more from price subsidies than poor farmers would. In addition, Chinese farmers have very little land, so any increase in land prices will have little impact on their income. Because of this, China cannot narrow the income gap between its cities and the countryside.

How then could the *san-nong* problem be solved? I will propose ideas and tie them together in a framework as our basic reference.

## 4 The Framework of Solving the *San-nong* Problem

To increase farmer income in a long-term, sustained, and effective manner, several aspects must be considered and are expected to coordinate with one another. The core is to transfer rural laborers from agriculture to non-agriculture, combined with the establishment of the universal market in the country and with the guarantee of science and technology. In this way, the income of farmers could increase consecutively, and the urban-rural income gap between the east and mid-west could gradually narrow.

### *4.1 The Transfer of Rural Laborers*

As mentioned earlier, the price and income elasticity for farm products are low, so it is difficult to increase income by improving production. However, if we divert rural laborers from agriculture to non-agriculture, they will change from suppliers of farm products to consumers of farm products. The supply curve of farm products will then move inward. Meanwhile, as farmers enter non-agricultural industries—either in cities or the countryside—their demand for farm products will increase, driving the demand curve outward. With the supply curve moving inward and the demand curve moving outward, price will naturally rise, and it will continue rising as more rural residents leave agriculture. Ultimately, the price increase will drive up the income level of farmers.

When farmers leave agriculture for a non-agricultural industry, they cannot take the land with them. Hence, those who remain in the countryside have more opportunities to expand their cultivated land area and increase production. In this way, we can overcome the limitations that the low-income and low-price elasticity of farm products have on increasing production and income.

Historical experience has shown that all countries, developed ones included, have similar problems during the early stage of their development. However, their rural-urban income gap has been much smaller than ours. In addition, farmer income is continuously increasing while that of urban workers and businessman is decreasing. Why is there no big gap? It is because of the tremendous decline of the rural population.

In the United States, for example, more than 50 percent of the population were farmers in 1876. More than a century later, only 2 percent consider themselves farmers. Europe experienced a similar change: 40 percent of the total population in many European countries after the World War II farmed for a living, but today that number has greatly diminished to just below 5 percent. After the World War II, 90 percent of Japan's total population were rural residents, but that number is now down to 4 percent. In Korea, the number was more than 60 percent in the 1950s but down to about 8 percent now. China's experience proved this.

After 1984, for example, income increases for farmers have been mostly connected with a farmer's non-agricultural work. From 1985 through the 1980s and early-1990s, township enterprises (xiangzheng qiye) soared, providing jobs for nearly 120 million of the rural population. Farmers were transferred from agricultural to industrial work within their hometowns, their income increased, and the *san-nong* problems were not grave.

From the early- to mid-1990s, migrant workers emerged in our rural labor adjustment. It is estimated that in 1994 and 1995, about 80 million migrant workers came to the cities. Rural income increased as a result of the migration from agriculture to non-agriculture, but after 1998, urban currency deflation, which resulted from the overall surplus of production capacity, led to rather scarce job opportunities, making it very difficult for migrant workers to find jobs. What's more, a number of those who had already migrated to the cities returned to the countryside because of an oversupply of laborers. Factories did not run at full capacity, and some were forced to close down. Originally, rural workers were diverted to township enterprises in their hometowns, but when the labor supply exceeded demand, township enterprises were the first to go bankrupt, forcing workers to return to agriculture. Therefore, the so-called *san-nong* problems were very grave after 1998. What "the countryside is so poor, and farmers so toilsome" reflects is a theme of discontinuity and a reversal of the process of the farmers' exodus.

The central government has realized that the transfer of rural laborers is the key to problems faced by farmers, including the *san-nong* problems. For example, the documents of the 16th National Congress and the 3rd Session of the 16th Central Committee of the Party, and the No. 1 document in 2004 all list the transfer of laborers as a focus.

Besides realizing the significance of this issue, however, we should put forward some specific policies and measures, for both the long- and short-term. For the short-term, production capacity can no longer be overly excessive as it has been since 1998. In 2003, a so-called overheating economy emerged but mainly in the real estate, steel, automobile and construction material sectors. According to the retail commodity price statistics from the National Statistic Bureau, the prices of 13 out of 17 product categories are actually declining, suggesting that the problem of excessive production has not been eliminated. It is found to occur largely within light-industry sectors and labor-intensive industries.

If China doesn't emerge from deflation quickly, few jobs will be created, diminishing the opportunity for farmers to migrate back to the cities. However, the products produced by excessive production capacity are still in very short supply in rural areas where the consuming power is low. Two reasons contribute to this dilemma: first, the income of rural residents is relatively low. In 2003, the disposable per capita income of urban residents was 8,742 *yuan*, while the net income of rural residents was 2,622 *yuan*—amounting to about 30 percent that of urban residents.

It is important to note that the countryside lacks almost any type of infrastructure system that would be associated with people's daily lives, such as water, electricity, and schooling. Therefore, I have been advocating the implementation of the public fiscal expenditure policy through *The New Countryside Campaign* for the past few years in order to improve the rural infrastructure throughout China. If production becomes excessive, the government's financial support is essential to boost the economy.

The Chinese government, however, had always invested all available funds into big urban infrastructures. If more money is put into rural areas to improve their infrastructure, I believe a consumption peak of electronic appliances will occur and this demand will suck in the excessive products in cities. *The New Countryside Campaign* will ameliorate the consumption environment of rural areas, stimulate consumption, create more jobs, save a lot of township enterprises, and increase the income of farmers. Even though the exodus of rural laborers may seem like one of the strategies to increase their income, the fact remains that 60 percent of the Chinese population reside in the countryside. An optimistic estimation suggests that by 2030, rural population will reach 500 million or 30 percent of the entire Chinese population. By 2030, the 500 million people shall also be living a modern life. Therefore, it is necessary and a must to invest in *The New Countryside Campaign*.

For the long-term, the most crucial thing is not only to divert rural laborers out but also to provide them with job opportunities in the cities. If they are diverted out without any job opportunities, the dispersed poverty problem in the countryside will be a concentrated poverty problem in the cities, making our economic development environment even worse. To provide rural laborers with more job opportunities, it is essential to develop labor intensive and mostly small- or medium-sized enterprises based on their comparative advantages. Former capital-intensive, modern-heavy and other similar industries must be abandoned. For labor-intensive small- or medium-sized enterprises, Zhejiang has provided China with a great example. His economy ranked very low in the past, but now all kinds of indexes suggest Zhejiang is the best nationwide after the three biggest cities, as it relies on its labor-intensive small- or medium-sized enterprises.

The Chinese government has now taken notice of the development of labor-intensive small- or medium-sized enterprises, but more coordination with government policies is needed. The coordination policies are as follows. First, provide our small- and medium-sized enterprises with a decent entry into various industries. The present financial system, regardless of the banks or stock markets, mainly supports large companies, but our most dynamic small- and medium-sized enterprises can hardly be financed. Third, education is extremely important. We are now promoting the nine-year obligatory education system nationwide, but we know rural residents have to pay for their basic education and when they go to cities, they also have to pay to receive professional education. Finally, after the diversion of rural laborers, stable and feasible arrangements should be made to allow those who stay in the countryside to expand their cultivated land area so that diverted rural laborers are able to sub-contract their land to those who stay behind.

### 4.2 The Establishment of Universal Farm Product Market

Besides diversion strategy, there should be something else to coordinate with it to narrow the income gap between different regions. One would be the universal farm products market nationwide. Not only industrial but also agricultural products should be uniform. Because China has such a vast territory, development levels and comparative advantages differ from west to east. For example, the comparative advantage of the eastern region is the relatively dense labor population, abundant resources, and complete infrastructures, so the eastern region should develop industries, especially the above-mentioned labor-intensive industries or the labor-intensive sectors within the capital-intensive industries. The middle region's comparative advantage is still agricultural production, whereas the western region relies on its mineral resources.

What kind of system shall we form? The eastern region wants to develop industries and it has a vast market and is closer to the international market. It is estimated that in the following 20 or 30 years, the eastern region will still be the most dynamic economic region in the country, serving as a national driving force and engine. Then how can we activate the engine to fuel the economic development of the middle and the western regions? For this, it is necessary to establish a nationwide universal market. For example, the eastern provinces, like Zhejiang, Jiangsu, Fujian, and Guangdong, have highly dense populations. People living there produced a lot of grains in the past, but with the rise of income, their industrial structure needs improvement. The eastern region will lose its comparative advantage if it continues to produce grain and other farm products. Therefore, people there should actually import grain and other farm products from the middle region.

At the same time, these following questions must be considered: When will the eastern region gradually steps out of grain production? Where should people there import grain from—from a domestic or overseas market? Without a nationwide universal market, foreign producers could take the grain production share that the eastern region gives way. In this way, it's difficult for the eastern region to boost the economy of the middle region. But with a universal market, the eastern region could give away grain production and increase its demand for grain from the middle provinces, and farmers from the major middle grain producing provinces will develop together with the eastern region and benefit from the development of the eastern region because of the increasing demand for commodity grain and the price rise of grain. The same principle also applies to the western region.

To establish the universal market nationwide, we should provide many necessary policies and measures to help with its establishment. In terms of policy, we should improve the land management system that it is suitable for the development of different regions. Quite often, as soon as grain production is reduced, people get panicky and every region is asked to maintain the basic grain sufficiency and protect their cultivated land. If the eastern region protects 85 to 90 percent of their cultivated land, it would be difficult for them to retreat from grain production and it may actually increase grain production. Therefore, we should establish some cultivated land management system to protect cultivated land rather than enforce a standardized measurement. Every year, with the development of industry, we have to give up some cultivated land, which is distributed equally across the country. One possible way is to set forth a quota in the country that only a certain amount of cultivated land can be taken each year. In the beginning, the quota is equally distributed, and different provinces can adjust the quota among themselves. Thus, the eastern region can give away some land so that the middle and western regions can produce more grain, which can be an effective way to narrow the gap between different regions.

Of course, besides the land system reform, to establish a universal market, every region should have some good circulating go-betweens (*liutong zhongjie*), which may actually achieve development if the government does not intervene. If one region's grain production declines, huge quantities of grain will flow in from other regions. When a grain shortage does occur, however, circulating channels are immediately shut off, and the entire country goes back to self-sufficiency again. In the name of protecting the interests of state-owned grain merchants, various obstacles are set up to regulate the grain circulating system, but in reality, these obstacles hindered the development of effective grain circulating go-betweens.

### *4.3 The Development of Agricultural Science and Technology*

In addition to establishing a universal market nationwide, we should emphasize on science and technology. Provided with the comprehensive diversion of rural laborers and the establishment of a universal market, through the advancement of science and technology, we can enhance agricultural production capacity, elevate the commodity ratio of farm products, increase income, become grain self-sufficient, and finally reach the supply-demand equilibrium.

Of course, from the perspective of comparative advantages, grain production is land-intensive, which is not our strength, but grain is not a completely commercialized product in any country, as it's politically sensitive. It is very important to enhance science and technology, because in the next 30 years, our annual per capita income increase will remain at an average of 7 to 8 percent. When income goes up, the demand structure of food will be affected—from mainly carbohydrate food to eggs, milk, meat, and so on. Our population is also on the rise. Starting with 1.29 billion right now, China's population is expected to reach 1.5 billion by 2030. All these additional people will clearly eat grain, and in the meantime, our cultivated land area will continue to shrink with economic development and industrialization, which encourages more land will be used to build factories, residential buildings, and roads. Considering this, farmers who remain in the countryside won't be able to produce enough products to meet the increasing demand, unless agricultural sciences and technologies in China can catch up.

It is also very important to improve agricultural science and technology after

China entered the World Trade Organization. After the entry, we are likely to integrate our farm products market, especially the labor-intensive products market, into the international market. Labor-intensive products, such as vegetables, fruits, and fresh flowers, are where our comparative advantage lies. If this integration is successful, our farmers can produce these products through structural adjustments in domestic and international markets. However, to enter the international market, we must have fine product lines as well as excellent quality products, which also rely heavily on science and technology.

I think we all understand the importance of agricultural science and technology. But the problem is how to advance them. According to experience at home and abroad, government's support is crucial. The main reasons are economic. First, the research efficiency of agricultural science and technology is low, and most agricultural science and technology are very difficult to commercialize. Second, the major beneficiaries of agricultural science and technology are consumers, who benefit from the augmentation of production capacity and the effective reduction of prices. Based on the principle of *who benefit who pay*, consumers should support the development of agricultural science and technology, but how would they support? Mainly by means of government taxation and then investing in agricultural science and technology using the tax revenue. If the government is willing to do this, I believe our agriculture has great potential to not only produce enough grain to feed the entire Chinese population but also compete in the international market with better products.

## Chapter 4

# Conflicts and Problems Facing China's Current Rural Reform and Development*

Xiwen Chen

This year marks the 26th year of China's rural reform. A lot of problems facing rural China have been solved during the 26 years of reform and development, but a lot still remains to be solved. Also, while some old problems are being solved, new ones are coming out. As a result, many conflicts and problems still exist in rural China today, some of which are rather serious. Recently, five major problems have become prominent.

### 1 Farmer Income

It has been very difficult for farmers to increase their income for some time. From 1997 through 2003, the average annual increase of the per capita income of rural reside was 4 percent. Judging from global indexes, we can say it is fairly good. If we look at the actual circumstances in China, however, we still see many problems. First of all, the increase of 4 percent failed to reach the goal set in the national *10th Five Year Plan*, which put forward a yearly 5 percent increase of farmer income in the *10th Five Year Plan* period, but three years have passed without reaching the goal. Second, in the past seven years, while the income of farmers has been increasing at 4 percent each year, the income of city residents has been growing at 8 percent, widening the gap between the urban and rural areas. During the six years after 1998, the total net per capita income of farmers has increased 532 *yuan*, whereas the disposable per capita income of urban residents has increased 3,312 *yuan* over the same period, suggesting an annual increase of 552 *yuan*. That is to say, the total increase of the net per capita income of farmers in six years is less than the income increase of city residents in a single year.

The difficulty that farmers face to improve their income arises from the fact that they not only failed to make much money from agriculture but often end up losing money as well. Right now, about 45 percent of the net income of Chinese farmers comes from agriculture, 18 percent down from that of eight years ago. The

* This article is based on a talk given at the annual Chinese Economists Society conference in June, 2004, Hangzhou, China and translated by Qingting Hu at Peking University.

percentage of agricultural income in the total income of farmers has been consistently declining, and the absolute amount of income has also been declining for seven consecutive years.

The highest percentage of farmer income from agriculture occurred in 1997, reaching 1,276 *yuan*, but that record had not been broken from 1998 through 2003, at least. Therefore, from this perspective, a key problem restraining agricultural income is the market for agricultural products. For example, up until the end of October 2003, the price of grain had been declining and remaining low for 84 consecutive months, suggesting that it is very difficult to expand the grain market. Other agricultural products face a similar problem. We once did an analysis, in which we compared the indexes of 2001 and 1996 and found that the disposable per capita income of city residents had increased by 2020 *yuan* in five years, but their expenditures on grain, vegetable oil, meat, and vegetables in 2001 was 131.2 *yuan* less than their expenditures in 1996. In this case, it is very difficult for farmers to increase their income from agriculture.

In addition, it is absolutely necessary for us to consider the diversion of farmers to non-agricultural industries in cities and towns. During this process, township enterprises have, in the past few years, increased their assets and production value and paid more taxes, but employment has remained flat. In 1996, 135,080 thousand people worked for township enterprises. Up through 2002, that number had still not been surpassed. In 2003, however, that number rose somewhat; 630,000 more people worked in township enterprises (*xiangzheng qiye*) that year than in 1996.

In the past seven years, township enterprises have barely increased the income of farmers. Hence, the "migrant workers' flood" (*mingong chao*) has become increasingly billowy as more and more rural residents rush into cities for work. According to the Statistics Bureau, the number of agricultural laborers who left for employment in the cities for more than half a year in 2003 was 113,900—23,400 of whom took their families with them. Therefore, about 150 million of the rural population left their homes to find work somewhere in the coastal region of China, where there are developed areas as well as large- and medium-sized cities.

It obviously has positive significance, but why are township enterprises no longer providing more jobs? Why are there severe employment contradictions in cities and towns? One of the most important reasons is that, ever since the late-1990s, the trend of technological innovation that was taking the world by storm had also left its distinct impact on China. Capital is replacing laborers on a large scale in the Second and Third Industries.

To increase the income of farmers, many things must be done, but two problems require special attention: (1) how to expand the agricultural products market and ensure reasonable prices; and (2) how to divert farmers towards employment, making more money from non-agricultural industries and urban employment. Obviously, tremendous problems exist in both aspects. It will be rather challenging to have them solved—whether it is now or in the future—so we shouldn't be expecting a sharp increase of farmer income in the near future. It is a long-term and formidable task.

## 2 Grain

China has witnessed a grain harvest for five years since the later half of the 1990s. At the end of the 1990s, grain supply exceeded its demand on a national level, and the stock piled up quickly. Thanks to the huge stock, in the past four years, the continuous decline of grain output has not affected the grain market or caused the grain price to climb. As a result, many people believe China has no grain problem, at least not a big one, yet the long-existing grain problem looms large again following the grain price rise at the end of 2003.

One important index is that the total grain output in 2003 was 861.3 billion *jin* (0.5 kg), but the forecasted total demand was 876.5 billion *jin*, suggesting a big gap between the supply and demand of grain. The gap has to be filled either by stock or import; otherwise, the market will react to it quickly. In economics, people believe that grain shortage will push the price to rise, which will lead farmers to grow more crops—naturally solving the grain problem. This logic is correct, but in practice, many problems complicate the solution.

When we say grain problems loom large, we do not mean we have a grain supply-demand problem now. With 2003's output plus stock, the total amount of supply still exceeds the demand. The situation, however, is different now from what it was a few years ago. Originally, we wouldn't sweat as the grain price fluctuated year-to-year, but what we need to consider is our grain producing capacity.

Many believe that there is not a significant grain problem because whenever grain prices would go up, grain output would increase accordingly. This analysis and judgment is based on the assumption that China's capacity to produce grain is adequate. By the end of the 1990s, there had already been three years in which the grain output exceeded 1 trillion *jin*, and while many still believe China's grain producing capacity is greater than 1 trillion *jin* a year, it may not be possible to produce that much grain today.

The exact estimate of the country's grain producing capacity needs to be carefully analyzed and studied, but with some basic data, we can make a few judgments. First, according to the Ministry of Land and Resources, the area of cultivated land in China was 1.851 billion *mu* (1 *mu*= 0.067 hectare) in 2003, which was 0.1 billion *mu* less than what it was in 1996. The findings of our investigation into this suggest that the 0.1 billion *mu* shrinkage is actually the most conservative estimate, which is far below the actual number. Although the exact amount of lost cultivated land cannot be accurately estimated, it is definitely more than 100 million *mu*. Only the *Returning Cultivated Land to Forest Campaign* has converted 108 million *mu* out of cultivated land by the end of 2003, so the exact number is unclear.

The second index is the grain seminating area. It was 1.49 billion *mu* in 2003—having decreased in size by more than 200 million *mu* from when it was 1.706 billion *mu* in 1998, the highest record in history. The third index is the total grain output. In 2003, China produced 863.1 billion *jin*, down from the historical record of 1,024.6 billion *jin* in 1998, which means grain production has been decreasing at a rate of 163.3 billion *jin* per year. The fourth index is the output of unit area. Calculated based on the seminating area, the highest output per unit area was 300 kg/*mu* in 1998. That number was 289 kg/*mu* in 2003, which is less by 11 kg/*mu*. The fifth index is grain possession per capita. The highest—824 *jin* per capita—occurred in 1996, but in 2003, it was only 667 *jin*. The sixth index is stock in which the number for this year has not yet been issued. The record was set in 2001 with about 52 million tons. It has apparently shrunk, but we do not know by how.

Nevertheless, since 2000, our grain output has never reached 920 billion *jin*, but our demand has always been more than 960 to 970 billion *jin*. The supply was further reduced to 860 billion *jin* in 2003. Therefore, we must use anywhere from the tens of billions to hundreds of billion *jin* of stocked grain each year, meaning that the current stock actually gives out more than it takes in. If the situation continues, China's storage will soon be exhausted. Therefore, if more grain is not produced as soon as possible, China will soon face a grain supply-and-demand crisis.

Our investigation shows the following: (1)In China's developed areas, which are also called the grain-selling areas, no one—from the decision makers to the grassroots officials, worries about grain supply. They all take the ability to buy grain as long as they have money for granted. The eight major grain-selling areas—Beijing, Tianjin, Jiangsu, Shanghai, Zhejiang, Fujian, Guangdong, Hainan—all essentially share this sentiment; (2) In the 13 major grain-producing areas, which export the grain, leaders believe they would suffer losses if they produced too much grain. If kept in stock, the excessive grain would take up capital, cost interest, and possibly cause serious losses. The ideal situation is just to produce enough grain to be self-sufficient and no more; and (3) Leaders in the 10 supply-demand balanced provinces care even less about the grain issue. They have never supplied grain to others, nor have they ever asked for it. They thought it is no one else's business, and they choose to look after themselves. No area is willing to produce more grain than they need, which is why I think China will have grain supply-and-demand issues sooner rather than later.

If a problem with China's grain production does occur, is it good to import from overseas? Would that be okay? Sure, we can think more about import, which would definitely be helpful for the adjustment of domestic indexes. The problem, however, would be concerning how much we can import from the global market and whether or not the import would destabilize China's economy, impair the employment and income of farmers—which is already in a tough situation—and lead the world into the "China Threat Theory." Therefore, many things should be carefully considered, especially if it is impossible to dodge grain problems. While it is not an emergency issue now, experience has told us that China would only realize the importance of the grain issue when they are suffering from hunger. When supply is ample and price is low, of course, nobody bothers to think about the grain problem since the grain industry makes no profit. It is more a matter of common sense.

## 3 Rural Land

There are two aspects about the land problem.

### *3.1 Rural Land System*

The first one is the problem with the system of rural land. China's rural land system is linked to China's basic rural management system. It is stipulated in our Constitution that in rural China, the basic management system is double-layered: land is collectively owned by farmers but contracted to individual households. However, at the grassroots level, few officials have read this provision, or even if they have, they forgot it very quickly. Therefore, some grassroots officials constantly make troubles with farmers' land, causing endless land contract conflicts. Because of this, the Rural Land Contract Law was passed in March 2003 in which there are two basic regulations: (1) during the contract period, the contract-granting party shall not be allowed to take back the contracted land; and (2) during the contract period, the contract-granting party shall not be allowed to adjust the contracted land.

Neither regulation, however, has been well implemented. The discussions concerning the rural land problem are now rather diverse. Some argue that since the collective ownership of land has never really worked, private ownership should be adopted instead. Actually, China has already adopted the private ownership system for many years. The private ownership of rural land as well as land commercialization had lasted more than 2,000 years, but neither had relieved Chinese farmers of their poverty. Some say that since private ownership would never work, we should go with a state ownership system. Others suggest something similar to the Permanent Rent System (*yongdianzhi*), but in my opinion, the best way is to carry the current Rural Land Contract Law through a series of system renovations, supervisions, and management. This is, of course, just one idea. A lot of work must still be done.

### *3.2 Requisition of Land*

The second problem encompasses the requisition of land (*tudi zhengyong*), which turns agricultural land into non-agricultural land. In this process, there are many defects in our current system. A premise must exist in China to turn agricultural land into non-agricultural land: the ownership has to be changed and only after the requisition by the government can it enter the urban construction land market. This is the basic policy, which was never a problem in the past when the urbanization process was slow and the scale of land ownership transfer was small. Also, in the planed economy era, the Chinese government would change a farmer's *hukou* (registered permanent residence) from agricultural to non-agricultural residence and provide that person with some commodity grain, a house, and a job. The government took responsibility for all of that, so farmers were fairly happy with the requisition of their land at that time. The situation, however, has greatly changed.

First of all, the urbanization process has sped up, and the requisition scale has gone up. In addition, the compensation for farmers whose land had been requisitioned doesn't fully account for their losses now in the market economy era.

Therefore, China's land system must be reformed. In the 3rd Session of the 16th Central Committee of the Party in October 2003, a clear reform direction was put forward. First, the premise of China's cultivated land system reform is to submit to the strictest protection system of cultivated land in the world. Because China has a population of 1.3 billion and a land area of 1.8 billion *mu*, if we do not adopt the strictest protection system, we may face a survival problem.

It is inevitable to take some farmland in the process of urbanization and industrialization, but the issues at stake are how to take as little land as possible and how to make up for the lost agricultural production capacity by means of further enhancing the productivity of the current land and reclaiming necessary cultivated land. To make sure the basic principles of land system renovation are to safeguard the interest of farmers and control the land requisition scale.

In addition, a key issue in reforming the land requisition system is to strictly differentiate the land for public use from the land for commercial use. The government's authority over land requisition should be limited to land for public use. As for land that is intended for commercial use, the government should play the part of a "night watcher" to supervise that its use is in accordance to the plan and purpose of the land. If a piece of land is allowed to be used for a non-agricultural purpose, developers and farmers are permitted to negotiate with each other within the scope of the plan, while the government is only responsible for strengthening the overall management. Of course, it is highly complicated to solve this conflict because a wide variety of interests are involved.

In order to clean and regulate the land market, the National Council issued a notice before the May Day of 2004 that suspended the auditing and approving of the transfer of agricultural to non-agricultural land for half a year, but the notice was objected everywhere upon its release. What is the real situation? The urban land reservation centers all over the country control 2.7 million *mu* of construction land. Within the hands of real estate agents throughout the country, about 40 percent of the approved land is not yet developed. Therefore, with such a large volume of land supply, there wouldn't be a problem if no new land was approved for half a year. However, the fact is that local government benefits from every *mu* it approves. Not to approve land for half a year means that the government wouldn't receive any benefits for half a year, so from this point of view, the notice was rejected, of course.

With so many conflicts and problems related to land, it is clear that we have problems in our current laws and policies and that reform is needed. However, part of the reason why we have such severe consequences is that some people turn a deaf ear to the existing policies and statutes. We often hear some government officials saying passionately: "To whom does the land belong? Doesn't it belong to the country?" The Constitution, however, stipulates that urban land belongs to the country, and rural land belongs to farmers collectively if not otherwise stipulated. If we do not memorize this sentence clearly, we could make a lot of mistakes. When discussing expropriating farmers' land, remember that you are talking about someone's possession. Government officials are not farmers, so they have no land ownership. When talking about other people's possessions, you have to consider the restraints of law on your liberty.

Here is the investigation of Zhejiang. At the turn of the century, the investment intensity of Zhejiang's non-agricultural land, which was converted from agricultural land, exceeded 800,000 million *yuan* every *mu*. By 2002, however, it had declined to 400 thousand *yuan*. Because of the excessive supply of land, even the owners of township enterprises and private enterprises have developed a strong sense of environmental protection. The area of a company's garden is larger than the company's workshop. This situation is due to the biggest problem in our land requisition system: I sell you land and I get a price for it. What a pleasure! The farmers, however, are the ones who suffer.

If China's land requisition problems are not solved, there will be tremendous hidden problems either for the protection of agricultural production or for the interests of farmers. Every year, a large area of land is taken, and many farmers are forced to leave without a job or social security. If the situation continues, the 20 million farmers who belong to the above category today will multiply into 30 or 50 million tomorrow. If the number is even higher, this society won't be stable.

## 4 Rural Social Affairs Development

The fourth problem is with the development of social affairs in the countryside, especially in education and healthcare. The reason these two areas are important is that they affect the improvement of the overall quality of farmers as well as the poverty this generation of farmers are facing, and whether or not the next generation of farmers can emerge from poverty. Considerable contradictions are facing the countryside. In comparison with the economic gap between the urban and rural areas, the contrast between rural and urban social affairs is far more striking.

In 2002, statistics show that the education expenditure of the whole country was 548.1billion, which includes financial expenditure—money spent by parents of the students—and various investments and donations from the society. According to the statistics of the Education Department, only 23.1 percent of the 548.1 billion *yuan* was used for rural areas. In other words, 76.9 percent was used for the city. Of course, a considerable part of the education in cities is non-compulsory education, such as high school, professional, and college education. However, the 360 million children who receive compulsory education are mostly in the countryside, making the educational resources distributed to the countryside far too limited.

In 2000, for example, the amount of fiscal money allocated to primary school children was 96 *yuan* per student in the city and 28 *yuan* per student in the countryside. For middle school children, the amount was 146 *yuan* per student in the city and 45 *yuan* per student in the countryside. The income ratio between urban and rural areas exceeded 3:1, and the educational expense for the compulsory education ratio between urban and rural areas also exceeded 3:1. Therefore, from this perspective, it is difficult for China's rural education to change in a profound way.

In 2003, the central government clarified that beginning that year any increase in spending on education, healthcare, and culture must be applied to the countryside, but this policy was never fully implemented because among those who participated in the distribution of educational resources, not many can speak on behalf of country kids, while college presidents have much louder voices.

The rural healthcare development in 2003 wasn't good either. Nevertheless, the Educational Law of the People's Republic of China is now in place to protect education, but no law exists to govern the healthcare practice in rural China. We can say to rural parents that your kids have to finish nine years of schooling; otherwise, it's illegal. But we can't say to village patients that it is illegal not to see a doctor. Commonly, sick people cannot afford to see a doctor in rural China. In 2002, the total fiscal expenditures from various levels used for rural hospitals came close to 6 billion *yuan*, accounting for only 15.5 percent of the total fiscal expenditures spent on healthcare nationwide. The majority of China's population lives in the countryside, but hardly any money has been spent on them.

Premier Wen asked China's health minister:

> Do you know how many farmers who die of diseases actually died in hospitals, and what is the percentage in cities? How many rural pregnant women deliver babies in hospitals, and what is the percentage in cities?

These two numbers were not included in the data system, so no one knew, not even the health minister. However, we can find it out if we go to the countryside. Only a very small percentage of farmers who died of diseases actually died in hospitals, and the percentage of rural pregnant women giving birth in hospitals was also very low. According to our estimate, no more than one-third of pregnant rural women deliver babies in hospitals; most of them give birth at home. Several indexes in a document were shocking: in the remote areas of central and west China, the mortality rate of pregnant women and lying-in women is 3.6 times that of women in coastal and developed areas; and the mortality rate of babies is four times that of babies in coastal and developed areas. This is extremely deplorable. A huge amount of medical resources are being wasted in cities on expensive medical equipment and prescription drugs; on the other hand, a lot of farmers lack the access to the fundamental medical resources. In addition, the document said that in mid-west China, 40 percent of farmers who need medical care couldn't afford it.

Therefore, if we do not speed up the education and healthcare development in rural China, it is destined that the next generation of farmers will be as poor as their parents. We should realize the importance of this issue and endeavor to speed up the development.

## 5 Safeguarding the Rights of Farmers

The fifth problem is safeguarding the rights of farmers. The biggest obstacle is that farmers are weak—not because their population is small but because they are too loosely organized. They have no organization, voice, or channel to help them to appeal in many places. Therefore, it is very important to speed up the building of farmer organizations.

Coincidentally, everyone who stays in the countryside belongs to an organization: the villagers' committee (*cunmin weiyuanhui*). As long as you are a farmer, you are a member. Apparently, the villagers' committee has not protected the rights of farmers very well. From the beginning of this reform, the Communism Party of China (CPC) and the central government realized that in order to develop China's rural economy, it is essential to safeguard farmers' rights. The 3rd Session of the 11th Central Committee of CPC opened the curtain of China's rural reform. At this conference, the decision to quicken China's rural and agriculture development was made and marked the beginning of this rural reform. Considering all the decisions that were made, it is clear that what farmers are now allowed to do had been prohibited then. For example, the Farm Output Quotas Fixing System (*baochan daohu*), also known as "fixing of farm output quotas for each household," was prohibited—according to a decision passed on December 22, 1978. However, if we completely follow the decisions that were made at that conference, then there would probably be no Farm Output Quotas Fixing System and no current rural reform, but hat doesn't mean this conference had no significance on rural reform. Essentially, Chinese leaders at that time simply did not know how to conduct rural reform, so it is not strange to find discrepancies between the decisions made then and the specific policies implemented later.

What is important is the basic principle proposed at the conference—to motivate the enthusiasm of farmers, their economic interests and democratic rights must be safeguarded. This has guided the relationship between the Party and farmers. For 26 years, the government has always taken this principle into consideration when constituting rural policies. Although the central government's policies may have generated different outcomes in the actual implementation, the intention has always been to safeguard the economical and political interests of farmers. As for the actual effects, however, the goal has not been attained in some aspects, such as safeguarding farmers' democratic rights.

What role can the villagers' committee play? In my opinion, the villagers' committee has managed the internal and social affairs of the community well, but it has done almost nothing to lead farmers to the market, develop productivity, and increase income. Therefore, since 2003, the National Congress has brought the establishment of Chinese Farmers' Professional Cooperative Economic Organization into its legislative agenda, which is undergoing the drafting process.

Rural China is facing numerous problems, but if we can manage to solve the above-mentioned five major ones, other minor tribulations will be easier to solve. When it comes to the solutions, however, a hundred people may have 99 different answers. Hence, it may take a long testing process to formulate an effective policy.

The central government and National Council have recently attached significant importance to agricultural and rural issues. At the closing meeting of the central government on rural affairs held on January 8, 2003, President Hu Jingtao addressed the conference and was the first to propose that the *san-nong* problems are the most important work among the important works of the Party. Premier Wen Jiabao reiterated in the Government Report at the 2$^{nd}$ Session of the 10$^{th}$ National Congress on March 5, 2004, the importance of the *san-nong* issue. The question, however, is if the government officials who control policies and resources will actually treat the *san-nong* issue as a priority. If so, many rural problems would be solved, but if they only pay lip service—doing, in effect, the exact opposite—rural problems will deteriorate from bad to worse.

Undoubtedly, many problems that have recently occurred in agriculture and rural areas are unprecedented. The dilemma with the income of farmers, which occurred when supply exceeded demand, has never happened before. The problem with rural land, which emerged during China's rapid industrialization, has not occurred frequently in the past.

Perhaps in early July 2004, the National Council will issue a new round of policies regarding tax and fee reform, which should eventually abolish agricultural taxes. One important question to consider would be how agricultural organizations and grassroots government will operate after the abolishment of agricultural taxes. How will rural social affairs develop? What would the relationship be between the rural government and farmers? How will farmers organize themselves?

These questions have never been raised before. Right now, it is imperative to assimilate the experiences and lessons of other countries and consult the suggestions of experts in order to form a more comprehensive and less defective policy system. No matter how perfect the policies and methods are, however, one thing is fundamental: we cannot rush to solve China's rural problems because in a country with such a huge population and vast territory, it takes painstaking efforts to fully carry out these policies and methods.

## Chapter 5

# China's Rural Economy and the Path to a Modern Industrial State

Scott Rozelle[*]
Jikun Huang

### 1 Introduction

The *East Asian Miracle* is generally regarded as one of the most successful development paradigms in the twentieth century. In the making of the miracle, Japan, Korea, and Taiwan, among other nations, all experienced rapid transformation from rural to urban societies based on industry rather than agriculture. During their takeoff periods, large portions of the rural population moved off the farm and into manufacturing jobs, fueling sharp rises in productivity and income. Almost as important, during the industrialization and urbanization phases, leaders were able to reduce poverty among those left in rural areas and maintain a healthy agricultural sector, thereby attenuating trends towards increased inequality (Johnston, 1970). The ability to increase—or at least maintain—the income levels of those left behind in rural areas during and after the initial waves of migration played a key role in giving the rural population the means to sustain the drive to modernization. The process of rapid urbanization and industrializes depended in no small way on the human capital and other investments made by rural households.

In many ways, China's development over the past two decades has been generating a new East Asian Miracle. Starting with a largely rural population that was largely engaged in farming, many rural residents have reoriented their livelihood strategies since the early-1980s. Off-farm work has emerged as a main source of income growth for many rural households (Lohmar, 1999; Kung, 2002). Migration has become the most common way for rural laborers to get a job off the farm (de Brauw *et al,* 2002). Nearly one hundred million migrants now reside outside their home villages. More than 75 percent of 16 to 20 year olds—three out of four—work off the farm, most working in cities far away from their homes. A

[*] The authors would like to thank Loren Brandt, Alan deBrauw, Klaus Deininger, Ruifa Hu, Songqing Jin, Keijiro Otsuka, Albert Park, Carl Pray, Tom Rawski and Linxiu Zhang for comments or for help on different parts of the manuscript. Rozelle is a member of the Giannini Foundation.

majority of the young workers, unlike those in the past, are now specializing in off-farm work. Few have worked a day on the farm in many years if ever. To an extent only experienced in other East Asian nations, a veritable flood of young and relatively well-educated workers have been flowing into China's cities, filling industrial jobs in recent years.

Despite the historical similarities, however, China is confronting a number of challenges, which in many ways exceed the complexity of those that were faced and overcome by Japan, Korea, and Taiwan (OECD, 2002). When Japan was in its period of rapid transformation in the pre- and post-World War II periods, it aggressively used trade barriers and other pricing measures to raise the returns to farming and increase the value of the assets of rural residents. Korea and Taiwan implemented similar policies in the 1960s and 1970s. Even though there is little doubt that leaders in these East Asian nations pursued the policies at a high cost to society, such trade and pricing practices—along with other investments—helped in keeping rural income and asset values high, contributing to the reduction of poverty and rise in rural income during the periods of rapid industrialization.

When rural households were endowed with greater income and wealth, they were undoubtedly better able to make the investments that allowed them and their children to continue an active and productivity-enhancing role in the process of industrialization and urbanization through the 1950s, 1960s, and 1970s in the case of Japan—through the 1980s and 1990s in the cases of Korea and Taiwan. For our study, it is important to note that trade and other agricultural protectionist policies in Japan, Korea, and Taiwan were implemented singularly without the aid of free commodity markets and without changing the fundamental structure of farms—neither in terms of operational, or ownership, size nor in terms of production patterns.

In contrast, China is experiencing the early stages of development in an environment in which a reliance on input provisions by government-sponsored marketing agencies and output price subsidies—through subsidies paid through government programs as a means to ensure a minimum standard of living for rural households—is no longer an option. Instead, China's WTO accession agreement and its own internal reforms have committed the nation to make its transition in an environment where producers and consumers, including those who work and live in poor rural areas, will need access to the factors of production, earning their income mainly through the markets at prices that are at, or near, internationally competitive levels.

In facing such challenges, the question naturally raised is whether or not China's rural economy is organized in such a way as to support the healthy transformation necessary for China to become a modern country. Without minimizing the difficulties China must overcome in order to create jobs for the rural labor force, we are primarily concerned with another dimension of the development process in this chapter: the income-earning and investment capacity of those left in the rural sector. The key question is if rural households will be able to use the resources at their disposal—mainly land and labor—to generate enough income and savings from farming and other enterprises that can be used to finance China's industrial transformation.

In the process of modernization, rural households need access to financial assets for several reasons. First of all, households require capital to finance moving themselves or their children to the cities when job opportunities present themselves. For those without the means to migrate in the immediate future, liquidity is needed to invest in the education of the household's children in order to increase their opportunities for employment in the future. In addition, rural households need a consistently increasing income as well as access to productive resources during periods of rapid transition so that they do not believe themselves to be disenfranchised or helplessly mired in poverty.

If farm households expect that their lives—or the lives of their children—will improve, they are less likely to partake in anything that would undermine the stability of their rural communities. If they do not believe that their lives, or living conditions, will get any better, however, the probability that some may turn to less productive, illegal, or violent activities that could undermine society. Since little has been published on this subject, we believe an effort is needed to understand if rural China is currently organized in a way that will support a healthy development process.

To overcome this failing in the literature, the overall goal of this chapter is to make an assessment of China's rural economy. In doing so, we will attempt to understand if rural producers are operating in an environment in which we should expect them to enjoy rising income and assets. In general, we will try to understand if rural producers have the means to increase the efficiency of their resource base, to expand that base, or both.

In order to accomplish this goal, we address three specific topics in our examination: (1) whether or not the farming operations of rural households have increased productivity over the past two decades, and if they have, then what the cause of that has been and if it will continue in the future, considering that a rise in productivity increases rural income by raising the efficiency of the production process; (2) in terms of rural China's development of commodity markets, if the markets are functioning, households can begin specializing in—as well as efficiently allocating—their resources, both of which would increase their income; and (3) given the importance of rural China's scarcest resource—land—the nature of land rental markets and how well they are operating must be explored, particularly for those rural households that have not yet migrated and need land—whether or not they can even gain access to it—thereby scrutinizing any and all linkages between land rental markets and off-farm employment.

In order to pursue such a broad range of objectives, we needed to narrow the scope of our analysis. Thus, we ignored a number of important issues. Above all, we are only examining a portion of rural China: the availability of technology, the nature of commodity, and land rental markets. If China's agriculture is becoming increasingly productive and commodity and labor markets function adequately, then when profitable opportunities happen to arise for rural households, farmers should be able to benefit from and enjoy the fruits of such investments in the form of rising income.

It is important to note, however, that although efficiency-enhancing technologies and well-functioning markets are necessary for a developing country in this new century, they are not sufficient. In addition, rapidly developing rural economies also need rural financial markets, a well-designed fiscal regime, and a system of rural governance, which will empower rural citizens to hold their government leaders accountable—resulting in complementary investments in public goods and institutional innovations that may raise the return on well-functioning land and labor markets. Despite their importance, we do not examine these particular aspects of the rural economy.

Rather if we find during the course of our analysis that China's research and development systems are creating efficiency-enhancing technologies and that the markets for commodities and cultivated land do function efficiently, these would be interpreted as good signs that the rural economy is developing. However, it should be understood that these are only the necessary elements for promoting the growth of rural income, which is, in turn, needed for the transformation of an economy—from rural to urban as well as agricultural to industrial. There are, of course, other investments and institutional changes involved but not discussed in this chapter.

## 2 Agricultural Productivity, Technology, and the Future Efficiency of Farming

Scientists and policymakers in the international community—in both developing and developed nations—recognize the importance that agricultural technology and its extensions have aided in promoting the expansion of supply and productivity in the world for the past thirty years. Grilliches (1957) and Alston (1998) have documented the importance of the total rising factor productivity in the agricultural sector of the United States. Hayami and Ruttan (1970) documented the role of agricultural technology in Japan's development, and in the developing world, Rosegrant and Evenson (1992) chronicled the importance of new, varying extension efforts on India's total factor productivity. Pingali, Hussein, and Gerpacio (1997) reviewed contributions made by the Green Revolution in South and Southeast Asia. In other words, early global economic growth is very much a result of agricultural productivity.

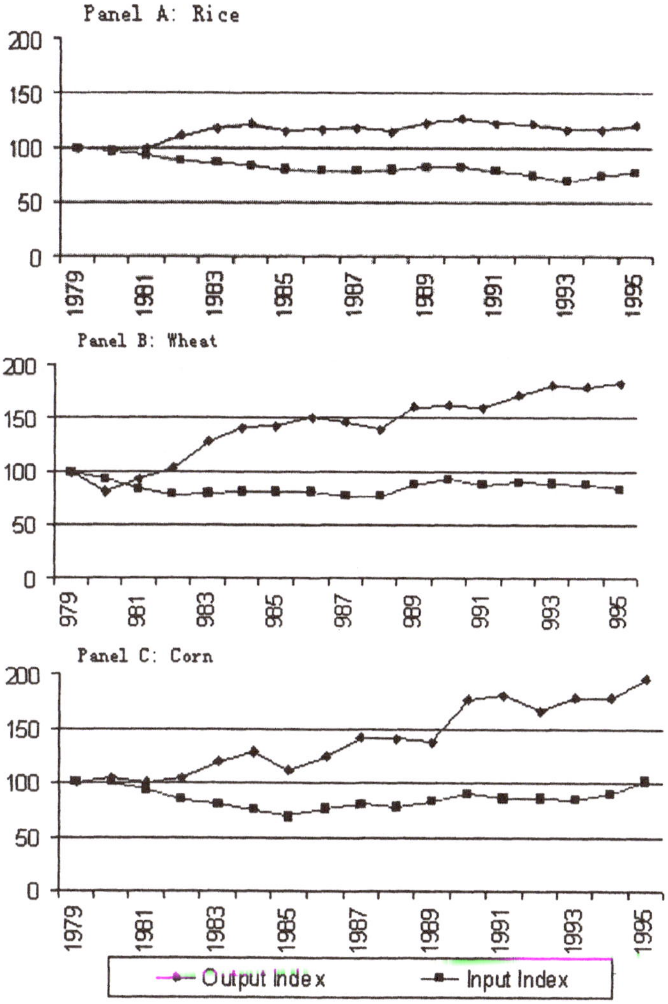


**Figure 5.1 Output and input indices for major rice, wheat and corn growing provinces in China, 1979-1995**

*Source*: Authors' calculation based on Divisia-Tornquist Formula, Jin et al. (2002).

While important in the rest of the world, little is known about the overall productivity of China's agricultural economy. Instead, more attention has been paid to the rise in partial productivity measures, such as yields and output. During China's reform period, the rapid and monotonic expansion of the real output of major food crops has ranked as one of the nation's great achievements, although a significant portion of that gain arises from the mobilization of inputs (Stone, 1993).

The outputs of rice, wheat, and corn rose sharply between 1982 and 1995 (Figure 5.1, upper line on each graph).

Rice production increased by 20 percent, wheat by 80 percent, and corn by 95 percent during the 1980s and early-1990s. At this point in China's development, however, technological improvements did not account for all the growth. Indices of aggregated inputs—such as measures of land, labor, and materials for rice, wheat, and corn—actually fell for all crops in the early-1980s (Figure 5.1, lower line on each graph). The slump in inputs as outputs were rising will itself lead to higher TFP measures. While land and labor fell in the early-1980s before stabilizing in either the late-1980s or early-1990s, material inputs—including fertilizer, pesticides, and other material factors—rose sharply at an annul rate of 32 percent for rice, 26 percent for wheat, and 30 percent for corn (China National Statistical Bureau, 2003). Lin (1992) and Huang as well as Rozelle (1996) had shown that the rise in purchased inputs accounted for a significant part of the increase in outputs during that same time period.

Even though input changes account for a substantial portion of the increase in output over the past twenty years, the future food supply increases in China may not be able to rely on inputs as much as before. Fertilizer and pesticide use nearly diminished in the 1990s. High levels of use in many of China's regions may mean that the decelerating trends could continue. Other correlating factors of development—such as rising wage-rates, environmental awareness, and resource limitations—imply that further pressure will be laid upon them to reduce inputs even more. Considering that agriculture in many countries is facing a worldwide input plateau, further output growth must then rely more on technological change. As the importance of technological change spreads, our need to understand TFP's past-performance as well as its determinants also rises.

## 3 The Record on TFP

Historically, estimates of China's cropping TFP have been controversial, arriving at significantly different conclusions. Poor data and ad hoc weights may rationalize the uncertainty over pre- and post-reform productivity studies as seen in the debates. In the past, researchers gleaned data from a variety of sources. Now, however, they warn readers of the poor quality of many of the input and output series (Stone and Rozelle, 1995).

To overcome this problem, we use data that have been collected over the past twenty years by the State Price Bureau. Using a sampling framework with more than 20,000 households, enumerators collected data on the costs of production for all of China's major crops. The data set contains information on quantities and total expenditures of all major inputs, as well as expenditure on a large number of miscellaneous costs. Each farmer also reports output and the total revenues earned from the crop.

Provincial surveys—by the same agency—supply unit costs for crops and have detailed information on input use. During the last several years, these data have been published by the State Development and Planning Commission ("The Compiled Materials of Costs and Profits of Agricultural Products of China," SPB, 1988-1998). The data have previously been used in analyses on China's agricultural supply and input demand (Huang and Rozelle, 1996; Rozelle, Huang and Rosegrant, 1996; World Bank, 1997). We use standard, modern methods to calculate TFP trends for China's agriculture.[1]

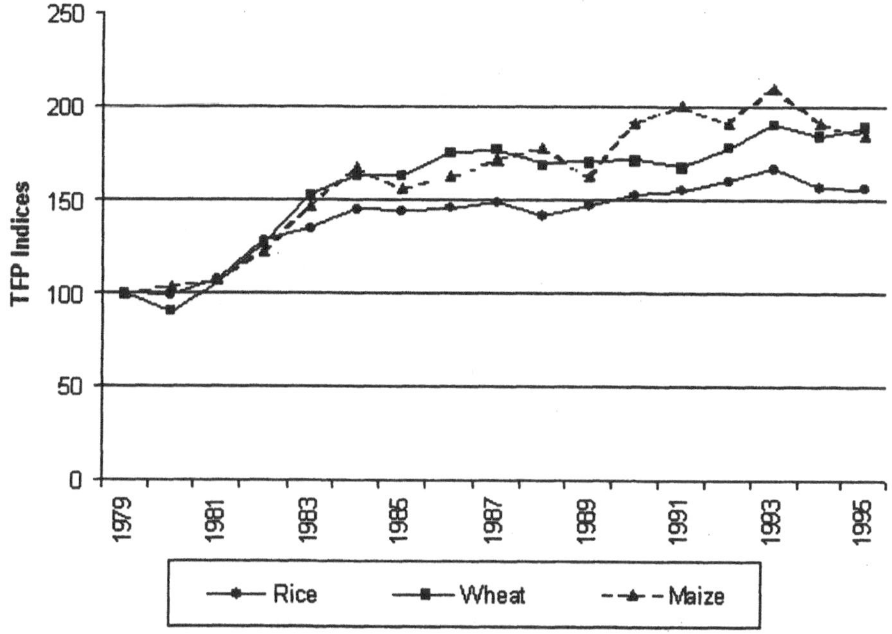


**Figure 5.2 Total factor productivity indices (sown area weighted average) for rice, wheat and maize in China, 1979-1995**

Although there are differences over time and across space, China's TFP has generally risen at a healthy rate of about 2 percent per year during the reform era (Figure 5.2). The national levels of TFP for all crops rose rapidly in the early-1980s, the earliest period of China's reforms. Such an unparalleled rise in TFPs, however, could not be sustained. In fact, for a period of five years in the late-1980s, there was stagnation in TFP growth. The average TFP of our sample

[1] Our methodological approach is similar to that of Rosegrant and Evenson (1992) in that we use standard Divisia index methods to calculate TFP. In essence, TFP measures the difference between aggregate output and aggregate inputs. It can be thought of as the rise in output that is not accounted for by inputs, and as such, is a measure of productivity from all (or total) factors.

provinces were at about the same level in 1990 as they were in 1985 for all crops. The rise in TFP, however, restarted itself in the 1990s. Even though TFP growth patterns for all the crops, aggregated to the national level, are similar, the trends of the various sample provinces—or even within a crop—vary markedly. For example, wheat TFP rises 3 to 4 percent annually in the Hebei and Shandong provinces, but less than 1.5 percent annually in Sichuan and Shanxi Provinces. Overall, however, a growth rate of 2 percent is above the rate of population growth and is considered strong by international comparisons, about the same as the US during the twentieth century and as Japan in the post-war period.

**Table 5.1 Decomposition of the sources of rice TFP growth in China**

| | | 1981-1984 | | | 1984-1995 | | |
|---|---|---|---|---|---|---|---|
| | TFP elasticities[1] | Factor annual growth rate[2] | Sources of growth Rate[3] | Sources of growth Percent[4] | Factor annual growth rate | Sources of growth Rate | Sources of growth percent |
| Varietal Turnover (VT2) | 0.28 | 21.47 | 6.01 | 63.61 | 7.81 | 2.19 | 197.01 |
| Extension | -0.02 | 2.03 | -0.04 | -0.43 | 3.96 | -0.08 | -7.14 |
| Flood Index | -0.01 | 29.02 | -0.18 | -1.93 | 9.26 | -0.06 | -5.19 |
| Drought Index | -0.02 | -13.17 | 0.21 | -2.26 | 1.24 | -0.02 | -1.80 |
| Irrigation Index | -0.34 | 0.70 | -0.24 | -2.58 | 1.29 | -0.44 | -39.50 |
| Residual[5] | | | 1.21 | 56.62 | | -0.30 | -143.94 |
| Actual growth rates | | | 9.45 | 100 | | 1.11 | 100 |

*Notes*:

1: TFP elasticity with respect to each factor is calculated on the basis of coefficients from Rice Model in Appendix 5.3.

2: TFP and factor growth rates are computed by a least square estimate. See Jin et al. (2002) for complete results.

3: Growth rate contributed by each factor is calculated by multiplying factor growth rate (column 2) by elasticity (column1).

4: The percentage of total TFP growth explained by each factor is the corresponding figure in column 3, divided by the total growth rate of TFP (which, e.g., for the period of 1981-84 was 9.45 percent).

5: The Residual (row 6) is simply the part that is unexplained by the included/measured factors and is equal to the Actual growth rate (row 7) minus the sum of the contributions that can be attributed to measured factors (rows 1 to 5).

To examine the relative impact of different factors, we reference the work of Jin et al. (2002) that produces estimates of the determinants of TFP change on China's provinces over time and then performs a decomposition exercise on rice, wheat and corn. According to the work of Jin et al. (2002) between 1981 and 1995, the TFP of China's rice (Table 5.1), wheat, and corn (Appendices 1 and 2) grew approximately 2 percent each year. However, since TFP growth was not constant over time, we conduct the decomposition analysis over two sub-periods: 1981 to

1984 and 1984 to 1995. Although institutional change is important, the rice decomposition results in Table 5.1 show that technology is a key factor driving the sharp increase in TFP during the early reform period. Improvement in technology contributed by far the largest share, augmenting the annual growth rate of TFP by 6.01 percent—63.61 percent of the total growth rate. Interestingly, expenditures on the extension of and investment in irrigation did not help TFP growth. The breakdown of China's extension system as well as the deterioration of the same irrigation systems that began in the early reform period already appear to have limited the impact on investments in extension and irrigation on TFP.

In the late reform period of 1984 to 1995, technology remains the most important source of TFP growth (Table 5.1). In fact, during this period, it is the only factor that underlies the positive growth of TFP during that period. If it had not been for other negative factors, technology would have caused TFP to grow by 4.17 percent instead of the actual 1.11 percent. In contrast, factors associated with the continuing breakdown of the irrigation system, above all, significantly reduced the growth of TFP. The decomposition analysis for wheat (Appendix 5.1) and corn (Appendix 5.2) find that the results are similar to those for rice.

## 4 Prospects for Future Technology-induced TFP Growth

The record of TFP growth in the past demonstrates the strength of China's institutional innovations and technological development in creating the rise of productivity. Future TFP growth, however, will only occur if China's agricultural research and development system is able to generate a series of new varieties that will increase the productivity potential that can be adopted by farmers. In this section, we first examine the quantity of varieties that is being produced by China's agricultural research system. We then look at the quality, and finally, we estimate the propensity of farmers to adopt the new varieties.

Building on one of the strongest research systems in the world, during the 1980s and 1990s, China's agricultural scientists and the extension system developed and disseminated technology throughout the People's Republic Period. Reform era breeders have turned out a constant stream of rice, wheat, and corn varieties (Table 5.2).[2] For example, each year in every province, breeders have had more than twenty rice varieties in use. Although the number of wheat and corn varieties was somewhat less, it is rising slowly over time.

[2] A "major" variety in our sample is any variety that covers at least 10,000 *mu* (or 667 hectares) in a province. Since our data base is built on this concept, we do not have full coverage. In fact, for the rice, wheat, and most of corn growing sample provinces, the proportion of area covered by "major" varieties exceeds 90 percent in each province. Only in some of the southern soybean provinces, does the coverage area fall.

**Table 5.2 Total and provincial averaged of the number of major varieties planted by farmers in China's rice, wheat and corn growing provinces, 1982-1995**

| | Rice | | Wheat | | Corn | |
|---|---|---|---|---|---|---|
| | Total | Average per Province | Total | Average per Province | Total | Average per Province |
| 1982 | 379 | 24 | 211 | 15 | 130 | 10 |
| 1983 | 333 | 21 | 274 | 20 | 130 | 10 |
| 1984 | 380 | 24 | 277 | 20 | 130 | 10 |
| 1985 | 424 | 27 | 313 | 22 | 156 | 12 |
| 1986 | 419 | 26 | 303 | 22 | 156 | 12 |
| 1987 | 373 | 23 | 313 | 22 | 156 | 12 |
| 1988 | 381 | 24 | 301 | 22 | 130 | 10 |
| 1989 | 365 | 23 | 337 | 24 | 143 | 11 |
| 1990 | 412 | 26 | 333 | 24 | 156 | 12 |
| 1991 | 395 | 25 | 350 | 25 | 156 | 12 |
| 1992 | 403 | 25 | 338 | 24 | 156 | 12 |
| 1993 | 392 | 25 | 341 | 24 | 182 | 14 |
| 1994 | 416 | 26 | 330 | 24 | 182 | 14 |
| 1995 | 391 | 24 | 311 | 22 | 208 | 16 |

*Notes*: 1. These are totals for the 16 rice growing provinces, 14 wheat-growing provinces and 15 corn growing provinces in our sample. The 16 rice growing provinces are Heilongjiang, Jilin, Liaoning, Hebei, Jiangsu, Anhui, Hubei, Hunan, Jiangxi, Zhejiang, Fujian, Guangdong, Guangxi, Yunnan, Guizhou, and Sichuan. Together the 16 rice-growing provinces make up more than 90 percent of China's rice sown area and output in 1995. The 14 wheat-growing provinces are Hebei, Shanxi, Jiangsu, Anhui, Shandong, Henan, Sichuan, Gansu, Guizhou, Heilongjiang, Hubei, Shaanxi, Yunnan and Xingjiang. The 14 wheat growing provinces account for 92 percent of China's wheat sown area and 95 percent of its output in 1995. The 13 corn growing provinces include Guangxi, Hebei, Heilongjiang, Henan, Jiangsu, Jilin, Liaoning, Shanxi, Shandong, Shaanxi, Sichuan, Xingjiang and Yunnan. The corn growing provinces account for more than 89 percent of China's soybean sown area and 92 percent of its output in 1995.

*Source*: Authors' data gathered from the Ministry of Agriculture.

**Table 5.3 Trend of sown area weighted averages of varietal turnover in China's rice, wheat and corn growing provinces, 1982-1995**[1]

| | Rice | Wheat | Corn |
|---|---|---|---|
| 1982 | 0.35 | n.a. | 0.47 |
| 1983 | 0.22 | 0.35 | 0.43 |
| 1984 | 0.20 | 0.26 | 0.40 |
| 1985 | 0.19 | 0.24 | 0.37 |
| 1986 | 0.28 | 0.27 | 0.41 |
| 1987 | 0.28 | 0.20 | 0.45 |
| 1988 | 0.26 | 0.19 | 0.34 |
| 1989 | 0.17 | 0.19 | 0.24 |
| 1990 | 0.24 | 0.21 | 0.24 |
| 1991 | 0.13 | 0.25 | 0.33 |
| 1992 | 0.29 | 0.22 | 0.32 |
| 1993 | 0.19 | 0.26 | 0.25 |
| 1994 | 0.25 | 0.23 | 0.32 |
| 1995 | 0.22 | 0.27 | 0.28 |

*Notes*: 1. See Jin et al. (2002) for definition and computation of varietal turnover.

**Table 5.4 Percentage change in price for every 1000 kilometers of distance from port**

| | Maize | Soybean | Rice |
|---|---|---|---|
| China-1998 | -4% | -10% | -10% |
| China-1999 | -4% | -11% | -9% |
| China-2000 | -3% | -8% | -7% |
| US-1998 | -5% | -3.50% | na |

*Notes*: 1. Figures for column 3 (Rice, China) for Table 5.2 (and similar regressions for 1998 and 1999); figures for columns 1 and 2 (maize and soybeans, China) from regression for maize soybeans for China that are similar to those for rice. Figures for US from spot market prices reported by the Chicago board of trade for 15 markets in 1998.

China's breeding efforts also have enhanced the quality of its seed stock. Using *experiment station yields* of each major variety during the year that the variety was certified, a measure of quality was developed—a variable we call the "yield frontier" variable. The yield frontier, which is created by using the *highest* yield of any *one* major variety in the field in each province during a given year, is a measure of the ultimate yield potential of the current technology used by farmers in all provinces of each province's research system. According to our measure, China's research system has created a steady stream of quality technology (Figure

5.3). On average, the yield frontier is moving up about 2 percent annually—a rate that, if continued into the future, would provide added productivity potential. Hence, from Table 5.2 and Figure 5.3 we see that China's research system has developed and appears to be developing a large quantity of quality varieties.

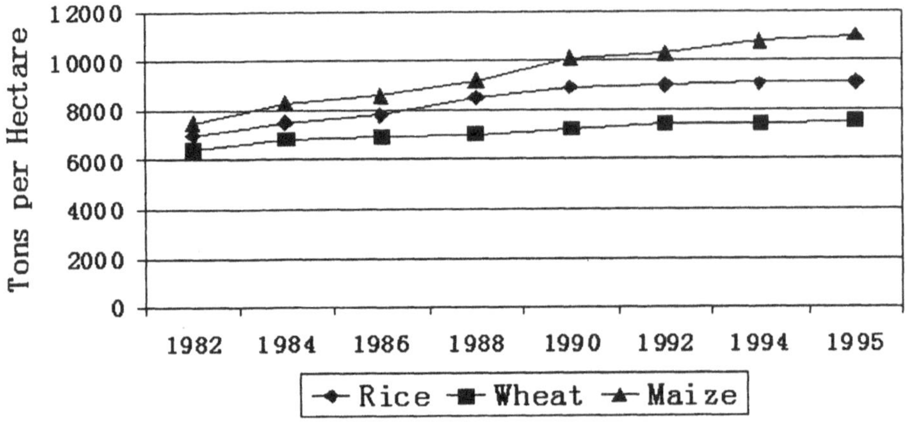


*Note*: Sown area weighted of sample provinces.

**Figure 5.3 Rise of "Yield Frontier" in China's experiment stations for rice, wheat, and maize in China, 1982 to 1995**

*Source*: Jin et al (2002).

Perhaps surprisingly, given the breakdown of the extension system during the reform era, new varieties have been not only produced by China's researchers, but adopted by farmers as well. In fact, China's farmers use new technologies in ways that are usually only seen in the most advanced agricultural economies. To examine this issue, we use a varietal turnover variable, which is a variable that measures the proportion of the average farmer's sown area that is planted to a new variety each year. Using this variable, we find that during the 1980s and 1990s, China's producers are replacing about 20 to 25 percent of their sown areas during each cropping season. In other words, about every four to five years, China's farmers are completely turning over their technology portfolios. Although such information is not widely reported in other countries, interviews with extension agents in the United States found that farmers in some of the most progressive states typically turn over their technology baskets about every three to four years, much like China's households. In contrast, according to interviews with national research administrators in India, we found that the typical Indian farmer changes their entire varietal basket about every eight to ten years.

**5 Plant Biotechnology Research Resources**

In addition to conventional agricultural technology that China's scientists and breeders are producing for the farm sector in the coming decades, officials also are making a strong commitment to plant biotechnology. As the world debates the promises and dangers of plant biotechnology, swinging between the optimism generated by a long list of breakthroughs and the pessimism caused by the backlash from consumer reticence in many parts of the world, a new source of plant biotechnology discoveries is emerging in what initially appears to be a most unlikely place: China. In addition, the discoveries being made are more than cosmetic transformations. China's research community has made a major investment into understanding the structure and function of the rice genome, the use of agrobacterium to transform the cotton and rice plant, and various new methods of transforming other crops.

Although China only started its national plant biotechnology program in the mid-1980s—a number of years after most other developed countries—since the launching of its program, it has grown quickly and taken a relatively unique path in the world. Unlike the rest of the world in which most plant biotechnology research is financed privately, China's government funds nearly all of the research. According to a survey that we did of twenty-two plant biotechnology laboratories, the Ministry of Science and Technology increased investment in plant biotechnology from 16 million *yuan* in 1986 to 92.8 million *yuan* in 1999. After a number of adjustments (see Huang et al., 2002), it is estimated that China's total investment in plant biotechnology in 1999 was $112 million (U.S. currency) in Purchasing Price Parity (PPP) terms. Expenditures of this level demonstrate the seriousness of China's commitment. In 1999, for example, China outspent all other developing countries combined.

China's leaders, however, have not stopped there, and in recent years, they have strengthened their commitment to plant biotechnology. In 2000, China's top leadership decided to more than quadruple the funding from 2000 to 2005. By 2003, according to a recent survey by the Center for Chinese Agricultural Policy, China was spending about $350 million (U.S. currency) in plant biotechnology and $570 million (U.S. currency) in total agricultural biotechnology—plant, animal and microorganism—in Purchasing Price Parity (PPP) terms. If the government meets its original goal, it will be spending far more than half a billion dollars per year, which would be close to outspending the U.S. government on plant biotechnology research.

Using those funds, China's scientists have applied advanced biotechnology tools to the field of applied plant science, regularly working on the synthesis, isolation and cloning of new genes and genetic transformations. After initiating a research program on rice functional genomics in 1997, researchers have used AC/DS transposons and T-DNA insertion methods to create rice mutagenesis pools. Biotechnologists also have initiated functional genomics research for arabidopsis. Our survey of China's plant biotechnology laboratories demonstrated that by 2000, there were more than fifty different plant species and more than 120 functional genes that have been used in plant genetic engineering. China has emerged as a global leader in the production of GM plants, even though it almost certainly lags behind the industrialized world in functional genomics research.

China's scientists have also generated an impressive array of new technologies. Between 1996 and 2000, China's Office of Genetic Engineering Safety Administration approved 251 cases of GM plants, animals, and microorganisms for field trials, environmental releases, and commercialization out of 353 applications. Regulators also approved 45 plant biotechnology applications for field trials, 65 for environmental release, and 31 for commercialization. In recent years, the pace of commercialization has slowed, but this is partly a reflection of China's leaders being careful, allowing its new regulatory system time to catch up with the rapid breakthroughs in the laboratories.

Breakthroughs on crops that have received little attention elsewhere—more than 40 percent of trials in the rest of the world involve GM corn—demonstrate the Chinese government's concern over food security. Transgenic rice resistant to stem borer (using Bt and CpTI genes), planthopper, and bacterial leaf blight (Xa21)—three of China's major rice pests—have already been through at least two years of successful environmental release trials. Researchers have moved GM wheat (BYDV resistant) to field and environmental release trials. China's scientists also experiment with GM potato, peanut, and horticulture commodities. The nation's public-dominated research system has given China's researchers a strong incentive to produce GM crops that increase yields and prevent pest outbreaks. In industrialized countries, 45 percent of all field trials are for herbicide tolerance and improving product quality, but only 19 percent is for insect resistance (Courmanche and Pray, 2001). In contrast, more than 90 percent of field trials target insect and disease resistance in China.

## 6 The Emergence of Commodity Markets

Price and market reforms have been key components of China's transition strategy in the nation's effort to shift from a socialist to a market-oriented economy. The policies, however, have only been implemented gradually (Sicular, 1995). For example, the original price and market reforms initiated in the late-1970s were modest in scope. At that time, they were only aimed at raising farm level procurement prices and allowing a small amount of local trade. These specific reform policies included: gradual increases in agricultural procurement prices toward market prices; reductions in procurement quota levels; the introduction of above quota bonuses for cotton, tobacco, and other cash crops; the negotiated procurement of surplus production of rice, wheat, corn, soybean, edible oils, livestock, and most other commodities at price levels higher than those for quota procurement; and flexibility in the marketing of surplus production in all categories of agricultural products by private traders. It is interesting that in the early years, little effort was made to transform the economy into one in which most resources and factors would be allocated according to market price signals.

Over time, the government's position on market reform has gradually evolved. As officials in charge of the overall economic reforms began to commit to the use of markets as the primary means to allocate resources for the economy in general, the commitment to allowing markets in agriculture also deepened (Sicular, 1995). Since the 1980s, China's reformers have further reduced the level of the mandatory delivery quotas, allowing farmers more freedom in their marketing decisions. Officials have also gradually commercialized the state grain system, reduced the rules prohibiting trade across provinces, and increasingly allowed the entry of private traders (Rozelle et al., 2000). If the grain system had followed through on its commitment to carry out all of the reforms, there is no reason to believe that markets would not have emerged earlier in the reform era.

The special status that many leaders afford agriculture and its role in national food security, however, has made the implementation of grain policy variable. In fact, there have been at least three cycles between the mid-1980s and late-1990s during which officials liberalized commodity markets and then retrenched. At different times, reformers have encouraged the development of inter-provincial grain markets and then blockaded grain shipments between provinces. Policies have urged specialization and structural change during some periods and promoted self-sufficiency in others. Also, even though private traders became a fixture in both the countryside and cities during the 1990s, they were prohibited from trading until 1998. Hence, while the overall the policy of China has been to encourage marketization, it is unclear if these roller coaster policies have actually hindered the development of well-functioning markets.

In making an assessment of the health of the rural economy, it is important to understand how well China's markets are functioning. Markets—whether classic, competitive markets or some workable substitute—increase efficiency by facilitating transactions among agents to allow specialization and trade and providing information through a pricing mechanism to producers and consumers about the relative scarcity of resources. With better markets, producers can increase their allocative efficiency and income.

In the rest of this section, we use data on the prices from the State Market Administration Bureau and the Jilin Oil and Grain Information Center to describe China's agricultural markets. To do so, we first plot the data over time and examine how prices move together within markets of the same geographic region as well as markets separated by long distances. Next, we examine the transportation gradients in China's rice, corn, and soybean markets. Finally, we use statistical tests to check for market integration.

## 7 Price Trends

According to out-price data, it appears as if China's markets appear to function relatively well despite the start-and-stop nature of marketing policies. For example, corn prices in northeast China track each other closely (Figure 5.4, Panels A and B). In Panel A, we plot the Dalian domestic price versus the prices in three Heilongjiang market sites, chosen because they are the farthest northeast from Dalian. While price levels in the different markets vary over time, the Dalian domestic price remains about \$127 (U.S. currency) per metric ton (*mt*) above the

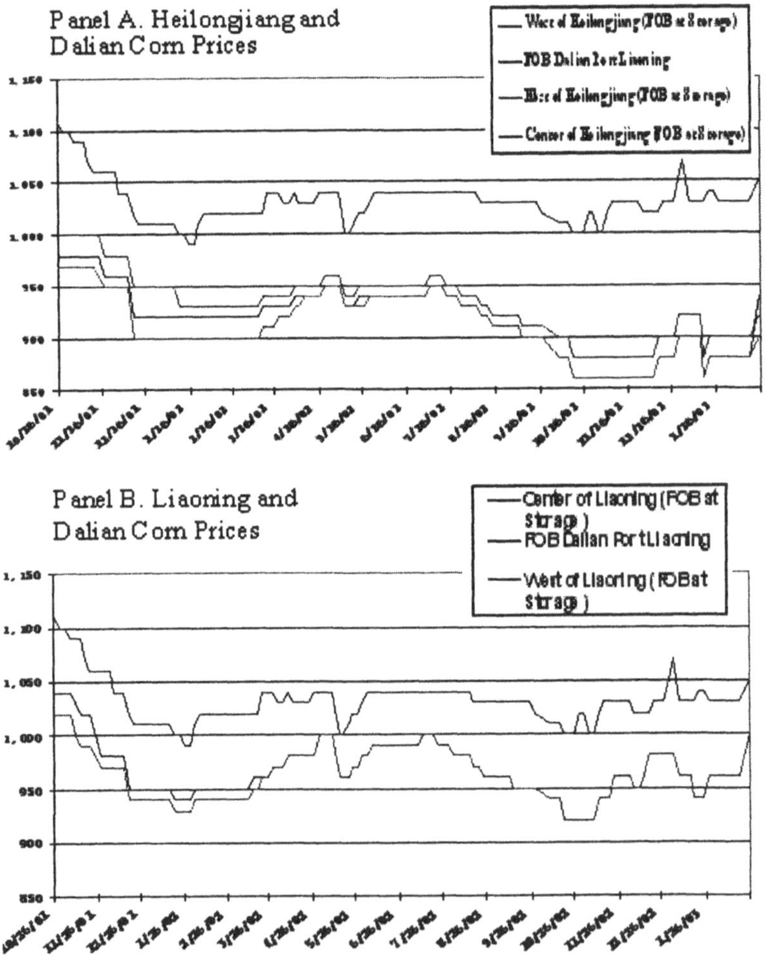


**Figure 5.4 Corn Prices in Heilongjiang, Liaoning and Dalian (RMB/*mt*), October 2001 to February 2003**

*Source*: Jilin Oil and Grain Information Center.

Heilongjiang price between December 2001 and February 2003. According to our interviews, the cost of shipping and handling for grain between Heilongjiang and Dalian is between $126 and $128 (U.S. currency) per *mt*. During the same period, the prices in each of the three Heilongjiang markets move together in almost perfect concert.

Similar patterns of price movement exist between the two markets in western and central Liaoning and Dalian (Panel B). In fact, the prices in the two Liaoning producing areas track each other even closer than the markets in Heilongjiang, a finding that perhaps is not surprising given the fact that Liaoning is a smaller province with better transportation and communication infrastructures.

Panel A. Guangdong and Dalian Corn Prices

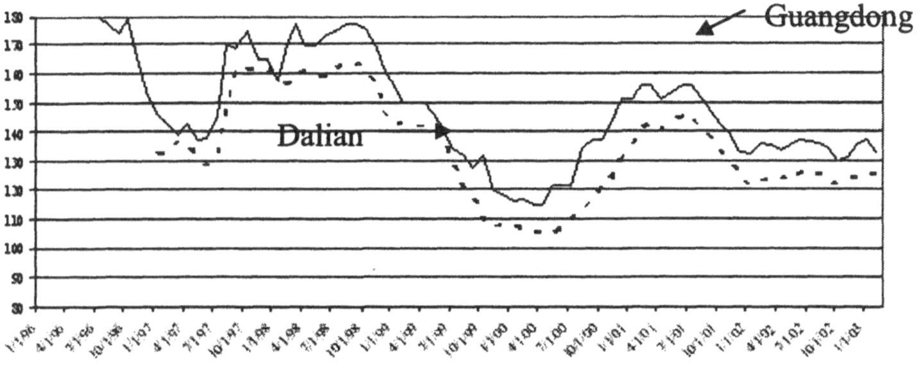


Panel B. Fujian and Dalian Corn Prices

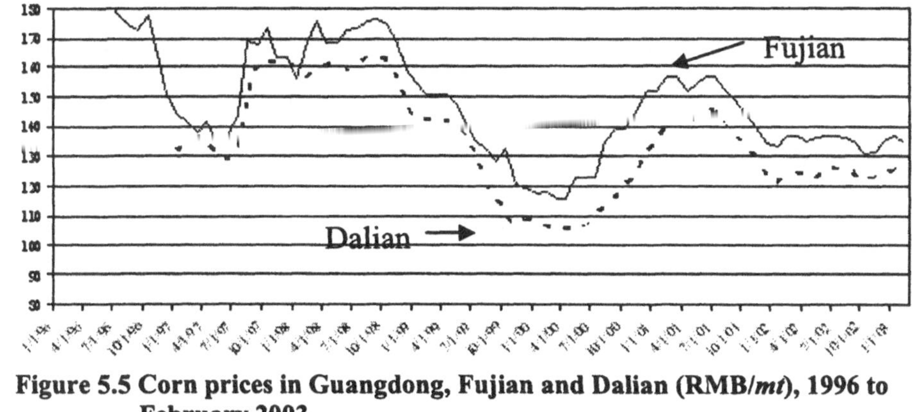


**Figure 5.5 Corn prices in Guangdong, Fujian and Dalian (RMB/*mt*), 1996 to February 2003**

*Source*: Jilin Oil and Grain Information Center.

The patterns of price movement among locations separated by greater differences within China display similar patterns of close co-movements (Figure

5.5, Panels A and B). While prices have moved together since the mid-1990s between Dalian and Guangdong as well as Dalian and Fujian, the tracking among markets appears to be even closer in recent years. Nearly every turning point, which is a shift from low to high or high to low, in Guangdong and Fujian can be found in the Dalian market. The results from Figure 5.5 (Panels A and B) mean that prices in Heilongjiang appear to depend on shifts in feed demand and corn availability in Guangzhou and Fujian when linked with those from Figure 5.4.

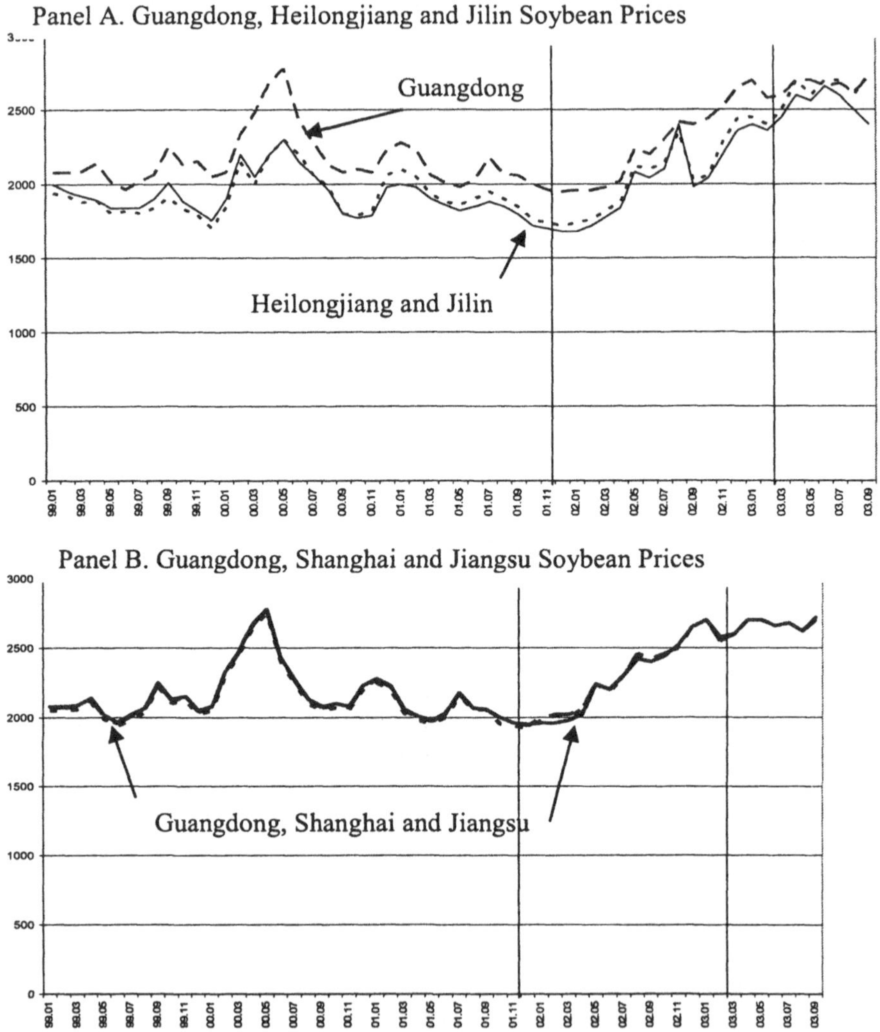


**Figure 5.6 Soybeans prices in Heilongjiang, Jilin, Guangdong, Shanghai and Jiangsu (RMB/*mt*), January 1999 to September 2003**

*Source*: Jilin Oil and Grain Information Center.

Similar patterns occur in the case of soybeans. The bottom two price series in Panel A (Figure 5.6) trace the price trends for soybeans in Heilongjiang and Jilin. In fact, the two series are almost indistinguishable from one another—with Heilongjiang prices slightly lower for just about the entire period. The Guangdong price (the top line in Panel A) also shows that prices move in concert with one another inside China's domestic market even though the markets are thousands of kilometers apart. In only two short periods, early 2000 and late 2002, does that gap between the two markets deviate from a fixed margin, which is about equal to the transport prices between the northeast and the south. Panel B in Figure 5.6 shows that prices appear to move in nearly perfect concert with one another in the south. In fact, the prices throughout the entire period are so close that it is difficult to distinguish the individual price series.

## 8 Transaction Costs and Transportation Gradients

When examining price relationships across China spatially, we can create transportation gradients. Transportation gradients plot prices according to the distance of each market from one of the nation's major ports. For example, Panel A in Figure 5.7 shows the relationship of corn prices between Dalian and those in Liaoning, Jilin, and Heilongjiang during post-accession period from December 2001 to February 2003.

The downward sloping gradient is high in the port and lower as markets move away from the port, which illustrates a price contour that is consistent with the existence of a functioning market. Indeed, the price in a market a thousand kilometers away from Dalian, such as the market in Jilin, is an average of RMB 70 per *mt* lower than the price in Dalian. This means that Jilin's corn price is about 6 percent lower than that of Dalian. The price in Heilongjiang is even lower, and the same pattern occurs when examining rice prices in south China (Figure 5.7, Panel B). In fact, similar figures can be shown no matter which crop is used and when (Huang et al., forthcoming).

Improvement in the quality of China's markets is further illustrated by comparing China's transportation gradients from different periods as well as comparing those from China with those of a market oriented economy, such as the United States (Table 5.5). In making these comparisons, we find three pieces of evidence that support the emergence of markets.

Panel A. Transportation Gradient, Corn in Northeast China, 2002

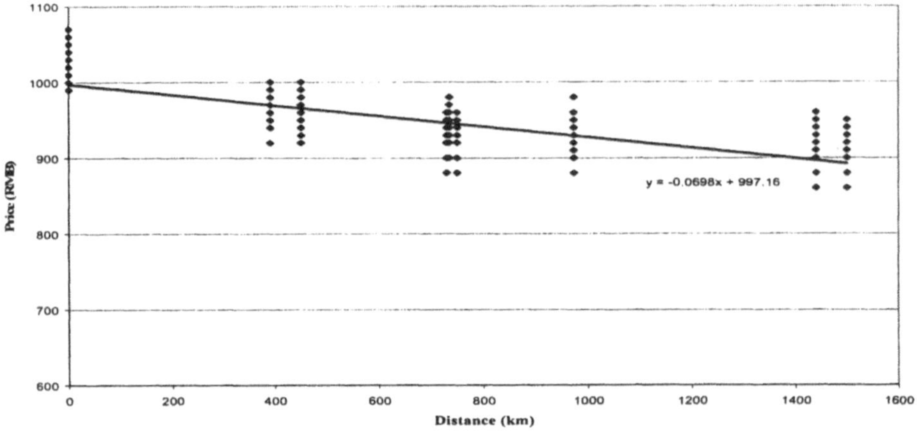


Panel B. Transportation Gradient, Rice in South China, 2000

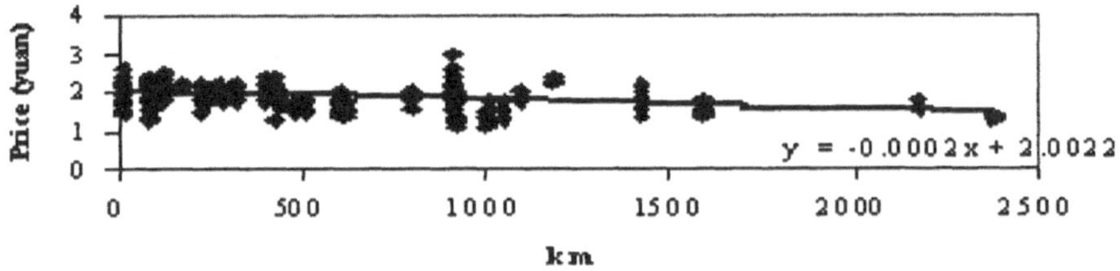


**Figure 5.7 Changes in corn prices across Northeast China as markets increase distances from the Port of Dalian, 2000-2003**

*Source*: Jilin Oil and Grain Information Center.

First, the magnitude of the transportation and transaction costs is similar to what was reported in Park et al. (2002). Using a completely different methodology—a method that uses a maximum likelihood estimator examining the price differences between markets when traders arbitrage away price difference between markets—almost identical estimates of transaction costs are found. Second, the transportation gradients are becoming less steep over time (rows 1 to 3). Although we cannot pinpoint the exact source of the fall in the transportation gradient, the patterns are consistent with a marketing environment in which there is an improving infrastructure and more competitive markets. Finally, the results show that the transportation gradients in China are similar to those found in the United States (Rows 1 to 3 versus Row 4). Plotting similar data and running a similar regression on corn in the Mississippi valley of the United States, we find patterns of spatial price-spread similar to those in China.

**Table 5.5 Percentage of market pairs that test positive for being integrated based on Dickey Fuller test in rural China, 1988-2000**

| Commodity | 1989-1995 | 1996-2000 |
|---|---|---|
| | (Percent of Market Pairs) | |
| Corn | 28 | 89 |
| Soybeans | 28 | 68 |
| Rice, Yellow River Valley (mostly japonica rice) | 25 | 60 |
| Rice, Yangtze Valley and South China (mostly indica rice) | 25 | 47 |

*Note*: 1. Results for two periods both use data from the State Market Administrative Bureau (SMAB). For results from 1989 to 1995 for corn and rice, see Park et al. (2002). Rice results are for the whole country in 1989-1995. Results from soybeans for 1989 to 1995 from Wang (1998). Results from 1996 to 2000 are by authors using Dataset 1.

In other words, assuming our findings are representative of average transportation gradients in China and the United States, these results show that the time in which China's inland markets were isolated by poor transportation and other infrastructure weaknesses may be past. Simply put, it appears as if the aggressive investment in roads and other infrastructure projects in the past decade have dramatically improved the ability of traders to move agricultural commodities, or at least staple crops, around China at costs that rival those of the United States.

## 9 Market Integration in China

In this section we use formal statistical-based tests to examine the degree of market integration in rural China's commodity markets. Using traditional co-integration analysis, we examine the extent to which prices in different pairs of markets move together over time, analyzing several time periods: the early-1990s using results from Park et al., 2002; the late-1990s; and post-2000. We use our price series for rice, corn, and soybeans. We can compare our more recent results with those in Park et al. (2002) that examine integration in the early-1990s because we use the same techniques and dataset.

*Results—Increasing Integration during the 1990s.* The results of the co-integration analysis illustrate that China's markets have indeed emerged steadily since the early-1990s. The first way to see this is to compare the results from the market co-integration analysis of the late-1980s and early-1990s to those of the late-1990s (Table 5.5). Midway through the reform era (1988 to 1995)—a time when markets were starting to emerge—between 20 and 25 percent of the markets showed signs that prices were moving together during the study periods and sub-periods (Park et al., 2002). According to the Park et al. findings, although there were many market pairs in which prices did not move together, there was evidence of rising integration between the late-1980s and mid-1990s.

Compared to the results from the early-1990s, China's markets have continued along their previous path of maturation despite stop-and-go marketing policies. Examining the co-movement of prices among pairs of markets in our sample, we see a significant increase in the fraction of market pairings that are integrated in the late-1990s. In fact, some markets in China are remarkably integrated. In the case of corn, for example, 89 percent of the cases had prices in one market move at the same time as in another (Table 5.5, Column 2). This is up from 28 percent in the early-1990s. The shares of market pairings that exhibit increasing price integration also rise for soybeans, japonica rice, and indica rice (Rows 2 to 4).

**Table 5.6 Cointegration tests on northeast corn markets and Dalian market**

| Region | Test Statistics | Lags | 5% Critical Value | Conclusion |
|---|---|---|---|---|
| *Augmented Dickey-Fuller Tests* | | | -2.89 | |
| 1. Center HLJ | -1.98 | 9 | | Each one is |
| 2. East HLJ | -1.99 | 9 | | unit root and |
| 3. West HLJ | -1.78 | 9 | | Proved to be |
| 4. Center JLN | -1.99 | 9 | | I(1), stationary |
| 5. East JLN | -1.72 | 9 | | at 1st |
| 6. West JLN | -1.62 | 9 | | difference |
| 7. Center LNG | -2.24 | 10 | | |
| 8. West LNG | -2.07 | 10 | | |
| 9. Dalian port | -2.80 | 16 | | |
| *Augmented Dickey-Fuller Tests for Pair Markets* | | | | |
| 1. Center HLJ/Dalian | -3.34 | 9 | | All pair |
| 2. East HLJ/Dalian | -3.49 | 9 | | markets are |
| 3. West HLJ/Dalian | -3.16 | 9 | | cointegrated |
| 4. Center JLN/Dalian | -3.49 | 9 | | Dalian market |
| 5. East JLN/Dalian | -3.24 | 9 | | is integrated |
| 6. West JLN/Dalian | -3.33 | 9 | | with all other |
| 7. Center LNG/Dalian | -3.98 | 9 | | regional markets. |
| 8. West LNG/Dalian | -3.84 | 9 | | |

*Notes:*

1. Augmented Dicky-Fuller test was implemented over the pair markets.
2. Guass program file "adf-test.prg" is used.
3. Data set used: dataset 2. Price series is bi-weekly and data are analyzed at the market level (that is, there are more than one observations per province)

*Results—Corn and Soybeans 2000 to 2003.* The results of the co-integration analysis for corn in the post-2000 period also support both our descriptive findings and conclusions of the transportation gradient analysis. In fact, markets in recent years have functioned remarkably well in terms of integration. For example, all pairs of markets in the northeast are integrated in a statistically significant way (Table 5.6). When compared to results of the late-1990s that are reported in Column 2 of Table 5.5, our analysis shows that during the post-2000 period, corn markets in China have continued to become more integrated. In addition, other pairs of key corn markets on the national level—for example, between Dalian and Guangzhou as well as Dalian and Fujian—are also integrated (results not shown). The integration of these markets is notable because in many cases, the pairs of markets are separated by more than a thousand kilometers, and integrated markets rose from 89 to 93 percent since the late-1990s.

Finally, soybean markets in the post-2000 period are also integrating rapidly (results not shown; see Huang et al., forthcoming). According to our results, nearly all of China's major soybean markets are now integrated with both the major market in China's main production region—Heilongjiang—and the major market in the China's main consumption region, Guangdong.

Taken as a whole, the integration analysis is consistent with our descriptive results and transportation gradient analysis: markets are performing better over time. Perhaps the most interesting finding is that market improvements have occurred despite the policy efforts of certain government leaders at certain times. The lesson appears to be clear: the power of markets has become so strong that they continue to show price integration despite policy intervention attempts. As such, leaders should try using markets to execute policy rather than working against them.

More fundamentally, our results also offer additional evidence of the power of China's gradual method of transition. As argued by McMillan (1997), China's gradual market reform has really been one of entry-driven competition. In the case of China, entry has come from both the commercialization of the state and emergence of a private trading sector. In doing this, China enfranchised millions of individuals to be involved in commodity trade. While this has produced a rise in integration and fall in transaction costs, which have been documented in the media, it has also eroded the state's power to control the markets with traditional command and control methods.

Our results suggest that if the nation's leaders want to control markets in the future, they are going to have to devise new ways to intervene—ones that use indirect methods instead of attempting to suppress traders. There are just too many traders to deal with now as shown by the integration trends that continued to increase even when the nation tried to stop trading.

## 10 Land Markets

In order for the rural economy as a whole to reap the benefits from better commodity markets and increased migration opportunities, well-functioning land rental markets are essential. As discussed above, it is imperative that households that have not been able to move into the migrant labor force—non-migrants—are able to gain access to additional land since the hands of China's policymakers are tied in terms of being unable to support agricultural prices at above-market rates. Active land-rental markets, however, can by no means be taken as given. There may be barriers to enter markets arising from high transaction costs and wealth constraints to asset ownership and education (deJanvry, Fafchamps and Sadoulet, 1991).

As a consequence, there are conceptual doubts about the ability of land markets to contribute to reducing poverty (World Bank, 2003). Since well-developed property rights are needed to facilitate the functioning of land markets, they will be of little use in the development of a nation. Mirroring the discussions in general development literature, scholars debate the nature of land markets in China (Benjamin and Brandt, 2002).

## 11 Data for Land Rental Market Analysis

To determine how well China's land markets are working, we use two datasets. First, we use data from a survey of 780 households from 31 villages in six counties in Hebei and Liaoning, conducted during the summer of 1995. Hebei and Liaoning provinces—located in north and northeast China, respectively—are two of China's major agricultural provinces, and the six sample counties are located in their major agricultural regions.

Most agricultural producers in the sample counties depend on grain or cash crop production. Farmers primarily grow corn, which accounts for about 70 percent of total sown area, but they also cultivate soybeans, rice, and cotton. For each of the surveyed households, detailed information on household characteristics and agricultural production activities were recorded. The total landholdings for each household were enumerated on a plot-by-plot basis. After obtaining basic information about each plot, two plots from each household were selected to investigate more thoroughly.

Other data used for the study came from China's rural Household Income and Expenditure Survey (HIES), a nationwide survey of rural households carried out annually by China's National Statistical Bureau (NSB). As in most household surveys, the sample uses a two-stage sampling procedure. In the first stage, sampling villages are drawn randomly from the survey. Sample villages in 2001 came from twenty-six provinces. In the second stage, ten households were drawn from each administrative village in the sample using equidistance sampling methodology. According to the NSB 2002 Survey Plan, the sampling error for the survey does not exceed 3 percent with a 95 percent confidence level.

While the main focus of the HIES is a detailed recording of the household's consumption and production activities, each year the survey team undertakes a series of special interviews with the household that provide information on several other variables. In 2001, the NBS added a one-time set of questions related to the household's land rental activities. In particular, enumerators asked households whether they rented land in or out, and if they did—what the size of the rental transaction was. We use a mixture of panel and cross-sectional data for our analysis in this chapter.

## 12 Transfer or Rental Rights

*Zhuanbao,* translated literally as "passing on a contract," refers to the transfer of land-use rights between two households and is comparable to the notion of land rental. In the 1980s and early-1990s, transfers were typically short-term and usually entailed the payment of a fee and/or the assumption of tax and quota liabilities by another household in return for the use of the land.

In 1995, 71.6 percent of villages reported that households had complete freedom to transfer land-use rights—about the same as in 1988 (Table 5.7, column 1). In the remaining 28.4 percent of the villages, households faced some sort of constraint, most often in the form of: restrictions on renting to non-villagers or requirements for households to obtain prior authorization from village leaders. Leaders, however, rarely impose a complete moratorium on rental transactions.

Despite the high percentage of villages reporting that households have unconstrained rights to permit other households to use their land, farmers rent in and out a remarkably low percentage of their land (Table 5.7, Columns 2 and 3). In 1988, only 0.5 percent of cultivated land was rented in rural China, and nearly 75 percent of villages reported no land rental. By 1995, although more than 75 percent of local leaders reported rental activities in their villages, farmers still rented less than 3 percent of their land, most of which occurs among relatives.

*China's emerging markets for cultivated land in 2001.* The descriptive statistics produced from the national-level data for 2001 are generally close to those for the overall figures generated by NSB, which are broadly supportive of our hypotheses on the productivity and equity effects of the emergence of land and labor markets in China. For example, Table 5.8 provides information for all of China as well as by region on household income composition, the participation of its members in different types of economic activities, and land endowment and rental market participation.

**Table 5.7 Non-residual property rights in China's villages, 1988 and 1995**

| Province | Unencumbered Right to Rent (% of Villages) | Percentage of Land Rented in 1988 | Percentage of Land Rented in 1995 |
|---|---|---|---|
| Zhejiang | 93.8 | 1.6 | 6.9 |
| | | (3.3) | (10.3) |
| Sichuan | 93.8 | 0.2 | 2.1 |
| | | (0.5) | (2.6) |
| Hubei | 59.4 | 0.3 | 3.6 |
| | | (1.1) | (8.3) |
| Shaanxi | 65.6 | 0.8 | 2.2 |
| | | (2.1) | (2.9) |
| Shandong | 46.5 | NA | 1.1 |
| | | | (1.8) |
| Yunnan | 66.7 | 1.3 | 0.9 |
| | | (0.5) | (2.2) |
| Hebei | 80.0 | 0.3 | 2.1 |
| | | (0.6) | (2.2) |
| Liaoning | 62.3 | 0.1 | 3.6 |
| | | (0.3) | (5.0) |
| Total | 71.6 | 0.6 | 2.9 |
| | | (1.8) | (5.8) |

*Notes*: 1. Standard errors are reported in parenthesis.
*Source*: Authors' data; Brandt et al. (2002).

Above all, the average rural income per capita levels for China (2681—Row 1) are almost the same as in the 2001 statistical yearbook publication (NSB, 2002). The national share of income from agricultural production at 37 percent and land holdings per capita at 1.62 *mu*—two variables also reported regularly in published statistical sources—are nearly the same as the published figures (NSB, 2002). Our data also show how diversified China's rural income sources were in 2001. Although agriculture still makes the largest contribution to the overall income of rural households at 37 percent, it is followed by income from local wage employment and migration at 25 and 9 percent, respectively, and local non-farm self employment (29 percent).

With information from the survey data, the emergence of land markets is confirmed. The 2001 rental market question from the NSB shows that 9.5 percent of households nationwide rented in land while 6.2 percent rented land out in 2001. Although there are considerable regional differences, there are still non-trivial amounts of rentals in all regions. About 10 percent of households rented land in China's central and coastal regions. About 7 percent of those in other parts of China did so. Clearly across China, land rental activities are becoming increasingly common, approaching those in more market-oriented economies.

**Table 5.8 Key indicators of labor and land market activity in China's main regions, 2001**

| | All China | North & Northwest | Coast | Central | South West |
|---|---|---|---|---|---|
| *Income level (Yuan) and composition (%)* | | | | | |
| Mean per capita income | 2681 | 2646 | 3894 | 2392 | 1794 |
| Agric. Production | 37 | 38 | 28 | 41 | 41 |
| Wage employment | 25 | 28 | 31 | 21 | 19 |
| Remittance | 9 | 6 | 10 | 13 | 8 |
| Non-farm self employment | 29 | 28 | 31 | 25 | 32 |
| *Participation in activities (%)* | | | | | |
| Households with non-farm enterprise | 10.7 | 7.3 | 14.4 | 11.1 | 9.2 |
| Households who migrate | 37.0 | 25.0 | 35.0 | 47.0 | 37.0 |
| Months in non-farm activity | 10.0 | 8.3 | 13.7 | 9.2 | 7.6 |
| Months spent in migration | 4.1 | 2.3 | 4.5 | 5.4 | 3.6 |
| *Agricultural endowments* | | 32 | 53 | 59 | 46 |
| Land endowment (*mu*) | 1.62 | 2.14 | 1.00 | 1.31 | 1.37 |
| Share of households renting-in | 9.50 | 7.10 | 9.40 | 10.40 | 7.50 |
| Share of households renting-out | 6.20 | 4.90 | 8.80 | 5.10 | 5.70 |
| Rented to own land ratio[1] | 0.51 | 0.48 | 0.59 | 0.50 | 0.44 |
| No of households in sample | 54590 | 12390 | 14680 | 14860 | 12660 |

*Notes*: 1. Only for households who are renting in.
The *North and Northwest* Region includes the provinces of Hebei, Shanxi, Liaoning, Henan, the *Coastal Region* includes Jiangsu, Zhejiang, Fujian, Shandong, and Guangdong, the *Central Region* includes Anhui, Jiangxi, Hubei, Hunan, and Guangxi, and the *Southwest* includes Sichuan, Guizhou, Yunnan, Shaanxi, and Gansu.
*Source*: Own computation from the NBS national 2001 household survey; Deininger et al., 2004

At a number of different levels of disaggregation, our data show not only rising levels of land rentals, but that there is a positive correlation among activities in land and labor markets. China's major regions, the ones that have the highest levels of migration—like the central and coastal regions—also have the highest levels of rentals (Table 5.8, Rows 8 versus 10). The correlation between the share of labor that is in the migrant labor force and the share of cultivated land that is rented is more than 0.80. It is more than 0.90 when including migration and other types of non-farm activities.

Moreover, trends at the regional level are supported by province-level data. For example, rental markets tend to be more active in the provinces where out-migration is most common, such as in Jiangxi, Henan, Hubei, Hunan, and Anhui provinces. The relationship would also be evident in the coastal region if the definition of non-farm employment was expanded to include both migration and local wage-earning. The correlation coefficient between migration and land rental at the provincial level is 0.54.

Examining the differences among households in Table 5.9—those that rent in or out and those that do not rent in or out (autarkic households)—supports the findings from Table 5.8 on the relationship between migration and land rentals as well as shows that the emergence of land markets helping those with less land endowments. The T-test results show that households that rent out land spend significantly more time in migration and have significantly less land holdings than those who rent in land—both tests are at a 1 percent significance level. According to our data, those that rent out have slightly larger per capita land endowments than the mean (Row 2). Participating in land markets can also be seen to allow those renting in to increase their operating area significantly above the average even though their original endowment is significantly below the mean (row 3).

Our data also indicate that land markets are pro-poor (Table 5.9). Households renting out, when compared to those that rent in, have the highest level of non-farm assets (557 versus 237—Row 5). Even more strongly, per capita income of those renting out (3024) is higher than those that rent in (2636—row 7).

**Table 5.9 Asset holdings and economic activities of households renting in and renting out land in 2001**

| | All | By households' rental market participation | | |
|---|---|---|---|---|
| | China | Rent in | Rent out | Autarkic |
| Number of household | 15873 | 3332 | 2590 | 9951 |
| Owned land per capita (*mu*) | 1.44 | 1.35 | 1.65 | 1.43 |
| Operated land per capita (*mu*) | 1.50 | 1.98 | 1.09 | 1.43 |
| Original value of agricultural assets (*yuan*) | 775 | 812 | 740 | 772 |
| Original value of non-farm assets (yuna) | 419 | 237 | 557 | 450 |
| Households owns draft animal (%) | 31 | 38 | 26 | 31 |
| Per capita income (Y/person) | 2686 | 2582 | 3024 | 2636 |
| Agricultural income (%) | 38 | 52 | 31 | 40 |
| Local wage income (%) | 33 | 27 | 35 | 31 |
| Non-farm self employment income (%) | 17 | 12 | 21 | 18 |
| Remittance income (%) | 11 | 9 | 13 | 11 |
| Months spent in migrating | 3.7 | 3.6 | 4.7 | 4.0 |
| Of which head (%) | 18.0 | 12.8 | 19.1 | 17.5 |
| Number of months in non-farm activities | 10.0 | 8.7 | 12.2 | 9.9 |
| Of which head (%) | 33.3 | 31.0 | 33.6 | 34.3 |

In addition, the descriptive evidence suggests a link between non-agricultural activity and participation in land rental markets (Table 5.9). It can be seen that once households allocate more of their available labor time to work off the farm, the propensity to rent out land increases. To see this, we note that households that rent out spend an average of 4.7 and 12.2 months in migration and non-agricultural self employment, respectively, as compared to 3.7 and 9.9 months for autarkic households (Rows 12 to 15). This illustrates the importance and potential link between land and labor markets.

In support of time allocation contours, income composition differs systematically between those who rent in and those who rent out (Rows 8 to 11). The former receive the most important share of their income from agriculture (51 percent) with lower importance of non-farm employment (40 percent) and remittances (9 percent). In contrast, the opposite is true for the latter who obtain 70 percent of their income from non-agricultural sources. Hence, our data strongly support a pattern of land rental that is not only making the sector more efficien—by providing land to households that are more focused on farming by shifting land from farmers that are participating in the non-farm sector, but pro-poor as well. Such a pattern is exactly what is needed in an economy, such as China's, that generates higher income for many households in the non-farm sector and at the same time, allows those that are left behind to access more land.

## 13 Conclusions

In this chapter, we have painted a positive picture of the state of rural China's economy in the first years of this new century, and in an era in which a large number of China's households are beginning to connect to the non-farm labor force, leaders and scholars are becoming concerned about whether or not this shift is sustainable. The fear is that after China's commitment to the WTO—during a period of time in which its leaders are not able to raise agricultural prices substantially as a way to support those left behind in rural areas—the rural economy is not organized in such a way that will allow the nation's sustained growth and structural transformation. In answering this question, we examined whether or not China's current system is able to raise the productivity of agricultural resources, provide a marketing environment that will allow for specialization and rational allocation of resources, and create markets for cultivated land that will allow households that still have not obtained non-farm employment access to more land for agricultural use.

In fact, we find that after looking at each of the three areas, China appears to be capable of generating long-term, sustained growth. In the future, technology-driven TFP growth will be one of the main forces raising returns in the agricultural sector. Its conventional system appears to be more than capable of generating new technologies—in terms of sufficient quantities and quality, both conventional and those created by biotechnology. The analysis of commodity markets showed that markets in China are becoming remarkably integrated—spatially and over time—between coastal and inland regions as well as between county market seats and villages, even in remote areas.

Finally, although the emergence of land markets has been fairly recent, they appear to have developed quickly in the late-1990s, allowing increases in both efficiency and equity. Land across China has begun to move from specializing in farming to being tied to the migrant labor force. The poor and those with fewer land endowments are also finding that land markets are providing them access to land. In summary, according to all three indicators—agricultural productivity, the emergence of commodity markets, and the emergence of cultivated land markets—China is making progress in beginning its structural transformation.

Of course, these accomplishments are not enough. They also do not mean that the lives of most farm families in China are completely fulfilled. China has a long way to go in making its rural environment a better place to live. At similar points in their development processes, Japan, Korea, and Taiwan launched enormous rural development campaigns aimed at making rural areas pleasant places to live in. Billions of dollars were invested. Typically, the investments were run through and managed by the villages themselves, requiring a transparent and accountable fiscal system. At the same time, other Asian countries developed ways to make financial markets more responsive to the demands of farmers. If China is to make progress on these fronts, which are almost certainly just as necessary as a steady supply of technology and well-functioning land and labor markets, leaders need to push fiscal and financial reforms forward—policy efforts that in the past have proven to be elusive. Therefore, from this perspective, China's efforts to increase farmers' access to technology and commodity markets as well as rental possibilities to date are necessary but not sufficient.

## References


Albert, P., Jin, H., Rozelle S. and Huang, J., 'Market Emergence and Transition: Transition Costs, Arbitrage, and Autarky in China's Grain Market,' *American Journal of Agricultural Economics*, 84, (1) (February, 2002): 67-82.

Benjamin, D. and Brandt, L., 'Property Rights, Labor Markets and Efficiency in a Transition Economy: The Case of Rural China' (Working Paper, University of Toronto, 2000).

Brandt, L., Huang, J.K., Li, G. and Rozelle, S., 'Land Rights in China: Facts, Fictions and Issues' *The China Journal* 40 (January, 2002): 67-97.

deBrauw, A., Huang, J., Rozelle, S., Zhang L. and Zhang, Y., 'The Evolution of China's Rural Labor Markets during the Reforms,' *Journal of Comparative Economics* 30 (2) (June, 2002): 329-353.

de-Janvry, A., Fafchamps, M., Sadoulet, S.E., 'Peasant Household Behaviour with Missing Markets: Some Paradoxes Explained' *Economic Journal* 101 (409) (November, 1991): 1400-417.

Hayami, Y. and Ruttan, V., 'Factor Prices and Technical Change in Agricultural Development: The United States and Japan, 1880 to 1960' *Journal of Political Economy* 78 (September-October, 1970): 1115-1141.

Huang, J.K., and Rozelle, S., 'Technological Change: Rediscovery of the Engine of Productivity Growth in China's Rural Economy,' *Journal of Development Economics* 49 (1996): 337-369.

Jikun, H., Pray, C., Rozelle, S. and Wang, Q., 'Plant Biotechnology in China,' *Science* 295 (January 25, 2002): 674-677.

Jin, S., Huang, J., Hu R. and Rozelle, S., 'The Creation and Spread of Technology and Total Factor Productivity in China,' *American Journal of Agricultural Economics* 84 (4) (November, 2002): 916-930.

Johnston, B., 'Agriculture and Structural Transformation in Developing Countries: A Survey of Research,' *Journal of Economic Literature* 8 (1970).

Julian, A., *Science Under Scarcity: Principles & Practice for Agricultural Research Evaluation & Priority Setting* (London: CABI, 1998).

Kung, J.K., 'Off-Farm Labor Markets and the Emergence of Land Rental Markets in Rural China' *Journal of Comparative Economics*, 30, (2) (June, 2002): 395-414.

Li, G., Rozelle, S. and Brandt, L., 'Tenure, Land Rights, and Farmer Investment Incentives in China,' *Agricultural Economics* 19 (1998): 63-71.

Lin, J.Y., 'Rural Reforms and Agricultural Growth in China,' *American Economic Review* 82 (1) (1992): 34-51.

Lohmar, B., *Household Labor, Migration and China's Rural Development* (Unpublished Ph.D. Dissertation, Department of Agricultural and Resource Economics, Davis: University of California, 1999).

McMillan, J., 'Markets in Transition', in Kreps, David and Kenneth F. Wallis, eds. *Advances in Economics and Econometrics: Theory and Applications, vol. 2,* (Cambridge: Cambridge University Press, 1997): 210-239.

MOA—Varieties, 'Statistical Compendium, China's Major Varieties' (Unpublished Statistical Volume, Beijing: Ministry of Agriculture, 1986-1997).

Pingali, P., Hossein, M. and Gerpacio, R., *Asian Rice Bowls* (London: CAB Publishing, 1997).

Rosegrant M.W. and Evenson, R.E., 'Agricultural Productivity and Sources of Growth in South Asia,' *American Journal of Agricultural Economics* (August, 1992): 757-761.

Rozelle, S., Huang, J.K. and Rosegrant, M., 'How China Will NOT Starve the World,' *Choice* (First Quarter 1996): 12-17.

Rozelle, S., Park, A., Jin, H. and Huang, J., 'Bureaucrat to Entrepreneur: The Changing Role of the State in China's Transitional Commodity Economy,' *Economic Development and Cultural Change* 48, (2) (January, 2000): 227-252.

Sicular, T., 'Redefining State, Plan and Market: China's Reforms in Agricultural Commerce,' *China Quarterly* 144 (1995): 1020-1046.

SPB (State Price Bureau), *Quanguo Nongchanpin Chengben Shouyi Ziliao Huibian* (National Agricultural Production Cost and Revenue Information Summary) (Beijing: China Price Bureau Press: 1988-1992).

Stone, B., 'Basic Agricultural Technology under Reform,' *Economic trends in Chinese agriculture: The impact of post-Mao reforms: A memorial volume in honour of Kenneth Richard Walker, 1932-1989*, With a foreword by Lord Wilson of Tillyorn. Studies on

Contemporary China, eds, Kueh,-Y.-Y.; Ash,-Robert-F. (Oxford; New York; Toronto and Melbourne: Oxford University Press, Clarendon Press, 1993) pp: 311-359.

Stone, B. and Rozelle, S., 'Foodcrop Production Variability in China, 1931-1985,' in *The School for Oriental and African Studies, Research and Notes Monograph Series*, Volume 9, London (August, 1995).

Wang, L., 'Soybeans, Diversity and Productivity in China', Unpublished Masters Thesis. (Beijing: Chinese Academy of Sciences, Institute of Agricultural Economics, 1998).

World Bank, 'At China's Table,' Monograph (Washington DC: World Bank, 1997).

World Bank, 'Rural Development in China: New Challenges in a New Landscape.' Report Written for the Government of the People's Republic of China (July, 2004).

ZGTJNJ, *Zhongguo Tongji Nianjian [China Statistical Yearbook]* (Beijing: China Statistical Press, 1980-98).

Zvi, G., 'An Exploration of the Economics of Technological Change' *Econometrica* 25 (1957): 501-522.

**Appendix 5.1 Decomposition of the sources of wheat TFP growth in China**

| | | 1981-1984 | | | 1984-1995 | | |
|---|---|---|---|---|---|---|---|
| | TFP elasticities[1] | Factor annual growth rate[2] | Sources of growth Rate[3] | Sources of growth Percent[4] | Factor annual growth rate | Sources of growth Rate | Sources of growth Percent |
| Varietal Turnover (VT2) | 0.33 | 19.00 | 6.26 | 49.29 | 8.23 | 2.72 | 247.27 |
| Extension | 0.09 | 2.33 | 0.21 | 1.65 | 3.96 | 0.36 | 32.7 |
| Flood Index | -0.03 | 9.60 | -0.29 | -2.26 | 3.36 | -0.10 | -9.09 |
| Drought Index | -0.04 | -19.18 | 0.77 | 6.03 | 3.66 | -0.15 | -13.6 |
| Irrigation Index | -0.29 | 0.17 | -0.05 | -0.41 | 1.71 | -0.50 | -45.50 |
| Residual[5] | | | 1.96 | 54.30 | | -3.7 | -211.78 |
| Actual growth rates | | | 12.72 | 100 | | 1.10 | 100 |

*Notes:*

1: TFP elasticity with respect to each factor is calculated on the basis of coefficients from Wheat Model in Appendix 5.3.

2: TFP and factor growth rates are computed by a least square estimate. See Jin et al. (2002) for complete set of results.

3: Growth rate contributed by each factor is calculated by multiplying factor growth rate (column 2) by elasticity (column1).

4: The percentage of total TFP growth explained by each factor is the corresponding figure in column 3, divided by the total growth rate of TFP (which for the period of 1981-84 was 9.45 percent).

5: The Residual (row 6) is simply the part that is unexplained by the included/measured factors and is equal to the Actual growth rate (row 7) minus the sum of the contributions that can be attributed to measured factors (rows 1 to 5).

## Appendix 5.2 Decomposition of the sources of corn TFP growth in China

| | | 1981-1984 | | | 1984-1995 | | |
|---|---|---|---|---|---|---|---|
| | TFP elasticities[1] | Factor annual growth rate[2] | Sources of growth Rate[3] | Sources of growth Percent[4] | Factor annual growth rate | Sources of growth Rate | Sources of growth Percent |
| Varietal Turnover (VT2) | 0.40 | 17.66 | 7.06 | 44.37 | 8.00 | 3.20 | 160.80 |
| Extension | -0.38 | 2.33 | -0.89 | -5.56 | 3.97 | -1.51 | -75.81 |
| Flood Index | -0.03 | 13.23 | -0.40 | -2.49 | 1.99 | -0.06 | -3.00 |
| Drought Index | -0.09 | -10.25 | 0.92 | 5.79 | 1.66 | -0.15 | -7.51 |
| Irrigation Index | 0 | 0.56 | 0 | 0 | 1.59 | 0 | 0 |
| Residual[5] | | | 4.30 | 42.11 | | -1.1 | -74.48 |
| Actual growth rates | | | 15.92 | 100 | | 1.99 | 100v |

*Notes:*

1: TFP elasticity with respect to each factor is calculated on the basis of coefficients from Corn Model of Appendix 5.3.

2: TFP and factor growth rates are computed by a least square estimate. See Jin et al. (2002) for complete set of results.

3: Growth rate contributed by each factor is calculated by multiplying factor growth rate (column 2) by elasticity (column1).

4: The percentage of total TFP growth explained by each factor is the corresponding figure in column 3, divided by the total growth rate of TFP (which for the period of 1981-84 was 9.45 percent).

5: The Residual (row 6) is simply the part that is unexplained by the included/measured factors and is equal to the Actual growth rate (row 7) minus the sum of the contributions that can be attributed to measured factors (rows 1 to 5).

**Appendix 5.3 Two-stage least squares estimates of the determinants of total factor productivity for rice, wheat and corn in China**

| | Rice | | Wheat | | Corn | |
|---|---|---|---|---|---|---|
| | TFP | Technology ($VT_2$) | TFP | Technology ($VT_2$) | TFP | Technology ($VT_2$) |
| *Technology Variables* | | | | | | |
| Varietal Turnover | 10.50 | | 26.86 | | 23.01 | |
| ($VT_2$) | (9.18)*** | | (6.02)*** | | (7.42)*** | |
| Extension | -0.01 | 0.0007 | -0.02 | 0.0005 | -0.06 | 0.0002 |
| | (1.66)* | (3.14)*** | (1.42) | (4.45)*** | (3.19)*** | (0.63) |
| *Weather, Irrigation,* | | | | | | |
| *and Period Dummy* | -8.44 | 0.03 | -98.29 | -0.12 | -14.62 | 0.04 |
| Flood Index | (1.70)* | (0.25) | (5.13)*** | (0.80) | (2.11)** | (0.33) |
| Drought Index | -21.29 | -0.73 | -52.54 | -0.06 | -40.35 | 0.002 |
| | (2.26)** | (2.91)*** | (3.19)*** | (0.42) | (6.02)*** | (0.01) |
| Irrigation Index | -91.82 | -2.32 | -118.91 | 0.18 | -11.61 | -0.15 |
| | (2.91)*** | (2.68)*** | (1.63)* | (0.31) | (3.20)*** | (2.46)** |
| D90-95 | 2.25 | -0.46 | 5.78 | -0.08 | 9.52 | -0.35 |
| (Index for 1990s) | (0.58) | (4.29)*** | (0.85) | (1.34) | (1.06) | (2.15)** |
| *Instruments* | | 0.02 | | 0.01 | | 0.02 |
| Research Stock | | (23.96)*** | | (20.52)*** | | (15.37)*** |
| CG Contribution | | 0.68 | | 0.004 | | 0.14 |
| | | (1.64)* | | (1.01) | | (0.20) |
| Yield frontier | | -0.003 | | 0.002 | | 0.0003 |
| | | (3.78)*** | | (4.20)*** | | (0.44) |
| # of Observation | 240 | 240 | 196 | 196 | 195 | 195 |

*Note*: 1. All regression equations include provincial dummies to hold constant unobserved fixed effects. For definition of variables, see Table 5.2 and methodological section. T-ratios in parentheses. ***, **, and * signify that the coefficients are statistically significant at the 1, 5, and 10 percent levels.

Chapter 6

# Rural Development Strategy in Western China under the WTO

Shenggen Fan

## 1 Introduction

After 15 years of continuous efforts, China was finally admitted to the World Trade Organization (WTO) in December 2001. During this period, China has witnessed considerable progress in economic liberalization and reforms even without being a WTO member. This process is in harmony with the general trend of globalization elsewhere, which, through the flows of trade, financial and human capital, technology and information across national boundaries, has led to and will continue to lead to a restructuring of the world economy.

As a result of its economic reform and integration into the global economy, China has achieved remarkable economic growth. Its total GDP has grown at nine to ten percent per annum, outperforming most of the countries in the world. The reform was initiated in the agriculture sector and has led to a rapid transformation in rural areas. Grain output increased from 305 million tons in 1978 to 508 million tons in 1999, with an annual growth rate of 2.5 percent per annum. Such growth is much faster than the population growth rate of 1 percent per annum.

The value added of agriculture rose at an even higher annual rate of 4.8 percent, due to increased diversification of agricultural production. The rapid growth in agriculture has led to an even more impressive reduction in rural poverty. At the beginning of the reform, about one-third of the rural population (or 260 million people) lived under the poverty line without access to adequate food supplies or income to maintain a healthy and productive life. In 2002, the number of rural poor had declined to 28 million, accounting for less than 3 percent of the rural population (MOA 2003). Many development indicators, including agricultural products possessed per capita and average calorie and nutrition intake, average life expectancy, the infant mortality rate, and the percentage of malnourished children, have reached or even surpassed the world average.

Over the last decade, the world has become increasingly globalized. Many countries have also begun to open their economies by lowering the barriers of trade, investment and migration. Various studies have shown a strong positive relationship between openness and economic growth and this relationship is particularly strong for low-income countries. Thus, it is almost certain that the

WTO accession will accelerate China's economic growth through more integration with the world economy and by taking advantage of globalization.

China's rapid economic growth, however, has not benefited everyone equally. In fact, income distribution and regional inequality are getting worse. The Gini coefficient has risen from 0.33 in 1980 to 0.46 in 2000. The income divide between the rural and urban sectors has become increasingly large. The average rural income was 60 percent of urban income in 1984, but the ratio declined to 33 percent in 2002. The income gap between the coastal areas and the western region has been widened dramatically over the last two decades. In 2002, the per capita GDP in Shanghai is nine or 10 times more than that of Guizhou.

With China's entry into the WTO, the less developed regions may suffer even more, as their economies are still predominantly agricultural. It is expected that agricultural prices will drop, leading to a decline in the income of farmers. With poor infrastructure and a shortage in human capital in less developed regions, it will be difficult for farmers to switch from grain production to other high value-added crops or to non-farm activities. All of these may lead to an even higher concentration of rural poor in these regions if proper government policies are not implemented.

This chapter will begin with a review of the potential impact of China's WTO entry on its regional development. In particular, we pay attention to how its WTO entry would affect agricultural production, farmer income, non-farm employment, and poverty in western China. We then synthesize the recent evidence of estimated returns to various public investments in western China, and finally, we discuss a future development strategy for western China to achieve higher growth and greater poverty reduction.

## 2 Potential Impact of WTO Entry on Western China

For a country as large and as geographically diverse as China, uneven regional development is anything but unexpected. The coastal area, endowed with favorable geographical and natural conditions, had been historically more developed than the country's interior. Over the years, China's development policies have exacerbated the unequal development across provinces.

Prior to the reform in 1979, China pursued a strategy of regional economic self-sufficiency, which significantly shaped regional economic outcomes. Each region was expected to be self-sufficient in terms of both food production and industrial goods. This policy severely distorted the allocation of resources, which in turn altered production efficiency, and worsened the imbalance in regional development. The introduction of economic reforms shifted away China's focus on developing the interior provinces. To attract foreign direct investment and to promote foreign trade, the government established special economic zones along the coast. The resulting rapid economic growth in the coastal provinces continued to widen the gap between the coastal and the interior regions.

Differences in economic development among regions can be gauged by their GDP per capita, the agricultural share in regional GDP, and rural income per capita (Table 6.1). In 2002, per capita GDP in the northwest and southwest averaged 5,000 to 6,000 *yuan*, or only about half the income level in the east, the northeast, and the north regions. The rural income per capita in northwest (1,744 *yuan*) and southwest China (1,894 *yuan*) was also considerably lower than both that of the east (3,203 *yuan*) and the national average (2,476 *yuan*). Moreover, the share of agriculture in the total GDP was larger in the northwest and southwest (18 and 21 percent, respectively) than in the east and north (12 and 10 percent, respectively), indicating that farming is still a major source of rural income in western China.

**Table 6.1 Major economic indicators by region, 2002**

| | Population | Per capita GDP | AgGDP/GDP | Per capita income Urban | Rural |
|---|---|---|---|---|---|
| | *(10000)* | *(yuan)* | *(percent)* | | *(yuan)* |
| North | 12,459 | 10,758 | 10 | 8,296 | 2,703 |
| Northeast | 10,715 | 10,813 | 13 | 6,315 | 2,509 |
| East | 36,761 | 12,266 | 12 | 8,823 | 3,203 |
| Central | 30,892 | 9,018 | 15 | 8,505 | 2,641 |
| Southwest | 25,039 | 5,144 | 21 | 6,872 | 1,894 |
| Northwest | 11,652 | 6,180 | 18 | 6,304 | 1,744 |
| China | 127,518 | 9,255 | 14 | 7,703 | 2,476 |

*Notes*: 1. North: Beijing, Tianjin, Hebei, and Shanxi; Northeast: Liaoning, Jilin, and Heilongjiang; East: Shanghai, Jiangsu, Zhejiang, Anhui, Fujian, Jiangxi, and Shandong; Central-South: Henan, Hubei, Hunan, Guangdong, and Hainan; Southwest: Chongqing, Sichuan, Guizhou, Yunnan, Tibet, and Guangxi; Northwest: Inner Mongolia, Shaanxi, Gansu, Qinghai, Ningxia, and Xinjiang.
*Source:* Authors' calculations based on data reported by China's National Bureau of Statistics, Statistical Yearbook of China, 2003.

The difference in the share of the rural labor force employed by the rural non-farm sector is also seen to contribute significantly to the regional gap in rural income. For China as a whole, about 29 percent of the rural labor force was engaged in non-agricultural activities in 1997, and the non-farm sector contributed to more than one-third of the income for rural residents. In the east, the non-farm sector employed 40 percent of the rural labor force compared with less than 20 percent in northwest and southwest China.

Therefore, with an overwhelmingly large share of the rural labor force employed in agriculture, labor productivity is low in China's western region. For example, labor productivity in the southwest was half of the national level. Poor natural resource endowments and weak infrastructure prevent agricultural land from reaching its yield potential, while the high illiteracy rate and the lack of investment and personnel in science and technology research restrain the adoption of new technology and the improvement of agricultural productivity. Table 6.2 presents major social and infrastructural indicators by region. The coastal region is the most developed with the best infrastructure and human capital as well as superior agro-climatic conditions.[1] The western region is the least developed, having poor natural resources and an inadequate social infrastructure. The central region falls in-between the other two.

**Table 6.2 Social and infrastructural development**

| | Coastal region | Central region | Western region | National |
|---|---|---|---|---|
| | | *1985* | | |
| Illiteracy rate (%) | 22.5 | 28.0 | 35.8 | 28.0 |
| Years of schooling | 4.8 | 5.1 | 4.5 | 5.1 |
| Road density (km/1000 km$^2$) | 221.9 | 122.9 | 69.1 | 111.1 |
| Irrigation (%) | 58.0 | 36.0 | 40.0 | 44.0 |
| Annual rainfall (mm) | 1097.6 | 716.7 | 506.9 | |
| | | *1996* | | |
| Illiteracy rate (%) | 8.6 | 11.4 | 19.8 | 12.1 |
| Years of schooling | 6.9 | 6.6 | 6.1 | 7.0 |
| Road density (km/1000 km$^2$) | 306.2 | 136.6 | 81.5 | 138.3 |
| Irrigation (%) | 62.0 | 45.0 | 46.0 | 51.0 |
| Annual rainfall (mm) | 1127.3 | 686.6 | 506.9 | |

*Sources*: China Statistical Yearbooks, various years.

The education and infrastructure indicators in the west not only are the lowest in all of China but also show the slowest improvement. For example, the illiteracy rate in the coastal area was 22.5 percent in 1985, while the rate in western China was 35.8 percent. In 1995, the rate in the coastal region declined to 8.6 percent, but in the western region, the rate declined to just 19.8 percent. In terms of infrastructure, the road density in coastal China in 1985 was 222 km per thousand square km while the density in western China was 69 km per thousand square km. In 1995, the density in the coastal area increased to more than 300, but it was still about 80 km per thousand square km in western China. The gap in social,

[1] The coastal region includes the following provinces: Hebei, Liaoning, Shandong, Jiangsu, Zhejiang, Fujian, Guangdong, and Guangxi. The central region contains Shanxi, Inner Mongolia, Anhui, Jiangxi, Henan, Hubei, and Hunan. The remaining provinces are classified as the western region. Tibet is excluded due to the lack of data. Hainan is included in Guangdong Province. Beijing, Shanghai, and Tianjin are excluded because of their small share of rural areas and population.

economic, and infrastructural conditions between coastal and western China has increased since the reforms.

**Table 6.3 Measures of openness by region**

| Province/region | Trade-GDP ratio (97-99 average, %) | Per capita Foreign Investment, 1999 (US$) |
|---|---:|---:|
| North | 22.3 | 430 |
| Northwest | 8.7 | 92 |
| Northeast | 20.5 | 559 |
| East | 40.1 | 1,452 |
| Central | 6.7 | 163 |
| South | 96.6 | 1,860 |
| Southwest | 7.1 | 121 |
| National Average | 33.8 | 615 |

*Notes*: 1. North: Beijing, Tianjin, Hebei, Shanxi, Shandong, Shaanxi, and Henan; Northeast: Liaoning, Jilin, and Heilongjiang; East: Shanghai, Jiangsu, Zhejiang; Central: Anhui, Jiangxi, Hubei, and Hunan; South: Fujian, Guangdong, Guangxi, and Hainan; Southwest: Chongqing, Sichuan, Guizhou and Yunan; Northwest: Inner Mongolia, Gansu, Qinghai, Ningxia, Tibet, and Xinjiang.
*Sources*: China Statistical Yearbook (2000).

The difference in the degree of openness across regions might contribute to the income gap across regions as well. After China adopted its "opening-to-the-outside-world" policy in 1978, the degree of openness of China's economy, measured both by trade and foreign capital flows, increased dramatically. For example, the trade-GDP ratio quadrupled from 8.5 percent in 1978 to 36.5 percent in 1999. However, due to differences in geographical and social economic conditions, the extent of openness varies sharply across the provinces and regions. In Table 6.3, we use the trade-GDP ratio and per capita foreign direct investment figures to measure the gap in openness across regions in China. The three-year (1997-99) average of the trade-GDP ratio was as high as 97 and 40 percent for south and east China, respectively, but as low as 7 to 9 percent for the southwest, central and northwest regions. Similarly, the per capita foreign investment in 1999 in the south and east was $1,860 and $1,452 (U.S.), respectively. However, it was only $90 and $121 (U.S.) in the northwest and southwest, respectively.

As a result of this biased development policy, poverty has been increasingly concentrated within western China. Regardless of the sources of the data, it is clear that the incidence of rural poverty is significantly higher in western China than anywhere else in the country. Based on the World Bank's estimates, the poverty rate averaged 19 percent and 11 percent in northwest and southwest China, respectively, in 1996, while the comparable figure for the whole country was 6 percent. In contrast, for that same year, only 1.2 percent and 2.6 percent of the rural population lived under the poverty line in the eastern and central regions, respectively. Moreover, the reduction in the incidence of rural poverty was not as dramatic in western China as it was in the other regions. Much to the contrary, rural poverty is increasingly concentrated in the western provinces. The southwest and northwest regions together accounted for about 70 percent of the rural poor in China in 1996—a 40 percent increase compared to 1988 (Table 6.4). In contrast, the central, eastern, and northern regions accounted for a declining share of the total number of rural poor in China.

Many scholars have modeled the potential impact of China's entry into the WTO on overall economic growth, trade flows, and agricultural performance. While the aggregate effect at the national level is positive, it does not imply that all of China would benefit equally or that some regions may even be hurt by it—given the gap in economic development and openness. Thus, a national level assessment is clearly not enough to understand the impact of WTO entry on China's economy, especially on agriculture and the well-being of the rural population. Diao et al (2003) was one of the first to use a CGE model with disaggregated regional production to simulate the effects of the WTO accession on the agricultural and rural economy at the regional level, particularly in the less-developed regions. The authors divided China into seven regions (for agricultural production), and 28 sectors, including 15 disaggregated agricultural sectors for grain, cash crop, livestock, and processed agricultural activities. They then utilized the model to simulate China's WTO accession effects by reducing or removing tariff (and tariff equivalent) protections in the model.

As expected—and similar to many other studies—China's WTO accession (by reducing or eliminating import tariffs) would benefit the economy at the aggregate level. While liberalizing agricultural trade (scenario 1) raises the GDP by 1.4 percent, liberalizing both agricultural and non-agricultural trade (scenario 2) leads to a double gain in the GDP by 3.7 percent. The regional analysis reveals large differential impacts on agricultural production. For example, wheat is expected to decline about 3 percent at the national level in both scenarios, but at the regional level, if only agricultural trade is liberalized, then wheat production falls much more in the central, south, and southwest regions than it would nationally. If both agricultural and non-agricultural trade is fully liberalized, the east becomes the fourth region where wheat production declines substantially. In north China, which is a major wheat production region, accounting for almost 60 percent of national wheat output, production falls by only 2.6 percent in the second scenario. About 10 percent of total wheat was produced in the northwest region. Given the limit in the choice of cropping mix, wheat production actually slightly rises in this region in both scenarios.

**Table 6.4 Regional distribution of rural poor**

| | Xian and Sheng (2001) | | | World Bank (2001) | |
|---|---|---|---|---|---|
| | Poverty incidence | Poverty incidence | | Share of national total | |
| | 1998 | 1988 | 1996 | 1988 | 1996 |
| *North* | | *15.2* | *4.6* | *9.8* | *7.6* |
| Beijing | 2.37 | 0.5 | 0.8 | 0 | 0.1 |
| Tianjin | 16.16 | 1.8 | 0.3 | 0.1 | 0 |
| Hebei | 39.11 | 14 | 3.9 | 5.8 | 4.1 |
| Shanxi | 44 | 22.1 | 7.5 | 3.9 | 3.4 |
| *Northeast* | | *10.2* | *4.7* | *4.6* | *5.1* |
| Liaoning | 13.04 | 8 | 2.9 | 1.5 | 1.3 |
| Jilin | 18.18 | 8.8 | 4.7 | 1.1 | 1.3 |
| Heilongjian | 22.84 | 13.6 | 6.7 | 2.1 | 2.5 |
| *East* | | *7* | *1.2* | *14.9* | *6.4* |
| Shanghai | 0.45 | 0.3 | 0.1 | 0 | 0 |
| Jiangsu | 12.37 | 4.5 | 0.1 | 2 | 0.1 |
| Zhejiang | 2.5 | 2.8 | 0.1 | 0.8 | 0.1 |
| Anhui | 27.64 | 10.3 | 2.7 | 3.9 | 2.7 |
| Fujian | 2.73 | 3.9 | 0.5 | 0.8 | 0.3 |
| Jiangxi | 9 | 8.5 | 0.7 | 2.1 | 0.5 |
| Shandong | 15.58 | 9.4 | 1.9 | 5.3 | 2.7 |
| *Central-South* | | *13.6* | *2.6* | *23.1* | *11.3* |
| Henan | 31.75 | 25 | 4.3 | 14.6 | 6.6 |
| Hubei | 16.33 | 11 | 2.7 | 3.6 | 2.1 |
| Hunan | 5.08 | 7.9 | 1.5 | 3.4 | 1.6 |
| Guangdong | 2.46 | 2.7 | 0.2 | 1.1 | 0.2 |
| Hainan | | 12.1 | 8.2 | 0.4 | 0.8 |
| *Southwest* | | *20.5* | *10.5* | *31.9* | *41.2* |
| Chongqing | | | 6.6 | | 3.2 |
| Sichuan | 21.49 | 16.7 | 7 | 12.8 | 9.7 |
| Guizhou | 42 | 23 | 12.8 | 5.3 | 7.6 |
| Yunnan | 36.45 | 23.8 | 22.9 | 6.2 | 15.3 |
| Tibet | 57.33 | 32.3 | 10.1 | 0.5 | 0.4 |
| Guangxi | 20.08 | 24.1 | 6.4 | 7.2 | 5 |
| *Northwest* | | *26.2* | *18.6* | *15.7* | *28.4* |
| Inner Mongolia | 19.78 | 17.3 | 9.3 | 2 | 2.6 |
| Shaanxi | 38.06 | 24.9 | 17.5 | 5.3 | 9.6 |
| Gansu | 49.7 | 38.4 | 22.7 | 5.7 | 8.9 |
| Qinghai | 35.52 | 22.4 | 17.7 | 0.5 | 1.2 |
| Ningxia | 28.39 | 24.7 | 18.5 | 0.7 | 1.4 |
| Xinjiang | 45.64 | 22.3 | 27.4 | 1.4 | 4.8 |
| *China* | *22.25* | *13.9* | *6.3* | *100* | *100* |

Given the regional difference in cropping mix (especially the difference in the share of non-farm income in the total rural income), the WTO accession has even larger regional differential effects on rural income. Four regions will benefit from the full liberalization, while less-developed regions will suffer. The total rural income declines by 2 and 0.1 percent in the northwest and southwest, respectively (Table 6.5). The northeast, which is the major soybean production region in China, will gain little due to a rapid decline in soybean production caused by the competition from imported soybeans and soybean oil. If only agricultural trade is liberalized, then the income falls in all regions because of the decline in agricultural income. In this scenario, the two less-developed regions suffer disproportionately more than the other regions since the rural income would fall by 9.4 and 8 percent in the northwest and southwest, respectively, compared to a 3.6 percent drop at the national level.

In more advanced regions, such as east and south China, non-farm income accounted for as much as 70 to 80 percent of the total rural income. In less-developed regions, however, the share was often less than 20 percent. The results show that returns in the non-agricultural activities rose more than those in agriculture, benefiting the advanced regions since their non-farm income ratio is high. Moreover, as the wage rate of non-farm labor increases more rapidly than that of the agricultural labor after liberalization, more labor will move from agricultural to non-agricultural sectors. This would further benefit the developed regions, considering that these regions have more non-farm employment opportunities. For the less-developed regions, however, as agriculture is still their main income source, rural households will gain very little from engaging in non-farm activities.

With the decline in agricultural prices and the majority of the rural labor force still in agriculture, rural income is expected to decline in these regions. Table 6.6 presents the impact on agricultural labor. If only agriculture is liberalized, about 7 percent of rural labor in the five regions would move from agriculture into non-agriculture. Meanwhile, fully liberalizing both agriculture and non-agriculture would reduce labor migration to about 2 to 4 percent in these regions. As a result of the decline in agricultural employment, rural income from agriculture would decline by 8 to 9 percent among all regions (if only agriculture is liberalized). If both agriculture and non-agriculture are liberalized, then rural income from agriculture may either decline slightly or rise as shown in Table 6.5. Rural income from non-agriculture, however, would rise in both scenarios, except for less-developed regions in which migration opportunities are limited.

Surprisingly, non-farm income would increase more in the central region than in either the east or south—the two most advanced regions in China. This is because in the base, non-farm employment accounted for 40 and 31 percent of the total rural labor force in the east and south, respectively, but only 27 percent in the central region. With trade liberalization, the speed of labor migration—and thus the increase in non-farm income—in the central region can be more rapid than in either the east or the south, even though the share of non-farm income in total rural income is still greater in the east and south than in central China.

**Table 6.5 Impact of WTO entry on farmers' income (% change from the base)**

| | EXP-1 | EXP-2 |
|---|---|---|
| *Rural Income* | | |
| North | -3.99 | 1.46 |
| Northwest | -9.39 | -1.98 |
| Northeast | -5.90 | 0.03 |
| Central | -4.32 | 1.43 |
| East | -0.93 | 2.89 |
| South | -1.17 | 2.94 |
| Southwest | -8.07 | -0.10 |
| *National Average* | *-3.55* | *1.64* |
| | | |
| *Agriculture* | | |
| North | -9.04 | -0.58 |
| Northwest | -9.39 | -1.98 |
| Northeast | -9.45 | -1.81 |
| Central | -8.17 | -0.36 |
| East | -8.99 | 0.00 |
| South | -8.38 | 0.76 |
| Southwest | -8.07 | -0.10 |
| | | |
| *Non-agriculture* | | |
| North | 2.75 | 4.18 |
| Northwest | | |
| Northeast | 3.16 | 4.73 |
| Central | 4.73 | 5.62 |
| East | 1.59 | 3.79 |
| South | 1.69 | 3.81 |
| *Southwest* | | |

*Notes*:
1. EXP-1: Eliminating agricultural tariffs.
2. EXP-2: Eliminating all tariffs.
*Source*: Diao, Fan and Zhang (2003).

**Table 6.6 Impact of WTO on agricultural labor (% change from the base)**

| | EXP-1 | EXP-2 |
|---|---|---|
| North | -6.73 | -2.06 |
| Northwest | | |
| Northeast | -7.35 | -3.76 |
| Central | -7.11 | -3.72 |
| East | -7.49 | -1.90 |
| South | -6.49 | -1.59 |
| Southwest | | |

*Notes*:
1. EXP-1: Eliminating agricultural tariffs.
2. EXP-2: Eliminating all tariffs.

*Source*: Diao, Fan and Zhang (2003).

In order to understand the robustness of the model results with respect to the assumptions about migration, Diao et al (2003) carried out an additional experiment that eases the constraint on labor mobility between agriculture and non-agriculture in less-developed regions—all other assumptions being the same as in the previous experiments. The results from this new experiment show that without migration constraint, about 3.8 and 4.8 percent of the labor force can move out of agriculture in the northwest and southwest, respectively, after full trade liberalization in both agriculture and non-agriculture. This allows rural income to rise in the southwest—increasing 0.5 percent as opposed to decreasing 0.1 percent without migration—and decline less in the northwest—decreasing 1.44 percent as opposed to 1.98 percent.

Comparing the results of this experiment to what the authors had obtained from the previous scenarios, it is clear that migration plays an important role in improving the income of rural households. Moreover, the decline in rural income within the less-developed regions further affects the poor people of these regions. The poverty ratio is already high in the less-developed regions. Therefore, the careful design of government policies and the use of its limited resources to avoid the adverse effects of the WTO accession on the less-developed areas deserve great attention from not only China's policymakers but researchers and international development agencies as well.

## 3 Returns to Public Investment in Western China

Public spending is one of the most important instruments the government can use to achieve its goals of growth, poverty reduction, and balanced regional development. However, as we mentioned in the previous section, government spending has been biased against western China despite the potential high returns from public investments. In this section, we synthesize the evidence on relative returns in growth and poverty reduction to different types of investments in western China.

For the past several decades, there have been many attempts to estimate the impact of public investment on economic growth and poverty reduction. A significant feature in the literature is that most of the previous studies have only considered one type of government spending or investment. It is difficult to compare the relative returns to both growth and poverty reduction of these spending or investment. In these empirical studies, most of them used a single equation approach, which has at least four disadvantages. First, many poverty determinants—such as income, production or productivity growth, prices, wages, and non-farm employment—are generated from the same economic process as rural poverty. In other words, these variables are also endogenous variables. Ignoring this characteristic leads to biased estimates of poverty effects. Second, certain economic variables affect poverty through multiple channels. For example, improved rural infrastructure will not only reduce rural poverty through improved agricultural productivity, but it will also affect rural poverty through improved wages and non-farm employment. It is very difficult to capture these different effects in a single equation approach. Third, including only one type of public investment in estimating poverty reduction will lead to an upward bias on the impact of that particular investment. Finally, it is difficult to rank the effects of different types of investments on both growth and poverty reduction.

In order to systematically assess the impact of different types of public investment on both agricultural growth and poverty reduction, several studies at the International Food Policy Research Institute have tried to estimate simultaneous econometric systems that consist of many equations. One of these studies conducted by Fan, Zhang and Zhang (2004) used the Chinese provincial level data over the last several decades and estimated the returns of various public investments on both growth and poverty reduction by Chinese regions. In their model to track the effects of public investment on poverty through various channels, rural poverty is first modeled as a function of growth in agricultural production, changes in rural wages, growth in rural non-farm employment, and changes in agricultural prices. Increases in agricultural production or wages should reduce poverty. Improvements in relative prices (a domestic term meaning trade variable) for agriculture are expected to benefit the rural poor in the case of China since the majority of farmers are either subsistence or net sellers of agricultural products.[2]

Agricultural production is modeled as a function of conventional inputs such as labor, land, fertilizer, machinery, and public investment variables, such as the use of high-yielding varieties, public irrigation, roads, electrification, and education. Rural wages and non-farm employment are modeled as functions of

---

[2] This differs from India where the rural poor may suffer form higher agricultural prices due to the fact that many of them do not have land or have little land and are net buyers of agricultural products, mainly grains.

growth in agricultural production as well as public investment variables. Numerous studies have shown the important linkage between agricultural and nonagricultural growth. Ignoring the effect of public investment on rural poverty through this linkage could lead to an underestimation of the poverty reduction effects of government investment in agriculture. A similar downward estimation bias could arise from overlooking the impact of improved infrastructure and education on wages and employment.

The next set of the equations in the model estimated the relationships between government spending and the physical stocks of public capital, considering the lead and lag effects of various investment. By taking derivatives with respect to each public investment variable, the marginal impact in growth and poverty reduction can be derived through the estimated equations.

The results from their report show that the government's production-enhancing investments, such as agricultural R&D, irrigation, rural education, and infrastructure—including roads, electricity, and telecommunications—contributed to not only agricultural production growth but a reduction of rural poverty and regional inequality as well (Table 6.7). However, variations in the magnitude of the effects are large among different types of spending and across regions. Based on actual investments in 2000 and the parameters estimated from the model, the authors calculated the marginal returns of various investments to growth in agricultural and non-farm production and reduction of rural poverty and regional inequality. These returns were calculated for the nation as a whole and for three different economic zones. Since the estimated returns are recent, they can serve as a direct input into the current policy debate.

Government expenditure on education had the largest impact in reducing rural poverty and regional inequality and had significant impact on production growth. Increased rural non-farm employment was accountable for much of this poverty- and inequality-reducing effect. Government spending on agricultural R&D substantially improved agricultural production. In fact, this type of expenditure had the largest impact on agricultural production growth, which is much needed to meet the increasing food demands of a richer and larger population. Benefits of agricultural production growth also trickled down to the rural poor. The poverty-reduction effect per unit of additional agricultural R&D investment ranked second after investment in rural education.

Government spending on rural infrastructure (roads, electricity, and telecommunications) had a substantial impact in reducing poverty and inequality, owing mainly to improved opportunities for non-farm employment and increased rural wages. Investments in irrigation had only a modest impact on agricultural production growth and even less impact on rural poverty and inequality, even after trickle-down benefits were allowed for. One finding that was particularly striking is the minimal impact of specifically-targeted government anti-poverty loans. In fact, the poverty-reducing impact of these loans was the least out of all the types of government spending considered in the study.

**Table 6.7 Returns to public investment in China, 2000**

| | Coastal | Central | Western | China |
|---|---|---|---|---|
| *Returns in total rural GDP* | | *(yuan per yuan invested)* | | |
| R&D | 5.54 | 6.63 | 10.19 | 6.75 |
| Irrigation | 1.62 | 1.11 | 2.13 | 1.45 |
| Roads | 8.34 | 6.90 | 3.39 | 6.57 |
| Education | 11.98 | 8.72 | 4.76 | 8.96 |
| Electricity | 3.78 | 2.82 | 1.63 | 2.89 |
| Telephone | 4.09 | 4.60 | 3.81 | 4.22 |
| *Returns in agricultural GDP* | | *(yuan per yuan invested)* | | |
| R&D | 5.54 | 6.63 | 10.19 | 6.75 |
| Irrigation | 1.62 | 1.11 | 2.13 | 1.45 |
| Roads | 1.62 | 1.74 | 1.73 | 1.69 |
| Education | 2.18 | 2.06 | 2.33 | 2.17 |
| Electricity | 0.81 | 0.78 | 0.88 | 0.82 |
| Telephone | 1.25 | 1.75 | 2.49 | 1.63 |
| *Returns in non-farm GDP* | | *(yuan per yuan invested)* | | |
| R&D | 6.71 | 5.16 | 1.66 | 4.88 |
| Irrigation | 9.80 | 6.66 | 2.43 | 6.79 |
| Roads | 2.96 | 2.04 | 0.75 | 2.07 |
| Education | 2.85 | 2.85 | 1.32 | 2.59 |
| *Returns in poverty reduction* | *(no. of poor reduced per 10,000 yuan invested)* | | | |
| R&D | 3.72 | 12.96 | 24.03 | 10.74 |
| Irrigation | 1.08 | 2.16 | 5.02 | 2.31 |
| Roads | 2.68 | 8.38 | 10.03 | 6.63 |
| Education | 5.03 | 13.90 | 18.93 | 11.88 |
| Electricity | 2.04 | 5.71 | 7.78 | 4.85 |
| Telephone | 1.99 | 8.10 | 13.94 | 6.17 |
| Poverty loan | 3.70 | 3.57 | 2.40 | 3.03 |

*Sources*: Fan, Zhang, and Zhang (2004).

**Table 6.8 Returns in GDP to road investment**

| | High Quality | Low Quality |
|---|---|---|
| | *(yuan per yuan)* | |
| *Returns in Total GDP* | | |
| Average | 1.55 | 5.99 |
| Northeast | 1.35 | 3.61 |
| North | 1.48 | 6.11 |
| Northwest | 1.13 | 1.44 |
| Central | 1.71 | 6.57 |
| Southeast | 1.61 | 18.63 |
| Southwest | 1.91 | 7.47 |
| South | 1.29 | 7.57 |
| *Returns in Urban GDP* | | |
| Average | 0.99 | 3.53 |
| Northeast | 0.95 | 2.33 |
| North | 0.97 | 3.70 |
| Northwest | 0.69 | 0.81 |
| Central | 0.90 | 3.18 |
| Southeast | 1.07 | 11.45 |
| Southwest | 1.05 | 3.78 |
| South | 0.88 | 4.78 |
| *Returns in Agricultural GDP* | | |
| Average | N.S | 1.48 |
| Northeast | N.S | 0.64 |
| North | N.S | 1.26 |
| Northwest | N.S | 0.45 |
| Central | N.S | 2.50 |
| Southeast | N.S | 2.85 |
| Southwest | N.S | 3.23 |
| South | N.S | 1.77 |
| *Returns in Rural Non-farm GDP* | | |
| Average | 0.65 | 5.34 |
| Northeast | 0.51 | 2.38 |
| North | 0.63 | 4.74 |
| Northwest | 0.45 | 1.19 |
| Central | 0.85 | 7.97 |
| Southeast | 0.75 | 15.01 |
| Southwest | 0.54 | 5.39 |
| South | 0.51 | 6.21 |

*Note*: 1. Except returns in agricultural GDP to high quality roads, all estimates are statistically significant at the 10% level.
*Sources*: Fan and Chan-Kang (2004).

**Table 6.9 Returns in poverty reduction to road investment**

| | High Quality | Low Quality |
|---|---|---|
| | *(number per 10,000 yuan)* | |
| *Returns in Urban Poverty Reduction* | | |
| Average | 0.05 | 0.19 |
| Northeast | 0.11 | 0.30 |
| North | 0.03 | 0.12 |
| Northwest | 0.15 | 0.19 |
| Central | 0.05 | 0.21 |
| Southeast | 0.01 | 0.15 |
| Southwest | 0.11 | 0.40 |
| South | 0.01 | 0.03 |
| *Returns in Rural Poverty Reduction, Official* | | |
| Average | 0.08 | 1.12 |
| Northeast | 0.04 | 0.36 |
| North | 0.07 | 0.97 |
| Northwest | 0.28 | 1.30 |
| Central | 0.05 | 0.64 |
| Southeast | 0.01 | 0.32 |
| Southwest | 0.40 | 5.70 |
| South | 0.02 | 0.45 |
| *Returns in Rural Poverty Reduction, Xian and* | | |
| Average | 0.31 | 5.67 |
| Northeast | 0.14 | 1.46 |
| North | 0.52 | 8.61 |
| Northwest | 0.59 | 3.39 |
| Central | 0.35 | 7.20 |
| Southeast | 0.10 | 4.70 |
| Southwest | 1.01 | 22.18 |
| South | 0.08 | 2.16 |

*Note*: 1. All estimates are statistically significant at the 10% level.
*Sources*: Fan and Chan-Kang (2004).

The returns of government spending on both production growth and poverty reduction are marked with large regional variation. In terms of returns to growth in agriculture, R&D, irrigation, education and rural telephones have the highest return in the western region. In terms of returns in rural non-farm GDP, it is still the coastal area where most of the investments have the highest returns. In terms of the poverty effects (for all types of investments), the west region has the highest return, followed by the central and the coastal regions as might be expected from the geographical distribution of the poor in China.

Out of all the types of investment, R&D and education generated the highest returns in the Western region, lifting 25 and 19 poor people, respectively, above the poverty line for every 10,000 *yuan* invested in 2000. In the central and coastal regions, R&D and education were also the most effective investments for reducing poverty, even though the actual number of poor people lifted out of poverty is lower than that of west China.

In the western region, investments in R&D and education generated the highest returns in terms of poverty reduction as well as in rural, agricultural, and non-farm GDP growth in 2000. In the coastal region, on the other hand, investments in education and roads yielded both the largest economic and poverty-reduction returns, while in the central region, education, R&D, and roads were the most effective investments. Therefore, targeting is very important as the magnitude of the effects differs among different types of investments as well as across regions.

However, the above study involved highly aggregated types of investment. This high aggregation may mask important differentials even with the same type of investment. For example, within education, primary education may have different impact on growth and on poverty reduction than higher education. Similarly, the different quality of roads may also matter. For this reason, Fan and Chan-Kang (2004) developed an analytical framework to estimate the effects of different types of roads on growth and poverty reduction in China by using provincial-level data for 1982 through 1999. The study differs from the previous study by Fan, et al, in two aspects: (1) it differentiates across different qualities of roads; and (2) it expands the effects of infrastructure investment on growth and poverty reduction to both the rural and urban areas.

The most significant finding of this study is the high returns from low quality roads, which are mostly rural roads. The marginal impact from lower-quality road investments is more than quadruple that of high-quality roads. Even in terms of the urban GDP, the return from low-quality roads, or rural roads, was greater than that of high-quality roads. While high-quality roads do not have a significant impact on agricultural GDP, low-quality roads can generate more than 1.48 *yuan* in the agricultural GDP for every *yuan* invested. Investment in low-quality roads also generates high return in rural non-farm GDP. Every *yuan* invested in low quality roads yields more than 5 *yuan* of rural non-farm GDP.

In terms of urban poverty reduction, the impact from low-quality roads is larger than the corresponding impact from high-quality roads. Likewise, the effects of low-quality roads on rural poverty reduction are larger than those from high-quality roads.

Another significant finding of the study is its trade-off between growth and poverty reduction when investing in different parts of China. Road investments often yield much higher economic growth in the eastern and central part of China, while they result in a much greater poverty reduction in western China. The western region, however, is diversified. Returns from the road investment on growth and poverty reduction are larger in the southwest region, one of poorest regions in China, than in the northwest region.

## 4 Development Strategy for Western Rural China

Throughout the history of economic development, one can observe that as a country moves from the low-income, or primarily agriculture, to the middle-income category (rapid industrialization period), regional inequality may increase. However, as the country continues to move to a higher income category, regional inequality will come down eventually[3]. China has reached the middle-income country status and will reach high-income country status in near future. One would expect regional inequality might come down, but this will not happen automatically. How China can maintain a high growth rate, which is much needed to increase the per capita income and to keep unemployment at bay, while having a more balanced regional growth will be a constant challenge that China must face in the future. High regional inequality will hinder future growth due to the lack of both demand from the vast low-income population in the west as well as the much-needed human capital (the poor cannot afford education and health care) for economic growth. In addition, it can trigger social and political instability, thereby making it impossible to achieve any long-sustained economic growth.

### *4.1 Promoting growth in rural sectors*

As Kanbur and Zhang have shown, the large regional gap in income comes from the inherent gap between the rural and urban sectors. West China lags behind mainly because agriculture—and the rural sector, in general—still accounts for large shares of the GDP. Lower productivity in the rural sector, particularly in the agricultural sector, has been the major reason of the low productivity for the overall economy.

Empirical evidence (e.g. Fan, Zhang and Zhang) has also shown that investment in rural areas can yield large returns. Therefore, the government should continue its efforts to increase overall investment in rural areas. Rural investment accounted for only 19 percent of the total government expenditures in 1997, but rural residents account for 69 percent of China's total population. Moreover, almost 50 percent of the national GDP was produced by the rural sector (agriculture and rural township and village enterprises) in 1997. The government's rural spending as a percentage of the rural GDP is only about 5 percent compared with 11.6 percent for the whole economy. China has implemented an urban- and industry-biased investment policy for the past several decades. As a result, the rural-urban income gap is gigantic and has increased over time. Any policies

[3] This is similar to the so-called Kuznets Curve.

against the rural sector will aggravate the existing disparity and should be discontinued.

In particular, the central government should re-direct its public resources towards the western region. West China shows the highest returns to all kinds of public investments targeted at reducing rural poverty and regional inequality. This is consistent with the national strategy to develop this region. In particular, investment in agricultural research, education, and rural infrastructure should be the government's top priorities. The most critical, however, is the universal and free primary education, ideally lasting for nine years, that is covered by the central government.

### *4.2 Correcting Government Regional Biased Policy*

In addition to biased regional investment policies, a predatory price policy on natural resources that has been used by the government has been the major culprit in the worsening of regional inequality. For the past several decades—particularly under the previous centrally-planned economy—natural resources, such as minerals, oil, gas, and even land, have been owned by the central government. These resources were shipped to the eastern regions at much lower prices or even free of charge, transferring rents to the coastal areas. The western provinces, although rich in these resources, benefited very little from the exploitation of these resources. Even worse is the latest reform of these state-owned enterprises, which left the millions of laid-off workers and degraded environment under the responsibility of local governments.

### *4.3 Promoting a More Sustainable and Environmentally Friendly Development in Western China*

China's agriculture has been growing at more than 4 percent per annum. However, this rapid growth has been achieved at the cost of a degraded environment and the overexploitation of natural resources. Soil and wind erosion, acid rain, water and air pollution, land degradation, soil salinization, desertification, deforestation, grassland destruction, and loss of biodiversity and wildlife habitat are widespread in China.

Western China's environment is fragile. Most of the soil that is prone to wind erosion, desertification and grassland destruction is concentrated in this region. The west also hosts the majority of China's wildlife and obviously embodies a significant potential for tourism in the future. This is all crucial for China's future economic development as well as the well-being of all Chinese. Therefore, the environment in western China needs to be preserved for future development.

### *4.4 Reforming the fiscal system for more equitable regional growth*

China is highly decentralized in its government spending. Local government accounts for more than 70 percent of all government spending. The central government plays a limited role in equalizing regional development through its financial transfer. Most of the transfer from the central government to the local governments is tax rebates, which is distinctly biased against the poor provinces in the western region of China. In fact, this may be one of the major reasons behind the increased regional inequality that began in 1988 when China introduced its new financial responsibility system. Under this system, every province would sign a contract with the central government in regard to each other's obligations and responsibilities. This system would give each province more incentives to develop its economy, so they can retain more revenues. Poor provinces, however, would suffer since their tax bases are low. As a result of this policy, the inequality in the per capita government budget has increased dramatically. For example, the gap in per capita budget spending between the richest and the poorest province has increased from 6.1 times in 1990 to 19.1 times in 1999 (Wong, 2003).

To reduce the regional inequality, the central government has to increase its ability in fiscal transfers to support the development of western China.

## 5 Conclusions

Over the past few decades, China has experienced rapid economic growth and a significant reduction in poverty. Regional inequality, however, has increased during this same period of time, raising many concerns among policymakers. Containing regional inequality is not only a social goal, but also a pre-condition to achieve sustained economic growth in the long-run.

A major source of regional inequality comes from both between and within China's regions, but the between-region inequality has increased much faster than the within-region inequality. When regional inequality is decomposed into different sectors, it is found that inequality within the rural sector is much larger than that within the urban sector. Moreover, the increase in regional inequality comes mostly from the much slower growth in the rural sector.

Therefore, the strategy to reduce regional inequality should focus on developing the rural sectors and increasing the central government's investment in education and infrastructure—all of which should occur in China's western region. In particular, the central government should gradually increase its education investment in the western rural areas to provide free education for all children through 9th grade. It should also correct the existing policy biases against the west China, such as those concerning the ownership and pricing of natural resources. Both explicit and implicit discriminatory policies against rural migrants in urban centers—including various kinds of registrations, excessive school fees for their children's education and health care—should be abolished so that rural labor in western China can migrate to work in the coastal and central regions. Since the western region of China is environmentally fragile and hosts a majority of China's natural wonders, protecting these natural resources should be an equally important priority to achieve long-term sustainable growth.

## References

China State (National) Statistical Bureau, *China statistical yearbook* (Beijing: China Statistical Publishing House, 2003).

Diao, X., Fan, S. and Zhang, X., 'China's WTO accession: impacts on regional agricultural income—a multi-region, general equilibrium analysis', *Journal of Comparative Economics* vol. 31 (2003): 332-351.

Fan, S., Zhang, L. and Zhang, X., 'Investment, Reforms and Poverty in Rural China', *Economic Development and Cultural Change,* Vol. 52, (2)(2004): 395-422.

Fan, S. and Kang-Chan, C., 'Road Development, Economic Growth and Poverty Reduction in China' (IFPRI Mimeo, 2004).

Ministry of Agriculture. 1985–2003. *China agricultural development report* (Beijing: China Agricultural Publishing House).

Ravi, K. and Zhang, X., 'Which Regional Inequality? The Evolution of Rural-Urban and Coastal-Inland Inequality in China from 1983 to 1995', *Journal of Comparative Economics* 27, 4 (December, 1999): 686-701.

Wong, C., *China: National Development and Sub-national Finance* (Beijing: CITIC Publishing House, 2003).

World Bank, *China: Overcoming rural poverty* (Washington, DC: World Bank, 2003).

Xian, Z. and Sheng, L., *PRC's Rural Residents with Consumption Less Than 860 Yuan: Targeting Group and Characteristics* (Memos, National Statistical Bureau, Beijing, China, 2001).

Chapter 7

# Taiwan's Agricultural Development: Experience and Lessons

Chia-Chu Hou
Jack W. Hou

## 1 Introduction

Many opportunities have opened up for foreign companies with China's entry to the WTO. The timeline differs for the various sectors of the market, and the expected impact on China's domestic economy is just as varied. Though many large companies around the world have shown tremendous interest in the service sector (financial and insurance, especially) and the promise of the world's largest consumer market, scholars and policy makers in China are increasingly concerned with the impact on China's agricultural sector.

China formally abandoned its "self-reliant" strategy for food production in the early 1970s, and embarked on a path that eventually led to the reform that changed the way of life for all Chinese, and indeed the world.[1] The success of China's reform is beyond doubt, and has generated a sizable literature both within China and across the world. Agriculture was the original cause of China's reform, and may be one of the reasons why we observe the current success compared to the stagnation of Russia (Hou and Hou, 2004).

It is well known that the first six years of China's Comprehensive Economic Reform was almost exclusively aimed at the rural agricultural sector. Its success is well documented with the impressive increase in food production and improvement of the livelihoods of the farmers. However, this two-tract system also benefited the urban industrial workers via the partial restoration of consumption choice (Fei and Hou, 1994; Hou 2004). However, these did not come without a cost, as the subsidy implicit in the two-tract system has put considerable strain on the central budget.[2]

---

[1] For a detailed discussion of how and why the Chinese leaders take the path away from Communism toward a market–oriented economy, refer to Hou, Mead, and Nagahashi (2005).

[2] Price subsidies did not appear till the reform began in 1978, and accounted for just under 1 percent of total government expenditure. By 2000, it had swelled to almost 10 percent. During this same period, the central budget balance changed from a 1 billion *yuan* surplus to an astounding 250 billion *yuan*, and the total cost of the price subsidy had ballooned to over 104 billion *yuan*, with the latest figures approaching 150 billion.

Since China is entering the WTO as an LDC, such subsidies are permitted under the WTO regulation, but it is perhaps beyond what the Chinese government can afford. In addition to this drain on the central budget, the cost disadvantage of certain agricultural production may persist even with the subsidy.

This chapter will begin with a brief outline of the problem and dilemma facing China. We will then look back into history and discuss the similar problem faced by Taiwan shortly after the Land Reform initiated by the Nationalist government after their retreat to Taiwan. Once this is established, we will discuss the policy that alleviated the problem and laid the foundation for the Taiwan "economic miracle" (growth with equity). We are most certainly *not* advocating a wholesale adoption of Taiwan's experience, as mainland China is very different from Taiwan (size is just one of the most obvious differences). Rather, we simply hope that Taiwan's success can inspire scholars and policy makers in formulating strategies that may work for mainland China, while Taiwan's failures serve as a lesson to development pre-emptive methods to avoid these pitfalls. We feel this is especially beneficial for the development of Western regions of China, and given the "Go West" strategy of the current stage of development, such organizations may be a useful element in the overall strategic planning for western China. We will share some specific thoughts at the end of the chapter.

## 2 WTO Admission and China's Rural Agriculture Economy

The domestic market of China will become increasingly open per WTO requirements. This has generated considerable excitement among many agriculture-exporting nations, such as the United States. Indeed, such was the sentiment expressed in a progress report on China's WTO accession talks by then Secretary of Agriculture, Ann M. Veneman (17 September 2001), "China's entry to the World Trade Organization will slash barriers to the sale of American agricultural products in the world's most populous country." U.S. total exports to China have grown from negligible levels to more than $28 billion in 2003 (twice as much as 1999). Based on the first quarter of 2004, overall trade volume may increase 25 percent. Agricultural exports in fiscal year 1999 were $1.1 billion and are expected to reach $1.6 billion in 2005 (Colby, Price, and Tuan, 2000).

The impact of WTO on China's agriculture is not entirely clear. Though the changes to Chinese agriculture are likely to be dramatic, but there is also evidence that the Chinese agriculture is more resilient than many give it credit for. The trade dispute between China and Japan/South Korea on its horticulture exports is evidence of China's strength in this area of agriculture. And despite an aggressive marketing campaign promoting US citrus products, California citrus growers are facing stiff competition from cheaper domestic producers. The prospect, however, for grain producers is much more bleak.

It is well accepted that the "origin" of China's economic reform was in the production of grain. Yet, China's domestically produced grain is not competitive against US production, either in terms of price or quality. With the accession into the WTO, many Chinese grain farmers will be forced to change their crop selection or cropping mix. This, however, raises many issues. To what should the farmers switch? How? Is the Chinese government ready to submit to a total reliance on imported grain to feed its 1.2 billion people?[3] These are all tough questions that need to be addressed.

Grain shortage was the original force that led the Chinese government toward the road of economic reform, and "self-reliant" grain production has long been abandoned, but the importance of producing a large quantity of grain domestically remains a top priority for the Chinese government. The prospect of feeding 1.2 billion people is a monumental task. The fact that China has been able to mostly accomplish this for the past 40 years is an amazing achievement in itself. With China's success in external trade and the accumulated foreign exchange surplus, feeding the people with imported grain is certainly feasible. But maintaining a sizable domestic grain production is desirable in many aspects. It gives the government some control over the supply; it stabilizes the economy, national security concerns, not to mention the historical heritage. Dynasties have fallen because of famine resulting from grain shortages, and besides, what will happen to the huge number of grain farmers?

The demand for grain is rather inelastic, thus even a slight increase in supply will reduce the price significantly. With the introduction of foreign competition, the current price subsidy policy will be a tremendous fiscal burden and will undoubtedly be beyond the range of feasibility. The proper way to confront this issue is from the side of cost effectiveness. From basic micro theory, we can characterize grain production as $Q = f$ (land, labor, capital, technology, entrepreneurship).

China has had a land shortage since the 10th century. To further add to the problem, the current average farm size is too small to utilize the increasing returns to scale inherent in large commercial agricultural production that has made the US such a successful food producer (despite the fact that less than 2 percent of the labor force is involved in agriculture). Labor is abundant, but China's labor-intensity in farming has exceeded the optimal level, and adding labor may only worsen the problem. In contrast, capital-intensity is too low, as many farmers are unable to afford modern mechanized farming, especially in the poorer inland areas. In addition, the farmers do not own the land, and hence really lack the incentive to

[3] The distinguished professor Du Run *yuan* sheng urged the government to look at the import of food with a more liberal attitude, "as China is land–scarce economy, the importation of food can be viewed as importing of land."

improve land quality. Combined with heavy taxes and the lack of finances,[4] the plight of the farmers is well known.

We specifically entered "technology" as a separate input (rather than have it infused into capital) as it involves more than just machines; it includes new systems, methods, crop rotation, and hybrid varieties. Though China is quite advanced in such research, the propagation to the small farmers is less than successful. With the guaranteed procurement by the government, many farmers act like tenants (but much better paid economically) and lack the entrepreneurship to maximize profit or truly commercialize their production.

How do we deal with this difficult situation? As the title of our chapter clearly indicates, we believe there are experiences that Taiwan can share with the Chinese farmers, and on the negative side, the problems facing the Taiwan agriculture sector n the last twenty or so years can also serve as a warning for preemptive policy (lessons to be learned).

Borrowing a page from the Chinese Communist Party, Chiang Kai-shek implemented a large-scale land reform immediately after his retreat to Taiwan (1949). This redistributed roughly 13 percent of the national wealth and laid the foundation for the "Taiwan Miracle" of rapid growth with income equality. However, it was evident almost immediately that the lot size was too small, and armers lacked the experience, expertise, and technical knowledge. To aid the farmers, and fully solidify land reform, the Council of Agriculture was established as a cabinet-level administration under the Executive *Yuan*. This became the agency responsible for agricultural policy in the central government.

The Council of Agriculture took a two-pronged approach. The government took the role of developing technology. There are now 30 government agencies that are actively engaged in agricultural research, of which the Agriculture Research Institute was the most exemplary. The Institute is under the jurisdiction of the provincial government (with six regional agriculture improvement stations) with the expressed role of experimenting and developing new agriculture-related "technology." As a second channel, the government encouraged and utilized the existing agriculture organizations as an instrument to disseminate the new innovations developed by the Institute and to promote cooperative efforts amongst the farmers. Due to the severe budget constraint the Taiwan government was facing at the time, it was vital that these agricultural organizations were not a drain on limited government resources. With this in mind, we now turn to the discussion of the Taiwan agriculture development.

---

[4] The direct taxes are really not that high, but when the various "fees" are added, the total effective tax rate is much too high. The troubled agriculture credit union cannot provide financing for the farmers, while the postal savings actually extract large amount of savings from the villages to finance urban development. Without landownership (hence no collateral), most farmers have little chance of obtaining loans to improve or even sustain their farms.

## 3 Historical Overview of the Farmer's Association (FA)

As can be seen, the problems facing the Taiwan farmers in the early 1950s are a mirror image of the problems facing the mainland Chinese farmers today, with the exception of land ownership and excessive taxes/fees which was resolved via Taiwan's land reform. The Taiwan Farmer's Association was designed to deal with the remainder of the issues. Taiwan's Farmer's Association (FA) is the continuation of the Agriculture Association and the Agricultural Union of the Japanese-occupied Taiwan. The Agriculture Association is made of tenants or sharecroppers. It was a spontaneous organization of tenants/sharecroppers to fight against the government. However, under the influence of the Japanese colonial government's economic policy, they evolved into a governing instrument. The president and the board of directors became government appointments and the Association morphed into a semi-governmental organization (Li, 1984).

The Agricultural Union, on the other hand, was a government-sponsored program from the start. It was built on the "Taiwan Production Union Regulations" proposed by the Colonial Governor of Taiwan in1913 (Hu, 2003). In modern terminology, this production union is what we term as a "cooperative." In 1933, realizing the small scale nature of agricultural production, the Colonial Governor initiated a series of actions (based on the aforementioned Regulation) forming a copulation of agricultural production, purchasing, sales, credit, and production utilization. This multi-functioning agricultural union formed the crude form of the Taiwan Farmer's Association.

After the retrocession of Taiwan (post-WWII), the government established the Agriculture Statute. The Agricultural Association was changed into the Farmer's Association. While its scope and organization was in the principle of the Agricultural Union, it was structured as a multi-function organization. The FA's main objectives are supply/marketing, propagate, credit, and husbandry insurance (which was added later). In 1974, however, the FA's scope of operations was redefined as an agent acting on behalf of the government or public/private organizations, under the revised Agriculture Statue.

The relationship between Taiwan's agriculture and economic development can be divided into two periods with 1973 being the breakpoint (Hou, 1980). Prior to 1973, Taiwan can be described as "nurturing industry with agriculture." It is in this period that Taiwan's agriculture blossomed and grew. After 1973, Taiwan moved into the era of "developing agriculture with industry." During this period, the main focus is on the direction of capital flows. In line with the objective of this chapter, we will examine only the earlier period where agriculture development played a major role.

The turning point in Taiwan's agriculture was 1952 when the production finally regained the pre-war level. In the next twenty years, agricultural production accelerated at an impressive rate. This was soon followed by the industrialization of Taiwan, clearly substantiating Rostow's theory that agricultural take-off was the prerequisite for the general economic take-off. During this period of "nurturing industry with agriculture," we can further divide into four phases: 1945–51, 1952–61, 1962–68, and 1969–72. In the first phase, agriculture was recovering from the ravages of WWII and going through radical structural changes (Hou, 1995), while in the last phase agriculture is already fading into the sunset. The prime of Taiwan's agriculture development was in phases two and three. For that purpose, we focus our discussion to the role of the farmer's association (FA) during this decade and a half.

Before we begin the detailed discussion of FA and its role in Taiwan's economic development, let us outline the main events in phases two and three. The second phases started in 1952 with the Taiwan government's implementation of its four-year economic construction plan. The policy objective focused on the development of agriculture with the aim of nurturing industry with agriculture. The policy instruments included land-to-the-tiller (which began in phase one and was completed in phase two) and the organization of the FA. The accomplishment included reform of the agriculture credit system, improvement of production technology, increased agriculture investment, and strengthening agriculture finances. The policy objective in phase three was still on agriculture development, with the instrumental focus also on the improvement of agriculture finances and technology.

The organization of functions of the FA during the second and third phase included (in descending order):

1. Rigorous classification of membership eligibility,
2. Maximize benefits to the farmers,
3. Dutifully perform government assigned functions.

The supply/marketing, propagation, and credit provision all showed vast improvements in phase two, establishing the confidence of the farmers in their FA. In the third phase, propagation was in the decline, but the financial and credit function of the FA continued to expand. The supply/marketing function also continued to grow, mainly benefiting from the increase in government-commissioned business (though the growth rate was down from phase two).

With this established, the rest of the chapter will refer to the "nurturing industry with agriculture" as *yesterday*, developing agriculture with industry" as *today*, while *tomorrow* refers to the revitalization of the Taiwan Farmer's Association.

## 4 Yesterday: Nurturing Industry with Agriculture (1945–73)

After the retrocession of Taiwan, organizations in the agricultural sector went through a period of confusion. The Agricultural Association was changed into the Farmer's Association, while the Agricultural Union was left unchanged. This allowed the coexistence of both systems, but was complicated by the fact that the president of the FA was also the chairman of the board of the Union. To alleviate this confusion, the government separated the two in 1948, but changed its mind and merged the two in February of the following year. Under the suggestion of American advisors, the formal reconstruction of the FA was initiated at end of 1951 and completed by the end of the next year. This reorganization established a Farmer's Association with practicing farmers as the main body. The organization chart has a tri-level structure, containing a total of 340 FAs:

Provincial-level Farmers' Association (1)
County / City-level Farmers' Association (22)
Township-level Farmers' Association (313).

FA membership was also defined during this reform. There are two types of membership: regular and supporting members. The former are actual cultivating farmers, while the latter are local residents that are not direct participants of the farming sector. The supporting members do not have the right to vote, but can be elected to the board of supervisors (though they cannot account for more than one-third of the total board). The members directly elect both the board of directors and the board of supervisors. The township FA has nine members on the board of directors, the county/city board is made up of nine to fifteen board members, while the provincial FA has fifteen to twenty-one board members. Each township FA is divided into two divisions: supply/marketing and credit (an insurance division was added later). It also has a propagation section and a treasury section. The county/city FA do not have the credit division, but both "sections" were elevated to departments. The provincial FA does not have the credit division either, but propagation and treasury were further elevated to division status.

The chairman (president) of the board (of directors) and the standing members of the board of supervisors are directly elected by the respective boards from the board members. There is an executive manager at every level of the FA. This manager is hired from the list of qualified candidates provided by the central government or the provincial government. All other employees are hired by the executive manager from the pool of candidates that have passed the qualification exam administered by the Taiwan Agriculture Council (TAC). Employees can come from various backgrounds, but those that work in propagation are almost exclusively from agricultural academies.

The supply/marketing division handles both, by definition, the marketing and the supply aspect of the FA. On the supply side, they are not only responsible for the procurement of production inputs such as fertilizers and pesticides, but also the provision of daily consumption goods for its farming members. Thus, many of the rural FAs also operate supermarkets to service its members. The sales side is the cooperative transportation and sales promotion of agricultural products. The credit division is to fill the void of financial services as most rural areas lack commercial banks or other financial institutions. The credit division of the FA accepts deposits from the community (including government and schools) and makes loans to needy farmers. This is the main contribution of the supporting members, as they have surplus funds that create the deposits in FA credit unions. This also simultaneously benefits local commerce and industrial development as these investment needs are also satisfied by loans from the credit unions of the FA, though the primary function of the FA credit union is direct loans to farming members.

The credit division of the farmer's association was the fastest growing area. According to Chu (1975), the deposit/loan growth rates were 21.2 percent and 20.2 percent during the first phase, respectively. The growth rate further increased to 26.4 percent and 25.2 percent in the second phase. The growth rate of the supply/marketing division's sales receipts were 14.2 percent and 10.3 percent in the first two phases, respectively. Growth rate from government commissioned business activities were 7 percent and 16.5 percent. By regulation, 60 percent of the profit from the credit relative business of the FA must be devoted to propagation activities. Despite this, the growth rate of propagation expenditures declined from 6.6 percent in the first phase to 6.0 percent in the second phase.

The above focused on the growth of the credit division, but the FA has other sources of income. According to the Agriculture Statute, there are eight sources of income: initiation fee (for joining the FA), annual membership dues, enterprise funds (specific to certain function within the FA), agriculture propagation, donations, government subsidies, profits from various FA businesses (such as warehouse, rice husking, etc.), and funding from various government commissioned projects. However, none of these income sources are as important as the profit from the credit division. The reason is quite simple. Unlike other financial institutions, the credit division of the FA has no shareholders or other financial obligations, hence the net earnings are pure profits for the FA. The reason it can operate as a financial institution is simply based on government authorization, which also led to special "preference" shown by various government agencies.

At that time, most banks were not allowed to have checking accounts or had strict requirements to qualify, while checks from the credit unions of the FA flooded the market. This attracted many small businesses depositors, as checks are a major instrument in smoothing out transactions between cash outlays and receipts. The main reason for this preferential treatment from the government was to use the profits from the credit division to support the agricultural propagation activities, as one may recall the regulation requires that 60 percent of the profit from the credit activities to be used to support propagation. This "relieved" the government from having to directly finance or subsidize many agriculture-related policies.

The agricultural propagation function is to transmit the new products, new varieties, new systems, new inputs, and new methods developed by the Agricultural Research Institute plus its six district (agriculture improvement) stations and other developmental agencies. These all fall in the category of propagation of technical innovations. During this period, the growth rate of technical improvements was 37.5 percent per annum (Wang, 1986). The annual growth rate of agriculture production was 8.25 percent, a clear indication of the importance and success of the technical improvements.

The broad definition of agriculture includes agricultural production, animal husbandry, fishing, and forestry. Forestry is exclusively the domain of the government, and our discussion of fishery will be limited to farm fishery, i.e. the narrow definition of agriculture. This can be divided into three areas (Li, 1984), and we will start with the technical innovations within agriculture crops.

### *4.1 Technical Improvements in Agricultural Crops*

Technical innovations can be categorized into new products, new inputs, new varieties, new systems, and new methods.

#### *4.1.1 New System: Crop Rotation System*

Due to the weather conditions, central and southern Taiwan has always been suitable for multiple harvesting. The original prevailing system was either rice-rice-sugar cane (or corn, soy bean, flax, horticulture, or tobacco) or rice-horticulture/sugar cane. The new multiple-cropping system developed by the Agricultural Research Institute improved the planting technology, and was able to extend the crop rotation to four crops: rice – squash – rice – sugar cane, or rice – yam (or wheat, potato) – rice – vegetable oil seeds. This new crop rotation system made it possible for multiple harvesting even in northern Taiwan. This new rotation system increased the multiple harvest index in Taiwan to 144.

#### *4.1.2 New Products*

This refers to the introduction of nonindigenous economic produce like asparagus, mushrooms, grapes and onions. The former two became prime exports in the 1960s, and even into the 1970s.

#### *4.1.3 New Varieties*

As in mainland China, Taiwan also has a strong emphasis on grain production. For Taiwan, grain refers almost exclusively to rice. The development of new rice varieties is not just to increase production quantity, but also to enhance its ability to resist pests and crop viruses. With this as the objective, the Taichung Agriculture Improvement Station introduced the Taichung Tsai-Lai rice No. 2. This allowed each hectare to produce 1104 kilos of rice in the first rotation and another 659 kilos in the second harvest. This variety of rice was propagated to all of Taiwan in 1959, and later adopted by the Philippine International Rice Center (with further improvement was later propagated to southeast Asia). In terms of Pong-Lai rice, the Tainan Agriculture Improvement Station developed the Tainan Rice in 1961. It has the characteristics of high yield, low fertilizer consumption, advanced pest-resistance capability, and broad climate adaptability. It was propagated the following year. In record-breaking speed (for propagation), it was introduced to the entire island within one year.

Major breakthroughs also occurred in other crops. In terms of corn, the Tainan-11 was the first economically viable anti-fungal variety in the world. Similar advances were made in the area of soybeans. Another major crop for Taiwan was sugar cane. In 1947, the Taiwan Sugar's Huwei Station introduced the Nc0310 variety. It had the characteristics of quick germination, increased sugar content, and high climate adaptability. This increased the per-hectare yield from 6 tons of sugar to 10 tons. The propagation was initiated in 1951 and reached 61.6 percent of sugar cane acreage after three years. The major improvement in the area of fruits was most substantial in the varieties of mango and guava. The size of the fruits was increased, and also with higher sugar content. The most profound development in this area was perhaps the introduction of the seedless watermelon, which was hailed as a major breakthrough and earned important hard currencies as they were targeted for exports. It is so widespread nowadays that it is difficult to find "seeded" watermelon in US supermarkets.

### *4.1.4 New Inputs: Pesticides*

The hot and humid climate of Taiwan is a hotbed for pests and fungus. To prevent and alleviate such damages, the FA took four approaches:

1. Regulate and demonstrate the usage of pesticides for different crops
2. Educate farmers on the economic efficacy of pesticides so as to induce voluntary adoption
3. Through economies of scale, provide pesticides to the farmers at an affordable price
4. Experiment and develop new pesticides for all major crops, and propagate such advances to the general farming sector

### *4.1.5 New Methods, New Technology*

The Agriculture Research Institute of the Taiwan Provincial government oversees all six regional Agriculture Improvement Stations. They are responsible for the development of new farming methods and related technology. Their research outcomes are then propagated and broadly adopted by farmers. Examples include the planting methods, demonstrations of correct fertilizer usage, and the use of plastic bags to protect seedlings (which shortened the seedling period by 8 to 20 days). In 1963, the propagation of mechanical harvesting machines, and the 1969 propagation of new rice seedling transplant machines (which was four times the speed of the previous technology) were hailed as a milestone in Taiwan's agriculture production.

Advances were made in other crops also. New varieties of yams, corn, and soybeans were introduced, while innovative planting methods were introduced for soybeans and corn. For economic crops, there was the increased density method for pineapples, new plastic bags for bananas (which prevented rotting and provided weight support), and the summer crop of horticulture.

### *4.2 Technical Improvements in Animal Husbandry*

The animal husbandry discussed here also includes poultry.

#### *4.2.1 Animal Husbandry*

The main categories are hogs and cattle. In 1950, a head of hog took one year before it could be delivered for slaughter. The total number of hogs slaughtered in 1950 was just over 900 thousand. By 1970, the head count was 4.3 million, and reached 6.3 million heads by 1974. This is the result of substantial innovations in the area of hog farming. The delivery time shortened from one year to six months, while the average weight increased from 84 kilos to 94 kilos. The feed-to-weight ratio (i.e. quantity of feed needed to produce one pound of pork) was reduced from 5:1 to 3.5:1. Furthermore, the pork was more lean with a thinner layer of surface fat, and the death rate of piglets was also dramatically reduced. The cumulative results of these technical innovations transformed hog farming from a subsidiary activity of farmers to a specialized industry. This created externalities in the sense that it led to the development of animal feed and pork-processing industries, which were pillar industries in Taiwan's early industrialization. As evidence of success in this hog industry, the United Nations even allocated funds to establish a scientific research center for hogs in Taiwan.

Amongst the innovations, new hybrid varieties of hogs were being developed. In 1950, the Berkshire breed was introduced from Japan and the US. These were cross-bred with indigenous hog breeds, which led to the first hybrid. This hybrid was then cross-bred with the Yorkshire breed, resulting in three more hybrid species. In 1967, after experimenting with three pure foreign breeds, it was found that the pairing of Landrace or Yorkshire sow with a Duroc-jeri boar resulted in a hybrid with the highest quality of pork.

Starting in 1951, the provincial Husbandry Research Institute began to study the preservation of boar sperm and artificial insemination. The propagation of artificial insemination began in 1957. By the early 1970s, more than one-third of the hogs were born via artificial insemination. In terms of fighting potentially devastating hog epidemics, major breakthroughs were achieved in 1950 and 1953. With new preventive shots, the hog epidemic incidence rate dropped from 0.13 percent in 1947 to 0.02 percent in 1965. The SPF Hog Research Center was established to further the research of disease-free hog species.

In 1963, the FA propagated a comprehensive hog-farming system, which utilized the superior hybrid breed of hogs (see above), using the new mixed feed, and innovated hog barns and management strategies to deliver maximum pork at minimum cost and loss (to epidemics). As evidence of the efficiency of this management strategy, even hog urine was used to generate fuel for farm use.

As for cattle, we will begin with the development of improved species. For working cattle (those that are used to plow fields and pull carts), cross-breeding of Kankrej and Sindhri breeds led to the development of a superior hybrid specie which had a larger body mass, heavier payload capacity, and more suitable for Taiwan's climate. The artificial insemination of dairy cows was propagated in 1957. Starting in 1959, frozen sperm of champion bulls were imported from the US and Japan. Via artificial insemination, these sperm were used to cross-breed with indigenous, Indian, and Western cow species to develop a breed that had superior body mass and served the dual purpose of dairy and meat supply.

To further improve the stock of dairy cows, a registry was established in 1963. In terms of disease prevention, the inspection and vaccination against tuberculosis and *Brucella abortus* began in 1954, with full vaccination of 4- to 8-month-old calves achieved by 1964. During the same period, over 700 varieties of grazing grass were imported to test for adaptability to Taiwan's climate with great success. Under such care, the cattle herd in Taiwan peaked at over 400 thousand heads, and even by 1977 Taiwan still had 187 thousand heads, of which dairy cows accounted for 23 thousand.

### *4.2.2 Poultry*

Taiwan's poultry is mainly made up of chickens and ducks, with an emphasis on the former. Taiwan's chicken farming has long been a primary business. In 1950, there was just over five million, which swelled to more than 14 million in 1977, and in excess of 35 million by 1997. During the same period, ducks increased from 2.6 million to 6.8 million, and eventually to 9.6 million in 1997. These impressive numbers were also the product of technical improvements.

Starting with 1950, Taiwan imported superior chicken stock from the US, Japan, and other nations. Via cross-breeding with indigenous chickens, the FA established chicken farming demonstration villages across the island in 1952 aimed at propagating the knowledge of chicken farming and management methods. In 1958, a poultry department was added to the provincial Husbandry Research Institute. The targeted mission was to carry out stock improvements of poultry, which was divided into egg-producing and meat-producing chickens. Vaccination procedures were also changed from the earlier blood vein injection to the more efficient muscle injection. Combined with improved efficacy in the vaccines, poultry epidemics were all but eliminated.

The innovations in duck farming also started with the improvement in the duck stock. This started with the introduction of Beijing duck breed from the US, and then the importation of fertilized duck eggs. After husbandry, experimental labs perfected the hatching technique, it was widely propagated to the farmers. In 1965, cross breeding of Australia white duck, US Beijing ducks, and local indigenous breeds resulted in three new hybrid species which had improved body mass and feed efficiency. In 1967, the Duck Research Center was established. Via artificial insemination, they perfected the white-feathered duck for export markets. To improve the feed-to-weight efficiency, a balanced combination feed was developed. This, combined with the conversion from free-range duck farming to barn or gated feeding, the raising period of meat-producing ducks was reduced by 15 to 20 days, and the egg-yielding ducks production efficiency was improved by 20 percent, with dramatic decreases in death rates.

### *4.2.3 Technical Improvements in Aquatic Fishery (Aquaculture)*

Taiwan's aquatic fishery can be divided into three types: slat water, fresh water, and coastal.[5] The scope of the aquatic production includes fish, shellfish, and seaweed. 1960 was a milestone year in the aquacultural history of Taiwan with the success of artificial incubation of fish hatchlings. By 1964, large-scale artificial incubation was possible for catfish, silver carp, and grass carp. The dependency of imported hatchlings was eliminated and the production level skyrocketed. Aquatic exports soon followed. This was greatly enhanced with the success in the incubation of dace and mullet (the former is a primary consumer fish, while the later is prized for its roe).

In 1966, several species of shrimp were successfully incubated, further expanding the aquaculture to the farming of high value-added shrimps. The technological improvement in the breeding and farming of freshwater eels led to spectacular growth in the eel farming industry. In 1968, the total tonnage of eel exports was about 17 tons (mostly to Japan), but by 1977 it had grew to 17,822 tons, earning an impressive foreign exchange of $150 million. The three major categories of technological advancements are all transmitted and propagated from top to bottom. This is best illustrated with the development of new varieties of rice. Under the guidance of the government agency (mainly the Agriculture Research Institute), the rice breed selection is done through three stages: original specie, hybrid specie, and selected variety. The regional agriculture improvement stations handle the maintenance and production of the original species, the hybrid species are then handed to the county/city government and the county/city farmer's association to reproduce and experiment. The chosen variety is then sent to township government and the township farmer's association to propagate.

The selected variety of new hybrid rice is given to the demonstration farmer to plant. The commissioned demonstrating farmer is typically an agriculture team leader. This is the true grass root of the organizational structure of the Farmer's Association. According to Regulation No. 23 of the Agriculture Statute, "The agriculture team of the farmer's association has a team leader and a deputy, elected from the team members. The term is for four years and can be re-elected." Further, by Regulation No. 35, "Agriculture team leaders must be present at the team

[5] The sea–faring fisherman have their own association, similar in spirit and organization to the Farmer's Association. It is perhaps also an experience that is worth sharing, but is beyond our scope here.

meeting. The team meeting is called by the team leader once every three months, and act as presiding president. Each team should have members no more than fifty." The team leader is typically one of the most experienced senior farmers in the area. When the supervisory levels have new technology or product variety to propagate, they typically go through the township farmer's association and request these team leaders to act as the demonstrating farmer. Once the team leader has successfully planted the rice, neighboring farmers are then invited to learn and replicate.

These technological improvements accounted for 39.13 percent of the Taiwan agricultural development. During this period, agricultural production reached its peak and also fulfilled its role in "nurturing industry via agriculture."[6] The contribution of the farmer's association is significant, with the propagation of new technological innovations being the most critical aspect, though other functions of the FA also had their respective contributions. The supply /marketing division was able to supply the member farmers agriculture material, fertilizer, pesticides with impressive returns to scale via its collective purchasing power. However, the marketing side did not perform as well under this monopolistic state and suffered losses. To sustain this function, the divisions took out loans from the credit division. By the end of 1954, the marketing divisions loan accounted for 3 percent of the total outstanding loans from the credit division.

The credit division of the FA is the frontline foot soldier in the financial sector of agriculture. Besides the deposit and loans of the FA itself, it also acts as the agent in transferring the loans made by the three major agricultural commercial banks (the Land Bank, the China Farmer's Bank, and the Taiwan Cooperative Bank) to the agricultural sector. The main reason for the intermediary agent role is due to the fact that the FA is the closest organization to the cultivating farmers. The credit division is also responsible for the discernment of the loans from the central government and other related official agencies (examples of the former is the consolidated agriculture loans, while the latter include the Grain Bureau's rice farmer loans). This last function demonstrates the role of the FA in transmitting government policy, combined with its role in propagation, clearly establishes the fact that the FA or farmer's association is actually a public juridical agent.

## 5 Today: Developing Agriculture with Industry (1973–Present)

During this period, there was no significant development in agriculture. Thus, it is perhaps more appropriate to call it as the " agriculture supported by industry" period. In the previous period, industry was still in its infancy. Agriculture was the main source for the government's current account expenditure and the capital account investment for the expressed purpose for establishing Taiwan's industrial

[6] Using a path analysis method, Hou and Appleton (1996) identified the agricultural sector as the "engine" of Taiwan's economic growth before 1965.

sector. In the second period (today), industry was well established and the tax revenue it generates is enough to cover the various government expenditures, including the subsidy system of fixed-price, guaranteed purchase of rice.

In addition to the above "support," the nonagriculture sector also shouldered the burden of reduced farmland tax, exemption of water fees for farmers, establishment of a farmer's health insurance program, and social security for elderly farmers. This can be seen as the repayment of the nonagricultural sector (industry and service) to the earlier aid the farmers provided them in the previous period. An alternative way to look at this relationship is to examine the direction of the flow of capital funds. In the previous period, capital flowed from the agricultural sector to the industrial sector, while in this period the direction is reversed. This is the practical meaning of the words "nurture" and "support." In the previous period, over time, the capital flow from the agricultural sector to the industrial side was diminishing, signaling the growth of the industrial sector. By now, the capital flow from industry to the agricultural sector was increasing as the result of a maturing industrial structure. This allowed the government to extract capital from industry to establish welfare policies for the agricultural sector.

The proposition here is that during the second period, the proper way to look at the agriculture-industry relationship is to examine the flow of capital. This leads to a rather interesting side point: the lack of respect for the true contributor and the over-inflation of the financial side. The development of agriculture depends on the work of the Agriculture Research Institute and its regional stations, but the township farmer's association does the actual propagation and is thus the wheel that moved Taiwan's agriculture forward. Yet, the propagation is a mere "section" in the organization of a farmer's association. In contrast, the credit service is a "division."

As discussed in the previous section, the credit division of the FA devotes 60% of its profit to propagation. This is the indirect contribution of the credit division to the development of agriculture, but it does not disguise the fact that the actual direct contribution remains in the propagation work. Why the lack of recognition of the propagation section and the over-emphasis of the other aspect of the FA? The reason is probably the financial accounts. The agriculture propagation function of the FA is a pure expenditure, while the other areas of the farmer's association all generate revenues.

By definition, the supply and marketing function generates at least some income. In the process of securing agriculture inputs with monopsonistic powers, it receives commissions from member farmers for the service they provide, and the same goes for their marketing activities. The credit division profits from the margin between the interest rate from loans and deposits, and they are also tax exempt. This is the main source of income for the FA. The insurance division mainly acts as an agent for government policy implementation, which generates income via commissions they receive from government agencies. In contrast, the propagation activities are a pure expenditure (cost of demonstration) and generate no income. Thus, as far as the FA is concerned, it is a "sacrifice fly" and not highly regarded within the farmer's association, hence only designated as a "section"; a notch below the other "divisions."

Let us now turn our attention back to the current period. During this time frame, the government showed numerous preferential treatments toward farmers. Even in the previous period there were many special tax advantages given to farmers mainly with the objective of providing relief for the peasants. Prior to the cancellation of the farmland tax, it was first converted from monetary tax to rice-equivalent in-kind tax. In 1974, the per tax dollar rice conversion was decreased from 27 kilos to 22 kilos, and further reduced to 17 kilos in 1977. Though this reduction took place in the period under examination, the reform in the concurrent (in conjunction with the tax) procurement began toward the end of the previous period.

The concurrent procurement was intended for the supplemental rations for the military, civil servants, and educators. The practice started in 1947, and was 12 kilos per tax dollar. The procurement price was below the market price and hence the difference was a real tax. Starting in 1972, the procurement price was set equal to the market price. In 1971, all farm-related structures of farmers and the FA-owned warehouse that was used for public grain storage were exempt from real estate taxes. In terms of income tax, the estimated cultivation cost was raised from 40 percent of revenue set in 1960 to 70 percent. This reduced the tax base from 49 to 30 percent, as most farmers' incomes were now below the tax-exempt level, the farmers basically did not have to pay any income tax.

Another major change was in commodity taxes. In 1971, the "Commodity Tax Regulations" was revised. A commodity tax was imposed on fruits with certain juice content, while drinks with a certain percentage of natural fruit juice were exempt from this commodity tax. This had a tremendous effect. By 1977, export of juice drinks rose from $0.72 million to $22 million. During the same period, domestic sales also increased from 10 million dozens to 36 million.

Major reductions were also made on farm related imports. In 1971, the tariffs on farm machinery was reduced from 13 to 7 percent, pesticides from 30 to 10 percent, fertilizer and corn/soybean designated for animal feed were also reduced in half. Starting in 1972, all man-powered or animal-powered vehicles exclusively designated for farm use were exempt from vehicle taxes. In the following year, with the introduction of the "Agriculture Development Regulations," capital gains tax on land purchased for the purpose of expanding family farms were reduced by 50 percent. During this period, cultivated farmland were exempt from land-price tax, the first transaction (usually between the farmer or FA cooperative marketing and wholesalers) were exempt from stamp and sales taxes.

Most of the tax reduction discussed above were implemented in the first period. Now we turn to the reform in the second period starting from 1973. To be more specific, the second period began 27 September 1972 with the introduction of "Directive to Accelerate the Development of Farming Villages" by the Executive Yuan. This is the most critical turning point since the Land Reform (1949–53). It contains nine major points:

1. Elimination of the rice-for-fertilizer system
2. Cancellation of the education fee attached to the farmland tax
3. Easing of the farm loans conditions
4. Reform of the transportation and marketing system of agricultural products
5. Accelerate the development of rural village public infrastructure
6. Accelerate the propagation of synthesized technical plantations
7. Promote agriculture specialization zones
8. Accelerate agriculture research and propagation efforts
9. Encourage the construction of factories in rural villages.

In recent years, Taiwan has had increased numbers of democratic elections. This has had a bad side effect of "black money" entering politics, and the farmer's association is often a hotbed for such activities. The reason being once one becomes the executive manager or the president of an FA, they control hundreds of millions and even billions of dollars in financial assets of the credit division, which can be used to "purchase" votes or influence elections.

The employees in the credit division of the FAs typically lack experience in other financial institutions, which results in a higher percentage of bad loans. In addition, as discussed earlier, FA credit unions do not have stockholders and operate simply on an executive order of the government. This implies a much-weakened supervisory control. The end result is an average 27 percent bad-loan rate across all FAs. Due to the severity of this problem, the Central Deposit Insurance Company have stationed personnel at some of the worst FAs credit divisions, and requested several banks to take over 27 credit unions of the FAs (Chu, 2003).

This has caused an immediate panic in the agricultural sector, and raised the questions of whether the FA can maintain its credit division, and whether this division can become independent. And, how to deal with the financial problems in the sector? To completely root out this problem of "black money," the easiest method is to split out all the credit function from the FA, and allow autonomy of credit sector. In other words, basically disallows the FA from having a credit division. This, however, creates another problem. Historically, the credit division is the "hen that lays the golden egg." How will a farmer's association survive without its credit division?

The "Directive to Accelerate the Development of Farming Villages" terms the farmer's association as the "farmer's group," but also alternates with the term of "farmer's organization." Both terminologies share common traits. First, both are group organizations formed by individuals. Second, they both imply a specific objective and function, and are the product of deliberate planning. There are, however, two layers of distinction between the two. First, the members and resources of an "organization" is formal and recognized, while not so for a "group." Second, when confronted with uncertainty and the need to restore order, the "organization" constrains the activity of its members, while a "group" is at the will of its members. Furthermore, an organization emphasizes the chain of command. The foundation of an organization is the formal establishment of such a hierarchy within the membership. For a group, such a hierarchy is generally unacceptable to its members.

Taiwan's FA is an "organization" in name, but a "group" in practice. It is this divergence that has clouded the role of the FA, and one of the main causes of why the credit division has such a high bad loan rate. To be more specific, the farmer's association is a farmer's group, and the purpose of establishing this group is to represent farmers. To secure privileges from government agencies on behalf of the farmers has led the group into the world of politics. However, a "group" does not have productive economic activities, such as the credit division of the farmer's association. That is in the realm of an organization (Chu, 2003). If it is an "organization," it should have certain control of the behavior of its members, such as the approval of loans. However, these loans are simply authorized by the executive manager or the manager of the credit division (whom, as mentioned earlier, is hired by the executive manager). Unfortunately, due to the aforementioned political nature of the "group," the credit division of the FA became the accomplice (or at least the hotbed) of the "black money," leading to excessive loans and massive bad debt, causing the current fragile state of the FA.

The time frame of this section is the "supporting agriculture with industry" period, but the term "today" mainly implies the 1990s to the first few years of the 21st century. During this decade and a half, the FA has weathered major changes in the political, economical, and social aspect of external environment surrounding it (Chu, 2003). On the political side, the FA is exhibiting a trend of political democracy. This pressure is coming from both external organizations and from groups within the farmer's association. Both groups stem from the 2000 election as the ruling party changed hands. Under the suddenly changed political climate, their influence on and within the FA has become more evident and more extensive.

The economic environment is the result of economic liberalization and globalization. Liberalization increased the competitiveness in the market and led to losses in the supply and marketing division of the FA. Part of globalization is the accession into the WTO. Since Taiwan enters as a developed economy, the impact to domestic agriculture will be dramatic (even more so than Mainland China). The social environment is the acceleration of urbanization as a consequence of economic development. Rezoning has allowed many land-owning farmers to become overnight millionaires, as farmlands turned from a productive factor into a money-making speculative instrument. As the speculative fad spreads across rural townships, the FA is inevitably infected, as it becomes the target of speculators, politicians and profiteers, leading to excessive loans, fraudulent loans, bad loans, and such; it's becoming worse by the day.

As a reflection of this changing environment, the financial situation is deteriorating for the FAs. In 1997, the total profit of the farmer's associations was $9.6 billion (NT), with 243 FAs exhibiting a profit. By 2001, the total combined loss was $500 million (NT), with 42 farmer's associations in the red.

## 6 Tomorrow: The Transformation of the Farmer's Association

The original intent of the Farmer's Association was to promote the welfare of farmers and protect the accomplishment of land reform. The hard labor of its various service sectors led to the phenomenal success of agricultural development in the "nurturing industry with agriculture" period. The propagation section did the most impressive work as they introduced new systems, new products, new varieties, new inputs, and new methods to the farmers. The propagation work was clearly the biggest contributor in this period, but their funding mainly came from the profit of the credit division. It can be thus said that propagation was the creator of the agriculture miracle, but the credit division was its benefactor. Unfortunately, in the later period of "supporting agriculture with industry", many shortcomings surfaced in the credit division of the FA, leading to the demise of the farmer's association becoming the hotbed for black money. This necessitates the reform of the FA, and the method of reform is in the timely transformation of the association.

On the transformation of the farmer's association, there are at least two views: the radical approach and the gradual approach. The former stems from organization theory and believe that the FA should be a pure farmers group, much like a labor union, solely as a representative of the farmers to fight for their rights and benefits without any of the current productive activities. They contend that these services can be replaced by other agencies. For example, the function of the credit division can be taken over by various credit unions, the post office, or various banks. Supply and marketing have been marginalized with economic liberalization, and could be done more efficiently with the many specialized cooperatives already in operation.

As for the all-important propagation function, in the age of information and the modern/commercial management of agriculture, the farmers themselves are eager pursuant of innovations. If we add farmers' mutual cooperatives and regional development cooperatives, then the propagation function can be replaced with legal entities in the form of foundations or government sponsored specific projects. The insurance function can also be replaced by the modern insurance system. The farmers' health insurance can be absorbed into the universal healthcare currently available for the general nonagricultural population, while the agriculture production insurance can be handled by farmers' organizations or professional insurance groups.

The above is a brief summary of the views of the radical approach. It essentially returns the FA to the format of the Japanese colonial era. In other words, the farmer's association will return to the form of an agricultural association. The only difference being that the old association (under Japanese rule) was made up of tenants, while it will now consist of autonomous farmers. The function it will serve is similar to the old agricultural union. This is effectively a dissection of the FA and totally erasing its glorious past.

In our opinion, the radical approach is not feasible. Now let us turn to the gradual approach that we advocate. The fundamental idea is to carve out the credit division and make it independent of the FA, and develop it into a regional agriculture bank. The process can be described as followed. The first step is to establish the Agriculture Bank, with the township FAs as its investors. According to the regulations, the necessary condition for the establishment of a new bank is that it must have a capitalization of no less than $10 billion (NT). There are currently 319 township farmer's associations, which comes out to approximately $30 million (NT) capital per FA.

With the Bank capitalized, the branches should be established based on the county/city administrative districts, with sub-branches distributed across the island. These third-tier sub-branches will be the charge of the township FAs, but the number must be less than the current number of such FAs. In other words, when separating the credit divisions from mother FAs, a consolidation effort must be made, merging three to five such credit divisions into a sub-branch of the Agriculture Bank. The guideline for this consolidation is to have at least one municipality within the area covered to serve as the branch bank headquarters. The original FA credit division will serve as township sub-branches. Other related guidelines include:

1. 40 percent of the annual profit of the township sub-branch will be transferred to the Agriculture Bank, while 60 percent will be retained by the sub-branch for regional use. This will cover the cost of agricultural propagation and the operational expenses of the township FA, and also provide economic incentive for the township sub-branch.
2. Each branch bank also divides their profits into two equal portions; one half is transferred to the Agriculture Bank, while the other half is retained profits. Of the retained portion, each branch banks keeps 40 percent for themselves, and then distribute the rest among the township farmer's association.
3. The function of the Agricultural Bank is much like the current Cooperative Bank.[7] The Bank itself engages in financial activities which will generate profits of its own, adding on the profit transfers from the branches and sub-branches, the total profit could be quite considerable. The Agriculture Bank can use part of this profit to subsidize the budget deficits that the FAs may have. More importantly, the Bank can use these profits to regulate the financial services of the branches and sub-branches. When the monetary market is tight, the Bank can evaluate the need of the braches/sub-branches and supply credit when needed. When the market is loose, they can accept excess deposits from the branches/sub-branches as time deposits in the Bank. And, if a branch or sub-branch is experiencing a financial crisis, the Bank can aid or bail out those in trouble.
4. The Agriculture Bank system can still employ the original employees of the credit divisions of the farmer's association, but must go through formal financial service training plus a six-month internship at more established commercial banks.

---

[7] The relationship between the Agriculture Bank and its branches is the same as the relationship between the Cooperative Bank and the various credit unions.

The management can come from senior/experienced employee from other established banks.

5. Taiwan's agriculture financial structure is lacking, as it does not have a formal system since there is no regulating agency within the central government. It is advisable to take advantage of this transformation of the credit services of the farmer's association to establish a Bureau of Agricultural Finances within the Council of Agriculture. It will be the Bureau's responsibility to manage and regulate the existing Farmers Bank and the Land Bank, in addition to the proposed new Agriculture Bank. It is especially vital that the Bureau conduct regular and unannounced audits of the branches and sub-branches of this new Bank.

The above moderate approach is to transform the credit division of the FA into a regional agriculture bank, regulated by the Bureau of Agriculture Finances. Under this method, the branch and sub-branches of the Agriculture Bank will operate just like a regular commercial bank, but the profits are still plowed back into the farmer's association to be used for propagation. The Propagation Section of the FA should be retained and elevated to a division. The insurance division can also be retained, but as a self-fulfilling unit. It already has the trust of the farmers and will truly be servicing the members. Thus, it may be advisable to rename it as the Service Division. Its function is to respond to farmer requests and act as an agent on behalf of specific tasks commissioned by the government or other related agencies.

In a similar fashion, the supply and marketing division should be changed into simply the marketing division. With the liberalization and globalization (WTO) of the markets, farmers can directly access the market to obtain both agricultural supplies and daily consumption items. There is no more need for the "supply" function if the FA, and should solely focus on the marketing of agricultural products and its processed goods. It may be more effective to establish a national farmer's association, or have the provincial farmer's association temporarily act in this function. The precise method can be summarized as follows:

1. Act as the "general" agent for the specialty products of each township farmer's association
2. Establish a sales network via enhanced communication between the township FAs, so as to introduce the specialty product of one farmer's association to all the other FAs. This stems from the personal experience of one of the authors. A few years back, we tasted preserved fruits produced by one of the township farmer's association in Hsinchu county. It was truly superb. When we tried to buy more later, we could not find it anywhere, and when we inquired with our neighboring FA, they had no knowledge of this product. Our proposal here is to first have trade (of specialty products) within the FA system, and then "export" to markets outside of the FA system. This will allow the specialty products of each farmer's association the ability to access a much bigger market.
3. For the implementation of the above objective, we can promote two separate

networks. One is to establish a specialized transportation cooperative that will transport the products of township FA's goods to relevant wholesale markets for agricultural goods or processed goods. This will allow a nationwide market for the farmer's association. The second channel is to establish a "farmer's market", located in urban centers and major junctions of traffic. The former is similar to the Taiwan Sugar Specialty stores, while the latter can be strategically located at (for example) rest areas on national highways or provincial highways.

## 7 Other Contributing Factors

As important as the farmer's association was, there are also other elements that contributed to the success of Taiwan's agriculture in the early years and in the intermediate period. They are not the main focus of this chapter, so we will only briefly outline them.

Much like we cannot live without the air we breathe, agriculture is impossible without water. The all-important irrigation was coordinated through a central organization that oversees 18 irrigation associations. Obviously, this is another experience that can be shared with the mainland Chinese also. China, especially the north and west, is under the constant threat of drought. The mighty Yellow River has even failed to reach the ocean in several occasions. The fact that part of the rationale for the Three Gorges Dam is to "transfer the south waters to the north" is clear testament to the importance.

Due to smaller lot size, Taiwan has modified mechanical farming machines to accommodate these special needs. For example, rather than use the monstrous plowing and harvesting machines commonly used in the US, Taiwan uses much smaller tractors. From the perspective of American farmers, plowing machines Taiwan farmers use look like lawn mowers. Such modification is needed for the mainland Chinese farmers also. The market demand is large enough that mainland Chinese industries will have the economy of scale to produce such "specialized" machinery at a cost much lower than what the Taiwan farmers had to face.

Even so, the price of owning such machines may be too expensive for the small farmer, and may not even be necessary. Again, we see an alternative in the Taiwan experience. Partially due to this capital expense and small farm size, partially because over time there was a drain of the agriculture labor force as young workers are lured to the city, cultivation sub-contractors came into existence. They are professional "guns-for-hire." The small family farmer can hire them to do basically everything farming-related; from plowing the fields to transferring the seedlings, from application of fertilizer/pesticides to crop harvesting.

Since they will attend to many individual farmers, they can fully utilize the returns to scale offered by farming machinery, making investments in such capital worthwhile. They are consummate professionals, and will have accumulated human capital through years of actual practice, making them much more productive than the average farmers. One only need to take one look at this and immediately see the potential for the Chinese agriculture sector. In case it did not occur to the reader, they are also intimately related to the FA as they obtain their capital through loans from the credit division and they serve a vital propagation function as new technology is developed.

Parallel to this is another often-overlooked point. As Taiwan became more and more proficient in agriculture, agriculture demonstration teams were often dispatched abroad. Many at the request of third-world countries, but also used as a tool to cultivate diplomatic relationship with foreign countries. Though this latter aspect is of no relevance for mainland China, such demonstration teams will still serve many beneficial functions. It will further stimulate domestic research and propagation efforts, express goodwill to third-world nations, and open markets for Chinese exports—a prospect definitely worth examining. Furthermore, the Western regions of China may be well served with the existence and efforts of such teams, as we will discuss later.

In addition to the farmer's association and the irrigation association, Taiwan has two more associations that are of interest. First, there is the fisherman's association. It parallels the farmer's association in many ways, and its contribution was also an integral part of Taiwan's economic success. Fish output was not only a source of much-needed protein for the population, but processed seafood products were also a major export category.

The fourth association is the Taiwan Provincial Fruit Marketing Cooperative. This is a single-purposed organization specializing in marketing fruits, and only farmers who grow fruits are eligible for the membership. This cooperative was instrumental in upgrading the farming structure from regular crops to high-yield economic ones. In addition to the many accomplishments of the Agriculture Research Institute described earlier, Taiwan was equally successful in fruit research. Among the most spectacular was the development of the seedless watermelon. When it was first grown, the seedless watermelon was exclusively exported to earn precious foreign exchange.

## 8 Conclusion: Experience and Lessons for China's West

China's economic reform began in rural agriculture, and indeed, many of the current achievements are built on the success of the early agricultural reforms (e.g. *bao chan dao hu*). This was not just a necessity when faced with the monumental task of feeding 1.2 billion people, but also deep-rooted in the Chinese heritage; historically, agriculture has been viewed as the foundation of the nation. However, under WTO rules, China's agriculture is facing an unprecedented challenge. The outcome is unclear, but the impact will undoubtedly be dramatic.

This chapter examines the development experience of Taiwan agriculture in hope of providing positive traits to be learned, and negative lessons to be avoided. Our focus has been on the Taiwan Farmer's Association. We detailed its historical origin and organizational structure, and showed how it was an irreplaceable contribution in the earlier period of Taiwan's economic development; we also highlighted handicaps in the latter stages. In terms of current negativities of the Farmer's Association, we outlined two competition methods in dealing with the problem, and added our own evaluation and recommendations.

Despite the problems of the farmer's association in the last decade and a half, the role it played in Taiwan's development is beyond doubt. The path and the success of the Taiwan experience clearly offers a lesson that the mainland Chinese agriculture can borrow, especially under the threat of cheap imports under WTO requirements. The current Chinese farmers are small in size, the spread of new technology is less than desired, and the cost of production may be too high to effectively compete with imports. Most of these are eerily similar to the condition facing the Taiwan agriculture sector after the retrocession. An organization in the style of Taiwan's Farmer's Association may go a long way in solving many of the problems facing the small Mainland Chinese farmers. Acting as a public advocate, this organization can better spread information, provide training, and act as consultants (or information clearing house).

The credit division can provide loans for many poor and not well-connected small farmers. As a coop, even small farmers can benefit from tractors and other modern production machinery. With a well-coordinated marketing organization, each area can specialize based on comparative advantage of soil, climate, rainfall, and market prices. These can improve the sustainability of farming; farmers may even become profit-seeking entrepreneurs. This may increase agricultural employment, which will in turn lessen the blind-migration toward the already over-burdened cities. The profitability of farming and the increased income of farmers will undoubtedly develop local commerce and clusters of industry, which may urbanize China in a more geographically even format.

The actual structure of such an organization obviously depends on the attitude of the central government and the need of the local farmers, but the experience of Taiwan is clearly an example well worth examining, if not mimicking. We fully understand the Chinese government's reluctance to add any more bureaucracy/agency, especially in light of a worsening budget deficit, plus the double threat of an aging population (old-age insurance) and a smaller labor force as a consequence of the one-child policy.[8] But that is precisely the attractiveness of the Taiwan experience. In our opinion, the budget cost of such programs should not be too high, and in many aspects they can be almost self-financed, while increased productivity and tax revenue should more than pay for the remainder.

However, state oversight is absolutely necessary. This is not just because the success of China's reform is significantly due to the guidance of the state (Hou and Hou, 2004), but also to plan ahead and prevent the pitfalls that plagued Taiwan in recent years. We do not profess to know how the Taiwan experience can be

[8] The central government may also be wary of the farmers becoming too strong of a political force. We feel, if properly organized and controlled, this should not be an issue, but we leave that to more qualified specialists to evaluate.

formulated into a system that fits the needs of mainland China. We simply hope that this presentation attracts the attention of policy makers and interested scholars to look into this proposition with serious intent and more in-depth analysis.

*The Farmer's Association as a Tool for the Development of Western China?*

We do, however, feel that this form of agricultural organization may be particularly beneficial for developing the western regions of China. Compared to the east/coastal regions, and even compared to the central regions, the west is vast in land size, much lower population density, agriculturally dominant, and until recently, suffering from significant outward migration (Bao, Hou, and Shi, 2005). Western China is also home to the vast majority of China's ethnic minorities. They are much more reliant on agriculture, and many live in more remote and isolated areas. They may well be the ones that benefit (and need) the most from services the Farmer's Association can provide. Hence, we will narrow our focus here and discuss in terms of the west; especially the ethnic minorities.

The main contribution of the Taiwan Farmer's Association can be summed into propagation of technology, supply of credit, coordinated provision of sales (of output) and supplies (both inputs and consumer essentials). In terms of technology, this should be the role of government and other research institutions. The research efforts of government (both central and provincial/regional) sponsored institutes and various major universities may have a harder time reaching the more remote and rural areas, especially in the western regions of China. Their remoteness, lack of human capital, minority status, and a host of other reasons are all contributing factors to this deficiency.

An efficient and practical way of propagating the new technologies is to borrow from Taiwan's agriculture demonstration teams. The provincial government (perhaps with partial subsidy from the central budget) can recruit experienced farmers from the more prosperous and advanced agricultural areas (e.g. Anhwei, Hunan of the central regions) to form demonstration teams. Given that there are severe labor surpluses in these areas (as evident of the net outward migration found in Bau, Hou and Shi, 2005), it should not be difficult to recruit qualified farmers, and it also augments the "Go West" national strategy.

To further enhance the technology and make it more regional specific (as the terrain and climate of the west is quite different from that of the central and east regions), incentives should be given to research institutes and universities to develop new crop varieties that are most suitable for the western provinces, design new crop rotation that will maximize the yield and optimize the sustainability of the land fertility. As the western regions of China are perhaps less fertile agricultural lands, improvements in animal husbandry may be just as important. Again, the Taiwan experience has taught us that significant strides can be made in these areas also, and may well become a major source of agricultural income for the rural farmers.

A major obstacle facing rural farmers is the absence of a proper channel to secure capital funds. This is, of course, not unique to western China or even China overall. For most developing nations, rural farmers have always faced this constraint. What puts Chinese farmers at a further disadvantage when compared to their comrades in other LDCs is that they do not own the land, and hence do not have collateral. With their land as collateral, the poor rural farmers in most LDCs at least have the chance of securing funds, even in an economy that is very pro-urban and usually not particularly friendly to poor rural peasants. Here, again, the Farmer's Association has an avenue that will relieve Chinese farmers from such dilemmas.

We acknowledge that similar institutions are in existence in China. The problem has been that these institutions have been quite successful in attracting the savings of rural China, but have not used them to develop rural areas. Rather, huge amounts of savings have been attracted to the coastal urban areas. Furthermore, these institutions have accumulated huge amounts of bad debt and are now facing financial collapse that may need the government's bailout.

The credit division of the Farmer's Association is different from the aforementioned rural credit unions in China. The Farmer's Association is "of the farmers" (owned by the farmers), "by the farmers" (governed by the farmers), and "for the farmers" (to serve the farmers). This can be clearly seen in structure of the Association. It does have the potential of abuse, and we have seen that in Taiwan. For that expressed purpose, we proposed to have a formal financial structure overseeing the credit division of the Farmer's Association, while still maintaining the "for the farmers, of the farmers, and by the farmers" nature of the Association. Done properly, this should improve the financial climate of the rural farming sector, despite the lack of collateral and the weak financial infrastructure. Recall, the Farmer's Association also serves as an insurance source.

Finally, the Farmer's Association also serves marketing and supply needs of its members. This may indeed be exceptionally important for the rural farming communities of Western China. The marketing aspect of the Framer's Association goes without saying, but the "supply" function of the association may prove to be even more valuable, at least in the sense of improving the quality of life for many of the remote rural villages. The Taiwan Farmer's Association (in the early stages of Taiwan's development") owned and operated "supermarkets" in the rural remote areas of Taiwan. These markets will provide important provisions for the rural communities (many of them being ethnic minorities), ranging from daily necessities to farming supplies such as fertilizers and pesticides. The large collective purchasing powers will be able to acquire these products at a price level affordable to these poor communities, expand the varieties, and guarantee both quality and quantity that these villagers may have never dreamed possible. Thus vastly improving their quality of life and productivity potential.

Though it has been stated earlier, we cannot conclude the chapter without reiterating the statement that we are most certainly not advocating a wholesale adoption of the Taiwan experience. There are too many differences between Taiwan and mainland China making this unfeasible. Taiwan is more-or-less a homogeneous land as far as weather and other agricultural conditions go. Mainland China, on the other hand, covers a wide range of terrain, precipitation, climate, and the like. Another major difference (which is directly related to the above) is the size. As the reviewer correctly pointed out, the assumption of a small economy is realistic for Taiwan, but not for mainland China. This has important implications that cannot be overlooked when designing development strategies.

For example, when Taiwan introduced asparagus as an export-oriented new crop (in the form of canned food), it was successful. But, if mainland China did the same, the sheer size of the production would cause the price to crash and harm the farmers that devoted their efforts in the endeavor. Rather than abandoning such efforts, however, we can revise the approach and still achieve similar results. For example, areas where the climate is especially suitable for asparagus, policies can still guide local farmers to utilize their comparative advantage and produce such economic crops. Rather than exporting the goods (which they still can do), target other areas in China that simply are not suitable for such crops.

As important as the early stages of the Taiwan experience ("yesterday"), the current problems in Taiwan ("today") are just as relevant. If mainland China can look ahead and take pre-emptive actions to incorporate the reforms we proposed ("tomorrow") at the onset, it will potentially be able to reap the benefits and avoid the later costs. After the decentralization of agricultural production from collectives to individual households, much like when Taiwan changed from landlord dominated farming to agriculture of the family tillers, mainland China also needs to establish its own farmers' organization in credit, marketing, and other public provisions. Much as most agree on this need, we are also in agreement that the government is very reluctant to let farmers organize their own autonomous coops, especially in fear of the politically powerful farmers' organizations in Taiwan, Japan, and the USA.

To this end, the Chinese government can separate the credit unit from the farmer's association from the start. The "Bank" will be chartered with strict and explicit guidelines that loans are to be targeted toward local, rural farmers in need, with the secondary objective of financing local/rural nonagriculture enterprises. In no way is the Bank allowed to conduct business with the urban areas. The Farmer's Association will be organized based on the principle: "of the farmers" (owned by the farmers), "by the farmers" (governed by the farmers), and "for the farmers" (to serve the farmers).

The government can replace the price subsidy with more targeted grants (much like how Taiwan used the US aid) aimed at promoting propagation in innovations in grain production, and guiding local farmers toward economic/cash crops that utilize their comparative advantage. Though promoting agricultural exports is not totally dismissed (as Taiwan enjoyed the friendly markets of Japan and the US), we feel this should not be the focus of mainland China. Rather, the objective should be to promote local and regional specialization, with surpluses "exported" to other regions of China. By lowering cost (through specialization), improving quality (propagation of new technology), lower transportation cost (relative to foreign imports), and the spirit of patriotism, we feel China's agriculture can survive foreign competition brought about by the WTO.

As farmers see and feel the care of the government (with "black money" taken out of the picture), we do not see the farmers' organization as a political threat to the central government. Rather, it will improve the standard of living for rural villages, reduce outward migration, and foster a more even income distribution across regions. These are all characteristics that would foster political stability.

Again, it is not our purpose to propose a strategy for developing a Farmer's Association style organization (though it did not stop us from making some proposals). We hope, however, that by demonstrating the structure and documenting the history/performance of the Taiwan experience, we can attract the attention of either pertinent government planners or influential scholars that are interested in taking a much deeper look at the potential of the Taiwan experience and lesson for western China, if not indeed for all of China.

## References


Bao, S., Hou, J.W. and Shi, A., 'Migration Scenarios and Western China Development: Some Evidence from 2000 Population Census Data' (working paper, to be presented at the Western Economic Association International's 6th Biennial Pacific Rim Conference, Hong Kong January 14–16, 2005).

Chu, Y.C., 'Taiwan's Farmer's Association: Where Do We Go from Here'? in Min–Ming Wu (eds), *Economic Status of Taiwan's Agriculture* (Taiwan: Taiwan Knowledge Bank, 2003).

Chu, M.Y., 'Taiwan Agricultural Cooperative and Economic development', in Yuh–hsien Yu (eds), *Essays on Taiwan's Agriculture Development* (Taipei: Lian Jing Publishing, 1975).

Colby, H., Price, J.M. and Tuan, F.C., 'China's WTO Accession Would Boost U.S. Ag Exports & Farm Income', *Agricultural Outlook*, 269 (March 2000): 11–16.

Fei, J. and Jack, W.H., 'The Comprehensive Economic Reform of The PRC (1978)', *Reform and Development in Deng's China*, Volume IV, The Miller Center Series on Asian Political Leadership (University Press of America: New York, 1994), pp.19–64.

Hou, C.C., 'Interactions Between Agriculture and Industry in the Economic Growth of Taiwan', *Proceedings for the Conference on Agricultural Development in China, Japan, and Korea* (Taipei: Academia Sinica, 1980).

Hou, C.C. and Hou, J.W., 'Evolution of Economic Development: Entrepreneurs, Market, and the State' (presented at the International Symposium on Private Enterprises and China's Economic Development, sponsored by the Chinese Economists Society (CES) and the Chinese Academy of Social Sciences (CASS). June 18–20, 2004).

Hou, J.W., *Modernization and the Chinese Experience* (Monograph, Long Beach: California State University, 1995).

———, 'Rural Reform and the Welfare Impact on Urban Workers: An Analytical Approach', in Aimin Cheng, Gordon G. Liu, and Kevin H. Zhang (eds),*Urbanization and Social Welfare in China* (England: Ashgate, 2004), pp,107–137.

Hou, J.W. and Appleton, J., 'The "Engine" of Taiwan's Economic Growth: A Path Analysis

Approach', *Singapore Economic Review*, 41(1) (1996): 25–46.

Hou, J.W. and Hou, C.C., Evolution of Economic Development: Firms, Market, and the State (presented at the International Symposium on Private Enterprises and China's Economic Development (The Chinese Economists Society and the Chinese Academy of Social Sciences). Beijing, China, June 18–20, 2004).

Hou, J.W., Mead, R.W. and Nagahashi H., 'Evolution of China's U.S. Policy (1965–72): Prelude to the Economic Reform', *the American Journal of Chinese Studies*, 12 (April 2005): forthcoming.

Hsiung, C.G., *Agriculture Development Strategy*, in K.Y. (Editor in Chief) Taiwan Economic Development Strategy Series (Taipei: Lian Jing Publishing, 1984).

Hu, C.Y., 'The Agricultural Cooperative of Taiwan: Where Do we Go From Here', in Min–Ming Wu (ed.). *Economic Status of Taiwan's Agriculture* (Taiwan: Taiwan Knowledge Bank, 1984).

Li, K.T., *The Evolution of Policy behind Taiwan's Development Success* (New Haven: Yale University Press, 1988).

Mead, R.W., Rural China Following WTO Admission (presented at the Western Economic Association Meetings, San Francisco, July 5–8, 2001).

Wang, Y.C., 'Technical Innovation and the development of Taiwan Agriculture', Journal of Taiwan Land Finance, also in Yuh–hsien Yu (ed.), *Essays on Taiwan's Agriculture Development* (Taipei: Lian Jing Publishing, 1986).

# Part 2
# The Performance and Potentials of China's Agriculture

Chapter 8

# Production and Productivity Growth in Chinese Agriculture: New National and Regional Measures*

Shenggen Fan
Xiaobo Zhang

## 1 Introduction

Agricultural output in China has been reported growing rapidly in the past several decades, particularly since the rural reforms that began in 1979. The State Statistical Bureau (SSB 1998) reported that from 1952 to 1997, output grew at 4.4 percent per annum. Up until 1978, the annual rate was 2.8 percent per annum. It then jumped to 6.5 percent per annum during the period from 1979 to 1997. This long-term growth rate was one of the highest worldwide during the same period.

There have been numerous literatures in explaining China's dramatic agricultural growth. Most studies (Weins, 1982; Lardy, 1983; Perkins, 1984; Tang, 1984; Lin, 1988 and 1992; Fan, 1990 and 1991; World Bank, 1991; Wen, 1993; and Zhang and Carter, 1997) on Chinese agriculture have used *gross value of agricultural output* (GVAO) as an indicator to measure growth in agricultural output. GVAO is reported by the State Statistical Bureau (SSB)—the official government agency specialized in collecting, measuring, and reporting statistics in China.[1] However, GVAO is usually measured in constant prices (or comparable prices as described by the Chinese statistical system) to represent total output in a particular year.[2] But constant prices may not be the appropriate weights in aggregating total output because the growth rates calculated from these constant prices may be seriously biased, especially when relative prices have changed (Diewert, 1976; Lau, 1979; and Jorgenson, 1995). Relative output prices in Chinese agriculture have changed dramatically over time and across regions since the economic reform in the late 1970s.

In more recent years, many scholars have also questioned the accuracies of

---

* Reprinted from *Economic Development and Cultural Change* (The University of Chicago Express), 2002, page 819-838.

[1] The agency has been renamed as National Statistical Bureau since 2000.

[2] The State Statistical Bureau has also recently published GDP growth for the agriculture sector. But it suffers the same problem as GVAO, i.e., measured in constant prices. See SSB, *Calculation Methods of China Annual GDP* (Beijing: China Statistical Publishing House, 1997).

livestock and fishery output in Chinese official statistics. For example, Zhong (1997), Lu (1998), and Fuller *et al.* (2000) estimated that major livestock output reported by SSB may have been overstated by as large as over 40 percent, and fishery output by 70 percent in 1996.

Biased estimates of production and productivity growth in Chinese agriculture may have serious consequences, as most previous studies have used these indicators to judge the performance of the agricultural sector and to measure the impact of the rural reforms in Chinese agriculture. Moreover, since the officially published output values measured in constant prices are also widely used in the regional inequality literature, a regional inequality index calculated based on official data may be misleading as well.

This chapter aims to properly measure national and regional growth in output, input, and total factor productivity in Chinese agriculture, and to reassess the impact of the recent policy reforms on production and productivity growth and regional inequality. The chapter is organized as follows. The next section will review some aggregation issues in production theory. We show how estimates of aggregate output and input, and therefore measured total factor productivity, can be biased as a result of using constant prices as weights. The third section will be devoted to the measurement of growth in output, input and productivity, and regional inequality in Chinese agriculture. We conclude the chapter in section 4.

## 2 Conceptual Framework in Output and Input Aggregation

The agricultural sector in China produces a great number of products including major staple grains like rice, wheat, and corn, major livestock products such as meat, eggs, and diary products, and horticultural and fishery products. Aggregation is often needed in order to compare the performance of the whole agricultural sector over time and across regions. Similarly, aggregation over inputs used in the agricultural sector is also necessary for number of reasons, such as providing information for measuring technical changes and efficiency improvement, and for measuring total factor productivity.

Agricultural output in the Chinese statistical reporting system is measured as gross value of agricultural output (GVAO) by summing production values of all products produced in the sector. Production value of a certain product is calculated by multiplying quantity by price. GVAO is often measured in current prices, and for the purpose of comparison across years, it is also measured and reported in constant prices.[3]

Many economists have pointed out that using constant prices to aggregate output may result in biased estimate of production growth. Despite these concerns, many countries and international organizations still report growth in output aggregated using constant prices. This potential bias is illustrated in Figure 8.1 where $Q_0$ represents a production possibility curve, which indicates the different combination of products $Y_1$ and $Y_2$, using the same amount of inputs.[4] Profit-maximizing producers choose different combination of $Y_1$ and $Y_2$ based on relative prices of the two products. Producers would choose point *a* in the production possibility curve when relative prices are $P_1$, and *b* when relative prices are $P_2$. If total output is aggregated using a liner aggregation of the two products weighted by their relative prices $P_1$, aggregate output at *a* (equals to output at b') would be greater than that at *b*. But if $P_2$ were used in the aggregation, output at *b* (equals to output at a') would be greater than that at *a*. Different output measures are obtained using different price weights, although producers only move along the same production possibility curve.

Figure 8.2 shows the potential bias that arises from input aggregation where $I_0$ represents an isoquant in which the same amount of output is produced using different input combination, $X_1$ and $X_2$. Cost-minimizing producers choose input combination based on relative input prices, $W_1$ and $W_2$. If producers face relative prices $W_1$, then the optimal combination of inputs would be at point *c*. If relative prices change to $W_2$, the optimal combination of inputs would be at *d*. This shift is the producers' response to input price changes (the substitution effect) along the same isoquant. But using different relative prices as weights yields different input aggregates. For example if relative prices $W_1$ are used as weights, aggregated input at *d* is greater than that at *c* (equals to output at *d'*). Conversely, if the relative price $W_2$ is used, aggregate input at *c* is greater than that at *d* (equals to output at c'). The resulting productivity index using these biased estimates of aggregate output and input is also biased even when there has been no change in quantities of either inputs or outputs.

---

[3] GVAO measured in current and constant prices are reported by various yearbooks published by State Statistical Bureau (SSB) and Ministry of Agriculture (MOA), for example, *China Statistical Yearbook* (SSB), *China Agricultural Yearbook* (MOA), *China Rural Statistical Yearbook* (SSB), and *China Agricultural Statistical Materials* (MOA). Since 1949, the SSB has measured output using five base prices, i.e., 1952 base prices for 1949-1957, 1957 for 1958-1970, 1970 for 1971-1981, 1980 for 1981-1990, and 1990 since 1990.

[4] Alston et al. have also demonstrated the potential bias in aggregation of inputs and outputs when technical change is both present and absent. See Alston, Julian M., George W. Norton, and Philip G. Pardey, *Science Under Scarcity: Principles and Practice for Agricultural Research Evaluation and Priority Setting* (Ithaca: Cornell University Press, 1995).

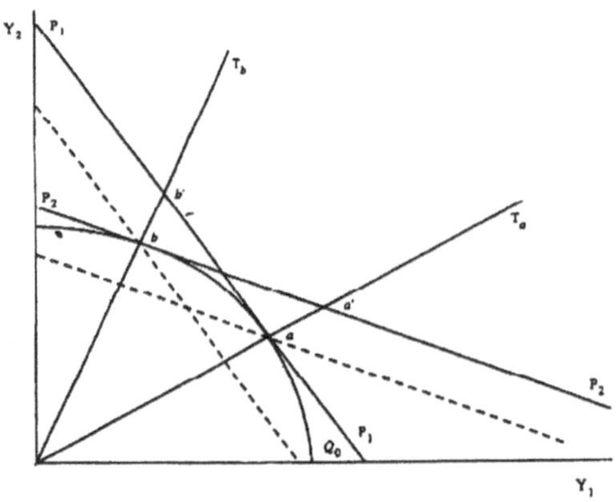


**Figure 8.1 Aggregation bias in output**

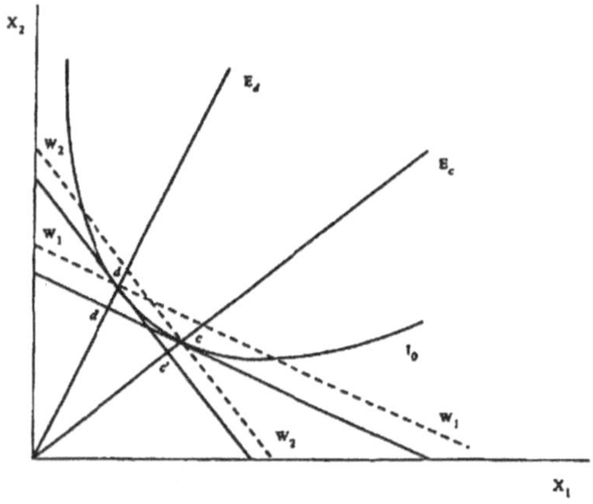


**Figure 8.2 Aggregation bias in input**

In order to minimize the potential bias caused by relative price changes, several approaches have been developed in the literature. The most commonly used method is the Divisa index. As Richter (1966) has shown, the Divisia index is desirable because of its invariance property: if nothing real has changed (e.g., the only quantity changes involve movements around an unchanged isoquant) then the index itself is unchanged. In practice, the Törnqvist-Theil (TT) index is usually used to approximate the Divisia index. The formula for a TT index of aggregate output is:

$$\ln QI_t = \Sigma_i 1/2*(S_{i,t} + S_{i,t-1}) * \ln(Y_{i,t}/Y_{i,t-1}), \quad (1)$$

where $\ln QI_t$ is the log of the aggregate output index at time $t$, $S_{i,t}$ and $S_{i,t-1}$ are output $i$'s share in total production value at time $t$ and $t$-1, respectively. $Y_{i,t}$ and $Y_{i,t-1}$ are quantities of output $i$ at time $t$ and $t$-1, respectively. The advantage of such an index is that rolling weights accommodate any substantial changes in relative prices over time. Diewert (1976) and Lau (1979) have proved that the TT index is exact for the more general class of translog aggregator functions. The TT index of aggregated input growth can be expressed in a similar way.

Based on the growth of aggregated output and input, total factor productivity (TFP) is defined as the difference of these two. Specifically, the TFP index can be written as follows:

$$\ln TFP_t = \Sigma_i 1/2*(S_{i,t} + S_{i,t-1}) * \ln(Y_{i,t}/Y_{i,t-1}) - \Sigma_i 1/2*(W_{i,t} + W_{i,t-1}) * \ln(X_{i,t}/X_{i,t-1}) \quad (2)$$

where $\ln TFP_t$ is the log of total factor productivity index, $W_{i,t}$ and $W_{i,t-1}$ are the cost shares of input $i$ in total cost at time $t$ and $t$-1, respectively, and $X_{i,t}$ and $X_{i,t-1}$ are the quantities of input $i$ at time $t$ and $t$-1, respectively.

## 3 Measures of Growth in Output, Input and Productivity, and Changes in Regional Inequality

### *3.1 Output Measures and Adjustments*

As defined by SSB, GVAO refers to total volume of output of farming, forestry, animal husbandry, and fishery in value terms, reflecting the scale of and the achievements made in agricultural production during a given period of time. The scope of official statistics on farming, forestry, animal husbandry, and fishery is as follows:

*Farming* is defined as cultivation of farm crops and other agricultural activities. Farm crops include grains, cotton, oil-bearing crops, sugar crops, bast fiber plants, tobacco, vegetables, medicinal herbs, melon and gourd crops, and cultivation and management of tea plantations, mulberry fields, and orchards. Other agricultural activities are defined as harvesting wild vegetation fruits, fiber, gum, resin, oil-bearing plants, grass, wild medicinal herbs, fungus plants, and rural household nonfarm activities.

*Forestry* refers to planting trees of various kinds (excluding tea plantations, mulberry fields and orchards), collection of forestry products, and cutting and felling of bamboo and trees by villages and other cooperative organizations under villages. *Animal husbandry* refers to raising and grazing of all animals except fishing and cultivating, and hunting and raising of wild animals. *Fishery* refers to cultivation and catching of fish and other aquatic animals and cultivation and collection of seaweed and other aquatic plants.

As indicated in the last two sessions, GVAO measured in constant prices cannot reflect the real growth of agricultural production. In this study, we use the TT index to measure production growth in Chinese agriculture for the past several decades. There are several hundred agricultural products covered by SSB, we try to cover as many as products as we can. In addition, adjustments have to be made to avoid double counting of livestock and fishery output. The following is a list of the commodities we covered and adjustments made to correct overstated output in this study.

*Crops* are divided into grain and cash crops. Grain crops include rice, wheat, corn, sorghum, millet, soybean, and tubers. Cash crops include cotton, hemp, jute, rapeseed oil, peanuts, sugarcanes, sugar beets, apples, bananas, citrus, grapes, pears, tea, tobacco, and vegetables. *Livestock* includes pork, beef, mutton, poultry, eggs, cow milk, and goat milk. Zhong (1997) found that meat output might have been overstated by 40 percent in 1996's official statistics by comparing consumption data from rural and urban households surveys and official reported meat production. Lu (1998) estimated that official meat and egg output was overestimated by 52 percent in 1995. Fuller *et al.* (2000) further estimated meat output by different types and found that 1996 official statistics overstated output of pork by 65 percent, beef by 139 percent, poultry by 239 percent, mutton by 87 percent, and eggs by 64 percent and most of livestock products were underreported back in 1985.[5] First Agricultural Census data also show that the inventories of large animals have been overstated by 30 percent, swine by 36 percent, goats and sheep by 40 percent. However, the inventory data does not reflect overstated number of animals slaughtered, and weight per head when slaughtered. Therefore, in this study, we use Fuller *et al.*'s estimates to adjust the official statistics for pork, beef, mutton, poultry, and eggs.[6] The SSB has

[5] The State Statistical Bureau adjusted its livestock production data for 1996 in 1998 *China Statistical Yearbook* based on the Agriculture Census. The pork output was adjusted downward by 28 percent, beef by 39 percent, poultry by 27 percent, and mutton by 32 percent.

[6] Fuller et al. adjusted official SSB data in two scenarios. In the first scenario, they assume that the proportion of total livestock products consumed outside of the household remains constant. Likewise, the yield of retail cuts from cattle, swine, and sheep carcasses remains constant over time. They also assume that the reported trade statistics are accurate and that stock levels remain constant. Finally, the ratio of production-based per capita consumption to survey averages over the 1985–1987 period is assumed to capture the inaccuracies introduced by away-from home consumption and stock changes; thus, this ratio is held constant near the 1985–1987 average. They construct the Scenario 2 estimates using Scenario 1 assumptions regarding carcass yields, stocks, and trade; however, the under-reporting caused by away-from-home (AFH) consumption in urban areas is assumed to increase proportional to the change in real per capita expenditures for urban households. Urban AFH consumption increases urban per capita meat consumption by 30 percent in 1993, rising to 35 percent in 1996, thus attaining a level roughly equivalent to average AFH consumption in the U.S. in 1970. Rural AFH consumption also rises proportional to the increase in real per capita expenditure for rural households, increasing rural per capita meat consumption by 1 percent in 1996. In this study, we use their scenario 2 estimates to adjust meat and egg output. The adjustments began in 1980 assuming that the overestimation or underestimation is zero, and then increases linearly to the level Fuller et al constructed for 1985 to avoid a disjoint.

adjusted its meat production data since 1996 beginning in 1998's China Statistical Yearbook. For 1997 livestock output data, we simply use the growth rate reported by SSB to extrapolate the output data, assuming there is no over reporting of growth in 1997. *Fishery products* are total weights of both sea and fresh water fish and other aquatic animals produced in a year measured in tons.[7] We use Lu's estimate of fishery output to adjust official fishery output.[8] *Forestry products* are excluded in this study. The exclusion of forestry does not bias estimate too much, because it accounts for only 3 percent of total SSB's GVAO in 1997.

The official quantity data are taken from various issues of *China's Statistical Yearbook* and *China's Agricultural Yearbook*. Prices are taken from *China Commodity Price Yearbooks* (various issues), *China Trade and Price Statistical Materials, 1952-83, China Domestic Marketing Statistical Yearbooks* (various issues), and USDA *Agricultural Statistics of the People's Republic of China, 1949-90*.

Table 8.1 reports various measures of output growth for China as a whole. The SSB index is reported by various official statistics without adjusting meat and fishery output. The constant price index was calculated by the authors using the official price and output data (no adjustments were made on meat and fishery data) and 1980 constant prices in aggregation. The TT1 is the output index constructed using the Törnqvist-Theil index approach and official statistics without adjusting meat and fishery output. The TT2 index is the Törnqvist-Theil index constructed by the authors using adjusted livestock and fishery output data. The difference between SSB index and index measured in 1980 prices is solely due to the commodity coverage because the methodology used in aggregating these two indexes are the same. When comparing SSB's GAVO and ours, we found the difference ranges from 20 percent in 1952, 1 percent in 1980, to 7 percent in 1997. Except for the 1950s, our coverage is reasonably good. The reason for large difference in the 1950s is due mainly to the fact that SSB's GAVO includes values of manurial fertilizer and rural household's small industry, and they are not in our commodity coverage and have been excluded from SSB's GAVO since 1957.

The difference between the index measured in 1980 prices and TT1 index is due to the aggregation bias as we have illustrated in the previous section. Prior to the 1960s, the difference between these two indexes is small, being less than 2 percent. But the disparity grew larger over time. Particularly since the reforms, the difference has grown from less than 8 percent in 1978 to more than 31 percent in 1997, implying that part of the rapid growth in agricultural output measured in constant prices may come from the aggregation bias. There have been rapid price changes in agricultural products in Chinese agriculture since the reforms. Some of the substitution effects (or

[7] It would be desirable to disaggregate fishery into individual products. But it is practicably impossible due to large number of various fishery products. It does not cause bias in aggregating total output to great extent because fishery accounts only 9 percent of total production value even in 1997.

[8] Lu estimated that official fishery output in China is over reported by 69 percent in 1997.

price effects) may have been captured as part of the production increase if constant prices are used in the aggregation.

The difference between TT1 and TT2 is due to the adjustments made to livestock and fishery output. The TT1 uses the official statistical meat and fishery data, while TT2 uses the meat and fishery data adjusted by the authors to avoid the over reporting of these outputs. The difference in 1981 is less than 1 percent, but gradually increased to 18 percent in 1997. Prior to 1988, agricultural production value was underreported while it was overstated thereafter due to the adjustment of livestock and fishery data.

Although still growing at a respective rate, the appropriately measured production growth is 4.6 percent per annum from 1979 to 1997, compared to 6.5 percent per annum reported by official SSB publications. In other words, the annual agricultural production growth reported by official statistics has been overstated as high as 1.9 percent per annum from 1979 to 1997.

**Table 8.1 Measures of output growth at the national level, 1952=100**

| Year | SSB | Constant Price | TT1 | TT2 |
|---|---|---|---|---|
| 1952 | 100 | 100 | 100 | 100 |
| 1953 | 103 | 100 | 100 | 100 |
| 1954 | 106 | 104 | 103 | 103 |
| 1955 | 114 | 114 | 112 | 112 |
| 1956 | 119 | 119 | 118 | 118 |
| 1957 | 129 | 120 | 119 | 119 |
| 1958 | 127 | 125 | 125 | 125 |
| 1959 | 110 | 111 | 111 | 111 |
| 1960 | 96 | 91 | 92 | 92 |
| 1961 | 94 | 81 | 82 | 82 |
| 1962 | 100 | 89 | 89 | 89 |
| 1963 | 112 | 98 | 97 | 97 |
| 1964 | 127 | 111 | 109 | 109 |
| 1965 | 137 | 121 | 118 | 118 |
| 1966 | 149 | 133 | 129 | 129 |
| 1967 | 151 | 137 | 133 | 133 |
| 1968 | 147 | 141 | 136 | 136 |
| 1969 | 149 | 147 | 141 | 141 |
| 1970 | 172 | 149 | 143 | 143 |
| 1971 | 188 | 154 | 147 | 147 |
| 1972 | 185 | 154 | 147 | 147 |
| 1973 | 200 | 166 | 157 | 157 |

| | | | | |
|---|---|---|---|---|
| 1974 | 207 | 175 | 165 | 165 |
| 1975 | 192 | 182 | 170 | 170 |
| 1976 | 190 | 180 | 167 | 167 |
| 1977 | 189 | 181 | 168 | 168 |
| 1978 | 206 | 200 | 185 | 185 |
| 1979 | 222 | 216 | 197 | 197 |
| 1980 | 225 | 223 | 202 | 202 |
| 1981 | 240 | 240 | 216 | 218 |
| 1982 | 267 | 263 | 235 | 238 |
| 1983 | 287 | 280 | 249 | 252 |
| 1984 | 322 | 310 | 272 | 275 |
| 1985 | 333 | 326 | 279 | 286 |
| 1986 | 345 | 331 | 283 | 293 |
| 1987 | 365 | 352 | 297 | 306 |
| 1988 | 379 | 365 | 299 | 300 |
| 1989 | 391 | 357 | 315 | 313 |
| 1990 | 421 | 421 | 343 | 339 |
| 1991 | 436 | 440 | 359 | 352 |
| 1992 | 463 | 469 | 375 | 363 |
| Continue: | | | | |
| 1993 | 500 | 514 | 400 | 375 |
| 1994 | 543 | 578 | 425 | 385 |
| 1995 | 602 | 638 | 465 | 408 |
| 1996 | 659 | 669 | 502 | 436 |
| 1997 | 693 | 685 | 522 | 441 |
| Annual Growth Rate | | | | |
| 1952-78 | 2.82 | 2.71 | 2.38 | 2.38 |
| 1979-97 | 6.53 | 6.63 | 5.56 | 4.57 |
| 1952-97 | 4.39 | 4.37 | 3.74 | 3.35 |

*Notes*: 1. The SSB index is reported by various official statistics without adjusting meat and fishery output. The constant price index was calculated by the authors using the official price and output data (no adjustments were made on meat and fishery data) and 1980 constant prices in aggregation. The TT1 is the output index constructed using the Törnqvist-Theil index approach with official statistics without adjusting meat and fishery output. The TT2 index is the Törnqvist-Theil index constructed by the authors with adjusted livestock and fishery output data.

Table 8.2 reports measures of output growth at the provincial level. Due to data unavailability, we were able to construct provincial growth index only after 1979. But this may not be a serious problem because overestimation of production growth predominantly occurred after the reforms. The constant price index represents measures of growth using the 1980 constant prices and official SSB output data without adjusting meat and fishery output. The TT2 index is measured by the authors using the Törnqvist-Theil index approach and the adjusted SSB output data. One significant finding from the table is that overestimation has mainly occurred in less-developed areas. For example, growth in GAVO in Guizhou and Qinghai has been overestimated by more than 4 percent per annum, and that in Gansu has been overestimated by almost 3 percent per annum. This implies that the difference in development level between less- and more-developed areas is actually larger than that calculated from the official statistics.

### *3.2 Measures of Inputs*

In order to aggregate total input, both quantities and prices of individual inputs are required. Quantities are easy to obtain as SSB has been consistently publishing these input data since the 1950s. But prices of inputs are not readily available. Certain statistical techniques are required to extrapolate price data for some inputs.

#### *3.2.1 Quantities of Inputs*

*Labor Input.* Labor input is measured in person-year equivalent of workers directly engaged in production of farming, animal husbandry, and fishery.[9] The labor of rural industry is excluded from agricultural labor input.

*Land Input.* Land input is measured as arable land. The official data on arable land are extremely inaccurate, and is reported to be understated by 30-40 percent from various sources. However, as long as the over reporting of land quantity is constant over time and the land input cost share is measured as residual as we will discuss later, the measure of input growth index will not be affected.

*Machinery Power Input.* It refers to total mechanical power of machinery used in farming, animal husbandry, sideline occupations and fishery, including ploughing, irrigation and drainage, harvesting, farm product processing and transportation, plant protection, stockbreeding, and fishery. It excludes machinery used for non-agricultural purposes such as township- and village-run industry, construction, non-agricultural transportation, scientific experimentation and teaching.

---

[9] Labor used in forestry production is excluded using the share of forestry production value in total agricultural production value.

**Table 8.2 Measures of output growth at the regional level, 1979-1997**

| Province | Constant Price | TT2 | Overestimation |
|---|---|---|---|
| *Annual Growth Rates* | | | |
| Hebei | 7.29 | 5.23 | 2.06 |
| Shanxi | 5.46 | 3.32 | 2.13 |
| Inner Mongolia | 10.09 | 7.27 | 2.82 |
| Liaoning | 6.23 | 4.49 | 1.74 |
| Jilin | 4.99 | 3.54 | 1.45 |
| Heilongjiang | 6.11 | 4.60 | 1.50 |
| Jiangsu | 5.91 | 4.41 | 1.50 |
| Zhejiang | 6.70 | 3.18 | 3.52 |
| Anhui | 8.37 | 5.00 | 3.36 |
| Fujian | 9.42 | 5.60 | 3.82 |
| Jiangxi | 7.68 | 4.79 | 2.89 |
| Shandong | 6.69 | 4.75 | 1.94 |
| Henan | 6.85 | 4.88 | 1.97 |
| Hubei | 6.51 | 4.33 | 2.18 |
| Hunan | 5.83 | 3.49 | 2.34 |
| Guangdong | 5.65 | 5.95 | -0.30 |
| Guangxi | 8.39 | 7.87 | 0.52 |
| Sichuan | 4.46 | 3.44 | 1.02 |
| Guizhou | 8.14 | 4.12 | 4.02 |
| Yunan | 6.77 | 5.59 | 1.18 |
| Shaanxi | 4.09 | 3.94 | 0.15 |
| Gansu | 7.85 | 4.77 | 3.08 |
| Qinghai | 6.66 | 2.61 | 4.05 |
| Ningxia | 9.32 | 6.84 | 2.47 |
| Xinjiang | 8.23 | 6.66 | 1.57 |
| National | 6.60 | 4.57 | 2.03 |

*Notes*: 1. The constant price index was calculated by the authors using the official price and output data (no adjustments were made on meat and fishery data) and 1980 constant prices in aggregation. The TT2 index is the Törnqvist-Theil index constructed by the authors with adjusted livestock and fishery data.

*Capital of Animals*. It is the sum of capitals for all animals. For draft animals and milk cows, 20 percent of current animal value is used as capital (assuming an animal can be used for 5 years). For hogs, beef cattle, sheep and goats, and poultry, the year-ending values of animal stocks for the previous year are used as capital input. For breeding animal stocks, 33.3 percent of the current values of animals are added to the capital assuming the animals can be used for 3 years.
*Chemical Fertilizer Input*. Chemical fertilizer is measured in standard weights. The standard weights are obtained by converting actual weights into the following standard: ammonium sulfate (20 percent nitrogen), super-phosphate (18.7 percent $P_2O_2$), and potassium sulfate (40 percent $K_2O$).
*Pesticide Input*. It is measured in standard weight, and includes both pesticides and fungicides.
*Seed Input*. Seed input is calculated based on the average seed use per hectare of sown area reported by the *Handbooks of Agricultural Technical Economics.*[10]
*Feed Input*. Total feed input is calculated based on number of animals and per day use of feed for each type of animals reported by the *Handbook of Agricultural Technical Economics*.
*Irrigation Input*. Irrigation input is the total irrigated area in agriculture, i.e., those areas that are effectively irrigated – level land which has water source and complete sets of irrigation facilities to lift and move adequate water for irrigation purposes under normal conditions.

### *3.2.2 Prices of Inputs*

*Labor Price*. Labor price is measured as wage per day. Wages for 1953, 1957, 1962, 1965, and from 1975 to 1997 annually are reported by State Price Bureau in its *Production Cost Survey.*[11] The gaps are estimated using geometric extrapolation. The annual labor cost is calculated by multiplying daily wage by number of working days per person.[12]
*Chemical Fertilizer Price*. Chemical fertilizer price is measured as yuan per standard ton. The data after 1977 are reported by *China Agricultural Development Report* (1995 -98), and those prior to 1978 are reported in the *China Trade, Marketing, and Price Statistical Materials, 1952-1983.*
*Pesticide Price*. Pesticide price is measured as yuan per standard ton. The data after 1977 are reported by *China Agricultural Development Report* (1995 -98), and those prior to 1978 are reported in the *China Trade, Marketing, and Price Statistical*

[10] Editorial Committee of the Handbook of Agricultural Technical Economics, Handbook of Agricultural technical Economics. Beijing: Agricultural Press.
[11] State Price Bureau, *Production* Cost Survey (State Price Bureau, 1953-98).
[12] The average number of working days is 300 in 1978, and then decline by 2 days per year. This is because farmers are working few days, and spend more time in non-farm activities or leisure. Therefore, number of labor-days used in agricultural production has declined for crop, cash and livestock production (*Production and Cost Survey*).

*Materials, 1952-1983.*

*Machinery Input Price.* Data on agricultural machinery price measured as yuan per horsepower after 1985 are reported in *China Marketing Statistical Yearbooks*. Those prior to 1985 are estimated by the author using price index of agricultural production materials reported in various statistical yearbooks published by SSB. When calculating the total cost of machinery use, 5 year-life span of machinery equipment is assumed, i.e., 20 percent of total machinery value is used as flow (or service) terms cost.

*Seed Price.* Procurement prices for grains, and cash crops are used as prices for seed.

*Feed Price.* Procurement prices for grains are used as prices for feed.

*Land Price.* Since there has been no land market in China, we use residual of total production value net of costs for labor, fertilizer, machinery, and irrigation on a per unit of land base as land price.

*Animal Stock Price.* Average prices for different types of animals are used as prices for animal capitals.

*Irrigation price.* This is measured as irrigation fee per irrigated hectare. Irrigation fee per hectare is reported by the *Production Cost Survey* (State Price Bureau, 1953-98), while irrigated areas are reported by various *China Statistical Yearbooks*.

### *3.2.3 Aggregation of Inputs*

Total input in agriculture is usually aggregated using the shares of inputs as weights.[13] Changes in input shares show that Chinese agriculture has experienced rapid technical transformation in the past several decades (Figure 8.3). Farmers have increased their use of modern inputs such as chemical fertilizer, pesticides, and machinery. The share of chemical fertilizer has increased from almost none in 1952 to more than 11 percent of the total production cost in 1997. The share of machinery has also increased from almost zero in 1957 to more than 5 percent in 1977. The declining share of machinery (3 percent in 1997) in recent years is mainly a result of more efficient allocation of inputs by farmers when production was decentralized to households. This is consistent with Fan and Ruttan's findings that a centrally planned economy often overuses capital because of the ideology belief. The rapid decline of pesticide use since 1982 is mainly due to the improvement of pesticide quality and more efficient application by farmers due to the change of production objectives from maximizing yield during the pre-reform period to maximizing profit during the reform period.

Meanwhile, the importance of traditional inputs like labor and land has declined rapidly. The land cost share declined from more than 53 percent in the 1950s to only 35 percent in 1997. The labor cost share first increased from 32 percent in 1952 to 45 percent in 1983, then declined again to 30 percent in 1997.[14]

---

[13] For example, Tang (1984), Wiens (1982), and Wen (1993).

[14] The factor shares presented here are roughly comparable with those reported by Fan (1990).

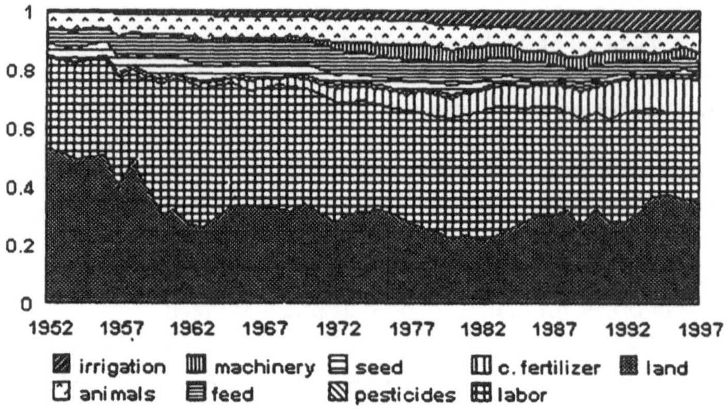


**Figure 8.3 Changes in input shares**

Total input is aggregated using both the TT approach and 1980 constant shares (table 8.3).[15] The 1980 constant share index overestimates growth in total input use by more than 1.18 percent per annum from 1952 to 1997. This bias was especially large during the pre-reform period (by 2.07 percent per annum). This is because the constant share index captures part of the substitution effects among inputs as input growth. Table 8.4 shows that the underestimation of inputs has less regional difference than the overestimation of output.[16]

We also constructed the aggregate input index using Wen's weights. The difference between his and our measures comes from both individual input use and shares used in the aggregation. But most of the difference comes from the weights. In

---

[15] Wen (1993) used the fixed weights in his measures: 0.35 for labor, 0.09 for capital, 0.36 for land, and 0.20 for current input. Later Jin *et al.* (1999), and Carter *et al.* (1999) either used Wen's weights or 1995 constant prices in constructing their TFP indexes at the crop level. See Jin, Songqing, Scott Rozelle, Erika Meng, Ruifa Hu, and Jikung Huang, "Genetic Diversity and Total Factor Productivity: The Case of Wheat in China," paper presented at the Symposium on China's Agricultural Trade and Policy: Issues, Analysis and Global Consequences, San Francisco, June 25-26, 1999; and Carter Colin, Jing Chen, and Baojin Chu, "Agricultural Productivity Growth in China: Farm Level versus National Measurement," paper presented at the Symposium on China's Agricultural Trade and Policy: Issues, Analysis and Global Consequences, San Francisco, June 25-26, 1999.

[16] The reason why 1980 constant share input index is different from Wen's (or Wien as his central case) is because our shares in 1980 are very different from those of Wen's. For example, in our paper, shares are: 0.199 for land, 0.422 for labor, 0.072 for chemical fertilizer, 0.011 for pesticides, 0.031 for seed, 0.107 for feed, 0.047 for machinery, 0.071 for animals, and 0.04 for irrigation. But for Wen, they are: 0.36 for land, 0.35 for labor, 0.09 for capital, and 0.2 for current input. Wen's land and labor shares are larger than those in our paper, and these two inputs grew relatively slowly than other inputs, leading to a slower growth in total input in Wen's aggregation.

fact, Wen's index is not that much different from the TT index up to 1964, implying that Wen's weights might be closer to the actual input shares in the 1950s and early 1960s.

*3.3 Measures of Total Factor Productivity*

Using estimated aggregate output and input growth; total factor productivity growth can be easily calculated. Again, both 1980 constant prices (or shares) and Törnqvist-Theil indexes are calculated at both national and provincial levels (tables 8.5 and 8.6). The TT1 index is the TFP index using the TT1 output growth index from Table 8.1 and the TT input growth index from Table 8.3, while TT2 is the TFP index using TT2 output growth from Table 8.1 and TT input growth index from Table 8.3. The 1980 constant price (share) index would underestimate total factor productivity growth by only 0.55 percent per year from 1952 to 1997, but this bias has great variations over time. The constant price (share) index would overestimate the decline in total factor productivity by more than 1.67 percent per annum from 1952 to 1978 and overstate the growth by more than 1.08 percent per annum from 1979 to 1997 when compared with the TT1 index. This overestimated total factor productivity growth after 1979 would exaggerate the effects of the rural reforms on productivity growth substantially. The difference between TT1 and TT2 is mainly due to the difference in livestock output between official statistics and adjusted output. Over reported livestock output would overestimate TFP growth by 0.98 percent per annum from 1979 to 1997.

**Table 8.3 Measures of input growth at the national level, 1952=100**

| Year | 1980 Shares | Wen (or Wein) | TT |
|---|---|---|---|
| 1952 | 100 | 100 | 100 |
| 1953 | 111 | 105 | 103 |
| 1954 | 119 | 109 | 106 |
| 1955 | 127 | 111 | 108 |
| 1956 | 135 | 114 | 112 |
| 1957 | 146 | 119 | 116 |
| 1958 | 144 | 112 | 107 |
| 1959 | 143 | 107 | 104 |
| 1960 | 146 | 108 | 106 |
| 1961 | 150 | 109 | 111 |
| 1962 | 162 | 115 | 116 |
| 1963 | 176 | 122 | 122 |
| 1964 | 189 | 129 | 128 |
| 1965 | 199 | 138 | 132 |

| | | | |
|---|---|---|---|
| 1966 | 215 | 150 | 139 |
| 1967 | 219 | 152 | 141 |
| 1968 | 216 | 147 | 140 |
| 1969 | 226 | 155 | 144 |
| 1970 | 240 | 164 | 150 |
| 1971 | 254 | 175 | 157 |
| 1972 | 261 | 181 | 160 |
| 1973 | 271 | 191 | 164 |
| 1974 | 274 | 190 | 165 |
| 1975 | 281 | 196 | 168 |
| 1976 | 284 | 200 | 169 |
| 1977 | 288 | 206 | 171 |
| 1978 | 301 | 228 | 179 |
| 1979 | 312 | 247 | 185 |
| 1980 | 316 | 257 | 187 |
| 1981 | 316 | 261 | 187 |
| 1982 | 322 | 274 | 191 |
| 1983 | 323 | 283 | 192 |
| 1984 | 324 | 286 | 192 |
| 1985 | 320 | 283 | 190 |
| 1986 | 326 | 296 | 193 |
| 1987 | 330 | 305 | 196 |
| 1988 | 336 | 317 | 199 |
| 1989 | 346 | 334 | 205 |
| 1991 | 362 | 365 | 214 |
| 1992 | 363 | 370 | 215 |
| 1994 | 368 | 399 | 218 |
| 1995 | 375 | 420 | 223 |
| 1996 | 380 | 437 | 227 |
| 1997 | 388 | 453 | 232 |
| Annual Growth Rate | | | |
| 1952-78 | 4.33 | 3.23 | 2.26 |
| 1979-97 | 1.22 | 3.42 | 1.25 |
| 1952-97 | 3.06 | 3.41 | 1.88 |

*Notes*: 1. The 1980 constant share index was constructed using the 1980 shares: 0.22 for land, 0.41 for labor, 0.072 for chemical fertilizer, 0.011 for pesticides, 0.031 for seed, 0.082 for feed, 0.047 for machinery, 0.081 for animals, and 0.040 for irrigation. The Wen index was constructed using the following weights: 0.35 for labor, 0.36 for land, 0.09 for capital (aggregation of both machinery and animal capitals), and 0.20 for current inputs (aggregation of chemical fertilizer, pesticides, seed, and feed). The TT index is constructed using the Törnqvist-Theil approach.

**Table 8.4 Measures of input growth at the regional level, 1979-1997**

| Province | 1980 Shares | TT | Overestimation |
|---|---|---|---|
| | *Annual Growth Rates* | | |
| Hebei | 1.33 | 1.42 | -0.09 |
| Shanxi | 0.91 | 0.87 | 0.04 |
| Inner Mongolia | 1.55 | 2.18 | -0.63 |
| Liaoning | 0.54 | 0.33 | 0.22 |
| Jilin | 1.58 | 1.82 | -0.25 |
| Heilongjiang | 1.06 | 1.24 | -0.18 |
| Jiangsu | 0.14 | 0.28 | -0.14 |
| Zhejiang | -0.43 | -0.46 | 0.02 |
| Anhui | 1.73 | 1.67 | 0.06 |
| Fujian | 0.74 | 0.83 | -0.09 |
| Jiangxi | 1.17 | 1.19 | -0.03 |
| Shandong | 0.81 | 0.78 | 0.03 |
| Henan | 1.72 | 1.90 | -0.18 |
| Hubei | 0.43 | 0.78 | -0.35 |
| Hunan | 0.80 | 0.70 | 0.10 |
| Guangdong | 0.09 | -0.07 | 0.16 |
| Guangxi | 1.44 | 1.65 | -0.21 |
| Sichuan | 0.75 | 0.82 | -0.08 |
| Guizhou | 2.63 | 2.49 | 0.14 |
| Yunan | 2.01 | 2.16 | -0.16 |
| Shaanxi | 1.40 | 1.67 | -0.27 |
| Gansu | 2.05 | 2.09 | -0.05 |
| Qinghai | 0.94 | 0.99 | -0.04 |
| Ningxia | 3.16 | 2.46 | 0.70 |
| Xinjiang | 1.38 | 1.60 | -0.22 |
| National | 1.22 | 1.25 | -0.03 |

*Notes*: 1. The 1980 constant share index was constructed using the 1980 shares. The TT index is constructed using the Törnqvist-Theil approach.

**Table 8.5 Measures of TFP growth at the national level, 1950-1997**

| Year | 1980 Constant Prices | TT1 | TT2 |
|---|---|---|---|
| 1952 | 100 | 100 | 100 |
| 1953 | 90 | 97 | 97 |
| 1954 | 87 | 97 | 97 |
| 1955 | 89 | 104 | 104 |
| 1956 | 88 | 105 | 105 |
| 1957 | 82 | 103 | 103 |
| 1958 | 87 | 116 | 116 |
| 1959 | 78 | 107 | 107 |
| 1960 | 63 | 87 | 87 |
| 1961 | 54 | 74 | 74 |
| 1962 | 55 | 77 | 77 |
| 1963 | 55 | 80 | 80 |
| 1964 | 59 | 85 | 85 |
| 1965 | 61 | 89 | 89 |
| 1966 | 62 | 93 | 93 |
| 1967 | 63 | 95 | 95 |
| 1968 | 65 | 97 | 97 |
| 1969 | 65 | 98 | 98 |
| 1970 | 62 | 95 | 95 |
| 1971 | 61 | 94 | 94 |
| 1972 | 59 | 92 | 92 |
| 1973 | 61 | 96 | 96 |
| 1974 | 64 | 100 | 100 |
| 1975 | 65 | 101 | 101 |
| 1976 | 63 | 99 | 99 |
| 1977 | 63 | 98 | 98 |
| 1978 | 67 | 103 | 103 |
| 1979 | 69 | 106 | 106 |
| 1980 | 71 | 108 | 108 |
| 1981 | 76 | 115 | 116 |
| 1982 | 82 | 123 | 125 |
| 1983 | 87 | 130 | 131 |

| | | | |
|---|---|---|---|
| 1984 | 96 | 141 | 143 |
| 1985 | 102 | 147 | 151 |
| 1986 | 102 | 146 | 152 |
| 1987 | 107 | 152 | 156 |
| 1988 | 109 | 150 | 151 |
| 1989 | 103 | 154 | 153 |
| 1990 | 119 | 163 | 162 |
| 1991 | 122 | 167 | 164 |
| 1992 | 129 | 174 | 169 |
| 1993 | 141 | 185 | 174 |
| 1994 | 157 | 195 | 176 |
| 1995 | 170 | 209 | 183 |
| 1996 | 176 | 221 | 192 |
| 1997 | 176 | 225 | 190 |
| Annual Growth Rates | | | |
| 1952-78 | -1.55 | 0.12 | 0.12 |
| 1979-97 | 5.34 | 4.26 | 3.28 |
| 1952-97 | 1.27 | 1.82 | 1.44 |

The regional difference in TFP growth is larger than that in both output and input growth due to overestimation of output and underestimation of inputs. In Guizhou, and Qinghai, TFP growth has been overestimated by over 4 percent per annum, when constant prices (shares) instead of TT indexes are used. This indicates that the official statistics have underestimated the difference in productivity growth between developed and less-developed region in Chinese agriculture.

### *3.4 Measures of Regional Inequality*

Multiplying the TT2 growth index with output values in 1980 prices, we can obtain adjusted output values expressed in 1980 prices. The adjusted values and official GVAOs in the 1980 prices can then be used for inequality analysis. Since each province varies by size, it does not make sense to calculate regional inequality using total outputs. Therefore, we use labor productivity to analyze the regional difference. The results show that official output data tends to understate the regional development gap. For instance, the gaps in labor productivity between the highest Jiangsu and the lowest Gansu provinces calculated from the adjusted data and official data are 5.9 and 4.5 times, respectively, in 1997. Similar bias applies to the estimate of regional inequality index as well.

**Table 8.6 Measures of TFP growth at the regional level, 1979-1997**

| Province | Constant Price | TT2 | Overestimation |
|---|---|---|---|
| | *Annual Growth Rates* | | |
| Hebei | 5.90 | 3.76 | 2.14 |
| Shanxi | 4.52 | 2.43 | 2.09 |
| Inner Mongolia | 8.42 | 5.03 | 3.39 |
| Liaoning | 5.61 | 3.97 | 1.64 |
| Jilin | 3.45 | 1.87 | 1.58 |
| Heilongjiang | 5.01 | 3.33 | 1.68 |
| Jiangsu | 5.68 | 3.94 | 1.74 |
| Zhejiang | 6.99 | 3.37 | 3.62 |
| Anhui | 6.57 | 3.34 | 3.23 |
| Fujian | 8.54 | 4.59 | 3.95 |
| Jiangxi | 6.44 | 3.54 | 2.90 |
| Shandong | 5.82 | 3.84 | 1.98 |
| Henan | 5.13 | 3.05 | 2.07 |
| Hubei | 6.00 | 3.45 | 2.55 |
| Hunan | 4.99 | 2.72 | 2.26 |
| Guangdong | 5.47 | 5.68 | -0.21 |
| Guangxi | 6.87 | 6.02 | 0.85 |
| Sichuan | 3.69 | 2.57 | 1.12 |
| Guizhou | 5.53 | 1.88 | 3.64 |
| Yunan | 4.78 | 3.49 | 1.29 |
| Shaanxi | 2.74 | 2.36 | 0.38 |
| Gansu | 5.78 | 2.79 | 3.00 |
| Qinghai | 5.66 | 1.67 | 3.99 |
| Ningxia | 6.16 | 4.40 | 1.76 |
| Xinjiang | 6.78 | 4.94 | 1.84 |
| National | 5.34 | 3.28 | 2.06 |

*Notes*: 1. The 1980 constant price (or share) index is constructed using the 1980 constant price output index and 1980 constant share input index. TheTT2 TFP index is constructed using the TT2 output index from Table 8.2 and the TT input index from Table 8.4.

Figure 8.4 graphs the Gini coefficients based on the two series. At least two features are apparent. First, the inequality index based on adjusted data is always higher than that based on official output data. Second, the rate of increase in regional inequality using the adjusted production value is much faster than that calculated from the official data. Using official output values, the estimated Gini coefficient increases by only 4 percent from 1980 to 1997, but it increases by 25 percent if the adjusted data are used. The results indicate that the extent of regional inequality is much more serious than previously thought.

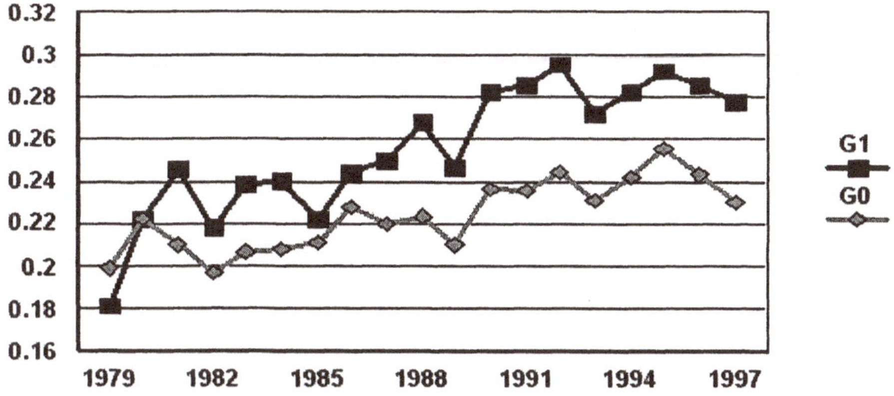


*Note*: G0 and G1 are Gini coefficients calculated from official SSB data and our TT output growth index, respective.

**Figure 8.4 Measures of regional inequality**

## 4 Conclusions

This study uses a more appropriate approach and adjusted livestock and fishery output data to measure growth in output, input and total factor productivity for Chinese agriculture based on detailed quantity and price information. Our results show that the official statistics overestimates both aggregate output and input, resulting in biased estimates of total factor productivity growth. Furthermore, the official data would overstate the impact of the rural reforms on both production and productivity growth. Nevertheless, both production and productivity still grew at respectable rates during the reform period.

The regional measures indicated that it is the less-developed areas where total output growth is overestimated and total input use is underestimated. As a result, growth in total factor productivity has been overestimated. This has several implications. First, the regional inequality in rural China may be larger than that calculated form official statistics. Second, the less-developed areas may have benefited less from the reforms than previously thought.

The overestimation of production and productivity growth may have serious policy consequences on searching the future sources of growth. The overestimation may exaggerate the impact of rural reforms and therefore underestimates the impact of technical change on growth, leading to underinvestment in agricultural research. The underestimated regional inequality may also lead to misinformed decision on more equitable development among regions.

## References


Chen, J. and Fleisher, B., 'Regional Income Inequality and Economic Growth in China,' *Journal of Comparative Economics*, Vol. 22 (1996): 141-164.

Diewert, W.E., 'Exact and Superlative Index Numbers,' *Journal of Econometrics*, 4 (1976): 115-146.

Fan, S., *Regional Productivity Growth in China's Agriculture* (Boulder: Westview Press, 1990).

———, 'Effects of Technological Change and Institutional Reform on Production Growth in Chinese Agriculture', *American Journal of Agricultural Economics*, Vol. 73, 2 (1991): 266-275.

Fan, S. and Pardey, P., 'Research, Productivity, and Output Growth in Chinese Agriculture,' *Journal of Development Economics* Vol. 53 (1997): 115-137.

Fan, S. and Ruttan, V., 'Technical Change in Centrally Planned Economies,' *Agricultural Economics* (The Journal of International Association of Agricultural Economists) 6 (1992): 301-314.

Jorgenson, D., *Productivity Volume 1: Post U.S. Economic Growth* (Cambridge, Massachusetts: The MIT Press, 1995).

———, *Productivity Volume 2: International Comparisons of Economic Growth* (Cambridge, Massachusetts: The MIT Press, 1996).

Kanbur, R. and Zhang, X., 'Which Regional Inequality? The Evolution of Rural-Urban and Inland-Coastal Inequality in China from 1983 to 1995,' *Journal of Comparative Economics*, Vol. 27 (1999): 686-701.

Lardy, R.N., *Agriculture in China's Modern Economics Development* (Cambridge: Cambridge University Press, 1983).

Lau, L.J., 'On Exact Index Numbers,' *Review of Economics and Statistics* Vol. 61, 1(1979): 73-82.

Lin, J.Y., 'The Household Responsibility System in China's Agricultural Reform: A Theoretical and Empirical Study', *Economic Development and Cultural Change* 36 (1988): 200-224.

———, 'Rural Reforms and Agricultural Growth in China', *American Economic Review*, Vol. 82, 1(1992): 34-51.

McMillan, J., Whalley, J. and Zhu, L., 'The Impact of China's Economic Reforms on Agricultural Productivity Growth', *Journal of Political Economy* 97(1989): 781-807.

Perkins, D. and Yusuf, S., *Rural Development in China* (Baltimore: The Johns Hopkins University Press, 1984).

Richter, M.K., 'Invariance Axioms and Economic Indexes,' *Econometrica* Vol. 34. 4(1966): 739-755.

State Statistical Bureau, *China's Statistical Yearbook* (Beijing: China Statistical Press, 1998).

———, *China Domestic Marketing Statistical Yearbook*, (Beijing: China Statistical Press,

1993-98); and USDA, *Agricultural Statistics of the People's Republic of China, 1949-90* (USDA 1993).

———, *China's Statistical Yearbook* (Beijing: China Statistical Press, 1981-98); and Editorial Committee of China's Agricultural Yearbooks, *China's Agricultural Yearbook* (Beijing: China's Agricultural Press, 1981-98).

Tang, A., *An Analytical and Empirical Investigation of Agriculture in Mainland China, 1952-1980* (Taibei: Chung-Hua Institution for Economics Research, 1984).

Tsui, K., 'China's Regional Inequality, 1952-1985,' *Journal of Comparative Economics*, Vol. 15 (April 1991): 1-21.

Wen, G.J., 'Total Factor Productivity Change in China's Farming Sector: 1952-1989', *Economic Development and Cultural Change* Vol 42 (1993): 1-41.

Wiens, T., 'Technical Change,' in Randolph Barker et al. (eds), *The Chinese Agricultural Economy* (Boulder: Westview Press, 1982).

World Bank, *China: Options for Reform in the Grain Sectors*, A World Bank Country Study, Washington, D.C.: World Bank (1991).

Yang, D.T. and Zhou, H., 'Rural-Urban Disparity and Sectoral Labor Allocation in China,' *Journal of Development Studies*, Vol. 35 (1999): 105-133.

Zhang, B. and Carter, C., 'Reforms, the Weather, and Productivity Growth in China's Grain Sector.' *American Journal of Agricultural Economics* Vol. 79 (November 1997): 1266-1277.

Chapter 9

# County-Level Agricultural Production Efficiency in China: A Spatial Analysis

Zhuo Chen*
Wallace E. Huffman

## 1 Introduction

China's access to the World Trade Organization (WTO) brings Chinese agricultural producers opportunities as well as the urgent message that they must compete with their foreign counterparts. Given limited per capita resources in China, Chinese agricultural producers need to have efficient production if they want to be competitive in the world market. Abdulai and Huffman (2000) compared the results of several agricultural efficiency studies and found that the average profit inefficiency score obtained by Wang, Wailes, and Cramer (1995) for China was higher than those for other countries. With China's accession to the WTO, we wonder how inputs are converted into outputs in China, how efficient Chinese agricultural producers are in their production, what factors contribute to their efficiency, and what kind of pattern their efficiency distribution exhibits. Answers to these questions will help researchers and policymakers to improve agricultural systems/policies and to find out whether or not institutional innovations are necessary.

In China, land is scarce and labor is abundant. Intuitively, the value of the marginal product of land is high relative to that of the marginal product of labor (Sen, 1960). Wan and Cheng (2001) obtained negative labor elasticities at sample means and their estimate of output elasticities of land were close to unity. Xu (1999) suggested that the role of industrial inputs in Chinese agricultural production might have been underestimated, and most of gains in total factor productivity were really

* Authors want to express their gratitude to Harwood Schaffer, Drs Daniel Monchuk, Holly Wang, Seong-Hoon Cho, and an anonymous referee for their comments. Thanks also go to participants at the *International Symposium on China's Rural Economy after WTO (Hangzhou)* and workshop attendants at Department of Agricultural Economics, The University of Tennessee, Knoxville. The usual disclaimer applies. Zhuo Chen thanks the Chinese Economist Society for providing Hangzhou conference travel grant.

attributable to the evolving mix of agricultural inputs. Widawsky et al. (1998) found that under the intensive rice production systems in eastern China, pesticide productivity was low compared to the productivity of host-plant resistance. Returns-to-scale is also of great interest to researchers and policy makers. Lin (1988) expressed his concern that gains from scale economies might be outweighed by additional monitoring costs in large-scale agricultural production. However, while the agricultural technologies in the 1950s were not suitable for large-scale production, the small farm and fragmented plots nowadays have been a hurdle for application of modern technologies. Yang (1996) found that increasing average plot size had a significant positive effect on productivity. Wan and Cheng (2001) concluded that no significant scale economies existed but argued that eliminating land fragmentation might lead to gains through fewer plot boundaries and access routes.

Estimating production efficiency and exploring its determinants provides intuitions on how well Chinese agricultural producers are doing their job and what factors are associated with their efficiency. Tian and Wan (2000) estimated national average efficiency scores ranging from 0.85 to 0.95 for several grain crops and cautioned that quite limited output growth could be attained through input injection and efficiency gains. Chen, Huffman and Rozelle (2003) applied a stochastic frontier model with farm fixed-effects using a panel of rural households in China and found that mechanization, specialization, and the highest education achieved by household members improve technical efficiency while land fragmentation reduces it. Wang, Cramer, and Wailes (1996) claimed that being a large farm is associated with positive and statistically significant profit efficiency gains.

Yet another feature of China's agricultural productions deserves careful investigation. With an area of roughly 9.6 million square kilometers, China displays significant geographical and economic variations across the country. Yang (1996) found that the levels of factor productivities for several crops are generally higher in the major producing areas than those in the fringe areas, partly due to more suitable natural conditions and higher levels of specialization. Yao, Liu and Zhang (2001) studied spatial disparity of grain production efficiencies in China using a panel dataset of 30 provinces (municipalities) for the period 1987–92 and found remarkable provincial and zonal differentials. In general, literatures agreed on the existence of regional disparity. While we acknowledge regional disparity and production inefficiency are serious concerns for Chinese agricultural producers, whether a region can share benefits of technology advances of its neighboring counties is also of great importance. As far as we know, none of previous studies has utilized geographic information and applied spatial econometric tools to study the spatial dependence in agricultural production in China. In addition, while most previous studies focused on province-level economic disparity, Herrmann-Pillath, Kirchert, and Pan (2002) argued that provincial aggregation might not represent the exact regional disparity of development for China and proposed a lower-level of aggregation, i.e. prefecture-level data, should be used. Using a county-level dataset, this study applies a two-step methodology to study the spatial dependence in the agricultural production efficiency in China. Provinces and counties are ranked by their technical efficiency. To go further beyond this, we associate efficiency scores with location information and examine the underlying spatial correlation. To our knowledge, no other study has applied a stochastic production frontier model to county-level data and/or examined the spatial dependence in the agricultural production efficiency of China.

The organization of this chapter is as follows. In section 2 we describe the data set. Section 3 estimates the stochastic frontier model. Section 4 undergoes the spatial analysis of the estimated efficiency scores. Conclusions are summarized in section 5.

## 2 Data

The dataset for our study is constructed based on a county-level socio-economic index survey conducted by State Statistical Bureau of China (SSB 2000) and a geographic information system of China (Liu et al, 1996). The SSB data set contains agricultural production and other socio-economic variables in 1999. There are 2159 counties (or its equivalent) in the data set but 157 observations are dropped due to missing values. These missing values are likely to be the counties that were not heavily engaged in agricultural production. Since they account for a small portion of the sample, data truncation problem is not a serious concern.

Descriptive statistics of the county-level agricultural production variables are reported in Table 9.1. A typical county has 71.66 thousand hectares of sown area. Average per hectare input uses are 2.36 agricultural laborers per year, 4.59 thousand watt equivalent of machinery, and 0.25 metric tons chemical fertilizer. Average per hectare output is 11.95 thousand Renminbi (RMB) *yuan* equivalent of agricultural products.[1] Input usages varied across China due to large geographic area spanned and different levels of economic development. Labor input has a relatively small dispersion while fertilizer usage and mechanic power use display wide variation. Geomembrane usage also varied significantly. It represents different levels of investments on cash crops, especially vegetables and fruits. An average county consumes about 329 metric tons of geomembrane.

Tables 9.2 to 9.4 list the first ten counties ranked by gross domestic product (GDP) per capita, agricultural output per hectare (monetary value), and sown area of all crops, respectively. Note that Yuxi city of Yunnan province is famous for its tobacco industry thus had an unusually high GDP per capita. The other nine counties are in the eastern and southern seaboard areas. The ten counties yielding the highest agricultural output per hectare are located in Zhejiang, Inner Mongolia, Liaoning and Fujian. Concentration of high value-added agriculture may underlie their high land productivities. Most of the ten counties with the largest sown area are in frontier provinces, e.g. Inner Mongolia, Qinghai. Counties from Hainan and

[1] As of May 2005, 1 RMB *yuan* = $0.12 approximately.

Sichuan province are on the list possibly attributable to their higher levels of multiple cropping indexes.

**Table 9.1 Descriptive statistics of county-level agricultural production data (2002 obs)**

| Variable | Unit | Mean | Std. dev. | Min | Max |
|---|---|---|---|---|---|
| Sown Area | 1000 Hectare | 71.66 | 50.87 | 0.19 | 320.02 |
| Population Density | 1000 Person/km$^2$ | 3.10 | 2.85 | 0.00 | 34.30 |
| Geomembrane use per hectare | Ton | 0.01 | 0.01 | 0.00 | 0.17 |
| Per Hectare Output and Input use | | | | | |
| Agricultural Output | 1000 *Yuan* | 11.95 | 54.91 | 0.02 | 2375.76 |
| Labor input | Person | 2.36 | 2.18 | 0.01 | 82.93 |
| Mechanic power | 1000 Watt | 4.59 | 38.03 | 0.03 | 1254.48 |
| Chemical Fertilizer | Ton | 0.25 | 0.16 | 0.00 | 2.46 |

Geographical conditions are crucial to agricultural production. We matched the location information (longitude and latitude) of Liu et al. (1996) with the SSB dataset to examine the spatial feature in the socioeconomic indexes of Chinese counties. This enables us to graphically illustrate spatial disparity in economic development of China. Figure 9.1 graphs GDP per capita of all counties. We observe an obvious spatial pattern of economic development. Three major economic zones exist, i.e. Bohai Bay area, Yangzi Delta area, and Zhujiang Delta area. Most counties' GDP per capitas are less than ten thousand RMB *yuan*.

**Table 9.2 Ten counties with highest GDP per capita**

| Province | County | GDP Per capita (Yuan) |
|---|---|---|
| Yunan | Yuxi | 59091.2 |
| Jiangsu | Taicang | 30234.7 |
| Fujian | Shishi | 29723.8 |
| Guangdong | Panyu | 29651.2 |
| Jiangsu | Kunshan | 29157.2 |
| Jiangsu | Wuxi | 28819.2 |
| Jiangsu | Zhangjiagang | 28700.4 |
| Guangdong | Nanhai | 28198.7 |
| Fujian | Jinjiang | 27261.5 |
| Guangdong | Shunde | 26806.1 |

**Table 9.3 Ten counties with highest output per hectare (Unit: 1000 *Yuan*/Hectare)**

| Province | County | Ag. GDP per hectare |
|---|---|---|
| Zhejiang | Shengsi | 2375.76 |
| Inner Mongolia | Sunite-Zuo | 481.48 |
| Liaoning | Changhai | 253.72 |
| Zhejiang | Daishan | 177.11 |
| Zhejiang | Dongtou | 163.28 |
| Inner Mongolia | Xiwuzhumuqin | 101.71 |
| Inner Mongolia | Xinba`erhu-You | 99.93 |
| Fujian | Pingtan | 98.59 |
| Zhejiang | Yuhuan | 92.43 |
| Fujian | Lianjiang | 59.07 |

**Table 9.4 Ten counties with largest sown area**

| Province | County | Sown area (Hectare) |
|---|---|---|
| Hainan | Baoting | 13321 |
| Inner Mongolia | Etuoke-Qian | 13290 |
| Hebei | Kuancheng | 13252 |
| Sichuan | Mao | 13233 |
| Guangxi | Dongxing | 13001 |
| Yunnan | Chenggong | 12932 |
| Guangxi | Heshan | 12841 |
| Shanxi | Daning | 12610 |
| Hunan | Lengshuijiang | 12500 |
| Qinghai | Tongde | 12422 |

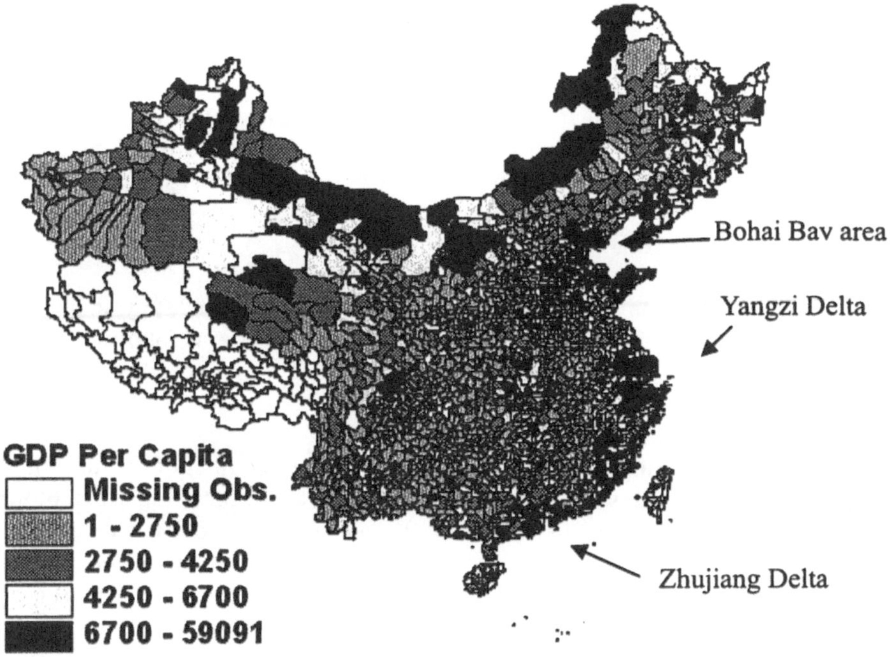


**Figure 9.1 GDP per capita across China (Unit: RMB *Yuan*)**

### 3 Technical Efficiency and Stochastic Frontier Model

Technical efficiency is defined as how well a producer does in minimizing input use for a given output level, or maximizing output with fixed input use. Technical efficiency scores can be estimated for a given production technology, and it can be explained by a set of explanatory variables, either by a two-stage procedure or integrated one-step estimation. This study uses the output-oriented measure since output maximization is more likely in China's agriculture.

The stochastic frontier function dates back to Meeusen and van den Broeck (1977), Aigner, Lovell, and Schmidt (1977), and Battese and Corra (1977). Their model can be summarized as: $Y = f(X;\beta)\cdot\exp\{V - U\}$ where $Y$ is a scalar of output, $X$ is a vector of inputs and $\beta$ is a vector of technology parameters. Jondow et al. (1982) extended the model by incorporating producer-specific efficiency effects.

Kumbhakar and Lovell (2000, p. 263) summarized several methodologies of incorporating inefficiency effects in stochastic frontier functions. Earlier researchers inserted exogenous variables into production frontier directly. This, however, cannot distinguish the impact of these variables on stochastic frontier from their impact on technical inefficiency. The "two-stage" approach has been used widely. A stochastic frontier function is fitted first and empirical measures of efficiency are generated. In the second step, efficiency scores are regressed on a set of firm-specific regressors. Kumbhakar and Lovell (2000) and Coelli (1996), among others, indicated that the two-stage approach has an inconsistency in that, in the first step, technical inefficiency scores are assumed not to correlate with the exogenous variables that are used to explain the efficiency in the second step. Coelli (1996) claimed that two-stage estimation is less efficient than single-step estimations, such as Battese and Coelli (1995), which is used in this study.

### *3.1 The Empirical Model*

Battese and Coelli (1995) extended Battese and Coelli (1993) by adding exogenous variable to explain technical inefficiency. Their model is as follows:

$$Y_i = X_i\beta + (V_i - U_i),\ i=1,..,N,$$

where: $Y_i$ is the natural logarithm of the agricultural output of the $i$th county; $X_i$ is a $k\times 1$ vector of regressors (depending on the functional form, logarithm of inputs and their interaction terms) of $i$th county; $\beta$ is a conforming coefficient vector.

$V_i$ is the random disturbance term that is assumed to be *iid* $N(0,\sigma_v^2)$. It is incorporated in the model to reflect random disturbance independent of $U_i$, which is a non-negative random disturbance term assumed to account for technical inefficiency in production. $U_i$s are assumed to be independently distributed and truncated at zero $N(m_i,\sigma_u^2)$ or as the more widely used notation $N^+(m_i,\sigma_u^2)$, where: $m_i = z_i\delta$. The relationship between $U_i$ and the output-oriented technical efficiency $TE_o$ is $TE^i_o = \exp(-U_i)$. $z_i$ is a $p\times 1$ vector of variables which may influence farm-level efficiency; and $\delta$ is an $1\times p$ parameter vector to be estimated. We define $\sigma^2=\sigma_v^2+\sigma_u^2$ and $\gamma=\sigma_u^2/(\sigma_v^2+\sigma_u^2)$.

Guilkey, Lovell, and Sickles (1983) compared three different functional forms for production frontier and concluded that translog specification provides better estimates of true technology parameters. Translog specification is also more flexible in permitting substitution effects among inputs than the other two functional forms. Therefore translog specification is used in this study. Our empirical model is formulated as:

$$\ln(Y_i) = \beta_0 + \sum_{j=1}^{4}\beta_j \ln(x_{ij}) + \sum_{j\le k}^{4}\sum_{k=1}^{4}\beta_{jk}\ln(x_{ij})\ln(x_{ik}) + \sum_{k=1}^{29}\beta_{d_k}D_k + V_i - U_i,$$

where subscript $i$ is county index and $j$, $k$ are inputs-use indexes. For county $i$, $x_{i1}$ is its labor use in agricultural production; $x_{i2}$ is total sown area for all crops; $x_{i3}$ is power equivalent of machinery used, and $x_{i4}$ is chemical fertilizer usage.[2] Their units are listed in Table 9.1. $D_k$s are the provincial dummy variables capturing the effects of different provincial policies and partial effects of the location variation. However, dummy variable approach usually assumes there is no correlation between the fixed-effects. Hence we are not able to investigate spatial dependence based on dummy variable estimates.

To explain inefficiency term $U_i$, we specify $m_i = \delta_0 + \sum_{k=1}^{3} \delta_k z_{ik}$, where $z_1$ is the geomembrane usage, $z_2$ is the population density, and $z_3$ is the square term of population density.[3] We use geomembrane usage as the proxy of cash crop activity. In addition, population density is assumed to be related to land quality and regional economic development. Historically, China's population density is higher where land is more fertile. We hypothesize a nonlinear effect of population density since population might be attracted to relatively fertile regions and share information and technology but overcrowding is detrimental to the agricultural efficiency. Extant literatures suggest that land tenure and farmer's experience and education are relevant to production efficiency (Huffman, 1977; Sadoulet and de Janvry, 1995). However, scant information on education stock and tenure is available at the county-level. We experimented using the number of students and the number of teachers (both normalized by total population) as proxy of education but no statistically significant relationship was found. Biases of coefficient estimates may arise if education and tenure variables are omitted. Exploratory studies suggest they are not correlated to education achievement when population normalized number of students is used as a proxy of education. Therefore, the omitted variable bias could be minimal. We admit that this remains to be an open question without further information on educational attainment. However, since our primary goal is to estimate county-level technical efficiency and to explore the underlying spatial dependence, omitted variable bias, as well as effects of nonfarm income (which is likely to be endogenous), could be put on our future research agenda until release of more information from SSB.

The particular frontier software used is FRONTIER 4.1 developed by Coelli (1996). A three-step estimation method in used to obtain the final maximum likelihood estimate.

---

[2] The quantity of chemical fertilizers is calculated by converting the gross weight into weight containing 100 per cent effective component (i.e. 100 per cent nitrogen content in nitrogenous fertilizer, 100 per cent phosphorous pentoxide contents in phosphate fertilizer, and 100 per cent potassium oxide contents in potash fertilizer).

[3] A discussant suggested using geomembrane as an input. This might have coincided with the debate on determining whether an explanatory variable should be included in the inefficiency term or in the production frontier. However, we have encountered convergence problems when pursuing the suggested approach. We also realize that geomembrane is only used on certain variety of cash crops thus indicates the structure of a county's agricultural sector. Therefore it is appropriate to treat geomembrane as a factor influencing efficiency rather than frontier.

### *3.2 Estimation Results*

For our estimated translog stochastic frontier function, likelihood ratio tests confirmed that labor, sown area, machinery power, and fertilizer individually make statistically significant contributions to the agricultural output (see Table 9.5).[4]

**Table 9.5 Likelihood ratio test for functional form and input effects**

| $H_0$ | Hypothesis | ln(lik) | $\lambda$ | d.f. | Inference[5] |
|---|---|---|---|---|---|
| H0: $\beta_{ij}$=0 | Frontier is of Cobb–Douglas Form | −795.17 | 211.00 | 10 | Reject |
| H0: $\beta_1$= $\beta_{1j}$=0 | Var. Labor does not affect production frontier | −736.35 | 93.40 | 5 | Reject |
| H0: $\beta_2$= $\beta_{2j}$=0 | Var. Sown area does not affect production frontier | −711.39 | 43.48 | 5 | Reject |
| H0: $\beta_3$= $\beta_{3j}$=0 | Var. Machinery power does not affect production frontier | −808.59 | 237.80 | 5 | Reject |
| H0: $\beta_4$= $\beta_{4j}$=0 | Var. Fertilizer does not affect production frontier | −779.73 | 180.10 | 5 | Reject |
| H1: Negation | Translog functional form | −689.65 | | | |

Coefficient estimates for the stochastic frontier are presented in Table 9.6. Output-input elasticities are evaluated for each county and we provide the summary statistics in Table 9.7. The mean elasticities are 0.237, 0.162, 0.246, and 0.239 respectively for labor, sown area, machinery power, and fertilizer. This yields a different pattern from the results obtained based on farm-level data set, e.g. Chen, Huffman, and Rozelle (2003) and Fleshier and Liu (1992), which show greater value for land elasticity and smaller labor elasticity (sometimes even negative, see, e.g. Wan and Cheng, 2000). The difference is mostly likely attributable to the nature of data. First, for household dataset, the lands are allocated by the village council and have a relative small spread. Meanwhile, since county-level measure of land aggregates all sown areas within each county's boundary, aggregated land displays a larger variation than household-level land quantity. In addition, many household-level production studies revealed that the surplus labor in rural China drove the marginal product of labor to nearly zero. The aggregate statistics may capture the contribution of labor on aggregate output. Lin (1992), using provincial data during the transition period of 1978–84, reported estimates of output elasticities of 0.67, 0.13, 0.19, and 0.07, respectively for land, labor, fertilizer, and

[4] Hypothesis that translog production function could be reduced to the simpler Cobb–Douglas form is rejected using a likelihood ratio test (see Table 9.5).

[5] The critical values correspond to 5 percent level of significance.

capital. His labor and fertilizer elasticity estimates are relatively close to ours. Second, we use the number of laborers rather than man-day as the unit of labor input. Both of the two indexes may associate with measurement errors. The effects of measurement errors on frontier estimation and output–input elasticities merit further studies. Third, the agricultural output is measured in monetary units and includes all agricultural activities. Land is relatively less important if we use the monetary value of outputs because labor-intense crops, e.g. vegetable and fruits, contribute to the outputs. The average scale elasticity is 0.884, and its standard deviation is 0.084. Therefore we cannot reject the null hypothesis that the agricultural production technology is constant returns to scale.

Our estimates of $\sigma^2$ and $\gamma$ are 0.684 and 0.905 respectively, and the estimate of $\sigma_v^2$ is 0.065. The estimate of $\sigma_v^2$ is much less than the estimate of $\sigma_u^2$ (0.619). *This implies that the asymmetric inefficiency component dominates the symmetric measurement error and other random disturbances.*

### *3.3 Technical Inefficiency*

The parameter estimates for determinants of technical efficiency are reported in Table 9.6. Technical efficiency is estimated as $T\hat{E}_o^i = \exp\left(-\hat{U}_i\right)$. The mean technical efficiency is 0.80. Roughly sixty percent of the counties have an efficiency score of over 0.80.

The lower part of Table 9.6 summarizes coefficients of inefficiency term. It shows that geomembrane usage has significantly improved technical efficiency. Geomembrane are mostly used on crops with high added-values, e.g. vegetables and fruits. Usage of geomembrane indicates better structure and orientation of agriculture within a county. Counties around wealthy municipalities may have good chances to produce and sell vegetables and other agricultural products. Intuitively, geomembrane usage accompanies positive efficiency gains.

The population density has a U-shaped effect on the efficiency. The turning point is about 20 thousand people per square kilometer. Higher population density usually associates with more fertile soil, better infrastructure, and more intense information exchange with other areas. Meanwhile, extremely high population density may induce severe land fragmentation thus drive technical efficiency in opposite direction. When the loss associated with increased land fragmentation outweighs the gains from land quality, infrastructure and information exchange, and population density have a negative effect on technical efficiency.

**Table 9.6 Maximum-likelihood estimates: county-level stochastic production frontier**

| Variables | Parameter | Estimates | *t*-value |
|---|---|---|---|
| *Frontier Estimates* | | | |
| Constant | $\beta_0$ | 10.683 | 11.23 |
| ln(labor) | $\beta_1$ | 0.299 | 1.49 |
| ln(Sown area) | $\beta_2$ | −0.044 | −0.15 |
| ln(Machinery) | $\beta_3$ | 0.651 | 3.66 |
| ln(fertilizer) | $\beta_4$ | −0.659 | −3.42 |
| $(\ln(\text{labor}))^2$ | $\beta_{11}$ | 0.035 | 2.63 |
| $(\ln(\text{Sown area}))^2$ | $\beta_{22}$ | −0.012 | −0.46 |
| $(\ln(\text{Machinery}))^2$ | $\beta_{33}$ | 0.028 | 2.94 |
| $(\ln(\text{fertilizer}))^2$ | $\beta_{44}$ | 0.012 | 1.11 |
| ln(labor)* ln(Sown area) | $\beta_{12}$ | 0.002 | 0.07 |
| ln(labor)* ln(Machinery) | $\beta_{13}$ | −0.046 | −1.94 |
| ln(labor)* ln(fertilizer) | $\beta_{14}$ | −0.014 | −0.53 |
| ln(Sown area)* ln(Machinery) | $\beta_{23}$ | −0.048 | −1.78 |
| ln(Sown area)* ln(fertilizer) | $\beta_{24}$ | 0.062 | 2.09 |
| ln(Machinery)* ln(fertilizer) | $\beta_{34}$ | 0.009 | 0.45 |
| *Inefficiency Terms* | | | |
| Constant | $\delta_0$ | −0.702 | −2.98 |
| Geomembrane usage | $\delta_1$ | −0.289 | −7.21 |
| Population Density | $\delta_2$ | −5.663 | −10.44 |
| Population Density square | $\delta_3$ | 1.390 | 5.88 |
| *Variance Estimates* | | | |
| | $\sigma^2$ | 0.684 | 8.90 |
| | $\Gamma$ | 0.905 | 71.23 |
| ln*(likelihood)* | | –689.65 | |

**Table 9.7 Elasticity estimates: county-level stochastic production frontier**

| Variable | Mean | Std. Dev. | Min | Max |
|---|---|---|---|---|
| Labor | 0.237 | 0.051 | −0.081 | 0.444 |
| Sown area | 0.162 | 0.043 | −0.168 | 0.355 |
| Machinery | 0.246 | 0.055 | 0.013 | 0.662 |
| Fertilizer | 0.239 | 0.077 | −0.255 | 0.397 |
| Scale | 0.884 | 0.084 | 0.298 | 1.068 |

## 4 Spatial Analysis of County-Level Technical Efficiency Scores

Table 9.8 lists the first 30 counties with highest efficiency scores and Table 9.9 provides the ranking of the 30 provinces by mean efficiency scores.[6] The national average efficiency score is comparable to that of Chen, Huffman, and Rozelle (2003) but much lower than that of Tian and Wan (2002). The tables also show severe regional disparity in the agricultural production efficiency in China. Well-developed provinces/municipalities, e.g. Shanghai, Jiangsu, Tianjin, Zhejiang, and Beijing, are on top of the list. It likely resulted from their relatively high per capita income boosting the demand and production of vegetable and fruits within province or city vicinity. Major agricultural producing provinces, such as Shandong, Anhui, Hebei, Hubei, and Hunan, have relatively high average efficiency scores. This agrees with Yao, Liu, and Zhang (2001), who observed strong spatial disparity of grain production efficiency in China from 1987 to 1992 using a provincial aggregated data. A brief examination on the distribution of technical efficiency across China confirms spatial disparity in technical efficiency, i.e. see Figure 9.2. We present the contour plot of technical efficiency in Figure 9.3, which shows a couple of peaks and valleys, indicating obvious spatial pattern.[7]

However, it is important to make a step further to examine spatial correlation of technical efficiency scores rather to stop with spatial disparity. Using a spatial econometrics model, Monchuk and Miranowski (2003) found that, in the American midwest, the employment rate of a county is correlated with economic growth rates of neighboring counties. With the determinants of the technical efficiency displaying spatial dependency, technical efficiency scores are likely to exhibit certain degree of spatial correlation (see, e.g. Druska and Horrace, 2004).

---

[6] We readily admit that this should not be treated as an absolute ranking of the provinces or counties but these results reveal the existence of the spatial disparity in agricultural production.

[7] The contour plot is generated with R (R development team, 2003).

**Table 9.8 Thirty counties with highest technical efficiency scores**

| Province | County Name | Efficiency Score |
|---|---|---|
| Liaoning | Changhai | 0.968 |
| Zhejiang | Yuhuan | 0.957 |
| Hebei | Fengnan | 0.954 |
| Shanxi | Qingxu | 0.954 |
| Inner Mongolia | Xiwuzhumuqin | 0.953 |
| Shandong | Rongcheng | 0.951 |
| Shanxi | Zhangzi | 0.949 |
| Jiangsu | Qidong | 0.945 |
| Hebei | Tanghai | 0.945 |
| Gansu | Linxia | 0.945 |
| Fujian | Pingtan | 0.944 |
| Shanxi | Linyi | 0.942 |
| Shandong | Jiaonan | 0.942 |
| Yunnan | Mengla | 0.941 |
| Zhejiang | Wenling | 0.941 |
| Hebei | Luannan | 0.940 |
| Heilongjiang | Mohe | 0.940 |
| Hebei | Yutian | 0.940 |
| Hebei | Luancheng | 0.940 |
| Henan | Xin | 0.940 |
| Zhejiang | Daishan | 0.939 |
| Hebei | Leting | 0.939 |
| Fujian | Changle | 0.939 |
| Fujian | Huian | 0.938 |
| Guangdong | Shunde | 0.938 |
| Shandong | Longkou | 0.938 |
| Fujian | Lianjiang | 0.937 |
| Shannxi | Chenggu | 0.937 |
| Shandong | Penglai | 0.937 |
| Chongqing | Jiangjin | 0.936 |

**Table 9.9 Provincial ranking by mean technical efficiency**

| Province | Mean | Std. Dev. | Observations |
|---|---|---|---|
| Shanghai | 0.90 | 0.03 | 4 |
| Jiangsu | 0.88 | 0.04 | 64 |
| Shandong | 0.87 | 0.05 | 94 |
| Tianjin | 0.86 | 0.03 | 5 |
| Henan | 0.86 | 0.07 | 116 |
| Anhui | 0.85 | 0.05 | 69 |
| Zhejiang | 0.84 | 0.08 | 64 |
| Beijing | 0.84 | 0.05 | 8 |
| Hebei | 0.84 | 0.09 | 139 |
| Hubei | 0.83 | 0.09 | 70 |
| Hunan | 0.83 | 0.08 | 90 |
| Guangdong | 0.82 | 0.09 | 77 |
| Jiangxi | 0.82 | 0.09 | 83 |
| Hainan | 0.81 | 0.08 | 11 |
| Chongqing | 0.81 | 0.11 | 27 |
| Fujian | 0.81 | 0.08 | 60 |
| Guizhou | 0.80 | 0.09 | 79 |
| Sichuan | 0.79 | 0.15 | 135 |
| Guangxi | 0.79 | 0.09 | 81 |
| Yunnan | 0.77 | 0.11 | 121 |
| Ningxia | 0.77 | 0.11 | 18 |
| Gansu | 0.77 | 0.12 | 73 |
| Qinghai | 0.76 | 0.10 | 16 |
| Shannxi | 0.76 | 0.18 | 91 |
| Jilin | 0.75 | 0.16 | 40 |
| Xinjiang | 0.75 | 0.12 | 82 |
| Liaoning | 0.75 | 0.16 | 44 |
| Inner | 0.74 | 0.14 | 76 |
| Heilongjiang | 0.74 | 0.13 | 66 |
| Shanxi | 0.71 | 0.23 | 99 |
| National average | 0.80 | 0.12 | 2002 |

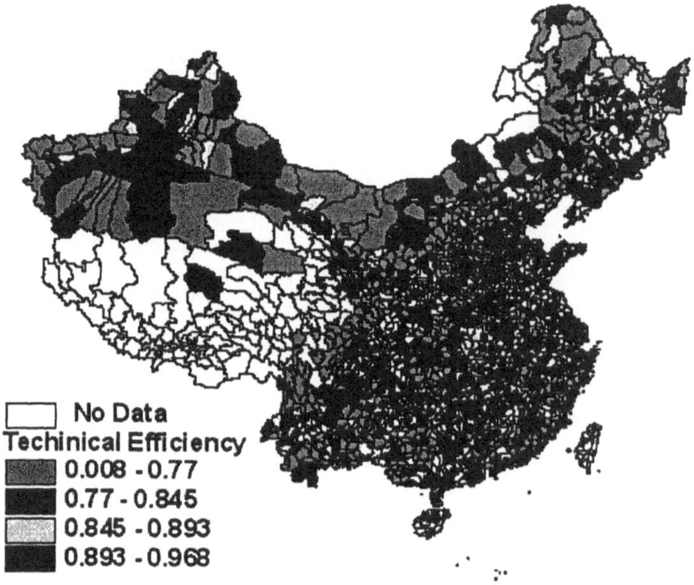


**Figure 9.2 County-level technical efficiency**

Several factors are related to the spatial correlation in technical efficiency. First, technology spillover and labor exchange among neighboring counties contribute to the technology change of a host county, see Jin et al. (2002) for a review on the creation and diffusion of agricultural technology as well as their interaction with total factor productivity. Second, infrastructure, information and human capital are likely to be spatially correlated. These factors affect agricultural production as well. Third, changes of land quality and/or population densities are relatively smooth across neighboring counties. Therefore county-level technical efficiency scores are likely to exhibit not only spatial disparity but also spatial dependence. With estimated county-level technical efficiency scores, we are able to investigate such spatial correlation.

The econometric approach we adopt in this study is similar to the usual two-stage method. Due to the extensive computation involved with spatial estimation, we refrain from estimating a technical efficiency model with spatial structure built-in within itself. Maximum likelihood estimation of a first-order spatial AR model takes unbearable amount of time for more than two thousand observations. Although it may subject to the same criticism of the usual two-stage procedure of explaining technical efficiency, given statistical properties of conditional likelihood maximization, estimates obtained using the two-step methodology provide a reliable intuition of the spatial correlation.

Denoting the vector of technical efficiency as $e$ (a $2002 \times 1$ vector), we apply a first-order spatial autoregressive (AR) model as following:

$$e = \rho We + \varepsilon$$
$$\varepsilon \sim N\left(0, \delta^2 I_n\right)$$

where $W$ is a symmetric first-order spatial contiguity weight matrix obtained by applying Delaunay triangulation routine. The routine picks out the three nearest counties based on the latitude and longitude coordinates of the county geographical center point. Delaunay triangulation computes a set of triangles such that no data points are contained in any triangle's circumcircle. Then neighboring counties are assigned a value of one in the appropriate row, see Pace and Barry (1999) for more details of the routine.

Computation details are described in LeSage (1999). The Matlab procedure obtains conditional maximum likelihood estimates using sparse matrix algorithm. Results in Table 9.10 show that there is strong spatial dependence among county-level technical efficiency scores. The spatial interaction ρ is estimated as 0.727 with a $t$-statistic of 39.84. The pseudo $R^2$ is 0.43, which suggests that a large percent of the efficiency variation can be explained by the spatial dependence model. Figure 9.4 plots the efficiency scores estimated by the stochastic frontier model and the fitted values predicted by the first-order spatial $AR$ model. Both residual plot and $R^2$ indicate the model has a good fit.

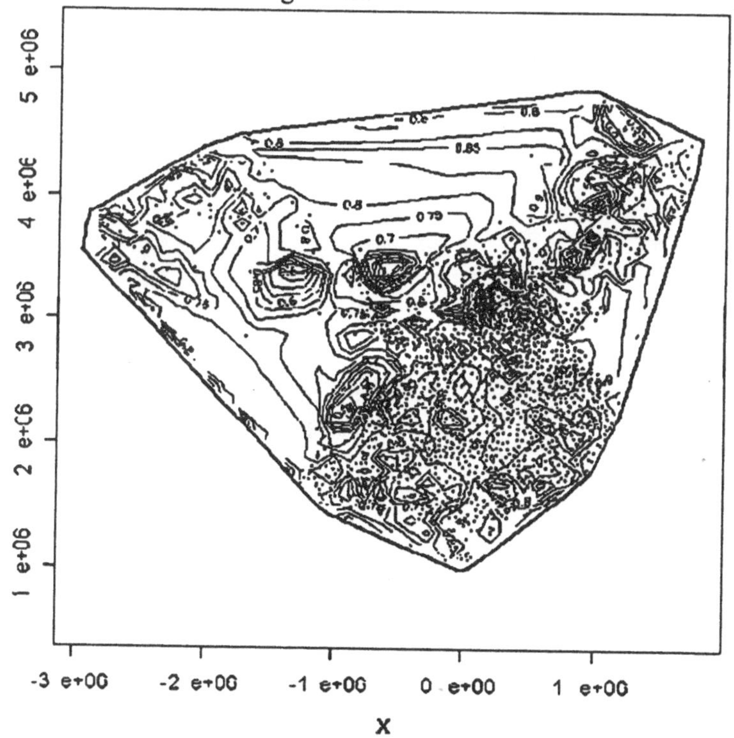


**Figure 9.3 Contour plots of county-level technical efficiency**

**Table 9.10 MLE estimates of first-order auto-regressive spatial model**

| Variable | Coefficient | Asymptotic *t*-stat | P-value |
|---|---|---|---|
| ρ | 0.727 | 39.84 | 0.00 |
| $\sigma^2$ | 0.009 | | |
| Diagnostic Statistics | | | |
| $R^2$ | 0.43 | | |
| log-likelihood | 1768.95 | | |

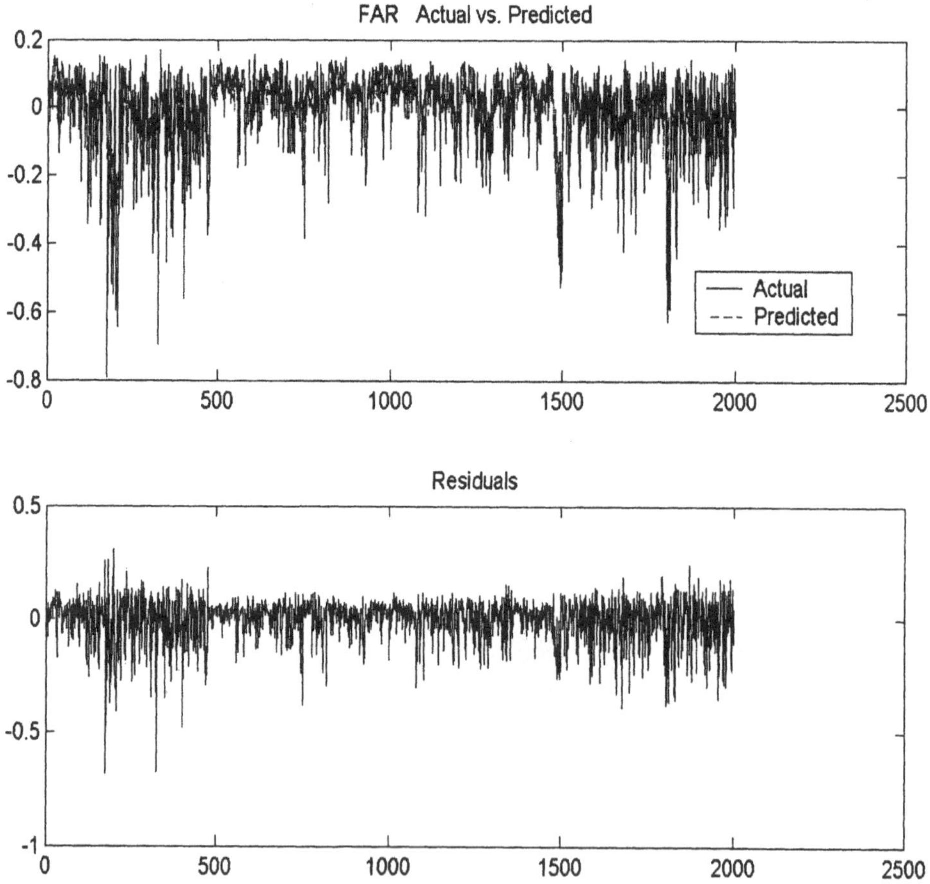


**Figure 9.4 Residual of first-order spatial AR model estimation**

Estimation results suggest that spillover effects of agricultural technology innovation of neighboring counties exist. Unlike that of manufacture industry, technology diffusion in agriculture sector is usually easier to take place for neighboring regions than for regions far away. When a county reviews and formulates its agricultural development strategy, polices of neighboring counties are good references. Agricultural extension stations can be benefited from information exchange with neighboring counties since it is easier to adopt new technologies and institutional innovations emerged in neighboring counties with relatively low cost. The hybrid rice and the household responsibility system are two examples that had been adopted in neighboring regions soon after they emerged and quickly spread all over the country. However, few studies addressed the agricultural extension system in China. Huang et al. (2000) concluded that lack of appropriate funding has greatly impacted the functioning of the agricultural extension system. To effectively promote new and efficient technologies among rural households, the Chinese agricultural extension system needs favorable policies and sufficient financial supports.

Results also suggest that regional protectionism may not benefit local welfares. The strong spatial dependence indicates that one county could collect spillovers of neighboring counties. However, Word Bank (2003) suggested that local protectionism had continued to be present in both coastal and inland provinces. Lee (1998) documented that earlier local protectionism was in the form of "trade wars" occurred frequently along borders between various administrative regions—usually provinces, sometimes counties. In the later 1980s, troops were deployed along the border between Hunan and Guangdong to prevent the outflow of rice from Hunan (Chao 1991, cited from Lee, 1998). Recent reports indicated that provinces and municipalities such as Beijing, Shanxi, Anhui, and Yunnan are among the most protected regions, and agriculture, especially tobacco, is among the most protected industries (cbiz.cn, 2004). Local protectionism not only violates consumer freedom of choice while creating opportunity for monopolization and corruption, it also sparks similar retaliatory actions hindering mutually beneficial economic interaction among various localities.

## 5 Conclusions

The objective of this study is to estimate technical efficiency in Chinese county-level agricultural production and investigate the spatial dependence in the estimated efficiency scores. Using data for 1999, we have estimated technical efficiency scores of 2002 Chinese counties and visualized the efficiency scores distribution. We find cash crop production improves technical efficiency while population density has a nonlinear effect on efficiency. Regions (provinces and counties) are ranked by their (mean) efficiency scores. Using a first-order spatial autocorrelation model, we obtain a strong and statistically significant coefficient estimate of spatial dependence in the estimated efficiency scores.

With China's economy becoming more and more integrated internationally and domestically, spatial dependence in agricultural production is expected only to grow stronger over time. Therefore more attentions should be directed to spatial studies of China's agriculture. County-level statistics with ample demographic and socio-economic information will enable us to take advantage of recent developments of spatial econometrics to explore broad scope of China's agricultural production. Household surveys with location information will help us to examine the pattern of spillover of agricultural technology based on non-aggregated data set, which is certainly another important direction for future research.

## References

Abdulai, A. and Huffman, W.E., 'Structural adjustment and economic efficiency of rice farmers in northern Ghana', *Economic Development and Cultural Change,* 48(3) (2000): 503–520.

Aigner, D., Lovell, C. and Schmidt, P., 'Formulation and estimation of stochastic frontier production function models', *Journal of Econometrics*, 6(1) (1997): 21–37.

Battese, G. and Coelli, T., 'Frontier production functions, technical efficiency and panel data: with application to paddy farmers in India', *Journal of Productivity Analysis*, 3(1/2) (1993): 153–169.

———, 'A model for technical inefficiency effects in a stochastic frontier production function for panel data', *Empirical Economics*, 20(2) (1995): 325–332.

Battese, G. and Corra, G.S., 'Estimation of a production frontier model: with application to the pastoral zone of eastern Australia', *Australian Journal of Agricultural and Resource Economics*, 21(3) (1977): 169–179.

Cbiz.cn, China tries to tackle local protectionism. Accessed May 16, 2005. http://www.cbiz.cn/news/showarticle.asp?id=2188, 2004.

Chao, C.M., 'T'iao–t'iao vs. K'uai–k'uai: a perennial dispute between the central and local governments in Mainland China', *Issues and Studies*, 27(8) (1991): 31–46.

Chen, Z., Huffman, W.E. and Rozelle, S., 'Technical efficiency of modern grain production on Chinese farms: a stochastic production frontier approach' (Paper Prepared for presentation at the American Agricultural Economics Annual Meeting, Montreal, 2003).

Coelli, T., 'A guide to FRONTIER version 4.1: a computer program for stochastic frontier production and cost function estimation' (Working Paper 96/07 Center for Efficiency & Productivity Analysis, Univ. of New England, Australia, 1996).

Druska, V. and Horrace, W., 'Generalized moments estimation for spatial panel data: Indonesian rice farming', *American Journal of Agricultural Economics*, 86(1) (2004): 185–198.

Fleisher, B.M. and Liu, Y.H., 'Economies of scale, plot size, human–capital, and productivity in Chinese agriculture', *Quarterly Review of Economics and Finance*, 32(3) (1992): 112–123.

Guilkey, D.K., Lovell, C. and Sickles, R.C., 'A comparison of the performance of three flexible functional forms', *International Economic Review*, 24(3) (1983): 591–616.

Herrmann–Pillath, C., Kirchert, D. and Pan, J., 'Prefecture–level statistics as a source of data for research into China's regional development', *The China Quarterly*, 172 (2003): 956–985.

Huang, J., Hu, R. and Sun, Z., 'Bring science and technology into rural households—establishing a new agricultural technology extension and innovation system', Agricultural Economic Issues (Rang kexue jishu jinru nongcun de qianjiawanhu—jianli xin de nongye jishu tuiguang chuangxin tixi, Nongye Jingji Wenti). 4(2000): 17–25 (in Chinese).

Huffman, W.E., 'Allocative efficiency: The role of human capital', *Quarterly Journal of Economics*, 91(1) (1977): 59–79.

Jin, S., Huang, J., Hu, R. and Rozelle, S., 'The creation and spread of technology and total factor productivity in China's agriculture', *American Journal of Agricultural Economics*, 84(4) (2002): 916–930.

Jondrow, J., Lovell, C., Materov, I. and Schmidt, P., 'On the estimation of technical inefficiency in the stochastic frontier production function model', *Journal of Econometrics*, 19(2/3) (1982): 233–238.

Kumbhakar, S.C. and Lovell. C., *Stochastic Frontier Analysis*, (Cambridge University Press, 2000).

Lee, P.K., 'Local economic protectionism in China's economic reform', *Development Policy Review*, 16(1998): 281–303.

LeSage, J.P., Applied econometrics using MATLAB, (Manual for the Econometrics Toolbox, 1999).

Lin, J.Y., 'The household responsibility system in China's agricultural reform: A theoretical and empirical study', *Economic Development and Cultural Change*, 36(3) (1988): 199–224.

———, 'Rural reforms and agricultural productivity growth in China', *American Economic Review*, 82(1) (1992): 34–51.

Liu, C., Yao, X. and Lavely, W., *China Administrative Regions GIS Data: 1:1M, County Level*, (Published and Disseminated by CIESIN, 1996).

Meeusen, W. and Van, den. B.J., 'Efficiency estimation from Cobb–Douglas production functions with composed error', *International Economic Review*, 18(2) (1997): 435–444.

Monchuk, D. and Miranowski, J.A., 'Spatial labor markets and technology spillovers –analysis from the U.S. Midwest' (Paper prepared for presentation at the American Agricultural Economics Annual Meeting, Montreal, 2003).

Pace, R.K. and Barry, R., 'Spatial statistics Toolbox 1.0'. Real Estate Research Institute (Louisiana State University, Baton Rouge, LA, 1999).

R Development Core Team, 'R: A language and environment for statistical computing', R Foundation for Statistical Computing (Vienna, Austria. ISBN 3–900051–00–3, http://www.R–project.org, 2003).

Sadoulet, E. and de Janvry, A., 'Quantitative Development Policy Analysis', The Johns Hopkins University Press (Baltimore, MD, 1995).

Sen, A.K., *Choice of Techniques*, Basil Blacewell (1960).

State Statistical Bureau, *County–Level Demographic and economic data: 1992, 1995, 1999*, http://www.stats.gov.cn/tjsj/qtsj/index.htm, 2002 (Accessed May 2005).

Tian, W.M., and Wan, G.H., 'Technical efficiency and its determinants in China's grain production', *Journal of Productivity Analysis*, 13(2) (2000): 159–174.

Wan, G.H. and Cheng, E.J. 'Effects of land fragmentation and returns to scale in the Chinese farming sector', *Applied Economics*, 33(2) (2001): 183–194.

Wang, J.R., Wailes, E.J. and Cramer, G.L., 'A shadow–price frontier measurement of profit efficiency in Chinese agriculture', *American Journal of Agricultural Economics*, 78(1) (1996b): 145–156.

Widawsky, D., Rozelle, S., Jin, S. and Huang, J., 'Pesticide productivity, host–plant resistance and productivity in China', *Agricultural Economics*, 19(1–2) (1998):203–217.

World Bank, China: Country economic memorandum— promoting growth with equity. Report No. 24169–CHA, Poverty Reduction and Economic Management Unit, East Asia and Pacific Region (2003).

Xu, Y., 'Agricultural productivity in China', *China Economic Review*, 10(2) (1999): 108–121.

Yang, H., 'China's maize production and supply from a provincial perspective' (Working Paper No. 96/7 Center for Asian studies, Chinese Economy Research Unit, The University of Adelaide, 1996).

Yao, S., Liu, Z. and Zhang, Z., 'Spatial difference of grain production efficiency in China, 1987–1992', *Economics of Planning*, 34(1–2) (2001): 139–157.

Chapter 10

# Impact of Land Fragmentation on Rice Producers' Technical Efficiency in Southeast China

Shuhao Tan
Nico Heerink
Arie Kuyvenhoven
Futian Qu

## 1 Introduction

China's entry into the WTO in December 2001 has since placed an increasing pressure on productivity and efficiency in Chinese agriculture. Significant increases in productivity and efficiency are needed to meet the challenges of increased foreign competition. Land fragmentation may act as a major bottleneck in this respect (Fleisher and Liu, 1992; Wan and Cheng, 2001; Zhang, 2002). Due to the high population pressure, the limited availability of arable land, and the prevailing system of land use rights distribution, landholdings in China are strongly fragmented. In 1999, farm households in China cultivated an average area of 0.53 *ha*, spread over 6.06 plots (Tan et al. forthcoming).

Land fragmentation may cause a loss of farmland area due to the use of land for marking boundaries, and a low efficiency in irrigation water management because of the irregular shape of numerous plots (Zhang et al. 1996). It may also cause time loss in travel and inconvenience in agricultural management (Nguyen et al. 1996).

In this chapter, we investigate to what extent rice production in China can be improved under existing technology. We do this by examining the factors responsible for technical efficiency in rice farming, and the relative importance of land fragmentation in this respect.

Rice is the most important crop in China. It is grown on 27 to 29 percent of the cultivated area and constitutes 41 to 45 percent of grain production. Moreover, it supplies 40 percent of caloric intake, and about 60 percent of the Chinese population consumes rice as a main staple food (Zhang, 2002). Rice farming is thus important for the generation of income and reducing poverty in large parts of China.

Empirical research on the impact of land fragmentation on China's agricultural productivity and efficiency is scarce. Available studies include Nguyen and Cheng

(1996), who used data from a household survey of 1,200 households in the Jilin, Shandong, Jiangxi, Sichuan, and Guangdong provinces between 1993 and 1994 in order to examine the impact of land fragmentation on the productivity of three major grain crops. Results indicated that there is a significant positive relationship between plot size and output for maize, wheat and rice. Wan and Cheng (2001) explored the impact of land fragmentation and returns to scale in the Chinese farming sector using the data set of the same rural household survey. Their main finding was that an increase in land fragmentation by one plot led to output losses of 9.8 percent for tubers, 6.5 percent for wheat, and less than 2 percent for other crops.

Earlier research undertaken by Fleisher and Liu (1992) used a survey data set of 1,200 households collected in the Jilin, Jiangsu, Henan, Hebei and Jiangxi provinces in 1987 and 1988. A Cobb-Douglas production function was applied to examine the effect of land fragmentation—measured by the number of plots—on productivity. They found that the number of plots had a negative impact on agricultural production. A 10 percent increase in the number of plots induced a 5.7 percent decline in output.

All these studies used simple partial measures of efficiency and fail to distinguish the productivity differential caused by land fragmentation and other factors like a farmer's age and education, among others. During the last two decades, many studies have analyzed agricultural efficiency with parametric methods (Kalirajan and Shand, 1986; Battese and Coelli, 1992; Kumbhakar, 1994; Battese and Coelli, 1995; Kebede, 2001; Daryanto and Battese, 2002).

In recent years, efficiency analysis with non-parametric methods has become increasingly popular (Chavas and Aliber, 1993; Sharma, 1997; Wadud and White, 2000; Krasachat, 2003). Coelli et al. (2002) provide a very good example of non-parametric methods to analyze the efficiency of rice cultivators in Bangladesh. Although they used one of the most exhaustive lists of farm-specific variables that any efficiency analysis has ever applied, they do not include land fragmentation in their research.

Among the numerous empirical analyses of agricultural efficiency, only a few have taken land fragmentation into account. A study by Hazarika and Alwang (2003) shows that plot size has a significant positive effect on the cost efficiency of tobacco cultivators in Malawi. Research in Bangladesh (Wadud and White, 2000) indicates that on average, farmers with greater plot size or less land fragmentation operate at a higher level of technical efficiency. Sherlund et al. (2002) test smallholder technical efficiency controlling for plot-specific environmental conditions for traditional rice plots in Côte d'Ivoire. They find that technical efficiency is higher for those who cultivate three or more rice plots. Recent research by Chen et al. (2003) examines the technical efficiency of Chinese grain farms, using a stochastic production frontier. The model is fitted to a panel data set covering nearly 600 farm households in nine provinces during the late-1990s. Land fragmentation was found to be detrimental to technical efficiency.

The aim of this chapter is to estimate the technical efficiency in different rice types in China and examine the impact of land fragmentation on rice producers' technical efficiency, while controlling all other factors. We focus on rice production and distinguish between double-rice—such as early rice and late rice—and one-season rice cultivation as production technologies and technical efficiency may differ considerably between them. A second difference with Chen et al. (2003) is the subdivision of fertilizer use into pure N, P and K contents in our study. This is expected to give more accurate technical efficiency scores, because nutrient requirements differ between different crops and rice types. Moreover, actual fertilizer applications often do not reflect these differences in nutrient requirements, leading to either overuse or underuse of specific fertilizer components in certain crops (see e.g. Huang, 1997).

The remainder of the chapter is as follows. Section 2 sets out the theoretical model. Section 3 describes the implementation of the model. Regression results are presented and discussed in section 4, and Section 5 summarizes the major conclusions and discusses some of the major implications.

## 2 Methodology

Three issues will be discussed in regard to methodology: (1) choosing between a non-parametric and parametric approach; (2) given a selected approach, choosing a functional form for the production function; and (3) selecting the method of estimation. We discuss the first problem in sub-section 2.1 and treat the second and third issues in sub-section 2.2.

### *2.1 Basic Model*

Choosing between a parametric and a non-parametric approach to measure efficiency has been controversial. Each has both strengths and weaknesses (Olesen, 1996; Coelli and Perelman, 1999). The parametric analysis deals with stochastic noise, and allows hypothesis testing on the production structure, efficiency, and so on. This method, however, has to specify a functional form for the frontier technology and impose a distributional assumption on the efficiency term. The non-parametric method does not impose such restrictions, but it assumes the absence of measurement, or sampling error. The choice between these approaches, therefore, depends upon the objective of the research, the type of farms that are analyzed and the availability of data.

In this chapter, we chose the stochastic frontier approach—a parametric method—to analyze the impact of land fragmentation on rice producers' technical efficiency. The main reason for this choice is that rice production in China is subject to weather disturbances and heterogeneous environmental factors, like soil quality and irrigation access. Moreover, the respondents may not have answered some of the questions accurately due to varied perceptions, for example, and may therefore have affected measured efficiency (Chen et al. 2003).

The stochastic frontier function was independently developed by Aigner, Lovell and Schmidt (1977) and Meeusen and Broeck (1977). Jondrow et al. (1982) extended it by incorporating producer-specific efficiency effects. Greene (1993) proposed various specifications for the distributional assumption. Following Battese and Coelli (1995) and assuming a half normal distribution of the one-sided error, the basic structure of the model for a cross-sectional data set can be expressed as

$$q_i = f(x_i; \beta) + \varepsilon_i \quad (i=1, 2, \ldots, N) \tag{1}$$

where $N$ is the number of household farms; $q_i$ is the production of the i-th farm; $x_i$ is a $(1\times j)$-vector of the input quantities of the $i$th farm; $\beta$ is a $(j\times 1)$-vector of unknown parameters; $\varepsilon_i$ is a composed error term, which can be decomposed as:

$$\varepsilon_i = v_i - u_i \tag{2}$$

where $v_i$ are stochastic random errors, which are assumed to be independently and identically distributed (iid) as N $(0, \sigma_v^2)$ and independent of the $u_i$, $u_i$ are non-negative random errors accounting for technical inefficiency (TIE) in production; they are assumed to be iid as half normal $N^+(0, \sigma_u^2)$ distribution.

Parameters $\beta$, $\sigma_v$ and $\sigma_u$ and TIE for each household will be estimated by running the stochastic frontier model. The resulting levels of technical efficiency (TE; TE = 1 − TIE) will be used to test the relative importance of land fragmentation by estimating the following equation:

$$TE_i = z_i \delta + \eta_i \tag{3}$$

where $TE_i$ is the predicted technical efficiency score of each farm household; $z_i$ is a $(1\times k)$ vector of variables which may influence the efficiency of a farm, including land fragmentation in our case; and $\delta$ is a $(k\times 1)$ vector of unknown parameters, and $\eta_i$ is a random disturbance term assumed to be idd as $N(0, \sigma_\eta^2)$.

### 2.2 Model Choice and Estimation Techniques

The choice of a functional form in parametric models has also been subjected to debate (Bravo-Ureta, 1993). Two production functions, Cobb–Douglas and translog, are commonly used in frontier production analysis. Some authors (Kopp and Smith, 1980) argue that functional specification has a discernible though rather small impact on estimated efficiency. Following Fleisher and Liu (1992) and Nguyen et al. (1996), we choose the Cobb–Douglas production function because of its simplicity, apparently good fit to Chinese agricultural data, and the relatively large number of inputs that we use in our analysis.[1]

Typical agricultural inputs like land area, labor and material inputs used in rice production are included in the production function. Fertilizer is separated into the three macro-nutrients (N, P, K) required for crop growth. Fertilizer application in China is commonly believed to be in severe unbalance. Farmers tend to use too much nitrogen and too little phosphorus and potassium. Some years ago, a so-called K-compensation project has therefore been launched in some areas of East China with assistance from agricultural extension agents.

We will estimate the specified model with the two-step technique. In the first stage, we estimate the frontier model by assuming a half-normal distribution of the inefficiency term to predict the technical efficiency scores and estimate the $\beta$ s; next we examine the determinants of technical efficiency by means of a censored normal (tobit) model. Alternatively, the so-called one-step method incorporates farm-specific factors affecting technical efficiency in the estimation of the production frontier[2] (Kumbhakar, 1991; Huang, 1994; Battese and Coelli, 1995). Although this method is preferable from a theoretical point of view, in the application to our data set it leads to highly unstable results.

## 3 Implementation

### *3.1 Sampling and Data Collection*

Data used for this research were collected during a household survey in three villages of northeast Jiangxi province. The three villages were chosen to reflect differences in degree of market access as well as agricultural and economic development.[3] All three show a high degree of variation in natural resource endowments, rural infrastructure, and land fragmentation and are assumed to be representative of a much larger rice-producing hilly area in Jiangxi and probably in neighboring provinces as well (see Kuiper et al. 2001 for details).

Banqiao is the smallest village with about 900 persons living in 220 households. It is located in a hilly area in which the upland area accounts for 60 to 70 percent of its total land. Market access is relatively good in this village since it is within 10

[1] In our research, nine inputs are distinguished. The use of a translog function will greatly complicate the hypothesis testing with respect to the impact of individual production inputs.

[2] Frontier 4.1 developed by Coelli (1996) is used to estimate the frontier function.

[3] The survey was designed and implemented under the project 'Strengthening Education and Research on Environmental and Resource Economics at Nanjing Agricultural University' (SERENA), financed by the Netherlands Ministry of Development Cooperation (SAIL program). The project is a collaboration between the College of Land Management, Nanjing Agricultural University, the Development Economics Group, Wageningen University, the Netherlands, and the Institute of Social Studies in The Hague, the Netherlands.

km of a major city, but the road conditions are poor between its hamlets and the main road. Irrigation conditions are adequate. Paddy fields can be easily irrigated with water from a reservoir, against payment of irrigation fees. In the dry land area, rain-fed agriculture is used for growing peanuts, fruits, and other cash crops.

Shangzhu is a remote village—taking about two hours from the county seat to reach the main hamlet. Sixteen hamlets are scattered over a mountain area, and some of them very difficult to reach. There are 472 households with 2,028 people. The main crops are rice and bamboo. Rice is planted on the terraces of the valley areas, while bamboo and fir (a kind of cash tree) are grown in the hilly areas. The terraces are well-constructed with stone, and are several hundred years old.

Gangyan is the largest village, consisting of 730 households—3,200 people. It is located in a plain area about 30 km from the county seat. Road conditions are good. The main crops in this village are rice and vegetables. Some tractors are used in this village. Most of the plots can be irrigated against paying irrigation fees.

Farmland—including irrigated land and dry land—per capita equals 1.89 *mu* in Banqiao, 1.36 *mu* in Shangzhu, and 1.21 *mu* in Gangyan. The surveyed households were selected at random. About 23 percent of the households were interviewed in each of the selected villages. The resulting 339 households were surveyed for the 2000 agricultural season. Detailed information was collected from 2,490 plots. Among the 339 households, 264 planted early rice, 206 one-season rice, and 261 late rice. The average number of plots is nearly the same in the three villages: 7.36, 7.44 and 7.36 in Banqiao, Shangzhu and Gangyan, respectively. The distance from the homestead to the plots is largest in the remote village of Shangzhu. It equals 13.7, 17.3 and 15.8 minutes for Banqiao, Shangzhu and Gangyan, respectively.

### *3.2 Variables Used and their Potential Impact*

The most frequently used variables in empirical analyses of technical efficiency are education and experience of farmers, contact with extensions, access to credit, farm size, land tenure, and other environmental and non-physical factors, like information and supervision, which may also influence the capability of the producer to utilize the available technologies. What indicators should be in the model depends on the relevant conditions in the research area and the availability of data.

In our case, the following factors will be used for explaining efficiency based on the initial test:

1. Household characteristics: age of household head, education of household head, household size, and savings;
2. Farm characteristics: land fragmentation indicators (number of plots, average plot size and average distance of plots to the homestead), oxen ownership and tractor use.

Within the same village, households face almost the same conditions with respect to extension and infrastructure. We, therefore, use village dummies to capture the impact of extension, infrastructure and other village-level variables.

**Table 10.1 Variable definitions and expected signs in TE equation**

| Variable explanation | Variable name | Unit | Expected sign |
|---|---|---|---|
| Age of household head | Age | Year | +/- |
| Education of household head | Edu | Year | +/- |
| Household size | Hhsize | Person | + |
| Number of plots | Nplot | | + |
| Average plot size | Psize | Mu | + |
| Average distance from plots to homestead | Dist | Minute | - |
| Dummy, =1 if household saves money | Dsave | | + |
| Dummy, =1 if household owns oxen | Dcat | | + |
| Dummy, =1 if tractor is used in rice production | Dtract | | + |
| Shangzhu village dummy | D1 | | - |
| Gangyan village dummy | D2 | | 0 |

Age may have both positive and negative impacts on technical efficiency, depending on whether older farmers are more experienced or slower to accept new technologies than young farmers. A higher level of education can lead to a better assessment of the importance and complexities of production decisions, resulting in a better arrangement of farming practices, but farmers with higher education may also tend to pay more attention to non-farm work, leading to lower efficiency. A larger household size usually implies more laborers and thus more time that can be devoted to timely irrigation, pest management, harvesting, and so on. In addition, larger families have more children or old persons for other supervision in agricultural production. Both situations imply a positive impact of household size on TE. Savings can reduce constraints on production, facilitating to obtain the inputs needed for production on a timely basis. Hence, it is supposed to improve the efficiency of farming.

Empirical studies of TE normally use farm size as one of the explanatory variables. In this study, we decompose farm size into number of plots and average plot size. The number of plots measures the scale effect, while the average plot size captures the impact of land fragmentation on technical efficiency. At a given average plot size, an increase in the number of plots is expected to have a positive scale effect on TE because larger farms have better opportunities to realize the economies of scale. For a given number of plots, the average plot size is also expected to have a positive impact on TE. Some technologies are inappropriate for use on (very) small plots. A larger average distance to the plots means less convenience in farming management, and therefore is expected to have a negative impact on TE. If a farm household owns oxen, it can prepare land more timely and carefully and hence is expected to be more efficient. Mechanization tends to increase technical efficiency, thus the expected impact of tractor use on TE is positive.

Shangzhu village has a poorer infrastructure, lower temperatures, and more sloping land than Banqiao village. Farmers in Shangzhu village may thereby be less efficient than their counterparts in Banqiao. Meanwhile, Gangyan village has no major differences in infrastructure climate or market access when compared to the village of Banqiao. However, the share of sloping land is higher in Banqiao—but much lower in Shangzhu—in comparison to Gangyan. The expected sign for the dummy variable for Gangyan village is therefore indeterminate. The variable definitions and anticipated signs of the impact of the explanatory variables on TE are summarized in Table 10.1.

### *3.3 Model Specification*

The above-mentioned data from the three villages are now used to analyze the technical efficiency of rice producers. Based on Equation (1), the model to be estimated is:

$$\ln(q_i) = \beta_0 + \sum_{j=1}^{9} \beta_j \ln(x_{ij}) + v_i - u_i \tag{4}$$

where $\ln(q_i)$ *is* the logarithm of rice output (either early, late, or one-season rice) on each farm, and $x_j$ are inputs used in each season's rice production and soil quality index.[4]

**Table 10.2 Variable definitions and expected signs in production function**

| Variable explanation | Variable name | Unit | Expected sign |
|---|---|---|---|
| Rice production per type of rice ($q_i$) | lnout | Jin | |
| Land area used ($x_1$) | lnland | Mu | + |
| Labor used ($x_2$) | lnlabor | Day | + |
| Seed used ($x_3$) | lnseed | Jin | + |
| Urea used ($x_4$) | lnurea | Jin | + |
| P fertilizer used ($x_5$) | lnpfert | Jin | + |
| K fertilizer used ($x_6$) | lnkcl | Jin | + |
| Herbicide and pesticide ($x_7$) | lnchem | Yuan | +/- |
| Oxen and tractor used ($x_8$) | lnoxen | Day | + |
| Soil quality index ($x_9$) | soildex | | - |

[4] We follow Battese (1997) to treat input levels that are equal to zero.

The variables $x_1$ to $x_8$ represent the rice planting area, labor use, seed, urea, P fertilizer, KCL, chemical inputs (herbicides and pesticides), and oxen and tractor use, respectively (see Table 10.2). $X_9$ is the soil quality index. In our survey, farmers were asked to categorize their plots as either good (with a score of 1), medium (with a score of 2), or bad land (with a score of 3) in terms of their perceptions on soil color, topsoil depth, soil texture, and workability. The soil quality index is derived by multiplying the size of a plot planted with early (late, or one-season) rice with its soil fertility score and dividing this score by the total land area planted with early (late, or one-season) rice. This index ranges from 1 to 3 in which the larger the value, the poorer the soil fertility.

All inputs in the Cobb-Douglas production function are expected to have a positive impact, except for the soil quality index. Herbicide and pesticide, however, may be negatively related to rice production if they are used for curative instead of preventive purposes For example, if they are used to control the damage caused by weeds and pests.

The efficiency model based on Equation (3) is specified as:

$$TE_i = \delta_0 + \delta_{ki}\sum_{k=1}^{9} z_{ik} + \delta_{mi}\sum_{m=1}^{2} d_m + \eta_i \qquad (5)$$

where $TE_i$ represents the efficiency score of each household obtained from Equation (4), and $\eta_i$ denotes the error term of the efficiency function. The *z* vector of variables represents factors that may influence farmer efficiency. The variables $z_1$ to $z_3$ represent demographic and human capital variables, such as age ($z_1$) and education ($z_2$) of the household head and household size ($z_3$). Variables $z_4$ to $z_6$ measure land scale and land fragmentation, such as number of plots ($z_4$), average plot size ($z_5$), and average distance of each plot to the homestead ($z_6$). The variable $z_7$ denotes whether a farming household has savings or not. Variables $z_8$ and $z_9$ are dummy variables, denoting if a rural household owns oxen and uses a tractor or not in rice production, respectively. Village-specific variables, like market access, extension services, and climate differences are represented by the village dummies $d_1$ and $d_2$ for Shangzhu and Gangyan, respectively.

### *3.4 Descriptive statistics of data used*

Table 10.3 shows the descriptive statistics for the variables used in the analyses. The average area used for rice cultivation is about 0.3 *ha* per household, with large variations among households. The corresponding rice production varies from about 100 kg to more than 10,000 kg, with an average value of about 1,500 kg for a four-to-five person household. This suggests that most of the farms are self-sufficient, while a few farms are market-oriented.

Average yields equal 4.3, 4.9, and 4.8 tons per *ha* for early, one-season and late rice, respectively. The labor and oxen inputs are relatively intensive, while fertilizer application is relatively low in one-season rice production. Early rice needs more applications of fertilizer and seed and slightly less herbicide and pesticide than late and one-season rice.

**Table 10.3 Descriptive statistics of variables used**

| | Early rice | | | | One-season rice | | | | Late rice | | | |
|---|---|---|---|---|---|---|---|---|---|---|---|---|
| | Max | Min | Mean | St.dev | Max | Min | Mean | St.dev | Max | Min | Mean | St.dev |
| *Variables for production function (per mu)* | | | | | | | | | | | | |
| Production | 8000 | 250 | 2863 | 1767 | 26400 | 150 | 2923 | 2551 | 14000 | 200 | 3634 | 2400 |
| Area | 16.0 | 0.4 | 5.03 | 3.03 | 33 | 0.40 | 4.70 | 3.63 | 23.0 | 0.30 | 5.62 | 3.47 |
| Labor | 179 | 5 | 60.94 | 32.4 | 269 | 1 | 65.5 | 47.7 | 307 | 4.59 | 59.6 | 39.6 |
| Seed | 34.0 | 0 | 7.05 | 5.16 | 62.8 | 0.07 | 6.41 | 6.79 | 47.1 | 0.35 | 7.46 | 6.79 |
| Urea | 1047 | 4 | 207 | 161 | 656 | 0 | 145 | 124 | 1486 | 0 | 227 | 194 |
| P-fertilizer | 1500 | 0 | 295 | 298 | 2343 | 0 | 165 | 251 | 2086 | 0 | 271 | 335 |
| K-fertilizer | 500 | 0 | 76.0 | 94 | 787 | 0 | 44.2 | 70.5 | 783 | 0 | 101 | 133 |
| Chemicals | 437 | 0.99 | 60.9 | 50 | 524 | 0 | 56.2 | 56.4 | 467 | 0.00 | 79.4 | 72.6 |
| Oxen | 17.5 | 0.31 | 4.13 | 2.97 | 62.1 | 0.52 | 5.73 | 7.03 | 26.8 | 0.33 | 4.07 | 3.03 |
| Soildex | 3.00 | 1.00 | 1.75 | 0.53 | 3.00 | 0.42 | 2.32 | 0.59 | 3.00 | 1.00 | 1.79 | 0.52 |
| *Values (per ha)* | | | | | | | | | | | | |
| Yield/ha | 8500 | 1731 | 4286 | 905 | 13125 | 1650 | 4873 | 1433 | 10500 | 1172 | 4786 | 1190 |
| Labor/ha | 829 | 58.8 | 211 | 110 | 1320 | 37.5 | 247 | 165 | 1265 | 30.3 | 187 | 125 |
| Seed/ha | 57.4 | 1.23 | 12.0 | 7.9 | 49.7 | 0.57 | 10.7 | 7.45 | 50.6 | 0.46 | 10.9 | 7.11 |
| Urea/ha | 1271 | 22.7 | 315 | 168 | 1125 | 0 | 262 | 169 | 1013 | 0 | 291 | 152 |
| P-fer/ha | 2720 | 0 | 442 | 385 | 1594 | 0 | 280 | 260 | 3651 | 0 | 369 | 405 |
| K-fer/ha | 626 | 0 | 109 | 107 | 707 | 0 | 74.4 | 78.5 | 1003 | 0 | 117 | 118 |
| Chem/ha | 1170 | 10.1 | 195 | 143 | 1025 | 0 | 202 | 145 | 915 | 0 | 217 | 134 |
| Oxen/ha | 37.5 | 1.58 | 13.4 | 6.77 | 77.6 | 1.88 | 18.2 | 11.5 | 100 | 1.12 | 12.3 | 8.80 |
| *Variables for technical efficiency model* | | | | | | | | | | | | |
| Age | 75 | 23 | 47.0 | 10.3 | 75 | 27 | 47.2 | 9.94 | 75 | 23 | 47.0 | 10.1 |
| Edu | 12 | 0 | 4.70 | 2.75 | 13 | 0 | 4.71 | 2.84 | 12 | 0 | 4.69 | 2.70 |
| Hhsize | 14 | 1 | 4.55 | 1.55 | 14 | 1 | 4.54 | 1.57 | 14 | 1 | 4.56 | 1.56 |
| Nplot | 15 | 1 | 3.13 | 2.10 | 9 | 1 | 3.21 | 2.12 | 15 | 1 | 3.69 | 2.34 |
| Psize | 9 | 0.25 | 1.90 | 1.11 | 8.00 | 0.34 | 1.55 | 0.94 | 9 | 0.30 | 1.79 | 1.10 |
| Dist | 35 | 1 | 12.6 | 6.76 | 75 | 0 | 20.5 | 12.4 | 45 | 1 | 12.8 | 7.35 |
| Dsave | 1 | 0 | 0.52 | 0.5 | 1 | 0 | 0.52 | 0.5 | 1 | 0 | 0.53 | 0.50 |
| Dcat | 1 | 0 | 0.64 | 0.48 | 1 | 0 | 0.64 | 0.48 | 1 | 0 | 0.65 | 0.48 |
| Dtract | 1 | 0 | 0.13 | 0.33 | 1 | 0 | 0.07 | 0.25 | 1 | 0 | 0.20 | 0.40 |

*Sources*: Based on the survey conducted by the SERENA project.

Land fragmentation and soil quality show substantial variation between the three rice types. On average, the respondent households used 3.13 plots to cultivate early rice in addition to 3.21 and 3.69 plots for the production of one-season and late rice, respectively. Households tend to use the best plots for early rice production—for example, the plots with best soil quality, shortest distance to the homestead, and largest plot sizes. On the other hand, they tend to use the plots with the smallest average size, largest distance, and lowest soil quality for one-season rice production.[5]

## 4 Empirical results

We first briefly discuss the results of the frontier function, and then discuss in more detail the results for technical efficiency.

### *4.1 Rice Farmers' Technical Efficiency*

The results of the three frontier models are presented in Table 10.4. Land has a very significant impact on the production of all three types of rice, confirming the fundamental importance of land availability for agricultural production in China. The estimated elasticity for one-season rice (0.914) is lower than the ones estimated for early and late rice (0.972 and 0.963, respectively). Most other variables are highly correlated (0.70 or higher) with land area, making it difficult to estimate their separate impact from that of land. This may explain why some explanatory variables (particularly labor and the use of oxen or a tractor) appear to have an impact opposite to production theory. For obtaining accurate estimates of technical efficiency, however, these inputs are left in the model.

Sub-ividing fertilizer use into its three major nutrient components offers interesting results, which indicate that the marginal productivity of N is positive in late rice and one-season rice but not in early rice. The marginal productivity of P is positive in early rice only, while the marginal productivity in K is positive only in late-rice production.

The sum of the estimated input coefficients is close to one for early rice (0.95) and late rice (0.94). For one-season rice, the sum is only 0.00. This means that the hypothesis that there are constant returns to scale is thus rejected for one-season rice, not for early or late rice. For early and late rice, this conclusion is consistent with the constant returns to scale in grain production found by Chen et al. (2003) and in Fleisher and Liu (1992).

[5] These findings also hold when the sample is disaggregated per village.

**Table 10.4 Results of frontier function**

| | | Early rice | | | One-season rice | | | Late rice | | |
|---|---|---|---|---|---|---|---|---|---|---|
| | | Coeff | z-value | Sig. | Coeff | z-value | Sig. | Coeff | z-value | Sig. |
| Constant | $\beta_0$ | 6.260 | 48.74 | *** | 6.89 | 42.25 | *** | 6.66 | 46.95 | *** |
| ln(land) | $\beta_1$ | 0.972 | 24.50 | *** | 0.963 | 18.23 | *** | 0.914 | 19.90 | *** |
| ln(labor) | $\beta_2$ | -0.0.33 | -0.10 | | -0.073 | -2.08 | ** | -0.057 | -1.97 | ** |
| ln(seed) | $\beta_3$ | -0.037 | -1.82 | * | -0.022 | -1.14 | | -0.001 | -0.04 | |
| ln(urea) | $\beta_4$ | 0.012 | 0.53 | | 0.062 | 2.19 | ** | 0.057 | 2.05 | ** |
| ln(pfert) | $\beta_5$ | 0.048 | 2.63 | *** | -0.022 | -0.67 | | -0.024 | -1.12 | |
| ln(kcl) | $\beta_6$ | -0.0003 | -0.02 | | 0.031 | 0.96 | | 0.051 | 2.31 | *** |
| ln(chem) | $\beta_7$ | 0.055 | 2.74 | *** | 0.006 | 0.24 | | 0.002 | 0.12 | |
| ln(oxen) | $\beta_8$ | -0.043 | -1.85 | * | -0.065 | -1.99 | ** | 0.07 | 2.67 | *** |
| ln(soil) | $\beta_9$ | -0.018 | -0.45 | | -0.084 | -1.43 | * | -0.184 | -3.71 | *** |
| $\ln\sigma_v^2$ | | -3.74 | -17.09 | *** | -3.59 | -13.50 | *** | -3.66 | -15.96 | *** |
| $\ln\sigma_u^2$ | | -3.15 | -8.85 | *** | -2.21 | -9.22 | *** | -2.41 | -10.65 | *** |
| $\sigma_v$ | | 0.154 | | | 0.166 | | | 0.16 | | |
| $\sigma_u$ | | 0.207 | | | 0.332 | | | 0.30 | | |
| Log likelihood | | | | 53.92 | | | -10.86 | | | 5.07 |
| Likelihood-ratio test of $\sigma_u$=0 | | | | 4.59 | | | 10.12 | | | 13.03 |
| Prob>=chibar2 | | | | 0 | | | 0.001 | | | 0 |
| Observations | | | | 264 | | | 204 | | | 261 |

*Notes*: 1. * represents significance at 10% level, ** at 5% level and *** 1% level. (NB: variables with either a plus-sign or a minus-sign in Tables 1 and 2 are tested one-sided)

Table 10.5 summarizes the technical efficiency scores obtained from the frontier model. The average technical efficiency for our sample is 0.85 for early rice, 0.79 for one-season rice, and 0.83 for late rice, suggesting that on average the respondents are able to obtain about 82 percent of the potential output by using the given mixture of production inputs. It also implies that in the short run, considerable room exists to improve rice yields for many households. The minimum efficiency levels are 0.61 for early rice, 0.57 for one-season rice and 0.54 for late rice. For households with the lowest efficiency levels, substantial output increases can still be reached with the amount of inputs they are currently using.

Also, Table 10.5 shows the frequency distribution of TE per rice type. About 50 percent of the farmers for all three rice types have TE scores between 0.80 and 0.90. One-season rice farmers have very few farmers with TE scores between 0.90

and 1.00 as compared to early and late rice farmers, while they have a relatively large number of farmers with TE scores lower than 0.70.

**Table 10.5 Technical efficiency scores of rice producers**

| Rice type | TE | | | 0.50-0.60 | 0.60-0.70 | 0.70-0.80 | 0.80-0.90 | 0.90-1.00 |
|---|---|---|---|---|---|---|---|---|
| Early rice | max | 1.00 | Cases | 0 | 9 | 55 | 131 | 69 |
| | min | 0.61 | | | | | | |
| | mean | 0.85 | Percentage | 0 | 3 | 21 | 50 | 26 |
| | stdev | 0.07 | | | | | | |
| One season rice | max | 1.00 | Cases | 3 | 23 | 78 | 96 | 4 |
| | min | 0.57 | | | | | | |
| | mean | 0.79 | Percentage | 1 | 11 | 38 | 47 | 2 |
| | stdev | 0.07 | | | | | | |
| Late rice | max | 1.00 | Cases | 2 | 16 | 68 | 130 | 45 |
| | min | 0.54 | | | | | | |
| | mean | 0.83 | Percentage | 1 | 6 | 26 | 50 | 17 |
| | stdev | 0.08 | | | | | | |

### *4.2 Results of TE Models*

The technical efficiency model, Equation (5), is estimated with a censored normal Tobit model. Regression results are presented in Table 10.6.

The age of the household head has a significant negative effect on TE in early and late rice. This suggests that older farmers operate farms in a less efficient way than their younger counterparts in double rice production. Compared to one-season rice, double rice production needs more complicated and timely decisions in nursery, harvesting (early rice), and transplanting (late rice).

Education is also found to have a significant negative effect on early rice but no significant effect on either one-season or late rice. This may be because farmers with higher education levels are more involved in non-farm employment and pay less attention to agricultural production. Due to climatic reasons, early rice needs special care during the growing season.

Household size has a significant positive impact in all three rice models. This conforms with findings from research in Mali (Audibert, 1997) that larger families tend to be more efficient than smaller ones. In our research area, the assistance provided by children or old people during peak seasons may explain this finding.

The number of plots and average plot size are found to have strongly significant positive impacts. This means that an increase in the number of plots—with average plot size remaining constant—has a positive (scale) effect on TE. Likewise, for a given number of plots, an increase in average plot size also has a positive effect.

**Table 10.6 Rice producers' technical efficiency determinants (censored normal Tobit model)**

| | | Early rice | | | One-season rice | | | Late rice | | |
|---|---|---|---|---|---|---|---|---|---|---|
| | | Coeff | z-value | Sig. | Coeff | z-value | Sig. | Coeff | z-value | Sig. |
| Constant | $\delta_0$ | 0.754 | 34.02 | *** | 0.620 | 21.73 | *** | 0.722 | 31.29 | *** |
| Age | $\delta_1$ | -0.001 | -2.96 | *** | 0.000 | 0.11 | | -0.001 | -3.41 | *** |
| Education | $\delta_2$ | -0.002 | -1.98 | ** | 0.000 | 0.02 | | 0.000 | -0.23 | |
| Household size | $\delta_3$ | 0.004 | 2.25 | *** | 0.005 | 2.40 | *** | 0.005 | 2.60 | *** |
| No. of plots | $\delta_4$ | 0.024 | 16.03 | *** | 0.024 | 13.74 | *** | 0.021 | 14.26 | *** |
| Plot size | $\Delta_5$ | 0.035 | 11.46 | *** | 0.040 | 10.77 | *** | 0.033 | 10.57 | *** |
| Distance | $\delta_6$ | 0.000 | -0.87 | | 0.000 | 0.08 | | 0.000 | -0.26 | |
| Dsave | $\delta_7$ | 0.005 | 0.87 | | 0.005 | 0.80 | | 0.002 | 0.35 | |
| Dcat | $\delta_8$ | -0.006 | -1.00 | | -0.010 | -1.40 | | 0.008 | 1.28 | |
| Dtract | $\delta_9$ | -0.014 | -1.66 | * | -0.008 | -0.56 | | -0.009 | -1.21 | |
| D1 | $\delta_{10}$ | -0.050 | -5.23 | *** | 0.003 | 0.18 | | -0.055 | -5.51 | *** |
| D2 | $\delta_{11}$ | -0.002 | -0.21 | | 0.002 | 0.10 | | 0.007 | 0.80 | |
| Adjusted R-square | | | | 0.669 | | | 0.595 | | | 0.668 |
| Log likelihood | | | | 4.59 | | | 340 | | | 447 |
| Observations | | | | 263 | | | 204 | | | 261 |

*Notes*: 1. * represents significance at 10% level, ** at 5% level and *** 1% level. (NB: variables with either a plus-sign or a minus-sign in Tables 1 and 2 are tested one-sided)

Distance to the plots does not have a significant impact on the TE for any of the three kinds of rice. This may be explained from the surplus of labor and scarcity of land in rural China, which induces farmers to cultivate far-away plots as efficient as plots nearby the homestead.

Savings and oxen ownership also do not have a significant effect on TE. This suggests that the impact of these two factors on more timely management is negligible. Whether a farm uses a tractor or not, however, does have a significant negative effect on TE in early rice. A possible explanation for this counterintuitive result is that the use of tractors at the start of the agricultural season causes soil compaction, a well-know problem in the research area.

Finally, the dummy variable for Shangzhu, the remote village, has a significant negative impact on TE in early and late rice but not in one-season rice. Because Shangzhu is located in a mountainous area, the growing season is shorter and one-season rice is much more common than double-rice as compared to the other two villages. The regression results indicate that when other relevant factors are controlled, farmers growing one-season rice in Shangzhu are as efficient as farmers growing the same crop in the other two villages with much better market access.

## 5 Concluding Remarks

Although rice producers in China have become more efficient and productive during the past decades by adopting high-yielding varieties (HYVs) and other productivity and efficiency building technologies (Carnahan 2002), China's entry into the WTO puts increasing pressure on productivity and efficiency in Chinese agriculture. Land fragmentation is regarded as a significant bottleneck to increasing productivity and efficiency and reducing poverty.

This chapter applied detailed household-, crop-, and plot-level data to investigate the impact of land fragmentation on rice producers' technical efficiency in a major rice-growing area in southeast China. The two-stage method is applied to double-rice and one-season rice production for this purpose. In addition, a stochastic frontier model is applied in which rice production is explained from traditional agricultural inputs and soil quality. The resulting technical efficiency scores are explained from rural household-specific factors using a censored normal Tobit model.

The frontier model results show that TE in one-season rice is lower than in double-rice production. The average TE scores (0.85 for early rice, 0.83 for late rice, and 0.79 for one-season rice) suggest that output increases of 15 to 20 percent can still be reached with the current amount of inputs. New technologies, however, will have to be introduced to realize further increases in rice productivity.

Results from the TE model suggest that land fragmentation plays an important role in explaining technical efficiency. Increases in average plot size have a significant positive impact on technical efficiency. Distance to the plots, however, has no significant impact on TE. Due to the surplus of labor and scarcity of land in rural China, farmers tend to cultivate far-away plots as efficiently as plots nearby the homestead.

As Carnahan (2002) has pointed out, increased rice production in China is expected through biotechnology techniques, integrated management of low- to medium-yielding rice fields (namely those with higher soil quality index), pest management and diseases, weed control, mechanization, and improved irrigation and water conservation over the long-term. All these measures are, to some extent, related to land fragmentation. If fragmented plots can be consolidated, the above-mentioned technology improvements can be much easier implemented. Therefore, a reduction of land fragmentation can substantially increase rice productivity and promote the international competitiveness of rice cultivation in China, thereby reducing rural poverty.

## References


Aigner, D.J., Lovell, C.A.K. and Schmidt, P.J., 'Formulation and Estimation of Stochastic Frontier Models', *Journal of Econometrics*, 6(1) (1977): 21-37.

Audibert, M., 'Technical Inefficiency Effects among Paddy Farmers in the Villages of The "Office du Niger", Mali, West Africa', *Journal of Productivity Analysis*, 8(4) (1997): 379-394.

Battese, G.E., 'A Note on the Estimation of Cobb-Douglas Production Functions When Some Explanatory Variables Have Zero Values', *Journal of Agricultural Economics*, 48(2) (1997): 250-252.

Battese, G.E. and Coelli, T.J., 'Frontier Production Functions, Technical Efficiency and Panel Data: With Application to Paddy Farmers in India', *Journal of Productivity Analysis*, 3 (1992): 153-169.

———, 'A Model for Technical Inefficiency Effects in a Stochastic Frontier Production Function for Panel Data', *Empirical Economics*, 20 (1995): 325-332.

Carnahan, J., 'Rice Culture.' http://web.ics.purdue.edu/~tstewart/ansc295K/China/Factsheets/Rice_Culture-Carnahan.htm, 2002.

Chavas, J.P. and Aliber, M., 'An Analysis of Economic Efficiency in Agriculture: A Nonparametric Approach', *Journal of Agricultural and Resource Economics*, 18(1) (1993): 1-16.

Chen, A.Z., Huffman, W.E. and Rozelle, S., 'Technical Efficiency of Chinese Grain Production: A Stochastic Production Frontier Approach' (Paper presented at the American Agricultural Economics Association Annual Meeting, Montreal, Canada, July 2003).

Coelli, T. and Perelman, S., 'A comparison of Parametric and Non-parametric Distance Functions: with Application to European Railways', *European Journal of Operational Research*, 117(2) (1999): 326-339.

Coelli, T., Rahman, S. and Thirtle, C., 'Technical, Allocative, Cost and Scale Efficiencies in Bangladesh Rice Cultivation: A Non-parametric Approach', *Journal of Agricultural Economics*, 53(3) (2002): 607-626.

Daryanto, H. and Battese, G.E. and Fleming, E.M., 'Technical Efficiencies of Rice Farmers under Different Irrigation Systems and Cropping Seasons in West Java' (PhD dissertation, Armidale, Australia: University of New England, 2002).

Fleisher, C.M. and Liu, Y., 'Economies of Scale, Plot Size, Human Capital, and Productivity in Chinese Agriculture', *Quarterly Review of Economics and Finance,* 32(3) (1992): 112-123.

Greene, W.H., 'The Econometric Approach to Efficiency Analysis', In: H. O. Fried, C. A. K. Lovell, and S. S. Schmidt (eds.), *The Measurement of Productive Efficiency*, (New York: Oxford University Press, 1993): 68-119.

Hazarika, J. and Alwang, J., 'Access to Credit, Plot Size and Cost Inefficiency among Smallholder Tobacco Cultivators in Malawi', *Agricultural Economics*, 29 (2003): 99-109.

Huang, C.J. and Liu, J.T., 'Estimation of Non-neutral Stochastic Frontier Production Function', *Journal of Productivity Analysis*, 4 (1994): 171-180.

Jondrow, J., Lovell, C.A.K., Materov, I.S. and Schmidt, P., 'On Estimation of Technical Inefficiency in the Stochastic Frontier Production Function Model', *Journal of Econometrics*, 19 (1992): 233-238.

Kalirajan, K.P. and Shand, R.T., 'Estimating Location-Specific and Firm-Specific Technical Efficiency: An Analysis of Malaysian Agriculture', *Journal of Economic Development*, 11 (1986): 147-160.

Kebede, T.A., 'Farm Household Technical Efficiency: a Stochastic Frontier Analysis—A study of Rice Producers in Mardi Watershed in the Western Development Region of Nepal' (MSc thesis, Ås, Norway: Department of Economics and Social Sciences, Agricultural University of Norway, 2001).

Kopp, R.J. and Smith, V.K., 'Frontier Production Function Estimates for Steam Electric Generation: A Comparative Analysis', *Southern Economic Journal*, 47 (1980): 1049-1059.

Krasachat, W., 'Technical Efficiency of Rice Farms in Thailand: A Non-parametric Approach' (Paper presented at the 2003 Hawaii International Conference on Business, Honolulu, Hawaii, June 18-21, 2003).

Kuiper, M., Heerink, N., Tan, S., Shi, X. and Ren, Q., 'Report of Village Selection for the Three Village Survey' (Working paper of SERENA project, Wageningen University, The Netherlands and Nanjing Agricultural University, P.R. China, 2001).

Kumbhakar, S.C., 'The Measurement and Decomposition of Cost-Inefficiency—the Translog Cost System', *Oxford Economic Papers*, 43(4) (1991): 667-683.

———, 'Efficiency Estimation in a Profit Maximizing Model Using Flexible Production Function', *Agricultural Economics,* 10(2) (1994): 143-152.

Meeusen, W. and Broeck, J. van den, 'Efficiency Estimation from Cobb–Douglas Production Functions With Composed Error', *International Economic Review*, 32 (1997): 715-723.

Nguyen, T., Cheng, E. and Findlay, C., 'Land Fragmentation and Farm Productivity in China in the 1990s', *China Economic Review*, 7(2) (1996): 169-180.

Olesen, O.B., Petersen, N.C. and Lovell, C.A.K., 'Efficiency and Frontier Analysis: Proceedings of a Research Workshop on State-of-the-art and Future Research in Efficiency Analysis - Special Issue - Introduction', *Journal of Productivity Analysis*, 7(2-3) (1996): 87-98.

Sharma, K.R., Leung, P. and Zaleski, H.M., 'Productive Efficiency of the Swine Industry in Hawaii: Stochastic Frontier vs. Data Envelopment Analysis', *Journal of Productivity Analysis*, 8(4) (1997): 447-459.

Tan, S., Heerink, N. and Qu, F., 'Land Fragmentation and Its Driving Forces in China', *Land Use Policy* (forthcoming).

Wadud, M.A. and White, B., 'Farm Household Efficiency in Bangladesh: a Comparison of Stochastic Frontier and DEA Methods', *Applied Economics*, 32 (2000): 1665-1673.

Wan, G.H. and Cheng, E., 'Effects of Land Fragmentation and Returns to Scale in the Chinese Farming Sector', *Applied Economics*, 33 (2001): 183-194.

Zhang, L., 'China's Rice Economy and Policy: With Implications to WTO Entry', (Workshop on Integrated Assessment of the WTO Agreement on Agriculture in the Rice Sector, 5 April 2002, Geneva, Switzerland, 2002) http://www.unep.ch/etu/etp/events/Agriculture/pps_china.pdf.

Chapter 11

# Future Prospects of Grain Supply and Demand in China: A Regionalized Multi-market Model Simulation

Wencong Lu

## 1 Introduction

Stable and sustainable growth in grain production is thought to be of fundamental importance for food security in China where farmland is scarce and the large population continues to grow, although at a decreasing rate. In the late 1990s, the Chinese grain market situation changed from a long-term deficit to nearly full self-sufficiency, which had at once brought an optimistic view on future grain security in China. However, the continuous decrease of domestic grain production since 1998 coupled with rapidly-reduced grain stocks—especially climbing domestic prices since 2003—has triggered new nation-wide concerns about future grain supplies in China. The key question being raised in political and academic circles is whether grain production can keep pace with expanding demand.

Since Lester Brown (1995) raised the question "Who will feed China,"[1] a number of simulation models, such as IMPACT (Rosegrant et al., 1995), CPPA (USDA, 1997), WFM (FAO, 1995), OECF (OECF, 1995), GTAP (Anderson et al., 1996), and GORLS (Kersten, 1998), have been applied to answer this question. A general review of these studies is provided by Fan and Agcaoili-Sombilla (1997). The results of the analyses included in this survey differ widely due to the model structure, parameters, data sources, and assumptions underlying the analyses. Recently, Huang (2004□developed a China's Agricultural Policy Simulation Model (CAPSiM) to simulate future grain demand and supply in China under some different scenarios, but the analysis treated China as one region. China is a very large country geographically; there are significant regional differences in regard to factors that affect production, consumption, trad, and prices of agricultural products. Therefore, it appears recommendable to take account of regional aspects in the deliberations on agricultural market developments in China. For this purpose,

[1] Brown (1995) holds that China's grain production will decrease dramatically due to losing farmland available caused by rural industrialization and water shortage while grain demand will increase much fast than the population. Finally Chinese grain import will rise dramatically and may exceed total supply capacity of the world market.

a regionalized agricultural multi-market model for China named "China's Agricultural Regional Market Equilibrium Model (CARMEM)" was developed to project production and consumption of agricultural products in China until 2010.[2]

In this chapter, only the results for wheat, corn, and paddy rice are presented. First, the model structure and data sources are described briefly. Second, the projection results—as obtained in two scenarios—are presented. Finally, some implications of future grain security and market policies are discussed.

## 2 Model Structure and Data Source

The model, CARMEM, is based on the Swopsim modeling framework as described in ERS-USDA in 1992 (Sullivan et al.) and on Tyers' GLS model in the form described in Tyers and Anderson (1992).[3] The model CARMEM covers various products from the grains-oilseeds-livestock sectors in China, which include wheat, corn, paddy rice, soybeans, rapeseed, cotton, sugar, roots and tubers, vegetable oils and meals, beef, mutton, pork, poultry, eggs, milk, and milk products. Processing is included for oilseeds and milk. The thirty-two provinces of the People's Republic of China are aggregated into seven regions, namely the north (Beijing, Tianjing, Hebei, Shanxi and Inner Mongolian), northeast ( Liaoning, Jilin and Heilongjiang), East China (Shanghai, Jiangsu, Zhejiang, Anhui, Fujian, Jiangxi and Shandong), central-south ( Henan, Hubei and Hunan), south (Guangdong, Guangxi and Hainan), southwest (Choqing, Sichuan, Guizhou, Yunnan and Tibet) and northwest (Shanxi, Gansu, Qinghai, Ningxia and Xinjiang). It is variable in terms of both the regional and commodity coverage. The model is embedded in a spreadsheet file, with one worksheet for each region and an additional worksheet for the market clearing mechanism.

In view of the fact that the performance of the Chinese agricultural market at current is essentially market-orientated, it is assumed that China's agricultural market is perfectly competitive and regionally integrated. There are no policy or technical barriers for domestic trade between different regions. Under this condition, the seven regional models are first established and then linked by international-national-regional price transmissions to be a regionalised model at national level. The model is solved either for the pre-fixed net-trade restrictions using the solver or by transmitting world market prices to the national and regional

---

[2] The model CARMEM is developed by Wencong Lu and Lutz Kersten (Institute of Market Analysis and Agricultural Trade Policy, German Federal Agricultural Research Centre, Braunschweig, Germany). Support from the German-Chinese Cooperation in Agricultural Research is appreciated.

[3] For more recent descriptions of Swopsim and the slightly modified GLS model, see Roningen (1997) and Tyers (1994), respectively. The model as applied here was first used as an auxiliary instrument to shift the supply and demand functions of a spatial quadratic programming model (Kersten, 1997).

markets. Therefore, the structure of the model CARMEM highlights the interdependence of agricultural production, consumption, trade, and price among different products and regions in China, and thus is capable to service as a research tool in the analysis of regional performance in Chinese agricultural market by changes in economic and policy structure of this country and its regions. The model is a system of supply and demand equations, price transmission, exogenous variables, and market equilibrium conditions, totally including more than 840 mathematic equations. Table 11.1 shows the main functions.

The current version of the model CARMEM is based on data from 2002 from different official statistics. The regional production of each product is taken directly from the "China Statistic Yearbook 2003" of the Chinese National Bureau of Statistics (NBS). The regional product-specific consumption is a sum of rural direct consumption, urban direct consumption, feed use, seed use, manufactured use and waste which are calculated from the statistical data in "China Statistic Yearbook 2003," "China Rural Household Survey Yearbook 2003," as well as the "Yearbook of China Prices and Survey of Urban Household" of the NBS and "China Domestic Balance of Agricultural Products" of the Chinese Ministry of Agriculture. Even though some of China's agricultural statistics somewhat lack fidelity, the statistical data used in the model are not revised in order to keep a comparability of the model results with the statistics. Because official statistic data—in terms of grain—stocks are not available, the results of the model simulation will not demonstrate here the national net trade, but only the information about grain deficit or surplus at the national and regional levels. The population growth rates toward 2010 are taken from the "Chinese Population Projection" by the National Population and Family Planning Commission of China. The elasticities and technical coefficients used in the model are based on empirical estimations. Feed demand coefficients and extraction rates are taken from past studies. The price scenario uses the world agricultural prices in current dollars as given by the World Bank.

## 3 Model Scenarios and Simulation Results

After a comprehensive agricultural policy reform initiated in the late 1970s —especially with the abolishment of the grain procurement quota policy in most Chinese provinces in 2001 and the reduction of agricultural protections by joining the World Trade Organization in 2001—a market-oriented mechanism for grain resource allocation has been established in China to some extent. To further advance grain market policy reform, China's domestic grain market will continue to be more integrated both nationally and internationally.

**Table 11.1 Main equations and the variables and parameters in the model CARMEM**

| | |
|---|---|
| Equations | (1) Supply: $S^{k}_{i,t} = S^{k}_{i,to}\left(1+a^{k}_{i,to}\right)\left(1+r^{k}_{i}\right)^{t}\prod_{h}\left(\frac{R^{h}_{i,t}}{R^{h}_{i,to}}\right)^{\eta^{kh}}$<br>(2) Demand: $D^{k}_{i,t} = D^{k}_{i,0}\left(\frac{POP_{i,t}}{POP_{i,0}}\right)\left(\frac{Y_{i,t}}{Y_{i,0}}\right)^{\delta^{k}}\prod_{h}\left(\frac{P^{h}_{i,t}}{P^{h}_{i,0}}\right)^{\varepsilon^{kh}}\prod_{l}\left(\frac{S^{l}_{i,t}}{S^{l}_{i,0}}\right)^{\varepsilon^{kl}}$<br>$D^{k}_{i,0} = SC^{k}_{i,0} + RC^{k}_{i,0} + F^{k}_{i,0} + I^{k}_{i,0} + Z^{k}_{i,0}$<br>(3) Price transmissions: $NP^{k}_{t} = NP^{k}_{t0}\left(\frac{WP^{k}_{t}}{WP^{k}_{t0}}\right)^{b_j}\left(\frac{EXR_{t}}{EXR_{t0}}\right)$<br>$P^{k}_{i,t} = P^{k}_{i,t0}\left(1+\lambda^{k}_{i,t}\left(\frac{NP^{k}_{t}}{NP^{k}_{t0}}-1\right)\right)$<br>(4) Exogenous variables: $Y_{i,t} = \frac{GDP_{i,0}\left(1+GDPR_{i,t}\right)^{n}}{POP_{i,0}\left(1+POPR_{i,t}\right)^{n}}$<br>(5) Equilibrium: $\sum_{i} S^{k}_{i,t} - \sum_{i} D^{k}_{i,t} - \sum_{i} \Delta ST^{k}_{i,t} = \sum_{i} NT^{k}_{i,t}$ |
| Variables and parameters | S = supply, a = shift factor, r = autonomous growth, R = producer price, to = base period, t = period, k, h = product, i = region, and η = supply elasticity, D = demand, POP = population, Y = income (GDP per capita), P = market price, SL = livestock products supply, f, g = product, δ = income elasticity of demand, ε = price elasticity of demand, γ = feed elasticity of demand, RC = rural direct consumption, SC = urban direct consumption, F = feed use; I = manufactured use and waste, Z = seed use, NP = national price for product, WP= world market price, b = transmission elasticity from the world market to the national market. λ = transmission elasticity from the national to the regional market, POPR = population growth rate, GDPR = GDP growth rate, EXR = exchange rate; ΔST = stock change; NT = net trade. |

With this background, China is clearly a country where the population and economic growth will continue at a high rate in the next decade. Therefore, it is necessary for a reasonable estimation of its changes in the agricultural market's supply and demand for the medium- to long-term. That way, the effect of farmland loss because of high economic growth on the agricultural production capacity, the impacts of a growing population, and the increasing income on food demand—including its structural shift—can be considered. Moreover, the impact of changes in the world market on China's domestic market has to be taken into account. Based on this reflection, two scenarios are used to simulate grain market developments toward 2010 (Table 11.2).

**Table 11.2 Assumptions for the model simulation scenarios**

| Assumptions | Baseline scenario | Price scenario |
|---|---|---|
| 1) Annual growth rate of GDP = 7.5% | O | O |
| 2) RMB exchange rate unchanged | O | O |
| 3) 1% farmland decrease in 2006 against the base year 2002 | O | O |
| 4) 2% farmland decrease in 2010 against the base year 2002 | O | O |
| 5) 13% world market price increase in 2006 against the base year 2002[4] | | O |
| 6) 21% world market price increase in 2010 against the base year 2002 | | O |

In the following sections, the results of the model simulation in the two scenarios are presented for the Chinese grain market at national and regional level.[5] In order to show the projected changes against the base year, the real grain market situation in 2002 is also presented in the following tables.

[4] According to the World Bank (2003), the world market price for almost all products covered in this model is expected to strengthen over the projection period in nominal terms after a continuous fall from 1997 to 2001 and a strong recovery in 2002. Here the projected world price increase by 13% in 2006 and by 21% in 2010 against the base year is used as the expected world prices in this model simulation.

[5] Due to the structure and specialty of the model CARMEM, the above simulated outcome has included the demand and supply, price and other derivative information of all 18 kinds of agricultural products in China and its seven regions in 2006 and 2010. This essay just concerns the relevant information about grain supply and demand.

*3.1 Grain Total*

Since 1998, China has experienced a remarkably consistent decrease in grain production. Total production of the three primary grains—wheat, rice, and corn—has fallen from 442 million tons in 1998 to 386 million tons in 2002. The fall in China's grain harvest is largely due to the reduction of the harvested area—62 million ha in 1998 down to 54 million ha in 2002. Yields, after a long period of increasing, have stagnated since the late-1990s. Several trends are converging to reduce the grain area, including the conversion of cropland for non-farm uses, the shift to higher-value crops, and a decline in double-cropping due to the abolishment of the grain procurement quota policy (as started in 2001 in the more prosperous coastal provinces). It is assumed that these changes are lasting.

On the other hand, grain consumption in China is expanding. It reached 459 million tons in 2002. The rate of grain self-sufficiency diminished to 89 percent with a domestic deficit of 38 million tons of which 66, 22, and 12 percent are wheat, rice and corn, respectively. This implies that China's domestic grain supply in recent years has depended considerably on the utilization of the large stocks. Thus, China's grain imports could be limited to relatively small quantities.

As shown in Table 11.3, production of wheat, rice, and corn is forecast to rise from 386 million tons in 2002 to 400 million tons in 2006 and 421 million tons in 2010 in the baseline. Aggregate grain demand is projected to reach 444 million tons in 2006 and 477 million tons in 2010. The gap between projected production and consumption implies a rising deficit so that the rate of grain self-sufficiency will fall from 90.9 percent in 2002 to 89.9 percent in 2010. In the price scenario, grain production is projected to reach 408 million tons in 2006 and 429 million tons in 2010 so that the deficit will fall below the level reached in 2002, and the self-sufficiency rate will rise by about 1.5 percent. It is thus expected that grain production will recover in China if the domestic grain market is further integrated into the world market. The total production capability of rice, wheat, and corn will exceed 400 million tons in the next decade. This notwithstanding, a deficit of about 34 millions tons will have to be covered by importing from international markets.

Except for northeast China, all six other regions were in a deficit in 2002. This applies to the east, south, and southwest, in particular, where the self-sufficiency ratio was 86, 68, and 77 percent, respectively. According to projections, grain production in north and northeast China will grow faster than consumption in both scenarios, which would result in an increasing surplus in the northeast and a slightly higher self-sufficiency ratio in the north.

**Table 11.3 Chinese regional grain market situation in 2002 and 2010 (million tons)**

| | | | North China | Northeast | East China | Central South | South China | Southwest | Northwest | National |
|---|---|---|---|---|---|---|---|---|---|---|
| 2002 Basis | | P | 40.7 | 52.8 | 109.4 | 78.5 | 27.9 | 52.2 | 25.0 | 386.5 |
| | | C | 45.9 | 35.9 | 127.7 | 80.6 | 41.1 | 67.5 | 26.3 | 425.0 |
| | | B | -5.2 | 16.9 | -18.3 | -2.1 | -13.2 | -15.3 | -1.3 | -38.5 |
| | | SSR | 88.7 | 147.1 | 85.7 | 97.4 | 67.9 | 77.3 | 95.1 | 90.9 |
| Baseline scenario | 2006 | P | 42.8 | 55.3 | 112.3 | 81.1 | 28.7 | 54.1 | 25.9 | 400.2 |
| | | C | 48.3 | 37.5 | 133.0 | 84.1 | 42.9 | 70.6 | 27.6 | 444.0 |
| | | B | -5.5 | 17.8 | -20.7 | -3.0 | -14.2 | -16.5 | -1.7 | -43.8 |
| | | SSR | 88.6 | 147.5 | 84.4 | 96.4 | 66.9 | 76.6 | 93.8 | 90.1 |
| | 2010 | P | 45.1 | 57.9 | 115.2 | 83.9 | 29.6 | 56.0 | 26.6 | 414.3 |
| | | C | 50.4 | 39.1 | 137.8 | 87.3 | 44.3 | 73.5 | 28.6 | 461.0 |
| | | B | -5.3 | 18.8 | -22.6 | -3.4 | -14.7 | -17.5 | -2.0 | -46.7 |
| | | SSR | 89.5 | 148.1 | 83.6 | 96.1 | 66.8 | 76.2 | 93.0 | 89.9 |
| Price scenario | 2006 | P | 43.6 | 55.6 | 114.6 | 83.6 | 29.5 | 54.8 | 26.3 | 408.0 |
| | | C | 48.4 | 37.5 | 132.7 | 83.7 | 42.8 | 69.6 | 27.5 | 442.2 |
| | | B | -4.8 | 18.1 | -18.1 | -0.1 | -13.3 | -14.8 | -1.2 | -34.2 |
| | | SSR | 90.1 | 148.3 | 86.4 | 99.9 | 68.9 | 78.7 | 95.6 | 92.3 |
| | 2010 | P | 46.6 | 58.3 | 117.7 | 87.0 | 30.3 | 56.6 | 27.3 | 423.8 |
| | | C | 50.5 | 39.0 | 137.8 | 86.8 | 44.3 | 72.4 | 28.5 | 459.3 |
| | | B | -3.9 | 19.3 | -20.1 | 0.2 | -14.0 | -15.8 | -1.2 | -35.5 |
| | | SSR | 92.3 | 149.5 | 85.4 | 100.2 | 68.4 | 78.2 | 95.8 | 92.3 |

*Notes*: 1. P = production, C = consumption, B = production - consumption, SSR = self-sufficiency rate in %.
*Source*: Own calculations based on the model CARMEN

Only under the price scenario is production in southwest, central-south, and northwest China expected to increase more than consumption so that the central-south would nearly reach its grain self-sufficiency and the southwest and northwest would raise their rate of grain self-sufficiency slightly. In both scenarios, the current gap between supply and demand in east and south China is expected to widen until 2010. The regional differences in the grain markets will be further exacerbated if increasing labor migration from western to south-eastern provinces is taken into account.

### *3.2 Rice*

Rice is the most important grain crop in China, contributing more than 40 percent of the total grain output. China's rice production, however, had declined from 199 million tons in 1998 to 175 million tons in 2002. Total consumption in 2002 reached 188 million tons, thus a domestic deficit of 12.5 million tons emerged (Table 11.4). Traditionally, China had been self-sufficient in rice with only small imports and exports.

According to the baseline scenario, it is expected that China will produce 180 million tons paddy rice in 2006 and 186 million tons in 2010—with a growth of 2.9 and 6.3 percent, respectively, against the base year 2002—and consume 194 million tons in 2006 and 209 million tons in 2010. The higher growth in consumption will lead to a rice deficit of increasing to more than 13.5 million tons. In the price scenario, China's paddy rice production is forecast to increase to 184 million tons in 2006 and 190 million tons in 2010 while consumption will slightly rise to 191 million tons in 2006 and 196 million tons in 2010. As a result, an increase in the rice self-sufficiency ratio by about 3 percent is expected. The total domestic deficit, compared with the baseline, will fall to about the half of the base year 2002. This suggests that China still has a relatively stable potential for the production of rice despite contracting farmland.

Rice is the main grain crop in East China where more than one third of total Chinese rice output is grown. In this region, its own production has been lower than consumption since the late-1990s. The baseline projection shows that east China will have a limited growth in rice production but a rising deficit toward 2010. The self-sufficiency ratio is forecast to fall from 95.7 percent in 2002 to 94.2 percent in 2010. On the other hand, as the price scenario shows, it is expected that the growth in production will be higher than in consumption so that the projected rice price change in the world market could lead to a 3 percent increase of the rice self-sufficiency ratio in the region East China.

In 2002, north China had the largest rice deficit of all regions, but its consumption accounted for only 6 percent of the national demand. According to the model results, the future relation between rice production and demand in north China will be constant, and the self-sufficiency ratio will remain at 11 percent.

**Table 11.4 Chinese regional rice market situation in 2002 and 2010 (million tons)**

| | | | North China | Northeast | East China | Central South | South China | Southwest | Northwest | National |
|---|---|---|---|---|---|---|---|---|---|---|
| 2002 Basis | | P | 1.3 | 17.0 | 60.4 | 39.3 | 25.6 | 28.9 | 2.6 | 175.1 |
| | | C | 11.6 | 15.7 | 63.1 | 37.8 | 25.9 | 28.4 | 5.1 | 187.6 |
| | | B | -10.3 | 1.3 | -2.7 | 1.5 | -0.3 | 0.5 | -2.5 | -12.5 |
| | | SSR | 11.2 | 108.3 | 95.7 | 104.0 | 98.8 | 101.8 | 51.0 | 93.3 |
| Baseline scenario | 2006 | P | 1.3 | 17.7 | 61.7 | 40.6 | 26.4 | 29.9 | 2.7 | 180.3 |
| | | C | 12.1 | 16.2 | 65.0 | 38.9 | 26.8 | 29.4 | 5.3 | 193.7 |
| | | B | -10.8 | 1.5 | -3.3 | 1.7 | -0.4 | 0.5 | -2.6 | -13.4 |
| | | SSR | 10.7 | 109.3 | 94.9 | 104.4 | 98.5 | 101.7 | 50.9 | 93.1 |
| | 2010 | P | 1.4 | 18.4 | 62.9 | 42 | 27.2 | 31 | 2.7 | 185.6 |
| | | C | 12.5 | 16.7 | 66.8 | 40 | 27.6 | 30.3 | 5.4 | 199.3 |
| | | B | -11.1 | 1.7 | -3.9 | 2 | -0.4 | 0.7 | -2.7 | -13.7 |
| | | SSR | 11.2 | 110.2 | 94.2 | 105.0 | 98.6 | 102.3 | 50.0 | 93.1 |
| Price scenario | 2006 | P | 1.3 | 17.5 | 63.1 | 41.6 | 27 | 30.9 | 2.8 | 184.2 |
| | | C | 11.9 | 16.0 | 64.3 | 38.4 | 26.7 | 28.9 | 5.2 | 191.4 |
| | | B | -10.6 | 1.5 | -1.2 | 3.2 | 0.3 | 2 | -2.4 | -7.2 |
| | | SSR | 10.9 | 109.4 | 98.1 | 108.3 | 101.1 | 106.9 | 53.8 | 96.2 |
| | 2010 | P | 1.4 | 18.1 | 64.3 | 43.1 | 27.8 | 32.3 | 2.9 | 189.9 |
| | | C | 12.2 | 16.4 | 65.9 | 39.2 | 27.3 | 29.5 | 5.3 | 195.8 |
| | | B | -10.8 | 1.7 | -1.6 | 3.9 | 0.5 | 2.8 | -2.4 | -5.9 |
| | | SSR | 11.5 | 110.4 | 97.6 | 109.9 | 101.8 | 109.5 | 54.7 | 97.0 |

*Notes*: 1. P = production, C = consumption, B = production - consumption, SSR = self-sufficiency rate in %.
*Source*: Own calculations based on the model CARMEM

As China's rice surplus regions in 2002, the northeast, southwest, and central-south will expand their rice surpluses because of higher production growth under each of the two scenarios. The southwest and central-south regions, in particular, show a more sensitive supply response to price changes. South China—where supply and demand of rice is almost in balance—will realize a higher production growth and thereby achieve a rice surplus in the price scenario.

### *3.3 Wheat*

Because of a declining tendency since 1998, China's wheat production dropped to 90 million tons in 2002—about 27 percent lower than what it had been in 1997—but consumption was above 115 million tons in 2002. This resulted in a deficit of 25.4 million tons or 57 percent of the total domestic grain deficit in 2002. The model results show that wheat production will rise to 93.3 million tons in 2006 and 96.5 million tons in 2010 in the baseline scenario (Table 11.5), but the growth in production will be still lower than in consumption so that the expected domestic deficit will expand to more than 27 million tons. In the price scenario, changes in the wheat market will be small so that, more or less, the domestic deficit will stay where it was in the base period. This implies that wheat production and consumption in China will tend to be stable in the next years. The rate of self-sufficiency will keep at a low level. To cover the expected domestic shortage, China will take its place in the world wheat market as a large importer if abundant stocks are not available.

Central-south is the only region with a wheat surplus in China. The region is projected to have a significant growth of production under both scenarios. Its current 4.5 million tons of wheat surplus could be maintained in the baseline scenario. North China is expected to achieve a higher growth in production than in consumption, so that its current deficit will be reduced and the supply and demand will be almost in balance. Northeast, northwest, and east China will keep their own deficit level of the base year until 2010. In the Southwest, where the deficit amounts to 50 percent of the national wheat deficit in 2002, the rate of wheat self-sufficiency will keep its current level with 38 percent under two scenarios. Therefore, a production expansion in this region will be of importance for future domestic market stability in China. Wheat demand in south China is expected to expand from 7 million tons in 2002 to 7.6 million tons in 2010, but the supply has to be imported from other regions and the world market since regional wheat production is very small indeed.

**Table 11.5 Chinese regional wheat market situation in 2002 and 2010 (million tons)**

| | | | North China | Northeast | East China | Central South | South China | Southwest | Northwest | National |
|---|---|---|---|---|---|---|---|---|---|---|
| 2002 Basis | | P | 15.3 | 1.1 | 29.2 | 24.2 | 0.1 | 8.0 | 12.0 | 89.9 |
| | | C | 16.4 | 6.0 | 30.2 | 19.7 | 7.1 | 21.2 | 14.7 | 115.3 |
| | | B | -1.1 | -4.9 | -1.0 | 4.5 | -7.0 | -13.2 | -2.7 | -25.4 |
| | | SSR | 93.3 | 18.3 | 96.7 | 122.8 | 1.4 | 37.7 | 81.6 | 78.0 |
| Baseline scenario | 2006 | P | 16.2 | 1.2 | 30.1 | 25.0 | 0.1 | 8.3 | 12.4 | 93.3 |
| | | C | 17.1 | 6.2 | 31.5 | 20.5 | 7.5 | 22.1 | 15.4 | 120.3 |
| | | B | -0.9 | -5.0 | -1.4 | 4.5 | -7.4 | -13.8 | -3.0 | -27.0 |
| | | SSR | 94.7 | 19.4 | 95.6 | 122.0 | 1.3 | 37.6 | 80.5 | 77.6 |
| | 2010 | P | 17.1 | 1.2 | 31.0 | 25.8 | 0.1 | 8.5 | 12.8 | 96.5 |
| | | C | 17.7 | 6.5 | 32.6 | 21.3 | 7.7 | 23.0 | 15.9 | 124.7 |
| | | B | -0.6 | -5.3 | -1.6 | 4.5 | -7.6 | -14.5 | -3.1 | -28.2 |
| | | SSR | 96.6 | 18.5 | 95.1 | 121.1 | 1.3 | 37.0 | 80.5 | 77.4 |
| Price scenario | 2006 | P | 16.2 | 1.2 | 30.5 | 25.6 | 0.1 | 8.2 | 12.4 | 94.2 |
| | | C | 17.2 | 6.2 | 31.6 | 20.4 | 7.4 | 21.6 | 15.3 | 119.7 |
| | | B | -1.0 | -5.0 | -1.1 | 5.2 | -7.3 | -13.4 | -2.9 | -25.5 |
| | | SSR | 94.2 | 19.4 | 96.5 | 125.5 | 1.4 | 38.0 | 81.0 | 78.7 |
| | 2010 | P | 17.2 | 1.2 | 31.6 | 26.7 | 0.1 | 8.6 | 12.8 | 98.2 |
| | | C | 17.9 | 6.4 | 32.6 | 21.0 | 7.7 | 22.3 | 15.8 | 123.7 |
| | | B | -0.7 | -5.2 | -1.0 | 5.7 | -7.6 | -13.7 | -3.0 | -25.5 |
| | | SSR | 96.1 | 18.8 | 96.9 | 127.1 | 1.3 | 38.6 | 81.0 | 79.4 |

*Notes*: 1. P = production, C = consumption, B = production - consumption, SSR = self-sufficiency rate in %.
*Source*: Source: Own calculations based on the model CARMEM.

### 3.4 Corn

In 2002, China produced 121.5 million tons of corn and consumed 122.1 million tons, which was a well equilibrated market situation. Under the baseline scenario it is expected that total corn production will grow by 4 percent to over 126 million tons in 2006 and 9 percent to 132 million tons in 2010 while demand will expand by 6 percent to 130 million tons and 12 percent to 137 million tons, respectively. A domestic deficit of 1.5 million tons in 2006 and 4.2 million tons in 2010 will come up in the price scenario. Therefore, although China's corn production will achieve high growth rates, it will not be able to keep pace with the higher demand expansion. China will become a net importer of corn in the projection period mainly because of a parallel expansion in animal production.[6]

The existing regional pattern of the corn market in China, which is characterized by a surplus in the north and a deficit in the south, will not be changed much in the scenarios. Northeast, north, and northwest, which produced more than 70 percent of the national corn output in 2002, are projected to further increase production. Moreover, the projected growth in these three regions will be higher in the price scenario than in the baseline situation, which reveals the price impact on production. Because of a higher growth in consumption, future corn surplus in the northwest will keep at the current level. At same time, the impact of price factors on corn demand in the southern regions is very small. Existing corn deficit in the southern regions is expected to widen rapidly as demand is expanding faster than production. This especially applies to Southwest and East China.

## 4 Conclusions and Policy Implication

The model results for the Chinese grain market indicate that production could follow total consumption in the upcoming years. Total production of paddy rice, wheat, and corn will increase to more than 400 million tons. A recovery of the growth in grain production could be realized if the World Bank's projected world market prices are transmitted into the internal market. However, the growth in production will be still lower than in consumption. The self-sufficiency ratio will be 92 percent. The domestic deficit would amount to about 35 million tons, to be compared with 38.5 million tons in 2002 when China had huge grain stocks available.

[6] The model simulation results also showed that total animal production in China is expected to grow by 6% in 2006 and 11% in 2010 in the baseline, and by 8% in 2006 and 13% in 2010 under the price scenario.

**Table 11.6 Chinese regional corn market situation in 2002 and 2010 (million tons)**

| | | | North China | Northeast | East China | Central South | South China | Southwest | Northwest | National |
|---|---|---|---|---|---|---|---|---|---|---|
| 2002 Basis | | P | 24.1 | 34.7 | 19.8 | 15.0 | 2.2 | 15.3 | 10.4 | 121.5 |
| | | C | 17.9 | 14.2 | 34.4 | 23.1 | 8.1 | 17.9 | 6.5 | 122.1 |
| | | B | 6.2 | 20.5 | -14.6 | -8.1 | -5.9 | -2.6 | 3.9 | -0.6 |
| | | SSR | 134.6 | 244.4 | 57.6 | 64.9 | 27.2 | 85.5 | 160.0 | 99.5 |
| Baseline Scenario | 2006 | P | 25.3 | 36.4 | 20.5 | 15.5 | 2.2 | 15.9 | 10.8 | 126.6 |
| | | C | 19.1 | 15.1 | 36.5 | 24.7 | 8.6 | 19.1 | 6.9 | 130.0 |
| | | B | 6.2 | 21.3 | -16.0 | -9.2 | -6.4 | -3.2 | 3.9 | -3.4 |
| | | SSR | 132.5 | 241.1 | 56.2 | 62.8 | 25.6 | 83.2 | 156.5 | 97.4 |
| | 2010 | P | 26.6 | 38.3 | 21.3 | 16.1 | 2.3 | 16.5 | 11.1 | 132.2 |
| | | C | 20.2 | 15.9 | 38.4 | 26.0 | 9.0 | 20.2 | 7.3 | 137.0 |
| | | B | 6.4 | 22.4 | -17.1 | -9.9 | -6.7 | -3.7 | 3.8 | -4.8 |
| | | SSR | 131.7 | 240.9 | 55.5 | 61.9 | 25.6 | 81.7 | 152.1 | 96.5 |
| Price scenario | 2006 | P | 26.1 | 36.9 | 21.0 | 16.4 | 2.4 | 15.7 | 11.1 | 129.6 |
| | | C | 19.3 | 15.3 | 36.8 | 24.9 | 8.7 | 19.1 | 7.0 | 131.1 |
| | | B | 6.8 | 21.6 | -15.8 | -8.5 | -6.3 | -3.4 | 4.1 | -1.5 |
| | | SSR | 135.2 | 241.2 | 57.1 | 65.9 | 27.6 | 82.2 | 158.6 | 98.9 |
| | 2010 | P | 28.0 | 39.0 | 21.8 | 17.2 | 2.4 | 15.7 | 11.6 | 135.7 |
| | | C | 20.4 | 16.2 | 39.3 | 26.6 | 9.3 | 20.6 | 7.4 | 139.8 |
| | | B | 7.6 | 22.8 | -17.5 | -9.4 | -6.9 | -4.9 | 4.2 | -4.1 |
| | | SSR | 137.3 | 240.7 | 55.5 | 64.7 | 25.8 | 76.2 | 156.8 | 97.1 |

*Notes*: 1. P = production, C = consumption, B = production - consumption, SSR = self-sufficiency rate in %.
*Source*: Own calculations based on the model CARMEM.

China will become a net importer of corn. Three-fifths of the grain deficit, however, is from wheat. The expected changes in the Chinese grain market also possess some regional characteristics as far as the regional results are concerned. An increasing grain deficit in east and south China will emerge. Northeast and north China will achieve a higher production growth mainly due to a rapid increase in corn production. The central-south will be able to improve its supply situation. The southwest and northwest will maintain the level of their existing deficit. The model results imply that Chinese grain security will remain a serious challenge in the projection period.

From the preceding grain market analysis, the following five points may be derived as important components of future grain market policies in China:

1. Strengthen farmland protection through legislation and the introduction of land markets: Though the legal system for farmland protection in China has been improved, high-yielding farmland has still been converted to non-farm use by rapid urbanization and industrialization in recent years.[7] As the Chinese economy continues to grow at high rates, the assumption of 2 percent farmland loss toward 2010 in the model simulation is still quite moderate if a loss of farmland on a similar scale as in the last decade will be the result. To stop the loss of farmland, the government should take legal measures to keep farmland in agricultural production, and it should also establish a market system for farmland exchange in order to raise the efficiency of land use. This will be not only an important prerequisite for maintaining the future capacity of grain production growth but also a key challenge for agricultural reform in China.

2. Domestic regional grain market integration and free trade: The model results show that there is a significant regional difference within China's domestic grain market. The integration of the domestic market into international markets will contribute to considerably improving the grain supply. The target of grain self-sufficiency at the regional level should be abandoned. The government should remove the existing internal trade barriers and integrate the regional grain markets as fast as possible, in order to allow free grain trade among the regions in China. For this purpose, the government should encourage private traders to enter the market, especially in the surplus regions. On the other hand, China should adapt the regional structure and scale of the state grain stocks to the changing market situation especially in deficit regions to improve the effectiveness of grain market stabilization policies.

3. Full impact of price changes on production growth: The model results demonstrate a significant effect of price changes on grain supply and demand in China. In particular in times of production shortfalls there is obviously a conflict between short-term stabilization through releasing stocks and medium- to

[7] According to the official statistics of the Ministry of Land and Resources of China, farmland totalled 123.4 million hectares by the end of 2003, dropping 6.7 million hectares since 1996. Urban expansion, industrial construction, and highway construction are all shrinking the land available for crops.

long-term adjustments through the response of supply and demand to market signals. Government policies should allow the market enough scope for adjustment by way of less intervention and more reliance on the market solution.

4. Establishment of international cooperation for grain-supply security in China: It must be expected that China's self-sufficiency in grains will fall below 95 percent in this decade. Normally, China would be able to procure the imports to cover the domestic deficit. However, there may emerge certain circumstances—be it natural, political, or otherwise—that could prevent China from importing the required quantities of grains. Therefore, first deliberations could go in the direction to use the WTO import quotas as a favorable starting-point on which to build a strategic cooperation in grain trade with other countries.

5. Establishing a grain market modeling analysis system to support policy making: Future Chinese grain market developments will be more influenced by a wide range of factors, such as population, climate, ecology, policy and world markets, internal and external economic developments, and exchange rates. Reasonably estimating future trends of China's supply and demand of grain and creating timely policy measures for ensuring grain security is of momentous current as well as strategic significance for Chinese economic and social development. For this purpose, Chinese central and provincial administrations should establish market research services to monitor, analyze, and project market developments at both the national and regional level.

## References

Anderson, K., et al. 'Asia-Pacific Food Markets and Trade in 2005: A Global, economy-wide Perspective' (Paper commissioned for the International General Meeting of the Pacific Basin Economic Council, May 20-22, 1996, Washington, DC).

Brown, L., 'Who Will Feed China: Make Up Call for a Small Planet' (New York: W.W. Norton and Company Inc, 1995).

ERS/USDA, 'International Agricultural Baseline Projections to 2005' (ERS Staff Paper No 9612, Washington DC, 1996).

Fan, F. and Agcaoili-Sombilla, M., 'Why Do Projections on China's Food Supply and Demand Differ' (EPTD Discussion Paper No.22. IFPRI, Washington DC, 1997).

Food and Agricultural Organisation of the United Nations, Impact of Uraguay Round on Agriculture (Rome, 1995).

Huang, J.K., 'Past and Future of China's Agriculture', *Management World*, 3 (2004).

Kersten, L., 'Spatial and Regional Model Analyses of the World Grain Market' (Braunschweig: German Federal Agricultural Research Centre, IflM-Arbeitsbericht, 1997).

———, 'Annotated Illustrations to China's Future Role in the World Grain Market' (Braunschweig: German Federal Agricultural Research Centre, IflM-Arbeitsbericht, 1998).

OECF, Prospects Grain Supply-Demand and Agricultural Development Policy in China, (OECF Discussion Papers No 6, Overseas Economic Cooperation Fund, Tokyo, Japan,

1995).
Roningen, V., 'Multi-Market, Multi-Region Partial Equilibrium Modeling', in Francois J.F., Reinert K.A. (eds) *Applied Methods for trade Analysis* (Cambridge: Cambridge University Press, 1997).
Rosegrant, M., Agcaoili-Sombilla, M. and Perez, N., 'Global Food Projections to 2020: Implication for Investiment', (Discussion Paper No.5., IFPRI, Washington DC, 1995).
Sullivan, J., Roningen, V., Leetma, S. and Gray, D., 'A 1989 Global Database for the Static World Policy Simulation (SWOPSIM) Modeling Framework' (ERS-USDA Staff Report No. AGES 9215. Washington, DC, 1992).
Tyers, R., and Anderson, K., 'Disarray in World Food Markets: A Quantitative Assessment' (Cambridge: Cambridge University Press, 1992).
Tyers, R., 'Economic Reform in Europe and the Former Soviet Union: Implications for International Food Markets' (IFPRI. Research Report 99. Washington, DC, 1994).
World Bank, 'Global Economic Prospects: Realizing the Development Promise of the Doha Agenda' (Washington, DC, 1993).

## Chapter 12

# How Well will China Handle its Demand for Grain when it Peaks?

Guanzhong James Wen*

### 1 Introduction

This study is to investigate whether China can meet its growing demand for grain mainly by its own effort when its grain demand peaks in about two decades. Traditionally, China's grain pressure mainly came from its huge and fast growing population against limited arable land resources. To a large extent, this pressure was dampened by the stagnation in the growth of its per capita income. However, since the late 1970s, the rapid industrialization, urbanization, and the ensuing rising per capita income have been increasingly exposing China to a new challenge: an increasingly meat-oriented diet.

Scholars have opposing views on how to interpret this new trend. Some scholars are very pessimistic, believing it highly unlikely that China can feed its population on its own in the future (Brown 1994, 1995, 2001, 2004). In this view, as a result of the much accelerated urbanization and industrialization, China has already lost—and will continue to lose—much of its arable land at a time when China has almost exhausted the potential to further enhance its grain yields—experiencing water shortage and other severe environmental deterioration.

Having a large amount of foreign reserves, China will soon become a big grain importer and thus drive up world grain prices. Most grain-exporting nations will react by restricting grain export under the pressure of the domestic consumers, leading to further reduction in the amount of grain available in the world markets and sharper rise in grain prices, resulting in severe starvation in many developing

* The author wants to thank three anonymous reviewers for their valuable comments, the Washington Center for China Study for its financial support, the China Center of Economic Research at Peking University, and the Research Center for International Trade at the Chinese Academy of Agricultural Science. His thanks also go to Xiwen Chen, Mai Lu, Justin Yifu Lin, Guoqiang Cheng, Jikun Huang, Feng Lu, Guoqing Song, Shuming Bao, and Hsi-Huang Chen, the Chinese Association for Eurasian Studies in Taipei, and the East Asian Institute and the East Asian Library at Columbia University. Last but not least, the author wants to thank his research assistants S. Michel and M. Guo for the excellent jobs they did. He is solely responsible for the views expressed in this report and the possible remaining errors.

nations who cannot afford to import. Some scholars are so pessimistic that they even believe that the shortage of food will develop in China and will cause its eventual collapse (Goldstone, 1995). If such reasoning is valid, the stability and order will be lost not only in China, but also in its adjacent areas.

Many disagree with the pessimistic school. The most optimistic view can be found in a research report conducted by the Chinese Academy of Sciences (1985). The other scholars are also optimistic, although to a less extent (Johnson, 1996; Lin, 1996; Huang and Rozelle, 1998; Mei, 1998). To everyone's surprise, China has enjoyed rapid growth in grain production since 1995. Its grain output peaked in 1998, reaching 508.39 million tons. The grain price dropped as a result of the excess supply. Farmers experienced increasing difficulty in selling their grain and gradually cut sown areas. As a result, grain output declined every year since 1999. By 2003, China's grain output dropped to 430 million tons, representing a reduction of 21.4 percent compared with that of 1995—the year when Brown alarmed the world that China would cause a grain crisis worldwide. This slide in grain production has rekindled the debate on China's capacity to feed its population in the long-run, and the government started to push farmers to produce more grain again. It is yet to see whether China will repeat the mistake committed in the late 1990s when overproduction significantly reduced the grain prices, worsening the income disparity between urban and rural areas.

This study uses a method different from the conventional one since what concerns people most is not the exact year-to-year gap between the supply and demand but whether China can feed itself when its population peak and high per capita income occur simultaneously. Hence, this study aims to find out whether or not China can handle the grain gap when it peaks. Our main results support the findings reached by many earlier studies such as Johnson (1996), Lin (1996), Huang and Rozelle (1998), and Mei (1998). Because the results of this report are obtained by a different method, they provide a strong corroboration to the earlier results.

In what follows, Section 2 discusses data and methodology. Section 3 aims to find out the time when China's demand for grain peaks. Section 4 assesses China's future potential in grain supply. Section 5 reports the main findings, and section 6 concludes the chapter.

## 2 Data and Methodology

### *2.1 The Required Supply-side Data if Using the Conventional Method*

A few words about why we use a different method: the conventional method estimates future supply by calculating various elasticities of supply with respect to prices of inputs and output, and with respect to the quantity of inputs. Therefore, one needs data on water resources, science and technology, labor, capital, land, technology, and government policies respectively. However, these data are often inaccurate or unavailable.

First, although the Statistic Yearbook of China (SYOC) provides irrigated areas each year at the provincial level, it does not provide data about how much water each province actually uses every year or to what extent China has been wasting its water. Second, data about technical progress are incomplete too. Currently, the SYOC only provides some scattering data about the financial expenditures on technology research and extension by the government. Third, it is unclear how many rural laborers are really engaged in grain production and at what speed they will leave the farming sector. Fourth, data on China's arable land is also a mystery. According to the SYOC, China has about 1.5 billion *mu* of arable land. However, on May 3, 1998, the Xinhua News Agency reported that the actual acreage of China's arable land is 1.95 billion *mu*—a 30 percent increase over the old figure (Lindert, 1998). While this new revelation of land acreage is useful, it does not tell us how the underreported acreage is distributed across provinces; what type of land has been underreported; and how the acreage of this type of land has changed over the years. Among the conventional inputs, only the data on capital is most easily available. Fifth, almost all the factor prices are incomplete, despite the fact that they are indispensable if using the conventional method. For example, in the absence of a real rental market for rural land, it is hard to estimate land price. Interest rates in China are still largely determined by the government rather than the capital market. Therefore, the interest rate does not reflect the true opportunity cost of capital. To predict the future output prices for the next 40 or 50 years is another thorny issue. Last but not least is the government factor. As Johnson (1996) points out, this factor may be the most difficult to predict. Since the implementation of the household responsibility system (HRS), the government policies have been wavering between the old planning practice and the new market-oriented approach. Every time, changes in policy orientation have always exerted a dramatic impact on grain production and consumption.

### *2.2 The Required Demand-side Data if Using Conventional Method*

In projecting China's future demand for grain, one conventionally needs to estimate the price and income elasticities separately for urban and rural areas before one can forecast the direct demand for food grain and indirect demand for feed grain from the urban and rural population in response to price and per capita income changes. However, it could be problematic to predict price changes of meat and grain over time. The data required by estimating income elasticity of demand for meat are also unavailable. For example, the 1996 per capita income measured in 1985 constant price was 2.44 times that of 1985 (Table 12.1). However, during the same period, the per capita meat consumption almost remains constant (Table 12.2). Obviously, we could very likely underestimate the future demand for meat if using the elasticities that are based on such data.

Another problem in using the conventional method is the difficulty in predicting how fast industrialization and urbanization will take place in China, and how the urban and rural shares in total income changes over time. Since it is almost impossible to foretell such trends, using past elasticities to forecast the future could be risky.

Data on feed are also problematic. As Lu (1998) points out, we do not even know how much pork and other types of meat China produces or consumes each year. China's meat production has been increasing at a much faster pace than its meat consumption, according to the SYOC (Table 12.3), especially for the past several years. [1] It is unclear if this reportedly widening surplus is real or not, but it is resulting in wild speculation about the feed-meat conversion ratio. Some estimates are as high as 6. Others are less than 2 (Xiao, 1996).

*2.3 Alternative Method*

Based on discussions above, we can see that it could be problematic to use the conventional method to project the future demand for—and supply of—grain. This is why I decided to use an alternative method and only focus on the period when China's grain pressure peaks, a period that worries most people. This method first simulates China's future demand for grain by using data from Taiwan and then estimates China's future supply based on an estimated average growth rate of the grain supply from 1985 through 1996. Four assumptions are made to avoid overestimating China's supply capability and thus underestimating its demand for grain. This method and the four assumptions permit me to significantly reduce the amount of data required otherwise by the conventional method without weakening the results.

The four assumptions include: (1) starting from 2020 everyone in China, urban or rural, will have a per capita GDP of $5,000 measured in the 1985 constant price; (2) everyone in China will adopt a diet similar to what we observe in Taiwan today; (3) starting from 2000 on, each province produces grain at a gradually reduced growth rate; and (4) in our central case, the grain-meat conversion ratio is 3 for China.

[1] The total meat consumption is the sum of the total meat consumption in urban and rural areas, i.e., the sum of the products of per capita meat consumption (Table 12.2) time population in urban and rural areas respectively.

**Table 12.1 Per capita GDP and per capita real GDP**

| Year | Total Population (10000) | Per Capita GDP | Urban Per Capita Consumption | Rural Per Capita Consumption | GDP Index[1] | Urban per capita consumption index[1] | Rural per capita consumption index[1] | GDP Index[2] | Real GDP[2] | Real per capita GDP |
|---|---|---|---|---|---|---|---|---|---|---|
| 1985 | 105851 | 846.9 | 802 | 347 | 192.9 | 147.5 | 194.4 | 100 | 8964.4 | 846.9 |
| 1986 | 107507 | 949.0 | 920 | 376 | 210.2 | 183.6 | 194.6 | 109.0 | 9768.4 | 908.7 |
| 1987 | 109300 | 1094.5 | 1089 | 417 | 234.3 | 172.0 | 207.9 | 121.5 | 10888.3 | 996.2 |
| 1988 | 111026 | 1344.6 | 1431 | 508 | 260.7 | 187.3 | 220.4 | 135.1 | 12115.2 | 1091.2 |
| 1989 | 112704 | 1500.3 | 1568 | 553 | 271.3 | 184.4 | 218.8 | 140.6 | 12607.8 | 1118.7 |
| 1990 | 114333 | 1622.3 | 1686 | 571 | 281.7 | 198.1 | 219.5 | 146.0 | 13091.1 | 1145.0 |
| 1991 | 115823 | 1866.5 | 1925 | 621 | 307.6 | 216.6 | 234.2 | 159.5 | 14294.7 | 1234.2 |
| 1992 | 117171 | 2273.4 | 2356 | 718 | 351.4 | 249.9 | 257.2 | 182.2 | 16330.2 | 1393.7 |
| 1993 | 118517 | 2922.3 | 3027 | 855 | 398.8 | 272.1 | 272.8 | 206.7 | 18532.9 | 1563.7 |
| 1994 | 119850 | 3901.5 | 3979 | 1138 | 449.3 | 283.3 | 290.6 | 232.9 | 20879.8 | 1742.2 |
| 1995 | 121121 | 4828.1 | 5044 | 1479 | 496.5 | 300.0 | 318.6 | 257.4 | 23073.2 | 1905.0 |
| 1996 | 122389 | 5604.6 | 5620 | 1756 | 544.2 | 307.5 | 349.5 | 282.1 | 25289.9 | 2066.4 |

*Notes*: 1. 1978=100; 2. In 1985 constant prices.

*Source*: All the data are adopted from SYOC of various years (1986-1997) unless indicated otherwise.

**Table 12.2 Direct and indirect per capita grain consumption (Unit: kg)**

| Year | Rural per capita grain consumptn | Urban per capita grain consumptn | Rural per capita meat consumptn | Urban per capita meat consumptn | Rural per capita poultry consmptn | Urban per capita poultry Consmptn | Rural per capita aquatic product consmptn | Urban per capita aquatic product consmptn | Rural per capita egg consmptn | Urban per capita egg consmptn | Rural per capita oil consmptn | Urban per capita oil consmptn |
|---|---|---|---|---|---|---|---|---|---|---|---|---|
| 1985 | 257 | 134.8 | 11.0 | 18.7 | 1.1 | 3.2 | 1.64 | 7.08 | 2.05 | 6.84 | 4.04 | 5.76 |
| 1986 | 259 | 137.9 | 11.8 | 21.6 | 1.1 | 3.7 | 1.87 | 8.16 | 2.08 | 7.08 | 4.19 | 6.24 |
| 1987 | 259 | 133.9 | 11.7 | 21.9 | 1.2 | 3.4 | 1.96 | 7.88 | 2.25 | 6.56 | 4.69 | 6.45 |
| 1988 | 260 | 137.2 | 10.7 | 19.8 | 1.3 | 4.0 | 1.91 | 7.07 | 2.28 | 6.87 | 4.76 | 6.69 |
| 1989 | 262 | 133.9 | 11.0 | 20.3 | 1.3 | 3.7 | 2.10 | 7.61 | 2.41 | 7.05 | 4.81 | 6.16 |
| 1990 | 262 | 130.7 | 11.3 | 21.7 | 1.3 | 3.4 | 2.13 | 7.69 | 2.41 | 7.25 | 5.17 | 6.40 |
| 1991 | 256 | 127.9 | 12.2 | 22.2 | 1.3 | 4.4 | 2.21 | 8.02 | 2.73 | 8.26 | 5.65 | 6.93 |
| 1992 | 251 | 111.5 | 11.8 | 21.4 | 1.5 | 5.1 | 2.25 | 8.19 | 2.85 | 9.45 | 5.85 | 6.65 |
| 1993 | 266 | 97.8 | 11.7 | 20.8 | 1.6 | 3.7 | 2.47 | 8.02 | 2.88 | 8.86 | 5.66 | 7.14 |
| 1994 | 257 | 102.0 | 11.0 | 20.2 | 1.6 | 4.1 | 2.68 | 8.53 | 3.03 | 9.68 | 5.66 | 7.53 |
| 1995 | 258.9 | 97.0 | 11.3 | 19.7 | 1.8 | 4.0 | 3.06 | 9.20 | 3.22 | 9.74 | 5.8 | 7.11 |
| 1996 | 256.2 | 94.7 | 12.9 | 20.4 | 1.9 | 5.4 | 3.37 | 9.25 | 3.35 | 9.64 | 6.07 | 7.13 |

*Source*: All the data are adopted from SYOC of various years (1986-1997) unless indicated otherwise.

**Table 12.3 Historical meat output**

| Year | Total Meat Output (10,000 tons) | Pork (10,000 tons) | Beef (10,000 tons) | Lamb (10,000 tons) | Poultry (10,000 tons) | Eggs (10,000 tons) | Aquatic Product (1,000 tons) | Cultivated Aquatic Output: Seafood (1,000 tons) | Cultivated Aquatic Output: Freshwater (1,000 tons) |
|---|---|---|---|---|---|---|---|---|---|
| 1985 | 1921 | 1655 | 47 | 59 | 160 | 535 | 7051.5 | 712.3 | 2377.7 |
| 1986 | 2105 | 1796 | 59 | 62 | 188 | 555 | 8236.0 | 858.0 | 2944.0 |
| 1987 | 2205 | 1835 | 79 | 72 | 219 | 590 | 9554.0 | 1100.0 | 3472.0 |
| 1988 | 2468 | 2018 | 96 | 80 | 274 | 696 | 10609.0 | 1424.0 | 3898.0 |
| 1989 | 2608 | 2123 | 107 | 96 | 282 | 720 | 11517.0 | 1576.0 | 4170.0 |
| 1990 | 2837 | 2281 | 126 | 107 | 323 | 795 | 12370.0 | 1624.0 | 4454.0 |
| 1991 | 3119 | 2452 | 154 | 118 | 395 | 922 | 13508.0 | 1905.0 | 4592.0 |
| 1992 | 3394 | 2635 | 180 | 125 | 454 | 1020 | 15571.0 | 2424.0 | 5334.0 |
| 1993 | 3499 | 2854 | 234 | 137 | 274 | 1180 | 18230.0 | 3087.0 | 6441.1 |
| 1994 | 4388 | 3205 | 327 | 101 | 755 | 1479 | 21431.3 | 3456.7 | 7850.4 |
| 1995 | 5200 | 3648 | 415 | 202 | 935 | 1677 | 25171.8 | 4123.0 | 9407.6 |
| 1996 | 5848 | 4038 | 495 | 240 | 1075 | 1954 | 32880.9 | 7639.0 | 10989.5 |

*Source*: All the data are adopted from SYOC of various years (1986-1997) unless indicated otherwise.

**Table 12.4 The total supply of grain and total demand for food grain (1985-96)**

| Year | Import (10,000 tons) | Export (10,000 tons) | Net Export (10,000tons) | Total Grain Consumption (10,000tons) | Total Grain Outpout (10,000tons) | Other Use (10,000tons)[1] | Rural Grain Consumption (10,000tons)[2] | Urban Grain Consumption (10,000tons)[3] |
|---|---|---|---|---|---|---|---|---|
| 1985 | 773 | 942 | 169 | 24584.8 | 37911 | 4549.32 | 21695.86 | 2888.939 |
| 1986 | 1533 | 717 | -816 | 25119.59 | 39151 | 4698.12 | 22016.87 | 3102.722 |
| 1987 | 1628 | 737 | -891 | 25360.23 | 40298 | 4835.76 | 22204.36 | 3155.875 |
| 1988 | 1045 | 357 | -688 | 25514.25 | 39408 | 4728.96 | 21768.6 | 3745.642 |
| 1989 | 1658 | 656 | -1002 | 26342.22 | 40755 | 4890.6 | 23011.72 | 3330.495 |
| 1990 | 1345 | 1086 | -259 | 26706.53 | 44624 | 5354.88 | 23472.66 | 3233.871 |
| 1991 | 1175 | 1364 | 189 | 26410.03 | 43529 | 5223.48 | 23174.43 | 3235.602 |
| 1992 | 920 | 1346 | 426 | 25780.33 | 44266 | 5311.92 | 22879.25 | 2901.074 |
| 1993 | 1372 | 583 | -789 | 26953.26 | 45649 | 5477.88 | 24294.71 | 2658.546 |
| 1994 | 752 | 1535 | 783 | 26411.23 | 44510 | 5341.2 | 23522.18 | 2889.048 |
| 1995 | 2081 | 214 | -1867 | 26590.85 | 46662 | 5599.44 | 23734.55 | 2856.301 |
| 1996 | 1200 | 144 | -1056 | 26438.71 | 50454 | 6054.48 | 23555.29 | 2883.426 |

*Notes:*

1: Industrial use + storage + seed.

2: Rural per capita grain consumption times rural population.

3: Urban per capita grain consumption times urban population.

*Source*: All the data are adopted from SYOC of various years (1986-1997) unless indicated otherwise.

Some explanations about the rationale of these assumptions are in order. The reason for the first assumption is based on a couple of considerations. As Column 8 in Table 12.10 shows, 2020 is the first year when the per capita income is approaching $5000. However, no one can know exactly how the population will distribute in urban and rural areas respectively over time or how their per capita income will change accordingly. The first assumption simplifies this situation.

The second assumption can help us avoid discussing tough questions, like how urban and rural diets evolve and what kind of diet will eventually prevail in the years to come. Such information should be contained in Taiwan's diet. As a typical Chinese society, Taiwan shares the same ethic, cultural, and diet background of the mainland China.[2] In addition, demand for food is very different from demand for luxury goods. As one's stomach is satiated, increase in income will not lead to significant increase in food consumption. Therefore, using data from Taiwan can greatly simplify our task. In Table 12.5, we can see that Taiwan's diet is a matured one with only minor changes at the margin. We will certainly not underestimate the mainland China's grain demand when using a diet that emerged at a per capita GNP of $10,000 or more for a society with a per capita GDP of only $5,000 or below.[3]

The third assumption is to avoid being criticized for overestimating China's grain production potential. China is still benefiting from technical progress and the restructuring product mix based on regional comparative advantages. However, to reflect the concerns about its environmental deterioration and severe water shortage, we assume that China's growth rate will decline over time.

[2] The main component of its population is from southern Fujian province. However, those who moved to Taiwan after 1949 came from every part of China, and have influenced the local diet profoundly, as evidenced by the fact that one can easily find almost all types of cuisine originated in mainland China. Since 1992 Taiwan's per capita GNP has been more than $10,000 measured in 1985 constant price. Taiwan's diet has also evolved into heavily meat-oriented (Table 12.5). As a result, the diet of a typical rural resident becomes very similar to that of a typical urban resident, as what we usually observe in highly developed nations. Both the urban and rural residents in Taiwan consume almost the same amount of meat, seafood and dairy products (Table 12.6).

[3] Readers may want to compare the diet that is reported by SYOC of 2001 (Table 10-8 and 10-23) with that of Taiwan. In 2000, a typical urban resident in mainland China consumes 82.31 kg grain, 16.73 kg pork, 3.33 kg beef and lamb, 5.44 kg poultry, 11.21 kg eggs, 9.87 kg aquatic products. In the same year, a typical rural resident in mainland China consumes 249.49 kg grain, 14.63 kg pork, beef and lamb, 2.85 kg poultry, 4.97 kg eggs, 3.92 kg aquatic products. Obvious, Taiwan diet (Table 12.6) is much more meat-oriented, and urban diet in mainland China is more meat-oriented than that of rural areas. By using Taiwan diet to simulate mainland diet and ignoring the difference between urban and rural, this study obviously will not underestimate China's demand for grain when its population peaks.

**Table 12.5 Taiwan's per capita GNP and per capita food consumption in 1987-1996**

| Year | GNP Growth rate | Per Capita GNP | Per Capita Pork Consmptn (kg) | Per Capita Grain Consumption (kg) | Per Capita Meat Consumptn (kg) | Per Capita Poultry Consmptn (kg) | Per Capita Milk Consmptn (kg) | Per Capita Aquatic Product Consmptn (kg) | Per Capita Egg Consmptn (kg) | Per Capita Oil Consmptn (kg) |
|---|---|---|---|---|---|---|---|---|---|---|
| 1987 | 111.9 | 5275 | 36.3 | 110.8 | 58.9 | 20.0 | 11.5 | 42.27 | 11.25 | 18.73 |
| 1988 | 107.8 | 6333 | 35.3 | 109.8 | 59.2 | 20.8 | 13.1 | 41.35 | 10.71 | 19.38 |
| 1989 | 108.0 | 7626 | 35.8 | 105.8 | 61.3 | 22.4 | 13.8 | 45.49 | 11.71 | 21.94 |
| 1990 | 105.5 | 8111 | 37.2 | 102.5 | 62.9 | 22.7 | 14.9 | 47.48 | 12.13 | 23.34 |
| 1991 | 107.6 | 8982 | 38.3 | 99.8 | 64.5 | 22.7 | 17.1 | 39.72 | 13.35 | 22.86 |
| 1992 | 106.2 | 10470 | 38.8 | 100.7 | 67.2 | 24.8 | 18.3 | 43.95 | 13.72 | 23.55 |
| 1993 | 106.0 | 10852 | 39.7 | 99.6 | 70.3 | 27.1 | 20.2 | 47.46 | 14.21 | 24.91 |
| 1994 | 106.1 | 11597 | 40.4 | 102.0 | 72.4 | 27.8 | 21.3 | 38.37 | 14.89 | 25.92 |
| 1995 | 105.9 | 12396 | 39.8 | 100.7 | 72.8 | 28.8 | 23.0 | 38.35 | 16.23 | 26.28 |
| 1996 | 105.4 | 12872 | 40.6 | 97.4 | 75.0 | 30.5 | 22.8 | 38.52 | 17.57 | 25.71 |

*Source*: Agricultural Planning and Development Committee, Taiwan, "Food Balance Table," 1987–1996.

**Table 12.6 Taiwan's urban and rural per capita grain and meat consumption (kg)**

| 1981 | | Grain | | | | |
|---|---|---|---|---|---|---|
| | Total | Rice | Wheat | Meat | Aquatic Product | Fruits |
| City | 115.5 | 86.9 | 28.6 | 46.8 | 42.9 | 105.5 |
| Town | 122.5 | 100.6 | 21.9 | 39.6 | 34 | 75.9 |
| Rural | 132.3 | 114.4 | 17.9 | 32 | 28.3 | 52.7 |
| Average | 122.8 | 99.4 | 23.4 | 40.1 | 35.8 | 80.5 |
| 1991 | | Grain | | | | |
| | Total | Rice | Wheat | Meat | Aquatic Product | Fruits |
| City | 96.5 | 61.1 | 35.4 | 70 | 45.5 | 122.3 |
| Town | 96 | 68.3 | 27.7 | 60.3 | 37.5 | 98.3 |
| Rural | 97.4 | 79 | 18.4 | 56.2 | 35.6 | 92.5 |
| Average | 96.5 | 67.6 | 28.9 | 63.5 | 40.4 | 107.2 |

*Sources*: Huang and Rozelle, *China's Grain Economy to the Twenty-first* Century, Beiing, China: The Chinese Agricultural Press, 1998, p.175 Table 10-1, p.176, Table 10-2.

The fourth assumption is based on international comparison. The typical conversion ratio that the U. S. Department of Agriculture (USDA) and elsewhere have adopted is 3.5 or 4. According to a recent report (Zhang 1998), the Center for Agricultural Research at the Ministry of Agriculture of China conducted a survey on 3,864 ordinary farming households and 120 households specializing in raising hogs (Table 12.7). This survey covered the following seven provinces: Jilin, Shandong, Jiangsu, Sichuan, Guangdong, Hunan, and Shaanxi. These provinces can be used to represent China's seven geographical regions, which would be northeast, north, east, southwest, south, central, and northwest China, respectively. Since the survey gives us the conversion ratios observed at the specialized households and non-specialized households in each of the reported provinces, we calculate the weighted average of the conversion ratio for each province, using the number of specialized households and that of non-specialized households as weights. Then we calculate the share of each of the seven provinces in the total meat production, using these shares as weights to obtain the national average conversion ratio. The result thus obtained is 2.31. We use this figure in our low case, 3 in our central case and 4 in our high case.[4]

**Table 12.7 Grain/meat conversion ratio**

| | Representative Provinces | Specialized Households | Non-Specialized Households |
|---|---|---|---|
| 1 | Shandong (North) | 2.14 | 3.11 |
| 2 | Jilin (Northeast) | 3.4 | 3.01 |
| 3 | Jiangsu (East) | 1.21 | 2.16 |
| 4 | Hunan (Central China) | 2.12 | 2.4 |
| 5 | Guangdong (South) | 2.03 | 1.36 |
| 6 | Sichuan (Southwest) | 1.14 | 1.79 |
| 7 | Shaanxi (Northwest) | 2.47 | 2.36 |

*Source*: Zhang (1998).

In Table 12.7, we can see that among the seven representative provinces, the specialized households in four provinces have a lower conversion ratio than their non-specialized counterparts (Shandong, Jiangsu, Sichuan, and Shaanxi, especially the former three). We also can see that in the remaining three provinces, the reverse is true. In Table 12.8, we find that these three provinces are, in fact, not important in meat production, judging by their shares in the total meat output. This implies that when the output produced by the specialized household becomes the main source of China's total meat output, the conversion ratio will not see a sudden jump as expected. Hence, using 3 as the conversion ratio in our central case is well-grounded.

In summary, among the four assumptions, three discuss future demand and are intentionally biased upward. The last assumption relates to the future supply and is intentionally biased downward. As shown in Sections 3 and 4, all the four assumptions are either based on direct estimates or relevant information. Therefore, one can justify these assumptions.

[4] An anonymous reviewer correctly pointed out that the amazingly low conversion ratio observed in China indicates that the actual amount of feed used in meat production might have been underestimated. While fully agreeing on this view, I would like to point out the following. Feed includes grain feed and non-grain feed. Compared with the grain/meat conversion ratio of 3.5 or 4 used by USDA, it is reasonable to use 3 as a proxy in China's context, given the fact that Chinese farmers use a lot more of non-conventional and often non-grain feed such as various types of vegetables, weeds, by-products from food processing, food leftovers from restaurants and family kitchens to feed hogs, thus can lower significantly China's grain/meat conversion ratio.

**Table 12.8 Provincial pork outputs and their national shares (Unit: 10,000 tons)**

| Province | 1995 | 1996 | Total | Share |
|---|---|---|---|---|
| Beijing | 23.9 | 24.6 | 48.5 | 0.006 |
| Tianjin | 12.2 | 13.1 | 25.3 | 0.003 |
| Hebei | 187.4 | 207.7 | 395.1 | 0.053 |
| Shanxi | 43.4 | 50.4 | 93.8 | 0.012 |
| Inner Mongolia | 47.7 | 59.1 | 106.8 | 0.014 |
| Liaoning | 141.6 | 152.9 | 294.5 | 0.039 |
| Jilin | 77.3 | 102.5 | 179.8 | 0.024 |
| Heilongjiang | 80.1 | 97.4 | 177.5 | 0.024 |
| Shanghai | 23.9 | 25 | 48.9 | 0.007 |
| Jiangsu | 195.9 | 201.4 | 397.3 | 0.053 |
| Zhejiang | 100 | 98 | 198 | 0.026 |
| Anhui | 136.7 | 157.5 | 294.2 | 0.039 |
| Fujian | 102.8 | 113.6 | 216.4 | 0.029 |
| Jiangxi | 188.5 | 189.6 | 378.1 | 0.05 |
| Shandong | 267.7 | 306.2 | 573.9 | 0.076 |
| Henan | 210.4 | 270.1 | 480.5 | 0.064 |
| Hubei | 239.6 | 261.1 | 500.7 | 0.067 |
| Hunan | 310.1 | 353.6 | 663.7 | 0.088 |
| Guangdong | 188.8 | 203.3 | 392.1 | 0.052 |
| Guangxi | 195.7 | 229.5 | 425.2 | 0.057 |
| Hainan | 18.4 | 19.1 | 37.5 | 0.005 |
| Sichuan | 526.3 | 547.3 | 1073.6 | 0.143 |
| Guizhou | 93.2 | 95.3 | 188.5 | 0.025 |
| Yunnan | 111.6 | 124.9 | 236.5 | 0.032 |
| Xizang | 0.6 | 0.7 | 1.3 | 0 |
| Shaanxi | 60.2 | 63.4 | 123.6 | 0.016 |
| Gansu | 44.3 | 47.4 | 91.7 | 0.012 |
| Qinghai | 5.6 | 5.8 | 11.4 | 0.002 |
| Ningxia | 6.3 | 6.6 | 12.9 | 0.002 |
| Xinjiang | 8.4 | 10.4 | 18.8 | 0.003 |

*Source*: The Agricultural Statistical Yearbook of China (1997), Table 6-43, p. 209.

## 3 The Time When China's Grain Demand Peaks

### *3.1 The Time when China reaches a Per Capita GDP of $5,000*

As mentioned above, the worst scenario that China may face is when its population peaks with a per capita income level of $5,000, an income level at which the population is assumed to adopt a diet that is similar to that of Taiwan today. Therefore, we have to first find out the approximate time when China's per capita income reaches this level.

Based on a report entitled "An Analysis of the Characteristics of the Various Stages of China's Future Economic Development and its Choices of Pillar Industries" (Qi et al 1997),[5] we can divide the entire period between 1996 and 2050 into three sub-periods. They are: 1996 to 2010; 2011 to 2030; and 2031 to 2050, respectively. During each of these three sub-periods, I assume that China's GDP growth rates will take high, medium, and low values. In the first sub-period, the high, medium, and low rates are 9.5, 8.5, and 7.5 percent, respectively. During the second sub-period, the three growth rates are 7.5, 6.5, and 5.5 percent, respectively. The three rates in the third sub-period are 6, 5, and 3.5 percent, respectively. Using these growth rates, we can project China's future GDP. The results are reported in Table 12.9. There are doubts on whether these growth rates are too high, but here is a reason to not revise these results downward. If the final results show that China can handle the grain gap under possible upwardly biased assumptions on the growth of income, it will reinforce the validity of the results.

### *3.2 The Time when China's Population Peaks*

Now consider when China's population may peak, which is another important factor that will affect how well China can deal with the maximum grain pressure. According to the summary volume of "The Population of China Towards the 21st Century" (Sun 1994), a 33-volume collection, there are three possible scenarios for China's population growth. In the high case, the overall birth rate for the nation as a whole will maintain at 1990's rate of 2.25 through 2050. In the medium case, the overall birth rate will decline from 1991's 2.04 to 1.89 in 2000, rise to 2 in the year 2010, and then maintain this rate through 2050. In the low case, the overall birth rate will first decline from 1991's 2.04 to 1.76 in 2000 and then maintain this level through 2050. Table 12.9 reports these three cases. Their size and timing population peaks are 1.601 billion in 2040 in high case, 1.502 billion in 2035 in the medium case, and 1.403 billion in 2025 in the low case.

---

[5] This research report is conducted jointly by the Research Center for Development at the State Council of China, the Institute of Mathematical and Technical Economic Research at the Chinese Academy of Social Sciences, and the People's University of China.

**Table 12.9 China's projected future GDP and population**

| Year | High Case GDP [1] (RMB) | Medium Case GDP (RMB) | Low Case GDP (RMB) | High Case GDP (US$)[2] | Medium Case GDP (US$) | Low Case GDP (US$) | High Case Population[3] | Medium Case Population | Low Case Population |
|---|---|---|---|---|---|---|---|---|---|
| 2000 | 36322.7 | 34694.2 | 33124.6 | 12354.7 | 11800.7 | 11266.9 | 1303 | 1282 | 1276 |
| 2005 | 57180.6 | 52168.1 | 47554.6 | 19449.2 | 17744.3 | 16175.0 | 1364 | 1328 | 1314 |
| 2010 | 90016.0 | 78443.0 | 68270.8 | 30617.7 | 26681.3 | 23221.4 | 1419 | 1373 | 1347 |
| 2015 | 129229.6 | 107473.6 | 89227.2 | 43955.6 | 36555.7 | 30349.4 | 1474 | 1419 | 1378 |
| 2020 | 185525.8 | 147248.2 | 116616.3 | 63104.0 | 50084.4 | 39665.4 | 1526 | 1460 | 1400 |
| 2025 | 266346.3 | 201742.8 | [illegible] | 90594.0 | 68620.0 | 51841.1 | 1563 | 1488 | 1403 |
| 2030 | 382374.5 | 276405.1 | [illegible] | 130059.3 | 94015.4 | 67754.3 | 1585 | 1500 | 1391 |
| 2035 | 511703.3 | 352770.7 | [illegible] | 174048.8 | 119990.0 | 80470.8 | 1597 | 1502 | 1367 |
| 2040 | 684774.5 | 450234.8 | [illegible] | 232916.5 | 153141.1 | 95574.06 | 1601 | 1500 | 1333 |
| 2045 | 916382.8 | 574626.4 | [illegible] | 311694.8 | 195451.1 | 113512.0 | 1594 | 1489 | 1288 |
| 2050 | 1226327.0 | 733385.0 | 396351.0 | 417118.0 | 249450.7 | 134816.7 | 1576 | 1469 | 1231 |

*Notes:*

1: 100 million RMB (in 1985 constant prices).

2: 100 million US$ (in 1985 constant prices).

3: million.

*3.3 The Time when China's Grain Demand Peaks*

Based on the various combinations of future GDP and the population sizes reported in Table 12.9, we have nine possible future per capita GDP scenarios. Table 12.9 shows that China's population peak will arrive by 2040 at the latest. Table 12.10 shows that the per capita GDP in China will reach $5,000 as early as 2020. Therefore, China's demand for grain can reach its peak at any time between 2020 and 2040. Before 2020, the grain pressure will not peak because its population is yet to peak. After 2040, due to a diminishing population and stabilized diet, the demand pressure will go down gradually.

Tables 12.9 to 12.12 report the projected demand for food grain and feed grain. Table 12.11 gives projected demands for feed derived from projected pork consumption—assuming that the per capita pork consumption is 40kg based on Taiwan data. Because of the various combinations of population growth and conversion ratios, Table 12.11 offers nine different scenarios as well as the total demand for feed—derived from the projected non-pork meat consumption in nine scenarios. Table 12.12 lists the detailed accounts of demand for feed derived from the consumption of non-pork meat.

Based on the data in Table 12.5, I assume the following per capita consumption and conversion ratios: poultry being 15kg and 2.6; milk 21kg and .32; egg 15kg and 2.6; aquatic products 34kg and 1.6kg—assuming that half of the aquatic products are cultivated; and beef and lamb 4 kg and 2.5, respectively. The per capita consumption figures are the averages of the corresponding numbers that are observed in Taiwan and listed in Table 12.5 for the period between 1992 and 1996.[6]

The conversion ratios were derived from various sources: aquatic products (compared with 0.8 by the OECF), poultry, and egg are the averages of the figures listed in Table 30 of Garnaut and Ma (1992); and the conversion ratio for milk is from Table 3.8 on p. 26 of the OECF report. I already discussed the conversion ratio for pork above.

Table 12.13 lists the total amount of feed demanded under three different pork conversion ratios in three population scenarios. As we can see in Table 12.13, the total demand for feed will peak in 2040. Table 12.15 lists grain's total supply and demand. The total demand is defined as the sum of the total demand for feed grain and food grain. The amount of seed use, industrial use, and possible loss is not included in the total demand. Therefore, we deduct 20 percent of the total supply to derive the effective supply of grain. In calculating the demand for food grain, we assume that the per capita consumption of food grain is 100 kg, based on the Taiwan data listed in Table 12.5.

---

[6] Compare Table 12.5 with the corresponding numbers given in footnote 5, we can see that using Taiwan's diet will not underestimate mainland China's demand for grain.

**Table 12.10 Projected per capita GDP (in 1985 constant US$ prices)**

| Year | High Population Growth | | | Medium Population Growth | | | Low Population Growth | | |
|---|---|---|---|---|---|---|---|---|---|
| | GDP High Growth | GDP Medium Growth | GDP Low Growth | GDP High Growth | GDP Medium Growth | GDP Low Growth | GDP High Growth | GDP Medium Growth | GDP Low Growth |
| 2000 | 948.2 | 905.7 | 864.7 | 963.7 | 920.5 | 878.9 | 968.2 | 924.8 | 883.0 |
| 2005 | 1425.9 | 1300.9 | 1185.8 | 1464.5 | 1336.2 | 1218.0 | 1480.2 | 1350.4 | 1231.0 |
| 2010 | 2157.7 | 1880.3 | 1636.5 | 2230.0 | 1943.3 | 1691.3 | 2273.0 | 1980.8 | 1723.9 |
| 2015 | 2982.1 | 2480.0 | 2059.0 | 3097.6 | 2576.2 | 2138.8 | 3189.8 | 2652.8 | 2202.4 |
| 2020 | 4135.3 | 3282.1 | 2599.3 | 4322.2 | 3430.4 | 2716.8 | 4507.4 | 3577.5 | 2833.2 |
| 2025 | 5796.2 | 4390.3 | 3316.8 | 6088.3 | 4611.6 | 3483.9 | 6457.2 | 4890.9 | 3695.0 |
| 2030 | 8205.7 | 5931.6 | 4274.7 | 8670.6 | 6267.7 | 4517.0 | 9350.1 | 6758.8 | 4870.9 |
| 2035 | 10898.5 | 7513.5 | 5038.9 | 11587.8 | 7988.7 | 5357.6 | 12732.2 | 8777.6 | 5886.7 |
| 2040 | 14548.2 | 9565.4 | 5969.6 | 15527.8 | 10209.4 | 6371.6 | 17473.1 | 11488.5 | 7169.8 |
| 2045 | 19554.3 | 12261.7 | 7121.2 | 20933.2 | 13126.3 | 7623.4 | 24199.9 | 15174.8 | 8813.0 |
| 2050 | 26466.9 | 15828.1 | 8554.4 | 28394.7 | 16981.0 | 9177.4 | 33884.5 | 20264.0 | 10951.8 |

**Table 12.11 Demand for feeder (unit: million tons)**

| | Pork | | | | | | | | | Other Meat[2] | | |
|---|---|---|---|---|---|---|---|---|---|---|---|---|
| | High Population Growth | | | Medium Population Growth | | | Low Population Growth | | | | | |
| Year | High Ratio[1] | Medium Ratio | Low Ratio | High Ratio | Medium Ratio | Low Ratio | High Ratio | Medium Ratio | Low Ratio | Populatn High Case | Populatn Medium Case | Populatn Low Case |
| 2000 | 208.5 | 156.4 | 120.4 | 205.1 | 153.8 | 118.5 | 204.2 | 153.1 | 117.9 | 176.4 | 173.6 | 173.2 |
| 2005 | 218.2 | 163.7 | 126.0 | 212.5 | 159.4 | 122.7 | 210.2 | 157.7 | 121.4 | 184.7 | 179.8 | 178.9 |
| 2010 | 227.0 | 170.3 | 131.1 | 219.7 | 164.8 | 126.9 | 215.5 | 161.6 | 124.5 | 192.1 | 185.9 | 184.3 |
| 2015 | 235.8 | 176.9 | 136.2 | 227.0 | 170.3 | 131.1 | 220.5 | 165.4 | 127.4 | 199.6 | 192.1 | 189.6 |
| 2020 | 244.2 | 183.1 | 141.0 | 233.6 | 175.2 | 134.9 | 224.0 | 168.0 | 129.4 | 206.6 | 197.7 | 193.9 |
| 2025 | 250.1 | 187.6 | 144.4 | 238.1 | 178.6 | 137.5 | 224.5 | 168.4 | 129.6 | 211.6 | 201.5 | 196.2 |
| 2030 | 253.6 | 190.2 | 146.5 | 240.0 | 180.0 | 138.6 | 222.6 | 166.9 | 128.5 | 214.6 | 203.1 | 196.3 |
| 2035 | 255.5 | 191.6 | 147.6 | 240.3 | 180.3 | 138.8 | 218.7 | 164.0 | 126.3 | 216.2 | 203.4 | 194.9 |
| 2040 | 256.2 | 192.1 | 147.9 | 240.0 | 180.0 | 138.6 | 213.3 | 160.0 | 123.2 | 216.8 | 203.1 | 192.6 |
| 2045 | 255.0 | 191.3 | 147.3 | 238.2 | 178.7 | 137.6 | 206.1 | 154.6 | 119.0 | 215.8 | 201.6 | 189.0 |
| 2050 | 252.2 | 189.1 | 145.6 | 235.0 | 176.7 | 135.8 | 197.0 | 147.7 | 113.7 | 213.4 | 198.9 | 184.0 |

Notes:

1: The grain/pork conversion ratio.

2: The feeder required for the production of beef, lamb, milk, poultry, eggs, and aquatic products. Also see the next table.

**Table 12.12 Feeder required in producing other meat (unit: million tons)**

| Year | Poultry | | | Milk | | | Eggs | | | Aquatic Products | | | Beef and Lamb | | |
|---|---|---|---|---|---|---|---|---|---|---|---|---|---|---|---|
| | Populat High Case | Populat Medium Case | Populat Low Case | Populat High Case | Populat Medium Case | Populat Low Case | Populat High Case | Populat Medium Case | Populat Low Case | Populat High Case | Populat Medium Case | Populat Low Case | Populat High Case | Populat Medium Case | Populat Low Case |
| 2000 | 94.9 | 93.3 | 93.3 | 8.8 | 8.6 | 8.6 | 50.9 | 50.0 | 49.8 | 17.7 | 17.4 | 17.4 | 13.0 | 12.8 | 12.8 |
| 2005 | 99.3 | 96.7 | 96.9 | 9.2 | 8.9 | 8.9 | 53.2 | 51.8 | 51.2 | 18.7 | 18.1 | 17.9 | 13.6 | 13.3 | 13.1 |
| 2010 | 103.3 | 100.0 | 100.0 | 9.5 | 9.2 | 9.1 | 55.3 | 53.5 | 52.5 | 19.3 | 18.6 | 18.3 | 14.2 | 13.7 | 13.5 |
| 2015 | 107.3 | 103.3 | 103.3 | 9.9 | 9.5 | 9.3 | 57.5 | 55.3 | 53.7 | 20.1 | 19.3 | 18.7 | 14.7 | 14.2 | 13.8 |
| 2020 | 111.1 | 106.3 | 106.3 | 10.3 | 10.0 | 9.4 | 59.5 | 56.9 | 54.6 | 20.8 | 19.9 | 19.0 | 15.3 | 14.6 | 14.0 |
| 2025 | 113.8 | 108.3 | 108.3 | 10.5 | 10.0 | 9.4 | 61.0 | 58.0 | 54.7 | 21.3 | 20.2 | 19.1 | 15.6 | 14.9 | 14.0 |
| 2030 | 115.4 | 109.2 | 109.2 | 10.7 | 10.0 | 9.3 | 61.8 | 58.5 | 54.2 | 21.7 | 20.4 | 18.9 | 15.9 | 15.0 | 13.9 |
| 2035 | 116.3 | 109.3 | 109.3 | 10.7 | 10.1 | 9.2 | 62.3 | 58.6 | 53.3 | 21.7 | 20.4 | 18.7 | 16.0 | 15.0 | 13.7 |
| 2040 | 116.6 | 109.2 | 109.2 | 10.8 | 10.1 | 9.0 | 62.4 | 58.5 | 52.0 | 21.8 | 20.4 | 18.1 | 16.1 | 15.0 | 13.3 |
| 2045 | 116.2 | 108.4 | 108.4 | 10.7 | 10.1 | 8.7 | 62.2 | 58.1 | 50.2 | 21.7 | 20.3 | 17.5 | 15.9 | 14.9 | 12.9 |
| 2050 | 114.8 | 109.0 | 106.9 | 10.6 | 9.9 | 8.3 | 61.5 | 57.3 | 48.0 | 21.4 | 20.0 | 16.7 | 15.8 | 14.7 | 12.3 |

**Table 12.13 Total feeder demand (unit: million tons)**

| Year | High Population Growth | | | Medium Population Growth | | | Low Population Growth | | |
|---|---|---|---|---|---|---|---|---|---|
| | High Ratio[1] | Medium Ratio | Low Ratio | High Ratio | Medium Ratio | Low Ratio | High Ratio | Medium Ratio | Low Ratio |
| 2000 | 384.9 | 332.8 | 296.8 | 378.7 | 327.4 | 292.0 | 377.4 | 326.3 | 291.1 |
| 2005 | 402.9 | 348.4 | 310.7 | 392.3 | 339.2 | 302.5 | 389.2 | 336.6 | 300.3 |
| 2010 | 419.2 | 362.4 | 323.2 | 405.6 | 350.7 | 312.8 | 399.8 | 345.9 | 308.7 |
| 2015 | 435.4 | 376.5 | 335.8 | 419.2 | 362.4 | 323.2 | 410.0 | 354.9 | 316.9 |
| 2020 | 450.8 | 389.7 | 347.6 | 431.3 | 372.9 | 332.6 | 417.9 | 361.9 | 323.3 |
| 2025 | 461.7 | 399.9 | 356.1 | 439.6 | 380.0 | 339.0 | 420.6 | 364.5 | 325.8 |
| 2030 | 468.2 | 404.8 | 361.1 | 443.1 | 383.1 | 341.7 | 418.8 | 363.2 | 324.8 |
| 2035 | 471.8 | 407.9 | 363.8 | 443.7 | 383.6 | 342.2 | 413.6 | 359.0 | 321.2 |
| 2040 | 473.0 | 408.9 | 364.7 | 443.1 | 383.1 | 341.7 | 405.9 | 352.6 | 315.8 |
| 2045 | 470.9 | 407.1 | 363.1 | 439.9 | 380.3 | 339.2 | 395.1 | 343.6 | 308.0 |
| 2050 | 465.6 | 402.5 | 359.0 | 433.9 | 375.2 | 334.7 | 381.0 | 331.7 | 297.7 |

*Note*: 1. the grain/pork conversion ratio.

## 4 Future Potential of China's Grain Production

### *4.1 The Response Function*

As mentioned before, it is difficult to obtain good estimates of input and output elasticities in China's context, considering the limited availability and quality of data. To avoid the difficulties previously mentioned—and to avoid the fluctuation in the actual growth rates—in what follows, I first estimated a response function to obtain the estimated average growth rate $\hat{g}_i$ for each province between 1985 and 1995.[7] These rates can then be used to project the future supply after some adjustment.

Based on climatic and geographical reasons, we grouped together: Beijing, Tianjin, and Hebei; Shanghai and Jiangsu; and Hainan and Guangdong. We dropped Tibet since its grain output is insignificant. Hence, in our data set, we have 25 time series and used the general least squared method (GLS) to estimate the parameters of the following population regression equation (denoted as 1):

$$\ln Y_{i,t} = \alpha + \beta_1 * \ln X_{1,i,t} + \beta_2 * \ln X_{2,i,t} + \beta_3 * \ln X_{3,i,t} + \beta_4 * \ln X_{4,i,t} + \beta_5 * \ln X_{5,i,t} + \beta_6 * \ln X_{6,i,t} + \beta_7 * \ln X_{7,i,t} + \beta_8 * \ln X_{8,i,t} + V_{i,t} \tag{1}$$

where $Y_{i,t}$ grain output (in 10,000t);
$X_{1,i,t}$ farm machinery (in 10,000kw);
$X_{2,i,t}$ irrigation areas (in 10,000*mu*);
$X_{3,i,t}$ areas affected by disasters (in 10,000ha);
$X_{4,i,t}$ areas sown to grain crops (in 10,000*mu*);
$X_{5,i,t}$ laborers engaged in grain production = agricultural laborers × $r$ (in 10,000)
(Letter $r$ is the share of areas sown to grain in the total sown areas)
$X_{6,i,t}$ real purchasing price index for agricultural goods = (nominal purchasing price index for agricultural goods)/ (retail price index of industrial goods in rural areas);
$X_{7,i,t}$ number of technicians in State-owned units (in person);
$X_{8,i,t}$ application of chemical fertilizers (in 10,000t).

The equation (1) is a response function, including the factors of production, output prices, and weather factor as its independent variables. The regression

[7] An alternative and much simpler way is to calculate the geometric average growth rate directly from the actual output of 1985 and that of 1996, although the result may suffer from bias. This is why I choose to estimate a response function to get the estimated average growth rate to reduce the impacts of random factors. In doing so, we only used the data covering the period 1985-1996. The period 1978-84 saw significant institutional changes when China gradually replaced the commune system with the HRS, and enabled China to have a one-time efficiency gain in its productivity. For this reason, this period is abnormal, and should be excluded.

results are listed in Table 12.14, where the sign 1 indicates that the estimates of the parameters are significant at the 5 percent level. All the variables are in logs.[8] Unless indicated otherwise, all the data were adopted from the SYOC of various years. Using the results reported in Table 12.14 we can thereby obtain the estimated annual grain output for each province between 1985 and 1996, designated as

$\hat{Y}_{i,t}$, $i$=1, ... 25; $t$ = 1985,... 1996.

In order to obtain the estimated average growth rate ĝ for this period, we assume that the grain output in each province from 1985 to 1996 grew in the following way:

$$\hat{Y}_{i,t} = \hat{Y}_{i,0} * (1+\hat{g}_i)^t \qquad (2)$$

**Table 12.14 Regression results**

| Independent Variables | Estimates | Standard Error | t-value |
|---|---|---|---|
| Constant | -0.43 | 0.49 | -0.87 |
| Labor engaged in Grain Crops | 0.02 | 0.08 | 0.31 |
| Irrigation Areas | 0.64 | 0.05 | 13.92* |
| Machinery | 0.07 | 0.03 | 2.32* |
| Application of Chemical Fertilizer | 0.14 | 0.02 | 7.25* |
| Areas affected by natural disasters | -0.06 | 0.01 | -5.31* |
| Areas sown to grain crops | 0.06 | 0.08 | 0.77 |
| Prices | 0.02 | 0.07 | 0.28 |
| Technology | 0.13 | 0.04 | 2.81* |

Using the results in Table 12.14, we can calculate the estimated output $\hat{Y}_{i,t}$ for both 1985 and 1996 with the Equation (2) to calculate the estimated average growth rate $\hat{g}_i$—noting that $t$ is equal to 12. We can then use this rate as a base with some adjustments to project the grain output in each province for years after 1996. The total supply of grain in a specific future year will be the sum of the projected outputs from all the provinces in that year.

[8] The data used in the estimation are available upon request.

### *4.2 Three Scenarios for Future Grain Growth*

Some of the provinces reached a rate higher than 3 percent during the period of time between 1985 and 1996.[9] In order not to overestimate China's future grain supply, we first lower their future growth rates $\hat{g}_i$ to 2 percent as the starting growth rates for the year 1997. By doing so, we actually control the national growth rate of grain production at a rate lower than 2 percent. We then further downwardly adjust the growth rates by considering the following three scenarios.

*Low case:* We assume that those provinces that had estimated average grain growth rates higher than 1 percent between 1985 and 1996 will lower their growth rates after 2010 by 0.9 percent every 10 years until their rates fall to 1 percent or lower.
*Medium case:* We assume that those provinces whose estimated average grain growth rates during that same time were higher than 1 percent will lower their growth rates after 2010 by 0.7 percent every 10 years until their rates fall to 1 percent or lower.
*High case:* We assume that those provinces whose estimated average grain growth rates were higher than 1 percent from 1985 to 1996 will decrease their growth rate after 2010 by 0.5 percent every 10 years until their growth rates fall to 1 percent or lower.

The above assumptions are extremely conservative and were made only to reflect concerns that China is suffering from shrinking arable land, deteriorating environment, and stagnating agricultural investment. In reality China still has great potential for increasing its grain yield made possible through technical progress and institutional innovation.[10] China's arable land has been underestimated by as much as 30 percent. China also has plenty of room to improve its water utilization efficiency if it acquires the technology used by some of the advanced nations.

In addition, we are at the eve of a major breakthrough in the field of biology, particularly in genetic engineering. China has achieved significant progress in agricultural technology in the past (Lin, 1991), so there is no reason to assume that China will lose its momentum in new technological advances after 2000. Our conservative assumptions only serve to demonstrate that even if the unfavorable growth rate we assumed above in grain production actually happened—supposing that the country could still handle the situation reasonably well—then China should not worry too much about its grain security.

---

[9] An anonymous reviewer correctly pointed out that the supply during this period "was achieved under the government grain policies. A relaxed policy, an increased opportunity of land from other competitive crops and urbanization, combined with increasing pressure of water shortage (the irrigation acreage is one of the few significant factors) in the next few decades may cause a lower supply growth rate." The downward adjustment in the future growth rate is exactly to reflect these concerns.

[10] China is a leading nation in genetic engineering. Its rural institutions, especially its land tenure system, still have rooms for efficiency enhancement (Wen, 1995).

**Table 12.15 The projected total grain supply and demand (unit: million tons)**

| | Total Consumption | | | | | | | | | Total Supply | | |
|---|---|---|---|---|---|---|---|---|---|---|---|---|
| | High Population Growth | | | Medium Population Growth | | | Low Population Growth | | | | | |
| Year | High Ratio[1] | Medium Ratio | Low Ratio | High Ratio | Medium Ratio | Low Ratio | High Ratio | Medium Ratio | Low Ratio | Production High Rate[2] | Production Medium Rate | Production Low Rate |
| I | II | III | IV | V | VI | VII | VIII | IX | X | XI | XII | XIII |
| 2020 | 603.4 | 542.3 | 500.2 | 577.2 | 518.9 | 478.6 | 557.9 | 501.9 | 463.3 | 665.9 | 653.8 | 642.0 |
| 2025 | 618.0 | 555.5 | 512.3 | 588.4 | 528.8 | 487.8 | 560.9 | 504.8 | 466.1 | 694.4 | 672.3 | 653.1 |
| 2030 | 626.7 | 563.3 | 519.6 | 593.1 | 533.1 | 491.7 | 557.9 | 502.3 | 463.9 | 724.3 | 691.4 | 664.6 |
| 2035 | 631.4 | 567.6 | 523.5 | 593.9 | 533.8 | 492.4 | 550.3 | 495.7 | 457.9 | 755.6 | 711.1 | 676.4 |
| 2040 | 633.0 | 569.0 | 524.8 | 593.1 | 533.1 | 491.7 | 539.2 | 485.9 | 449.1 | 788.4 | 731.4 | 688.5 |
| 2045 | 630.2 | 566.5 | 522.5 | 588.8 | 529.2 | 488.1 | 523.9 | 472.4 | 436.8 | 822.7 | 752.4 | 701.1 |
| 2050 | 623.1 | 560.1 | 516.6 | 580.8 | 522.1 | 481.6 | 504.1 | 454.8 | 420.8 | 858.7 | 774.1 | 714.0 |

Notes:

1: the grain/pork conversion ratio.

2: see the discussion in Section IV about the growth rate in grain production.

**Table 12.16 The projected consumption of food grain (unit: million tons)**

| Year | Population High Growth | Population Medium Growth | Population Low Growth |
|---|---|---|---|
| 2000 | 130.3 | 128.2 | 127.6 |
| 2005 | 136.4 | 132.8 | 131.4 |
| 2010 | 141.9 | 137.3 | 134.7 |
| 2015 | 147.4 | 141.9 | 137.8 |
| 2020 | 152.6 | 146 | 140 |
| 2025 | 156.3 | 148.8 | 140.3 |
| 2030 | 158.5 | 150 | 139.1 |
| 2035 | 159.7 | 150.2 | 136.7 |
| 2040 | 160.1 | 150 | 133.3 |
| 2045 | 159.4 | 148.9 | 128.8 |
| 2050 | 157.6 | 146.9 | 123.1 |

## 5 Main Findings

The main findings of this study support the optimistic view. China is highly unlikely to fail to meet the grain demand of its population. Despite the highly unfavorable assumptions we made in our projection, the results show that China is able to stand the test reasonably well even during a period when it faced its maximum grain pressure. Tables 12.13, 12.14, and 12.15 report the various cases. More specifically, Table 12.17 reports nine cases where the grain growth rate is assumed to be low, and the population growth and conversion ratio take high, medium, and low values. Table 12.18 reports nine cases where the grain growth rate is assumed to be medium, and the population growth and conversion ratio take high, medium, and low values. Finally, Table 12.19 reports nine cases where the grain growth rate is assumed to be high, and the population growth and conversion ratio take high, medium, and low values.

There are twenty-seven scenarios altogether. Among them, the maximum pressure case is reported by Column 2 of Table 12.17 where low supply coincides with high population growth and high conversion ratio. If this scenario really happens in 2025, the total deficits in grain supply will amount to 95.5 million tons. This gap represents 14.9 percent of the domestic supply of that year.[11] In other words, China still maintains a grain self-sufficiency rate of 85 percent, a rather high rate when compared to many other nations.

[11] In column XIII of Table 12.15 we can see that the grain supply of year 2025 is projected as 642.0 million ton.

**Table 12.17 The grain gap between the total consumption and the low case total supply[1] (unit: million tons)**

| Year | High Population Growth | | | Medium Population Growth | | | Low Population Growth | | |
|---|---|---|---|---|---|---|---|---|---|
| | High Conversion Ratio[2] | Medium Conversion Ratio | Low Conversion Ratio | High Conversion Ratio[2] | Medium Conversion Ratio | Low Conversion Ratio | High Conversion Ratio[2] | Medium Conversion Ratio | Low Conversion Ratio |
| 2020 | -89.8 | -28.7 | 13.4 | -63.7 | -5.3 | 35.0 | -44.3 | 11.7 | 50.3 |
| 2025 | -95.5 | -33.0 | 10.1 | -65.9 | -6.3 | 34.7 | -38.4 | 17.7 | 56.4 |
| 2030 | -95.1 | -31.7 | 12.1 | -61.5 | -1.5 | 39.9 | -26.3 | 29.4 | 67.7 |
| 2035 | -90.4 | -26.5 | 17.6 | -52.8 | 7.3 | 48.7 | -9.4 | 45.4 | 83.2 |
| 2040 | -82.2 | -18.2 | 26.0 | -42.3 | 17.7 | 59.1 | 11.6 | 64.9 | 101.7 |
| 2045 | -69.4 | -5.6 | 38.4 | -27.9 | 31.7 | 72.8 | 37.0 | 88.5 | 124.0 |
| 2050 | -52.0 | 11.1 | 54.6 | -9.6 | 49.2 | 89.7 | 67.1 | 116.3 | 150.4 |

*Notes*:

1: In this low grain supply case, all the numbers listed in this table are derived by finding the differences between the numbers in column XIII in table 12.15 (after 20% deduction for the amount of seed use, industrial use, and possible loss) and the respective numbers in columns of High Population Growth. Note that those provinces whose grain growth rates in the period 1985-1996 were higher than 1% are supposed to lower their growth rates by 0.9% every ten years starting from 2010 until their rates fall to 1% or below.

2: The high, medium, and low grain/pork conversion ratios are 4, 3, and 2.31 respectively.

**Table 12.18 The grain gap between the total consumption and the medium case total supply[1] (unit: million tons)**

| Year | High Population Growth | | | Medium Population Growth | | | Low Population Growth | | |
|---|---|---|---|---|---|---|---|---|---|
| | High Conversion Ratio[1] | Medium Conversion Ratio | Low Conversion Ratio | High Conversion Ratio | Medium Conversion Ratio | Low Conversion Ratio | High Conversion Ratio | Medium Conversion Ratio | Low Conversion Ratio |
| 2020 | -80.3 | -19.3 | 22.8 | -54.2 | 4.2 | 44.5 | -34.9 | 21.1 | 59.8 |
| 2025 | -80.2 | -17.7 | 25.5 | -50.5 | 9.0 | 50.1 | -23.1 | 33.0 | 71.7 |
| 2030 | -73.6 | -10.2 | 33.5 | -40.0 | 20.0 | 61.4 | -4.8 | 50.8 | 89.2 |
| 2035 | -62.6 | 1.3 | 45.4 | -25.0 | 35.1 | 76.5 | 18.5 | 73.2 | 110.9 |
| 2040 | -47.9 | 16.1 | 60.3 | -8.0 | 52.0 | 93.4 | 45.9 | 99.2 | 136.0 |
| 2045 | -28.3 | 35.4 | 79.4 | 13.1 | 72.7 | 113.8 | 78.0 | 129.5 | 165.1 |
| 2050 | -3.9 | 59.2 | 102.7 | 38.4 | 97.2 | 137.7 | 115.2 | 164.4 | 198.4 |

*Notes*: 1. In this medium grain supply case, all the numbers listed in this table are derived by finding the differences between the numbers in column XII in table 12.15 (after 20% deduction for the amount of seed use, industrial use, and possible loss) and the respective numbers in columns of High Population Growth. Note that those provinces whose grain growth rates in the period 1985-1996 were higher than 1% are supposed to lower their growth rates by 0.7% every ten years starting from 2010 until their rates fall to 1% or below.

**Table 12.19 The grain gap between the total consumption and the high case total supply[1] (unit: million tons)**

| Year | High Population Growth | | | Medium Population Growth | | | Low Population Growth | | |
|---|---|---|---|---|---|---|---|---|---|
| | High Conversion Ratio[2] | Medium Conversion Ratio | Low Conversion Ratio | High Conversion Ratio | Medium Conversion Ratio | Low Conversion Ratio | High Conversion Ratio | Medium Conversion Ratio | Low Conversion Ratio |
| 2020 | -70.7 | -9.6 | 32.5 | -44.6 | 13.8 | 54.1 | -25.2 | 30.8 | 69.4 |
| 2025 | -62.5 | 0.0 | 43.2 | -32.8 | 26.7 | 67.8 | -5.4 | 50.7 | 89.4 |
| 2030 | -47.3 | 16.1 | 59.9 | -13.7 | 46.3 | 87.7 | 21.5 | 77.1 | 115.5 |
| 2035 | -27.0 | 36.9 | 81.0 | 10.6 | 70.6 | 112.1 | 54.2 | 108.8 | 146.5 |
| 2040 | -2.4 | 61.7 | 105.9 | 37.6 | 97.6 | 139.0 | 91.5 | 144.8 | 181.6 |
| 2045 | 27.9 | 91.7 | 135.6 | 69.4 | 129.0 | 170.1 | 134.3 | 185.8 | 221.3 |
| 2050 | 63.8 | 126.8 | 170.3 | 106.1 | 164.9 | 205.4 | 182.9 | 232.1 | 266.1 |

*Notes*:

1: In this high grain supply case, all the numbers listed in this table are derived by finding the differences between the numbers in column XI in table 12.15 (after 20% deduction for the amount of seed use, industrial use, and possible loss) and the respective numbers in columns of High Population Growth. Those provinces whose grain growth rates in the period 1985-1996 were higher than 1% are supposed to lower their growth rates by 0.5% every ten years starting from 2010 until their rates fall to 1% or below. Table 12.14 lists the grain output of each province in 2000 and after at a five-year interval. The growth rates that are used in our calculation are reported in Table 12.14.

2: The high, medium, and low grain/pork conversion ratios are 4, 3, and 2.31 respectively. Unless otherwise, all the data are adopted from the Statistical yearbook of China of various years.

Column 2 of Table 12.18 reports a scenario where the grain growth rate is medium, but the population growth rate and conversion ratio are high, requiring China to import 80.3 million tons of grain in 2020. This means that China's self-sufficiency rate will be almost 88 percent.[12] Although the amount of imports reduces by 15 million tons in comparison to the previous case, the maximum grain pressure occurs in 2020, five years earlier.

In column 2 of Table 12.19, we can see that if the population, grain growth, and conversion ratio are all high, China will need to import 70 million tons of grain in 2020. These three cases are the most unfavorable scenarios among all simulated. If China can survive in these three scenarios, then there is no reason to doubt China's capability to feed itself in other scenarios.

Among all simulations, the maximal import requirement is 95.5 million tons, and will take place in 2025. While this figure looks big, it is only equivalent to 14.9 percent of China's total supply, or 15.5 percent of China's total demand.[13] In other words, China can still maintain a self-sufficient grain rate as high as 85 percent—a rate that would be viewed as very high in many other nations. If China can lower its self-sufficient rate to this point, it will be very beneficial to its environment without causing too much of a disruption to the world market for two reasons: (1) this is unlikely to happen; and (2) the world will have more than fifteen years to prepare for this possible scenario.

The results of this study show that it is groundless to believe that China is doomed to face a severe grain shortage in the future or that the world grain market is doomed to face disarrays because of China's possible hunger for grain imports. Only policy blunders or institutional wrong doings in China could lead to such a disaster. However, such a prospect is highly unlikely given that China is actively and successfully reforming its economic and social institutions.

The second finding is that whether or not China needs to import a large amount of grain actually depends on three factors: the population growth rate, conversion ratio, and growth rate of grain production. For example, Table 12.17 shows that the maximum grain pressure will occur in 2025 in the amount of 95.5 million tons. However, if the population grows at a medium rate, other things remain same; the peak gap will fall to 65 million tons in that year. If the population grows at a low rate, other things remain unchanged; the peak gap will be 44 million tons in 2020. Hence, population growth is still very relevant in reducing grain pressure in the future.

Overall, the grain situation depends mostly on the value of the conversion ratio. For instance, Table 12.17 tells us that the grain gap will be 95.5 million tons if we assume low grain growth, high population growth, and that the conversion ratio takes a high value of 4 between 2020 and 2025. In our central case where the

[12] In column XII of Table 12.15, we can see that the supply of 2020 will be 653.8 million tons.

[13] See column II of Table 12.15 where we find that corresponding to this scenario, the total demand will be 618.0 million tons in 2025.

conversion rate takes the value of 3 even if a high population growth is combined with a low grain growth, the grain gap will fall to 33 million tons in 2025. Since 4 is the value used by the USDA, compared to the value of 3.5 that is also used by the USDA, 4 is definitely on the higher side in China's context. This is why we choose 3 as the conversion ratio for the central case. But even if it were 4, China still can maintain a self-sufficiency rate of 85 percent—a high rate for any nation.

## 6 Concluding Remarks

On its way toward modernization, China is still facing many traps and pitfalls. The results of this study, however, show that a future famine is certainly not one of them. China did experience a serious famine from 1958 to 1961 in which about 30 million people, mostly farmers, died of hunger (Ashton et al 1984). Because of this as well as the fact that China has had numerous famines historically, many are still deeply worried about history repeating itself and a famine in China triggering a world-wide food crisis. According to recent studies (Yang, 1996; Chang and Wen, 1997), the great famine of 1958-61 was entirely a man-made disaster. The communal dining halls that were imposed on farmers first triggered a rampant grain waste in consumption and later deprived farmers of any incentive to work hard and produce more. This unprecedented famine would never have occurred had farmers not been driven to join communal dining halls.

In the early-1980s, China wisely replaced the inefficient commune system with the much more efficient HRS. Since then, more than a hundred million young, relatively better-educated farmers have left the farming sector. In addition, China has lost a significant amount of arable land as a result of urbanization and industrialization. These trends will continue in the future, and some of these changes are unfavorable to grain production. For example, China's population has doubled since the mid-1950s, and its per capita grain possession has increased from less than 300 kg in 1952 to 400 kg in 1997.

As long as China can avoid committing severe policy mistakes and institutional blunders, the current HRS will enable the country to mainly rely on its own efforts and resources to feed its population, as the results of this study show. It is unwarranted to use the 1958-61 famine as proof that another famine is likely to happen again in the future. China now embodies a totally different, and much more efficient, agricultural institution.

I have no intention to make grain security sound like something unimportant to a nation with a huge and growing population base, such as China. However, it is harmful if one becomes obsessed with grain security. For example, between 1998 and 2003, China resumed a state monopoly on grain purchasing—as was reflected in its grain circulation reform—at a time when China was enjoying a large amount of grain surplus. Such unnecessary government intervention in grain production and circulation is obviously driven by the fear of a possible food shortage. Such interventionist and protectionist policies are harmful to the long-term productivity of China's agriculture. The current agricultural policies and regulations overemphasize the importance of grain production at the expense of other crops, the environment, and the income of farmers. These policies and regulations reflect a baseless fear of famine, a blind belief in a high self-sufficiency rate, and a lack of trust in market mechanisms. Such policies are also ignoring the right of farmers to pursue a maximizing of their income.

Many well-known overseas agricultural economists (Chen, 1994; Johnson, 1996) have pointed out that the main problem in China's agriculture can be found in its government policy and rural institutions. I hope that the results of this study help alleviate the unsubstantiated fear among policymakers and restore their confidence in the HRS and market mechanisms.

Now that the WTO formally accepted China as a member, China is facing great challenges as well as opportunities. It is time to raise questions, such as: should China organize its grain production according to the market signals, or should it single-mindedly increase its grain production out of an unnecessary apprehension of grain shortage? Should the purpose of China's grain production be mainly a means to increase the income of farmers, or a way to demonstrate to the world its capability to maintain a high grain self-sufficiency at any expense, including its ecology and environment? Do Chinese farmers have the rights to choose what to produce according to their local comparative advantages and market signals so that they can maximize their income and welfare as everyone else, or do they belong to a lower class that has to follow every whim of local government officials?

At a time when China's environment has been deteriorating and the income disparity between rural and urban areas widening, it is worthwhile to give some serious thought to these questions. Unless they can be correctly answered, it is likely that the obsession with grain security will drive China to repeat the same mistake that we saw within the past few years, resulting in a grain surplus and an even further worsening of the rural-urban income disparity.

## References

Agricultural Planning and Development Committee of Taiwan, '*The Food Balance Sheet*' (Taiwan, 1987-1996).

Ashton, B. et al, 'Famine in China 1958-61', *Population and Development Review,* Vol. 10, (December, 1984) pp.613-645.

Brown, L., 'How Could China Starve the World: Its Boom is Consuming Global Food Supplies', *Washington Post* (August 28, 1994).

———, *Who Will Feed China? Wake up Call for a Small Planet* (New York: W.W.Norton and Co, 1995).

———, 'Worsening Water Shortages Threaten China's Food Supplies' (Earth Policy Institute, October 4, 2001, http://www.mindfully.org/Water/China-Water-Shortage.htm).

———, 'China's Shrinking Grain Harvest: How Its Growing Grain Imports Will Affect World Food Prices' (Earth Policy Institute, March 10, 2004, http://www.earth-policy.org/Updates/Update36.htm).

Chang, G.H. and Wen, G.J., 'Communal Dining and the Chinese Famine of 1958-1961', *Economic Development and Cultural Change*, Vol. 45 (1) (1997):1-33.

Chen, H.H., 'An Analysis on the Problems faced by the Mainland China' (paper presented at the Seminar on China's Rural Development at Columbia University, October, 1994).

Cheng, G. et al., 'An Estimation of China's Supply of and Demand for Feed', *Issues in Agricultural Economy* (5) (1997): 25-29.

Chinese Academy of Agriculture, 'The Summary of the Comprehensive Study on the Development of China's Grain and Economic Crops (Beijing: 1985).

Chinese Statistics Bureau, 'The Statistical Yearbook of China (SYOC)' (Beijing□The Statistical Publishing House of China, Various years).

Fan, S., 'Production and Productivity Growth in Chinese Agriculture: New Measurement and Evidence', *Food Policy*, Vol. 22 (3) (1997): 213-228.

FAO, 'Demand Prospects for Rice and Other Foodgrains in Selected Asian Countries' (Rome: Food and Agricultural Organization Economic and Social Development Paper No. 97, 1991).

Garnaut, R. and Ma, G., *Grain in China: A Report* (Australia: East Asia Analytical Unit, Department of Foreign Affairs and Trade, 1992).

Goldstone, A.J., 'The Coming Chinese Collapse', *Foreign Policy* (99) (Summer, 1995): 35-52.

Huang, J. and Rozelle, S., 'Technological Change: Rediscovering the Engine of Productivity Growth in China's Rural Economy', *Journal of Development Economics*, Vol. 49 (1996): 337-369.

———, *China's Grain Economy Toward the 21th Century* (Beijing: The Agricultural Publishing House of China, 1998).

Huang, J., Rozelle, S. and Rosegrant, M.W., 'China's Food Economy to the Twenty-first Century: Supply, Demand, and Trade', *2020 Vision Discussion Paper* (19) (Washington, D.C.: IFPRI, 1997).

Huang, P. and Yu, J., 'A Study on China's Grain Balance in the period 2000-2030 and its Solution', *The Manager's World* (February, 1997): 153-159.

Johnson, D.G., 'Does China Have A Grain Problem?' *China Economic Review*, Vol. 4 (1) (1996): 1-4.

Lin, J.Y., 'The Household Responsibility System Reform and the Adoption of Hybrid Rice in China', *Journal of Development of Economics*, Vol. 36 (1991): 353-372.

———, 'Institutional Reforms and Dynamics of Agricultural Growth in China', *Food Policy*, Vol. 22 (3) (1997): 201-212.

Lin, J.Y., Huang J. and Rozelle, S., 'China's Food Economy: Past Performance and Future's Projection' (working paper series No. E1996001, Beijng: China Center for Economic Research, Peking University, 1996).

Lindert, P.H., 'The Quality and Quantity of China's Farmland Since the 1930s' (a paper presented at the Working Meeting on the Strategy and Action Project for Chinese and

Global Food Security organized by the Millenium Institute, Washington D.C., February, 1998).

Lu, F., 'How Much Meat, Egg, and Aquatic Products Are We Producing?' (Working Paper series No. C1998005, Peking: China Center for Economic Research, Peking University, 1998).

Mei, F., 'Expectations and Strategies for Food Security in China by the Early 21st Century' (a paper presented at the Working Meeting on the Strategy and Action Project for Chinese and Gloabla Food Security organized by the Millenium Institute, Washington D. C., February, 1998).

The Ministry of Agriculture of the PRC, 'The Report on China's Agricultural Development 1997' (Beijing: The Agricultural Publishing House of China, 1997).

OECF, *Prospects for Grain Supply-Demand Balance and Agricultural Development Policy in China* (OECF Discussion Paper No.6, September, 1995).

Qi, J., Li, J., Wang, T. et al., 'An Analysis of the Characteristics of the Various Stages of China's Future Economic Development and its Choices of Pillar Industries' (The first draft of a joint report by the Research Center for Development at the State Council of China, the Institute of Mathematical and Technical Economic Research at the CASS, and the People's University of China, 1997).

Sun, J., The summary volume of a 33-volumed collection entitled 'The population of China Towards the 21st Century' (Beijing: The Statistical Publishing House of China, 1994).

The Study Group on Grain at the Central Planning Committee, 'The Issues in China's Grain production and Their Solutions during the Period of Ninth Five -Year Plan', *Economic Reform and Development*, (12) (1995): 3-8.

Wen, G.J., 'Total Factor Productivity Change in China's Farming Sector: 1952-1989', *Economic Development and Cultural Change*, Vol. 42, (1) (October, 1993): 1-41.

———, 'The Land Tenure System and the Saving and Investment Mechanism: The Case of Modern China', *Asian Economic Journal* (November issue, 1995): 233-259.

World Bank, *Agriculture* to *the Year 2000.* A World Bank Country Study (Annex 2 to China's Long- term Development Issues and Options, Washington, D. C: the World Bank, 1990).

Zhang, X., 'A Comparative Analysis on Household Husbandry Production and its Performance' (Beijing: the Center for Agricultural Research at the Ministry of Agriculture of China, 1997).

# Part 3
# Agricultural Risk Management

Chapter 13

# Agricultural Income Risk and Acreage Decision in China: Analysis of the Alternative Relationship between Soybeans and Corn

Qingsen Mao

## 1 Introduction

In China, rural households earned 2366.4 *yuan* of net income per capita in 2001, which is five times larger than what it was in 1985—397.6 *yuan*. Rural household incomes consist of wage income, transfer income, property income, and income from household business. The income from household business, which occupies the largest portion of overall rural household incomes, is earned mainly from the planting sector, which accounted for 34.2 percent of the total rural household income in 2001. The ratio of income from the planting sector of total rural household incomes had been about 50 percent between 1985 and 1995. However, it has diminished dramatically to about 35 percent in the last decade. Nevertheless, income from the planting sector is still the most important source of income for rural households in China.

During the last several years, however, rural household incomes have increased slowly and become unstable due to agricultural overproduction that has made the sale of agricultural products difficult. The improvement and stabilization of rural household incomes is one of central topics among Chinese leaders at present.

In order to solve the rural household income problems mentioned above, the Chinese government launched an agricultural structural adjustment program that has been running since the mid-1990s. It encourages rural households to convert their current farm products into those with a more competitive edge and higher profitability, such as fruits, vegetables, fisheries and livestock, among others. However, as a result of rapid production, even these agricultural products have struggled against significant price drops brought about by an oversupply in some provinces (Oshima, 2003). Thus, this kind of conversion seems to be effective only in the short-term in regard to solving the income problems of rural households. It is doubtful that ongoing agricultural structural adjustments work well or not from the standpoint of promoting and maintaining steadily increasing incomes for farmers are working in the long run.

Citing a USDA report (Tuan *et al.*, 2000), Tuan points out that, among the main agricultural products in the planting sector, only rice can keep a comparative advantage while others, including wheat, soybeans, corn and others, have been losing their comparative advantage in the world market since the mid-1990s (Ruan, 2003). After China's admission into the WTO, the international market began to have a greater effect on certain products in the domestic market; farmers producing soybeans and corn felt a much greater impact from this new competition (Ke *et al.*, 2002). Thus, the income risk is believed more serious for Chinese farmers.

Diversification is considered one of the strategies for coping with market uncertainty and income risk. In China's agricultural history, abundant cropping systems were formed in addition to the main cropping system of rotation. Cropping systems, including intercropping, compound cropping, and so-called *taozhong* (the staggering of cultivation periods among different crops), are used all over China. A number of studies on Chinese cropping systems tend to argue for yield improvements through biological means but offer little discussion in regard to their roles from an economical standpoint (Shen and Liu, 1983; Huang *et al.*, 1997). As the income of farmers grows increasingly unstable, however, it is necessary to consider the function of China's cropping system in terms of not only improving the yield but also reducing the income risk for farmers. This chapter analyses the effect of the agricultural income risk on the acreage decisions made by farmers through the estimated supply response of soybean farmers, taking the mixed-cropping of soybeans and corn as an example since they are usually cropped together in China.

The composition of this chapter is as follows. The next section examines the cropping system of soybeans and corn and then analyzes their production stability during the period of time from 1986 to 2002. Following their production conditions, a model is established in Section 3. The estimation procedure and data used in the estimations are highlighted in Section 4, followed by the estimation results in Section 5. The sixth and final section draws conclusions and offers some policy implications.

## 2 Soybean and Corn Production in China

Soybeans and corn are widely cultivated in China and their acreages in 2002 were 12.5 million and 24.6 million hectares, respectively. North and northeast China as well as Inner Mongolia are the main regions of production for these two crops. Soybeans and corn are cultivated with mix-cropping, according to their biological characteristics (Shen and Liu, 1983). Because corn requires more nourishment, planting it alongside soybeans allows it to take advantage of the nitrogen that soybeans naturally produce. On top of that, soybeans prefer a cooler environment with less sunlight, and corn can provide that exact environment with its tall stalks. Moreover, while these two crops are cultivated together, their cropping weights differ according to soil fertility. Soybeans are cultivated with more weight than corn in a land of low productivity and vice versa if the land has high productivity.

China has a long history of mix-cropping soybeans with corn. In 1976, the mixed-cropping acreage of soybeans and corn covered more than half of total mixed-cropping acreages in Heilongjiang province. That same year, the acreage of mixed-cropping soybeans and corn were about 80 percent of soybean acreage in Sichuan province (Shen and Liu, 1983). Now, the areas for the intercrops of corn and soybeans are still considerably large (Tan and Xin, 2001). For instance, 40 percent of corn acreages are intercropped with soybeans in the northern China.[1]

However, crop acreage is not only decided biologically but economically as well. Results from several rural surveys in China and Japan support this point (Buck, 1964; Hosono, 1955). In spite of the existence of a rotation system that has come into wide use in China, the mixed-cropping systems seem complicated. In addition to agricultural and technological factors, such as soil condition, irrigation, weather, and damage caused by diseases and harmful insects, farmers must consider economic factors, such as family consumption, agricultural income, profitability, and market risk, among others.

For soybeans and corn, their planting ratios are affected by their profitability independence of soil fertility (Aubert and Zhu, 2002). The Household Responsibility System (HRS), which was introduced in rural areas in the early 1980s, provides an environment where Chinese farmers can determine what and how much they would cultivate after they finish the governmental procurement allocation. It is natural that farmers adjust their crop ratios based on the comparative profitability of different crops.

Figure 13.1 shows the acreage trend of soybeans and corn from 1986 up through 2002, taking the year 1986 as a base of one. In most years, it is clear that the acreage expansion of one crop is accompanied by the acreage reduction of the other crop, even though they have their own trends. This figure hints at the alternative relationship between soybeans and corn.

Table 13.1 indicates the production stability of soybeans and corn from 1986 to 2002. Corn has a larger acreage and higher yield than soybeans. Corn acreage and yield are 334.8 million *mu* and 334.7 kg per *mu*, respectively. Soybean acreage and yield are 124.7 million *mu* and 109.7 kg per *mu*, respectively. Corn, however, has a lower price average of 17.3 *yuan* per 50 kg compared to 42.1 *yuan* per 50 kg of soybeans. After deducting production costs and agricultural taxes per *mu* (44.7 *yuan* per *mu* for corn and 25.7 *yuan* per *mu* for soybeans), farmers earn a higher real agricultural income from corn—74.8 *yuan* per *mu*—than soybeans, which is 62.9 *yuan* per *mu*. However, the agricultural income from corn seems more precarious than soybeans. After eliminating the time trend, the coefficient of variance (CV) is utilized to indicate a crop's degree of flexibility. Compared with soybeans, corn can be considered a "high risk but high return crop" because the CV of real agricultural income from corn is 36.3 percent and 25.2 percent for soybeans.

[1] Cited from the web: http://www.chinamaize.com.cn/mtymk/048.htm.

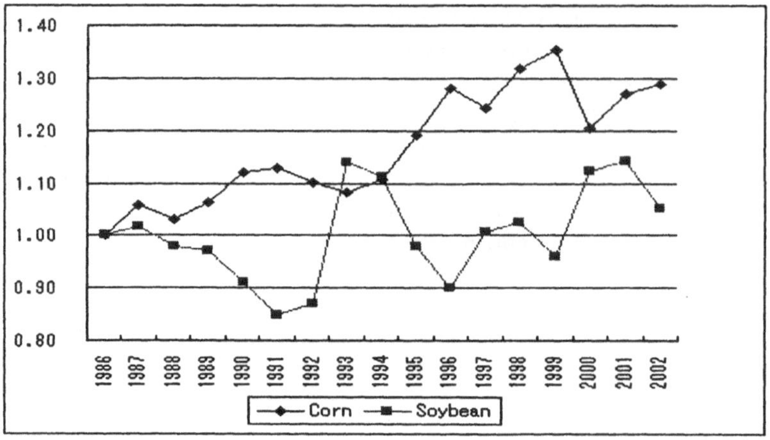


**Figure 13.1 National acreage trend of soybeans and corn, 1986-2002 (Year1986=1)**

*Source*: various issues of Rural Statistical Yearbook of China

**Table 13.1 Production stability of soybeans and corn, 1986-2002**

| | | Mean | | Coefficient of Variation (%) | |
|---|---|---|---|---|---|
| | | Soybeans | Corn | Soybeans | Corn |
| Acreage | (10,000mu) | 12,470.1 | 33,477.3 | 8.3 | 4.1 |
| Yield | (Kg/mu) | 109.7 | 354.7 | 5.5 | 4.2 |
| Real Average Price | (Yuan/50kg) | 42.1 | 17.3 | 16.4 | 21.5 |
| Real Production Cost | (Yuan/mu) | 25.7 | 44.7 | 7.9 | 5.4 |
| Real Agricultural Income | (Yuan/mu) | 62.9 | 74.8 | 25.2 | 36.3 |

*Notes*: 1. Agricultural income=Gross income-Production costs-Agricultural taxes. 1 mu=1/15 hectare. Average price and agricultural income are deflated by national CPI (base year =1985) in rural areas; Production costs together with agricultural taxes is deflated by national price index of agricultural production materials; The coefficients of variation are calculated after being eliminated time trend.

*Source*: various issues of Rural Statistical Yearbook of China, China Statistical Yearbook, Comprehensive Materials on National Cost and Profit of Agricultural Products compiled.

Moreover, the division of the agricultural income variance per *mu* into the three components of yield, product price, and per *mu* production costs, including agricultural taxes, makes it clear that the uncertain condition of agricultural income for both soybeans and corn result mainly from the instability of product price. The

CV for the average price of soybeans and corn is 16.4 percent and 21.5 percent, respectively, whereas the CV of yield is only 5.5 percent for soybeans and 4.2 percent for corn while the CV of production costs is just 7.9 percent for soybeans and 5.4 percent for corn. Price instability accounts for 92.1 percent of agricultural income uncertainty for soybeans, and 82.7 percent for corn.

## 3 Empirical Model

This section establishes a model for estimating the supply response of soybean farmers. The estimation is based on the Nerlovian model (Nerlove, 1958). There is a long time span in agricultural production; therefore, agricultural price and yield is an unknown for farmers at the beginning of every production period. It turns out that farmers are uncertain about their agricultural income. Farmers will establish a production plan basing on past information about price, yield or agricultural income. The model is set as follows.

$$A_{i,t,s} = \beta_0 + \beta_1 R^e_{i,t,s} + \beta_2 R^e_{i,t,c} + \beta_3 V^e_{i,t,s} + \beta_4 V^e_{i,t,c} + \mu_{i,t} \quad (1)$$

$$R^e_{i,t,s} = \sum_{h=0}^{2}(1-\theta)\theta^h R_{i,t-h-1,s},\ 0<\theta<1 \quad (2)$$

$$R^e_{i,t,c} = \sum_{h=0}^{2}(1-\lambda)\lambda^h R_{i,t-h-1,c},\ 0<\lambda<1 \quad (3)$$

$$V^e_{i,t,s} = \sum_{h=0}^{2}(1-\delta)\delta^h (R_{i,t-h-1,s} - R^e_{i,t-h-1,s})^2,\ 0<\delta<1 \quad (4)$$

$$V^e_{i,t,c} = \sum_{h=0}^{2}(1-\varepsilon)\varepsilon^h (R_{i,t-h-1,c} - R^e_{i,t-h-1,c})^2,\ 0<\varepsilon<1 \quad (5)$$

Equation (1) states that farmers in province $i$ decide soybean acreage ($A_s$) in period $t$ according to the expectation for agricultural income from soybeans ($R^e_s$), expectation for agricultural income form corn ($R^e_c$), expectation for agricultural income risk from soybeans ($V^e_s$) and expectation for agricultural income risk from corn ($V^e_c$). $\beta_1$,$\beta_2$,$\beta_3$ and$\beta_4$ denote the degree that the soybean supply responds to agricultural income expectation and risk. $\mu$is the regression residual.

Equation (2) illustrates farmers' expectations for agricultural income from soybeans ($R^e_s$) based on the weighted average of past agricultural income from soybeans ($R_s$). Similarly, equation (3) states the expectations of farmers for agricultural income from corn ($R^e_c$) based on the weighted average of past agricultural income from corn ($R_c$). $\theta$ and $\lambda$ are the parameters for composing the weighted average of past agricultural income from soybeans and corn, respectively. The longer the period for expectation, the greater the weighting is. Farmers are assumed to make such expectations back to period $h$. Since the period for analysis in this chapter is only 17 years, here farmers' expectation is assumed to be based on the past 3 periods only, namely, $h = 0, 1, 2$.

Equation (4) shows how farmers anticipate agricultural income risks for soybeans ($V^e_s$). Given that $R^e_s$ is the expected value of agricultural income for soybeans in the last section, ($R_s$- $R^e_s$) can be taken as the variation of agricultural income for soybeans.[2] Supposing that farmers estimate agricultural risk the same way as agricultural income expectation, equation (4) expresses the process by which farmers expect agricultural income risk for soybeans (Just, 1974). Similarly, equation (5) shows how farmers anticipate agricultural income risk for corn ($V^e_c$). $\delta$and $\varepsilon$are the parameters composing the weighted average of past agricultural income risk for soybeans and corn, respectively. $\delta$ and $\varepsilon$ have the same definitions as$\theta$ and$\lambda$. Also, it is assumed that $h = 0, 1, 2$ for the short period analyzed.

The substitution of equations (2) through (5) into equation (1) and rearrangement gives equation (6), which can be used for estimations.

$$A_{i,t,s} = \beta_0 + \beta_1 L_1 + \beta_2 L_2 + \beta_3 L_3 + \beta_4 L_4 + \mu_{i,t}$$

where

$$L_1 = \sum_{h=0}^{2} (1-\theta)\theta^h R_{i-t-h-1,s} \tag{6}$$

$$L_2 = \sum_{h=0}^{2} (1-\lambda)\lambda^h R_{i-t-h-1,c}$$

$$L_3 = \left\{ (1-\delta)\left[R_{i,t-1,s} - \sum_{h=0}^{2}(1-\theta)\theta^h R_{i,t-h-2,s}\right]^2 + \delta(1-\delta)\left[R_{i,t-2,s} - \sum_{h=0}^{2}(1-\theta)\theta^h R_{i,t-h-3,s}\right]^2 + \delta^2(1-\delta)\left[R_{i,t-3,s} - \sum_{h=0}^{2}(1-\theta)\theta^h R_{i,t-h-4,s}\right]^2 \right\}$$

$$L_4 = \left\{ (1-\varepsilon)\left[R_{i,t-1,c} - \sum_{h=0}^{2}(1-\lambda)\lambda^h R_{i,t-h-2,c}\right]^2 + \varepsilon(1-\varepsilon)\left[R_{i,t-2,c} - \sum_{h=0}^{2}(1-\lambda)\lambda^h R_{i,t-h-3,c}\right]^2 + \varepsilon^2(1-\varepsilon)\left[R_{i,t-3,c} - \sum_{h=0}^{2}(1-\lambda)\lambda^h R_{i,t-h-4,c}\right]^2 \right\}$$

## 4 Estimation Method and Data

In equation (6), if the value of $\theta$,$\lambda$,$\delta$ and $\varepsilon$ is known, each value of $L$ can be calculated and thus equation (6) takes on a linear form and can be estimated by the OLS. Here, the value of $\theta$,$\lambda$,$\delta$ and $\varepsilon$ can be found with the search procedure (Maddala, 1998). Each value of$\theta$,$\lambda$,$\delta$ and $\varepsilon$ in the range (0,1) is substituted into $L$s in intervals of 0.1. Given different values of each $L$, regression for equation (6) is run. The suitable value of $\theta$,$\lambda$,$\delta$ and $\varepsilon$ is chosen when the sum of the squared residuals is minimized and the corresponding value of $\beta$s is obtained as the least squared estimate. In order to capture the supply response elasticities, $L$s in equation (6) takes a natural logarithm.

Soybeans and corn are cultivated in nationwide. Because China is so large, it is necessary to consider regional differences in the supply behaviors of farmers (Mao, 2002). Due to the limitation of data availability, only data covering the 17-year-period between 1986 and 2002 in the following 11 provinces are used: Anhui, Jiangsu, Hebei, Shanxi, Inner Mongolia, Shangdong, Henan, Shaanxi,

---

[2] Cited from the web: http://www.aweb.com.cn/2004/2/16/200421682946.htm.

Liaoning and Heilongjiang. These provinces are China's main areas of soybean and corn production. In 2002, the total acreage of soybeans and corn in these provinces occupied 78.8 percent and 74.1 percent of national acreage, respectively.

The necessary data for regression are soybean acreage and agricultural income from soybean and corn. The data of soybean acreage can be obtained from various issues of the *Rural Statistical Yearbook of China* compiled by the National Bureau of Statistics of China (NBSC). The agricultural income is computed by subtracting production costs and agricultural taxes from the gross income. This combination is then deflated by the consumer price index (CPI) of rural areas in each province using 1985 as the base year. Data of gross income, production costs, and agricultural taxes are colleted from various issues of the *Comprehensive Materials on National Cost and Profit of Agricultural Products*, compiled jointly by the former National Development and Planning Committee and other organizations. For the CPI in rural areas, data from 1985 to 1998 are obtained from the *Comprehensive Statistical Data and Materials on 50 Years of New China* compiled by the NBSC, and those from 1999 to 2002 are collected from *China Statistical Yearbook*, issues from 2000 to 2003, compiled by the NBSC. Since the CPI data for rural areas in Shaanxi are only available after the year of 1994, the CPI for urban areas in this province will be substituted because it is believed that there is little difference between the prices in rural and urban areas in that province.

## 5 Estimation Results

### *5.1 Panel Unit Root Tests*

Normally, before estimation, the time series data need to be tested on whether they are stationary or not. Otherwise, the regression would be spurious if the data were nonstationary. There are various unit root tests for individual time series data. Both the well-known Levin-Lin (LL) and Im-Pesaran-Shin (IPS) tests can be used for unit root problems in the panel data because unit root tests based on panel data are generally considered to be more effective than those based on individual time series data (Levin *et al.*, 2002; Baltagi, 2003). The LL test assumes the autoregressive coefficient to be identical across cross-sections; in contrast, the IPS test relaxes the restrictive assumption of the LL test and assumes that the autoregressive coefficient may vary across cross-sections.

The panel unit root tests are conducted for soybean acreage, soybean agricultural income, and corn agricultural income after they are changed to natural logarithms. The procedure is carried out in two ways. One includes time trends, and the other does not. The unit root tests begin with level data. If the null hypothesis of unit root existence is not rejected for the level data, the same procedure is continued with the data taking a different form. Table 13.2 summarizes the results of the panel unit root tests. The hypothesis for most variables can not be rejected for the level data no matter whether the LL test or the

IPS test is utilized. However, it can be rejected for the data taking the first difference for both the LL test and the IPS test. Therefore, the regression for equation (6) must be run with data of taking the first difference.

**Table 13.2 Panel unit root test results**

| | | Soybean acreage (LnAs) | | Corn income □LnRc) | | Soybean income □LnRs□ | |
|---|---|---|---|---|---|---|---|
| | | C | C+T | C | C+T | C | C+T |
| Level data | LL test | -3.34*** | -3.88*** | -1.75** | 0.48 | -1.24 | 1.77 |
| | IPS test | -2.28*** | -0.29 | -0.12 | 0.32 | 0.73 | 1.52 |
| First difference | LL test | -7.68*** | -4.17*** | -5.54*** | -4.17*** | -5.54*** | -1.84** |
| | IPS test | -5.69*** | -4.41*** | -6.68*** | -4.41*** | -4.31*** | -2.27* |

*Notes*: 1. C and T denote constant and trend respectively. Hypothesis for test is the existence of unit root. Coefficients with *** are statistically significant at 1% level, ** are at 5% and * are at 10%.

### *5.2 Panel analysis results*

Both fixed-effect and random-effect models are applied for the panel data analysis. Table 13.3 reports the regression results. The minimum value of the residual sum of squares is 2.667 for the fixed effects and 2.817 for the random effects. Corresponding to the minimum residual sum of squares, two models have the same suitable value for $\theta,\lambda,\delta$ and $\varepsilon$ by accident, which is 0.7, 0.7, 0.9 and 0.9. Not much difference was found between the fixed effects and the random effects, but the result of Hausman's specification test suggests that the null hypothesis that the unobserved specific factors do not correlate with each explanatory variable can not be rejected. Therefore, the random effect model is selected. The reasons for no fixed effects are partly due to the fact that the most provinces analyzed in this study are in north China. The small size of cultivated land may be another reason for the no fixed effects among provinces. For random effects, the variance components can be divided into variance both between and within provinces. The former equals 0.0014, and the latter equals 0.0242. Thus, the variance between provinces only accounts for 0.0014 / (0.0014 + 0.0242) = 5.5 percent of random variation. Variance within a province explains 94.5 percent of the random variation.

Adjusted R-squared value for the random effects is 0.156. This small value can be explained by the following two reasons: (1) the period for regression becomes short because the agricultural income and its risk are expected. Note $L_3$ and $L_4$, for instance, express agricultural income risk expectations in equation (6). In order to expect an income risk for the past third period, it is necessary to trace the data back to the past sixth period.

**Table 13.3 Panel estimation results**

| | Fixed Effects | Random Effects |
|---|---|---|
| Constant ($\beta_0$) | - | 0.011 |
| | | (0.549) |
| Expectation of Agricultural Income for Soybeans ($\beta_1$) | 0.473*** | 0.441*** |
| | (3.059) | (3.110) |
| Expectation of Agricultural Income for Corn ($\beta_2$) | -0.582*** | -0.565*** |
| | (-4.263) | (-4.481) |
| Agricultural Income Risk of Soybeans ($\beta_3$) | -0.050* | -0.046* |
| | (-1.386) | (-1.394) |
| Agricultural Income Risk of Corn ($\beta_4$) | 0.055** | 0.055** |
| | (1.818) | (1.941) |
| Parameter to expect soybean agricultural income ($\theta$) | 0.7 | 0.7 |
| Parameter to expect corn agricultural income ($\gamma$) | 0.7 | 0.7 |
| Parameter to expect soybean agricultural income risk ($\delta$) | 0.9 | 0.9 |
| Parameter to expect corn agricultural income risk ($\varepsilon$) | 0.9 | 0.9 |
| Sum of Squared Residuals | 2.667 | 2.817 |
| Adjusted R-squared | 0.117 | 0.156 |
| DW | 2.137 | 2.019 |
| Hausman's specification test | $Chi^2(4)=0.383$ | P-value=0.984. |
| Variance components for random effects | | |
| Variance between provinces | - | 0.0014 |
| Variance within province | - | 0.0242 |

*Notes*: 1. The numbers in parentheses are t-values. Coefficients with *** are significant at 1% level, ** are at 5%, * are at 10%. Variance components for random effects are computed from large sample formula.

Additionally, the data take the form of the first difference. Therefore risk expectation only can be made after 1993. Data limitation affects the estimated results; (2) income would not be the only factor influencing the acreage decisions of farmers. Furthermore, corn is the alternative crop for soybeans. The value of the adjusted R-squared can be improved when more data is available. However, the estimated results are still meaningful in regard to analyzing the effect of the agricultural income risk on a farmer's soybean acreage decisions.

The estimated results show that Chinese farmers behave rationally during agricultural production, allocating more lands to soybean production when the agricultural income from soybeans is expected to rise. However, they will reduce the lands for soybean production when the agricultural income from corn is expected to rise, which means farmers shift some land to corn production. Furthermore, farmers will reduce soybean acreage when agricultural income from soybeans is expected to be more risky. Meanwhile, when agricultural income from corn is expected to be more risky, more soybeans will be cultivated. The result implies that the multi-cropping systems are useful in not only improving yield but also reducing the agricultural income risk of farmers.

However, note that the acreage decisions made by farmers respond much more to income expectations than to income risk. For a 10 percent increase in soybean agricultural income expectation, the acreage for soybeans increases by 4.41 percent; likewise, the acreage for soybeans decreases by about 5.65 percent for a 10 percent increase in the agricultural income expectation from corn. Whereas, 10 percent of the increase in an agricultural income risk from soybeans and 10 percent of decrease in that from corn only changes the acreage by a 0.46 percent decrease and a 0.55 percent increase, respectively.

It is interesting that farmers respond little to income risk in spite of the existence of the large agricultural income risk as was seen in Section 2. The explanation for that may be that in rural areas, market information is incomplete and increases the difficulty of forecasting income risks. Information resources largely exist among organizations, such as governments, institutions, and companies, among others, but it is difficult for farmers to obtain partly due to their lack of effective channels to the organizations and partly due to their low educational levels (Zheng and Shang, 2004).

According to a survey of a fixed rural observation village conducted by the Ministry of Agriculture in 2003, only about 11 percent of laborers per rural household have received an education beyond senior year in high school.[3] Such low educational levels seem to be an obstacle for Chinese farmers to forecast market risk. The difficulty in risk forecasting hints at some answers to the question of why farmer incomes grow slowly and are unstable even though they cultivate according to the multi-cropping system and behave rationally. Considering the problems that the superfluous phenomena emerge even in the competitive and profitable agricultural products, it is often said that the reasons for sales difficulties for some fruits, vegetables and meats lie in the fact that many farmers plant agricultural products only by chasing the market or following someone else blindly and that they do not understand the market situation well. Because of such actions taken by many farmers, the problems of overproduction are difficult to avoid (Xia *et al.*, 2002).

## 6 Conclusions and Policy Implications

This chapter, focusing on the alternative relationship between soybeans and corn, analyzes the acreage decisions of soybean farmers. Agricultural incomes from soybeans and corn are risky, and the income risk is mainly caused by price uncertainty for these products. Chinese farmers behave rationally in terms of supply response to agricultural income expectations and agricultural income risk. The multi-cropping systems in Chinese agriculture are not only helpful for yield

[3] Cited from the web: http://www.rcre.org.cn/RCRE/gdgc/gdgcdata.htm.

improvement but also helpful for reducing farmers' agricultural income risk. However, farmers respond more to the income expectation than to income risk.

This chapter suggests that, besides the encouragement of cultivating agricultural products with more competitiveness and a higher profitability, the government should create an environment under which farmers can easily access market information. Market information will lead farmers to supply more competitive and profitable products as a result.

## References


Aubert, C. and Zhu, X.G., *Economic Research of China's Soybeans* (*Zhongguo Dadou JInji Yanjiu*, Chinese) (The Agricultural Press of China, 2002).

Baltagi, B.H., *Econometric Analysis of Panel Data* (John Wiley & Sons, Ltd, 2003).

Buck, J.L., *Land Utilization in China* (Paragon Book Reprint Corp, 1964).

Hosono, S.O., *Pulses Production and Commercialization in Hokkaidou* (*Mamerui no Seisan to Syouhinka*, Japanese) (Cereals Encouragement Committee, 1955).

Huang, G.Q., Zhang, T.L. and Zhao, Q.G., *The Cropping System in Southern China* (*Zhongguo Nanfang Gengzuo Zhidu*, Chinese) (The Agricultural Press of China, 1997).

Just, R.E., 'An investigation of the importance of risk in farmers' decisions', *American Journal of Agricultural Economics*, 56(1) (1974): 14-25.

Ke, B.S., He, X.R. Tian, W.M., *WTO and Chinese Agriculture* (Chinese) (Agricultural Press of China, 2002).

Levin, A., Lin, C.F. and Chu, C.S., 'Unit root tests in panel data: asymptotic and finite-sample properties', *Journal of Econometrics*, 108 (1) (2002): 1-24.

Maddala, G.S., *Introduction to Econometrics* (Prentice Hall International, 1998).

Mao, Q.S., 'Empirical analysis of rice farmers' supply response to price in China (Japanese)', *Proceeding of Annual Conference of the Agricultural Economics Society of Japan* (2002): 323-326.

Nerlove, M., *The Dynamics of Supply: Estimation of Farmers' Response to Price* (The Johns Hopkins Press, 1958).

Oshima, K., *Imported Vegetables and China's Agriculture* (*Yunyuu Yashayi to Tyuugoku Nougyou*, Japanese) (Ashisyobou Press, 2003).

Ruan, W., *WTO and Chinese Agriculture* (*WTO to Chyugoku Nougyou*, Japanese) (Tsukuba Shobo, 2003).

Shen, X.N. and Liu, X.H., *Multicropping System* (*Duoshu Zhongzhi Zhidu*, Chinese) (The Agricultural Press of China, 1983).

Tan, X.Y. and Xin, X., *Market Analysis for the Main Agricultural Products in China* (*Zhongguio Zhuyao Nongchanpin Shichang Fenxi*, Chinese) (The Agricultural Press of China, 2001).

Tuan, F.C., Cheng, G.Q. and Peng, T.J., *Comparative Advantage and Trade Competitiveness of Major Agricultural Products in China* (ERS/UDSA, 2001).

Xia, Y.X., Zhao, W.J. and Chen, X.W., *Farmers' Income, Burden and Structural Adjustment* (*Nongmin Shouru, Nongmin Fudan and Jiegou Tiaozheng*, Chinese) (Agricultural Press of China, 2002).

Yan, S.P., *The Challenge of Peasant Country, as one of Series of Modern Chinese Economy* (*Nouming Kokka No kadai*, Japanese) (Nagoya University Press, 2002).

Zheng, H.W. and Shang, C.M., *Thinking about information market development problems in rural China* (*Woguo Nongcun Xinxi Shichang Fayu Wenti De Sikao*, Chinese). Problems on Agricultural Economics (Nongye Jingji Wengti, Chinese, 2004).

Chapter 14

# Reforms, Risks and Crop Diversification in Chinese Provinces: Commercial Crops versus Grain Crops

Weiyong Yang*

## 1 Introduction

Historically, China is an agricultural country in which agriculture is predominant in the national economy. For political and economical reasons, the Chinese cropping system has been characterized by a high concentration of grain crops since 1949. Hence, the cropping structure was very rigid and under-diversified. However, the cropping system has experienced a general trend of on-farm diversification from grain to commercial crops over time despite frequent fluctuations. In other words, an increasing amount of land has been allocated to cash crops, such as jute, sugarcane, peanuts, vegetables, and fruits in place of cereals, like rice and wheat. This trend became more pronounced in the post-Mao period—1978 onward—when the opening-door policy to international trade and the market-oriented reforms were implemented.

The objective of this chapter is to understand the trend of grain-commercial crop diversification, especially in this post-Mao period, and assess the respective roles of different factors driving this agricultural diversification, paying attention to two particular questions: whether or not the agricultural diversification is a rational profit-maximizing behavior of agricultural decision-makers under a more market-oriented system; and if it is an *ex ante* mechanism to cope with abundant risks in rural China where credit and insurance markets are either absent or imperfect.

Recently, the adjustment of cropping structure has received more attention in China. It is an issue greatly impacts not only rural income and employment, which have both stagnated in recent years, but also the rural environment that has deteriorated after a long period of intensive mono-cropping practices. Furthermore, the recent entry into the World Trade Organization requires China to adjust its cropping structure due to the intensification of international competition.

* The author expresses his gratitude to Sylvie Demurger, Jean-Louis Combes and Martin Fournier for their insightful comments.

Consequently, understanding the driving forces behind cropping-pattern changes is of great relevance for the rural development of China.

This chapter is organized as follows. Section 2 presents the evolution of cropping structures since 1952 by dividing it into two sub-periods. The third section consists of a theoretical analysis of crop-choice determinants with an emphasis on the significance of institutional reforms and risk factors. Section 4 describes the data and variables, and Section 5 presents and interprets the subsequent econometric results. The sixth and final section concludes the chapter and suggests some policy implications.

## 2 Evolution of the Cropping Structure

China's cropping patterns over the past fifty years have generally been characterized by a decrease of grain's share of total sown area in favor of commercial crops, such as rapeseed, jute, vegetables, and fruits. Grain has dropped from 88 percent in 1952 to 68 percent in 2001 (SSB, 1990 and 2002). This is a significant reduction, considering the continual growth of a large population at an annual rate of 1.6 percent during that same time span. However, frequent political and economical changes made this evolution very uneven, allowing us to divide it into two distinct sub-periods: the collectivization period from 1949 to 1978 and the reform period from 1978 to present day.

### *2.1 The Collectivization Period*

Since 1958, People's Communes—composed of an average of 5,000 households (Lin, 1999)—have been established throughout rural China. Under this system, all production, distribution and consumption decisions are made according to pre-established plans, depressing rural markets and fairs. The prices of agricultural products were kept artificially low in order to finance industrialization in urban areas.

The painful memories of the frequent famines during the war era before 1949 and embargos imposed on China by western countries made the Chinese government extremely sensitive to food self-sufficiency issues. Besides a direct control of the pricing system, four additional policies were used to influence the supply of grain: (1) a strict plan to the sown area of crops; (2) a compulsory quota procurement system; (3) subsidies on agricultural inputs; and (4) an incentive policy called "three links," which rewarded peasants who fulfilled the state grain quota with a fixed quantity of high quality fertilizer, oil, and cash advances (Davis and Wang, 2000). The result was the high proportion of grain in the sown areas, which was always more than 80 percent throughout this period, as shown in Figure 14.1.

The increase of agricultural production during the first half of the 1950s led the government to reduce the land area allocated to grain. More importantly, however, the cropping decision was substantially distorted by largely fake yield data during the Great Leap Forward between1958 and 1960. Consequently, grain's share of sown land registered an impressive drop from 88 percent in 1953 to 81 percent in 1960, the year when the whole country suffered from a severe famine.

In 1961, the government readjusted the cropping structure by an increase of grain's sown area. The deterioration of international relations—particularly with the former Soviet Union—seemed to justify this. After a moderate increase in the mid-1960s at the beginning of the Cultural Revolution, grain experienced a decreasing trend which would become more pronounced during the reform period.

### *2.2 The Reform Period*

In 1978, China entered a transitional period marked by numerous market-oriented reforms. In the countryside, the household responsibility system was introduced in agricultural production and applied to the whole country by 1983, which led to the dismantling of the People's Communes. Grain decreased rapidly at the beginning of the 1980s—falling from 80.3 percent in 1978 to 75.8 percent in 1985—followed by two episodes of slight increases corresponding to two reform setbacks, one in 1986 and another between 1989 and 1991. During the 1990s—except for a stagnation period in 1996 and 1997 due to the implementation of the provincial governor's grain responsibility system—the commercial-grain crop ratio in terms of sown area rose steadily, particularly in recent years (Table 14.1). As a result, grain's share of total sown area continued to fall to 68.1 percent in 2001 (Figure 14.1).

However, this national evolution hides large disparities among the different regions of China, as shown in Figures 2 and 3. Figure 14.2 shows that there is a great difference between the north and the south. Between 1978 and 2001, the commercial crops always occupied a more important place in the cropping system in south China than in the northern regions where the economic reforms were less advanced. In addition, as suggested in Table 14.1, these two regions reveal divergent evolution patterns over time despite similar upward trends (the commercial-grain crop ratio increased at an annual rate of 2.9 percent in both regions). From 1978 to 1988, the ratio increased more rapidly in the north—3.6 percent per year—than in the south at 1.8 percent per year, narrowing the gap between the two regions.

The trend, however, reversed itself in the following period as the importance of commercial crops continued to rise in the south and stagnate in the north. The gap between the two regions was widened once more during the 1990s, but in recent years, the cropping-structure adjustment tended to accelerate in the north.

**Table 14.1 Annual change rate of the commercial crop-grain crop ratio**

| Periods | National | South | North | East | Center | West |
|---|---|---|---|---|---|---|
| 1978-2001 | 2.9% | 2.9% | 2.9% | 3.3% | 2.0% | 4.1% |
| 1978-1988 | 2.6% | 1.8% | 3.6% | 2.5% | 1.5% | 5.4% |
| 1989-1991 | 1.7% | 3.3% | 0.04% | 2.1% | 1.3% | 2.3% |
| 1992-1995 | 2.2% | 3.4% | 0.8% | 1.6% | 2.3% | 2.6% |
| 1996-1997 | 0.3% | 1.6% | -1.8% | 0.7% | -1.6% | 2.3% |
| 1998-2001 | 6.5% | 5.6% | 8.0% | 9.3% | 5.4% | 4.7% |

*Notes*:

1. The commercial crop-grain crop ratio is measured as the ratio between sown area of commercial crops and that of grain crops.
2. These rates are annual geometrical mean for each region.

*Source*: *China Statistic Yearbook*, 1981-2002.

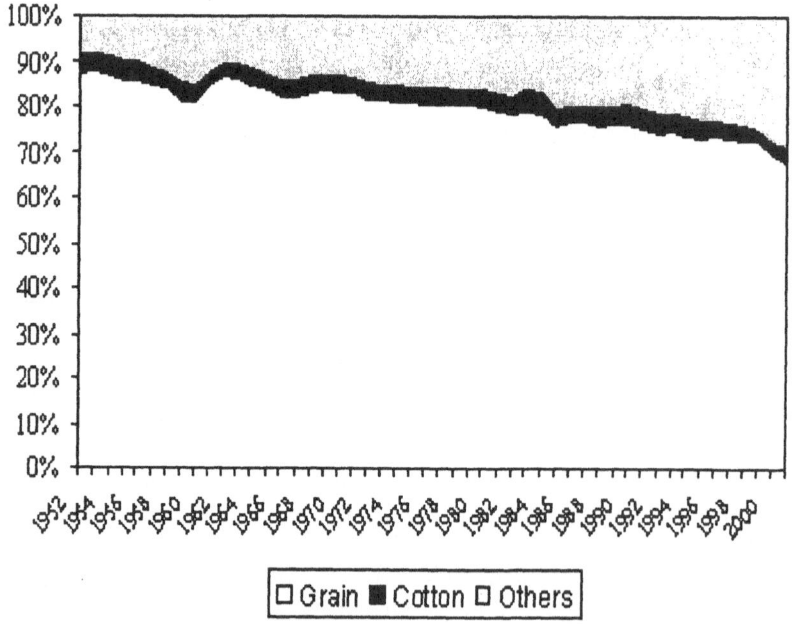


*Note*: 1. Other crops include rapeseed, sesame, peanut, jute, sugarcane, tobacco, vegetables, fruit plants, etc…

**Figure 14.1 Evolution of the cropping structure 1952-2001**

*Source*: SSB, 1981,1985 and 2002.

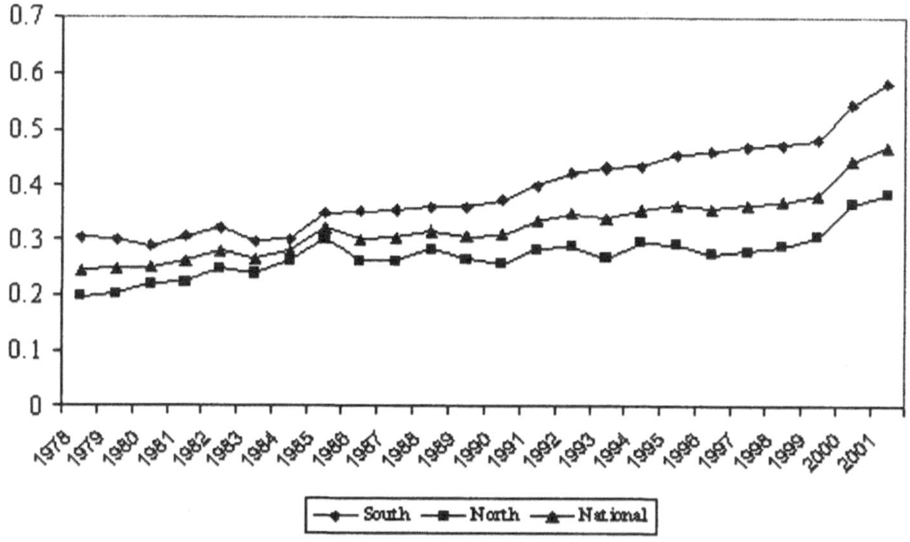


*Notes*:
1. The ratio is defined as in the notes of Table 14.1.
2. The North includes 16 provinces: Beijing, Tianjin, Hebei, Shanxi, Inner Mongolia, Liaoning, Jilin, Heilongjiang, Anhui, Shandong, Henan, Shaanxi, Gansu, Qinghai, Ningxia and Xinjiang; The South is composed of the 13 remaining provinces (Tibet is excluded): Shanghai, Jiangsu, Zhejiang, Fujian, Jiangxi, Hubei, Hunan, Guangdong, Guangxi, Hainan, Sichuan, Guizhou and Yunnan.

**Figure 14.2 Regional evolution of the commercial crop-grain crop ratio (1): north and south**

*Source*: SSB, 1981-2002.

Figure 14.3 reveals that disparities among east, central, and west China are also important. From 1978 to 2001, the west, which had the greatest diversity of natural conditions among the three regions, experienced the fastest adjustment in favor of commercial crops at an annual average rate of 4.1 percent, followed by the east where economic reforms were the most advanced with 3.3 percent, and finally central China, which is the traditional grain production region with 2.0 percent. As a result of the differences in adjustment speed, the west has caught up the central regions since the mid-1990s. The east has preserved its leading position since 1986—further consolidated by a sharp rise of its commercial-grain crop ratio by 9.3 percent per year between 1998 and 2001. The factors generating these temporal and spatial disparities are explored in the next section.

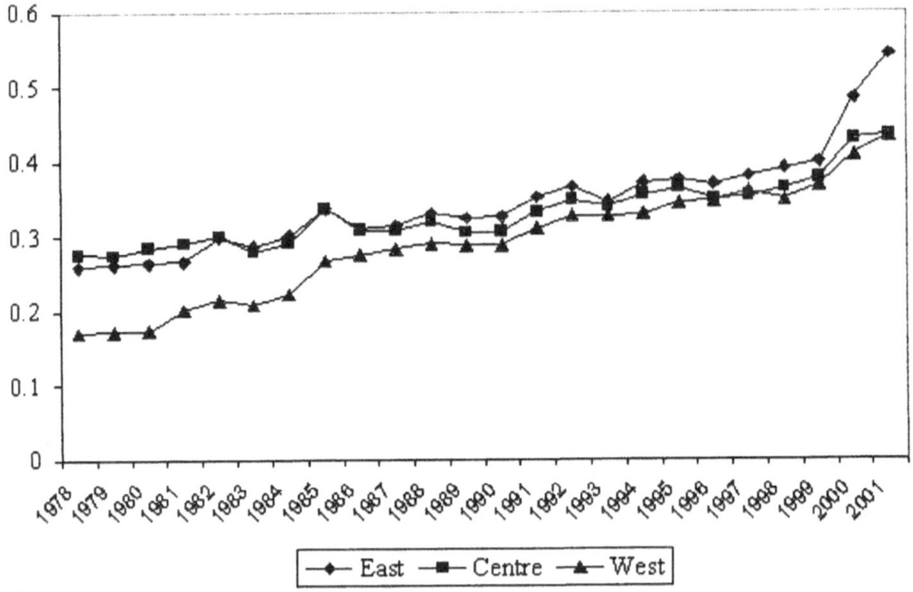


*Notes*:
1. The ratio is defined as in the notes of Table 14.1.
2. The East includes 12 coastal provinces: Beijing, Tianjin, Hebei, Liaoning, Shanghai, Jiangsu, Zhejiang, Fujian, Shandong, Guangdong, Guangxi, Hainan; The Center: Shanxi, Inner Mongolia, Jilin, Heilongjiang, Anhui, Jiangxi, Henan, Hubei, Hunan; And the West (without Tibet): Sichuan, Guizhou, Yunnan, Shaanxi, Gansu, Qinghai, Ningxia and Xinjiang.

**Figure 14.3 Regional evolution of the commercial crop-grain crop ratio (2): east, center and west**

*Source*: SSB, 1981-2002.

## 3 Determinants of Commercial Crop versus Grain Crop Choice: Reforms and Risks

Crop choice may be influenced by a great number of socio-economic factors and natural conditions. In our analysis, we focus on two important factors, institutional reforms and risks.

### *3.1 Reforms and Crop Choice*

We focus on two main institutional changes which marked the reform period from 1978 onward. One is the introduction and the development of market mechanisms in a planned economy, and the other is the opening-up policy of foreign trade. Market development may make the crop-choice decision more sensitive to relative prices of crops, and the intensification of international competition induced by the open-door policy pushes China to readjust the cropping structure according to its comparative advantages.

### *3.1.1 Price Reforms and Agricultural Product Market*

In the agricultural sector, the reforms started with price reforms in the late-1970s. The "two-track" price system was introduced in the procurement system of agricultural products, with a quota price and an above-quota price for the extra-quota sale of grain to the Chinese government, generally 30 to 50 percent higher. Besides several increases of quota prices and above-quota prices—by 17 percent in 1979 and 41 percent in 1980 (Lin, 1992)—the government reduced by the procurement commitments of grain 20 percent, from 37.75 to 30.32 million tons between 1979 and 1983 (DDZGLSGZ, 1988). Since the government continued to provide grains at a low ration-price for urban residents, heavy subsidies became more unbearable in the mid-1980s. Hence, the government abandoned the "two-track" price system in 1985 and replaced it with a unique "proportional" price, which is a weighted average of the quota price and the above-quota price. This new price corresponded to an increase of 35 percent compared with the former quota price, but a decrease of 10 percent with respect to the above-quota price. Therefore, a decrease of grain's marginal return, which might partly explain the impressive increase of sown area of commercial crops such as tobacco, jute, fruits, and vegetables in 1985—24.2 percent of total sown area against 21.7 percent in 1984.

At the same time, markets reappeared in rural areas and gradually became an important outlet for the agricultural surplus of rural households. At the end of 1978, sales of agricultural surplus at local fairs were allowed after fulfillment of the state quota, even though quantity and types of the marketed products were still controlled by the government (CCP, 1978). In 1995, 37 percent of grain produced that year was sold through the market channel (Davis and Wang, 2000). According to Ke (1995), an average of 350 kg of grain was sold through the markets by an agricultural household each year. After one decade of reforms, the number of market places in rural China, including countryside fairs, retail markets, and wholesale markets had doubled, from 29,882 in 1977 to 58,775 in 1987. All these changes made agricultural production more sensitive to the evolution of both prices and market conditions. However, this market development process was interrupted during the retrenchment period of 1989 to 1991 in which the state procurement system with low quota price was strengthened.

The 1990s were characterized by the liberalization of the commercialization system of agricultural products and vigorous development of the market system. On the one hand, market infrastructure developed steadily—the number of market places continued to rise from 72,579 in 1990 to 88,576 in 1999 (including 26,414 specialized markets of agricultural products). On the other hand, administrative controls were substantially reduced. In 1992, about 20 percent of the counties in

China had already removed the quota imposed on peasants (ZGSYNJ 1993; Rozelle et al. 1997). In 1991, the government significantly raised the sale price of grain, which had been kept very low and unchanged for 26 years, and in the next year, the purchase and sale prices were unified before the entire liberalization of the grain purchase and sale prices in 1993. Meanwhile, the contractual procurement system was replaced by the state grain purchases contingent on prevailing market conditions.

However, imperfections of the market system in the early stage of its development made the prices very unstable. Between the end of 1993 and mid-1995, the price of rice and corn rose by 75 and 60 percent, respectively. To stabilize food prices in the mid-1990s, price controls were imposed on cities, and the quota procurement system (with a purchase price lower than the market price) was reintroduced in rural areas. These sharp rises of the price of grain and an impressive increase of grain imports—from 9 million tons in 1994 to more than 20 million tons in 1995—revived the government's worries about food security, leading it to re-emphasize grain production in the following years by introducing a provincial governor's grain responsibility system consisting in putting the province's grain self-sufficiency responsibility on the shoulder of provincial governors. Under this policy, the provinces in grain deficit had to increase the grain's sown area whatever their natural or agronomic conditions. As a result, the grain's share in the total sown area increased slightly from 73.4 percent in 1995 to 73.9 percent in 1996.

In summary, agricultural production, including crop choice, became less controlled by state administrative measures and more guided by market conditions, especially market prices during the reform period. Consequently, we can expect that with the development of the market system, crop choice decisions will be increasingly made according to the relative prices between commercial crops and grains.

### *3.1.2 Trade Opening-up Policy*

With the implementation of the open-door policy in 1978, China has been more actively participating in the international food trade as shown in Figure 14.4. Grain's trade ratio (the sum of grain's import and export divided by the national production of grain) rose during the reform period an average of 4.4 percent from 1978 to 2001 against 2.9 percent from 1953 to 1977. The opening policy can influence crop choice decision in two ways: (1) the participation in international food markets allows China to equilibrate its national food market, making the government less sensitive to food security issues; and (2) international competition brought by this policy and its recent entry into the WTO forces China to adjust the structure of its agricultural production according to its comparative advantage. Given China's factorial endowment—characterized by the abundance of labor and relative scarcity of land resources—China must reduce the share of land-intensive grain crops that are still overwhelmingly dominant in its cropping structure and increase the importance of labor-intensive crops, such as vegetables and fruits. Therefore, with the trade opening-up, we expect an increase in the share of commercial crops in the total sown area to the detriment of grain crops.

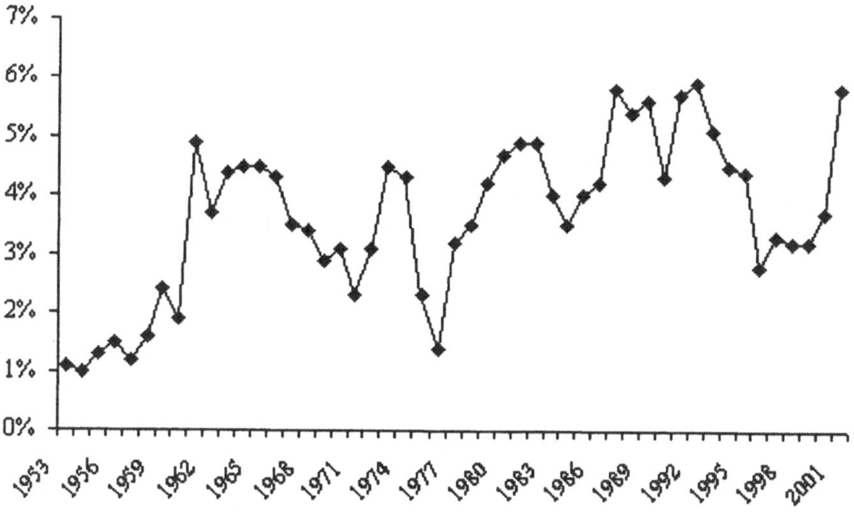


*Note*: 1. The grain's trade ratio is calculated by dividing the sum of grain's import and export by national grain's production (in percentage).
**Figure 14.4 Evolution of grain's trade ratio over 1953-2001**
*Source*: SSB (1994-2002) and Cook, Yao and Zhuang (2000).

*3.2 Risks and Agricultural Diversification*

Rich literature about risks and agricultural diversification (Chavas and Holt, 1990; Rosenzweig and Binswanger, 1993; Newbery and Stiglitz, 1981; Kurosaki, 1995 and 1997, Fafchamps, 1992) has pointed out that, due to the lack of *ex post* risk-management mechanisms, like insurance and credit markets, agricultural diversification constitutes an important *ex ante* instrument for risk protection.

In China, risks are abundant in agriculture. During the transitional period, market prices of agricultural products are very volatile due to the incompleteness of the reforms and the numerous imperfections of the nascent market system. This agricultural price variability may have serious consequences on the income and welfare of rural households. The development and integration of the market system, however, are expected to reduce these price risks over time.

On the other hand, the climatic risks, especially natural calamities, are an important determinant of the yield (Zhang and Carter, 1997; Yang, 1994). From 1978 to 2001, natural disasters, such as floods and droughts, affected an average of 30.8 percent of the total sown area each year and caused severe consequences in

15.5 percent of the total sown area with a yield reduction of at least 30 percent, compared to a normal year (SSB 1990 and 2002).

For rural households, the incidence of risks tended to increase during the reform period. The dismantling of the People's Communes, which played a risk-polling role in rural area, and the introduction of the household responsibility system in agricultural production led to a transfer of the risk burden from collectives to the individual agricultural households. Moreover, the withdrawal of the state in public programs, such as irrigation maintenance and other agricultural infrastructures, [1] might accentuate the incidence of climatic risks and make agricultural production more exposed and vulnerable to climatic hazards. Therefore, the diversification trend in the Chinese cropping system may be considered a rational strategy in order to cope with the risks. According to Fleisher and Liu (1992), the multi-cropping system is the best way to prevent a crop failure in Chinese agriculture.

Following Dixit (1993), we formalize the analysis within a simple framework of portfolio theory. We consider the case where a decision-maker allocates, according to risks, his land resources between two kinds of crops—commercial and grain—with the proportion $\alpha$ ($0 \le \alpha \le 1$) and $1-\alpha$, respectively, in order to maximize agricultural profits. Hence, the object of the portfolio decision is the cultivated land which is an important productive resource, measured as sown area instead of monetary value.[2] The risks produce a random return of agricultural production:

$$\tilde{R} = \mu + \eta \tag{1}$$

where $\mu$ is the expected value of the random return $\tilde{R}$, and $\eta$ denotes the random component of the return, which follows an identical and independent distribution, with E ($\eta$) = 0, and $\sigma^2$ as the variance of the agricultural return. Hence, the expected utility-equivalent, certain return is given by

$$\bar{R} = \mu - \frac{1}{2} g(\alpha) A \sigma^2 \tag{2}$$

where $A$ is the absolute risk aversion coefficient. To simplify the analysis, we suppose that the return $\mu$ only depends upon the land allocation parameter $\alpha$, and the prices of the two crops, $p_1$ for the commercial crop products and $p_2$ for grains,

$$\mu(\alpha, p_1, p_2) = p_1 \alpha q_1 + p_2 (1-\alpha) q_2 \tag{3}$$

[1] For the period 1952-80, on average, the expenditures for agricultural fixed capital formation accounted for 4.3 percent of total government budget, but this share fell to 2 percent during 1981-97 (SSB 2000).

[2] No explicit prices are available for collectively owned land due to the lack of land market in China.

$p_2$ being normalized to 1, then $p$ is the relative price between commercial crop products and grains, and Equation (3) becomes :

$$\mu(\alpha, p) = p\alpha q_1 + (1-\alpha)q_2 \quad (4)$$

The factor $g(\alpha)$ ( $0 < g(\alpha) \leq 1$ ) measures the effect of diversification. By definition, diversification reaches its highest level when $\alpha$ equals 0.5 and its lowest level when $\alpha$ takes the value of 0 or 1. Considering these properties, we suppose that $g(\alpha)$ takes a quadratic form as below:

$$g(\alpha) = \alpha^2 - \alpha + z \quad (5)$$

where $z$ can be any value satisfying $0 < g(\alpha) \leq 1$.

By introducing Equations (4) and (5) into Equation (2), we obtain

$$\overline{R} = \alpha p q_1 + (1-\alpha)q_2 - \frac{1}{2}(\alpha^2 - \alpha + z)A\sigma^2 \quad (6)$$

The problem then becomes the maximization of the agricultural profit (Equation 6) by choosing an appropriate value of $\alpha$.

The first order condition gives:

$$\alpha = \frac{1}{2} + \frac{pq_1 - q_2}{A\sigma^2} \quad (7)$$

From Equation (7) we can see that $\partial\alpha / \partial p > 0$. It means that when the price of commercial crop products increases with respect to grains, land will be reallocated from grain crops to commercial crops. Concerning an increase of risk ( $\sigma^2$ ) induced by a greater incidence of climatic hazards or more volatile prices, two cases are considered according to the sign of the return difference between the two crops $pq_1 - q_2$.

1. If $pq_1 - q_2 \geq 0$, then, $\alpha \geq 1/2$, and $\partial\alpha / \partial\sigma^2 < 0$. When commercial crops are already dominant, a risk increment will lead to a reallocation of land from commercial to grain crops. However, this is not the case in China since $\alpha$ is always below 0.5 in all provinces between 1978 and 2001.[3] Therefore, we consider the second case instead.
2. If $pq_1 - q_2 < 0$, then $\alpha < 1/2$ and $\partial\alpha / \partial\sigma^2 > 0$. When grain crops dominate the cropping pattern—as is the case in China—a risk increment will increase the value of $\alpha$ toward 0.5.

In both cases, a risk increment will lead to a greater diversification.

[3] Except Shanghai municipality and Xinjiang province where $\alpha$ exceeded slightly 0.5 in the recent years, which means a specialization in commercial crops rather than a diversification, as pointed out by an anonymous referee. In order to avoid confusions about the concept of diversification, we exclude these observations (only seven of the 460 observations) from our analysis. The empirical results do not change with this sample adjustment.

As pointed out by several studies, the existence of other risk protection possibilities will reduce the necessity for agricultural diversification through crop adjustment. Rosenzweig and Binswanger (1993) and Dercon (1996) found that the magnitude of risk effects diminishes with the initial wealth if the risk aversion coefficient (*A* in the above equations) is decreasing in respect to wealth and if wealth facilitates an ex-post consumption smoothing. For example, livestock can be an effective risk-protection mechanism for its good liquidity and synergies existing between cropping and husbandry (Townsend, 1994; Udry, 1995; Deaton, 1991; Reardon et al. 1988 and 1992; Kurosaki, 1995 and 1997; Reardon and Taylor, 1996).

Likewise, off-farm activities, in particular the rural industry, can reduce the necessity of on-farm diversification in two ways: (1) stable and cash incomes from rural industry can reduce the riskiness of the total household income; and (2) an income increase induced by these non-agricultural activities may decrease risk aversion of rural households and make them less vulnerable to risk. Additionally, a well-developed and maintained irrigation system can also reduce the incidence of climatic risks and make agricultural production more resistant to climatic hazards.

In summary, the agricultural diversification can be viewed as a process toward a greater flexibility regarding risks in the cropping system and a higher sensitivity to market conditions. Hence, the on-farm diversification factors can be summarized in the following function:

$$\alpha = \alpha(P, G, R, S) \qquad (8)$$

where *P* represents the relative price between commercial crops and grains. *G* is a vector of reform variables, including a market-development index and an opening-up policy indicator, *R* is risk indicators and risk-related variables, and *S* structural variables, such as the rural population ratio, agronomic factors, and rural household characteristics. The function will be estimated with provincial panel data described in detail in the next section.

## 4 Data and Variables

The data set used for the empirical analysis is composed of twenty-nine provinces from 1985 to 2001. Due to the lack of a consistent data series, Tibet is excluded from the database. The data came from China's officially published yearbooks: *China Statistical Yearbook*, *Township and Village Enterprises Yearbook of China*, *Rural Statistical Yearbook of China*, *China Statistical Yearbook of Price and Urban Household Income and Expenditure*, *China Regional Economy: A Profile of 17 years of Reform and Opening-up*, and *Comprehensive Statistical Data and Materials on 50 years of New China*. Using these data, a series of variables are constructed for the estimation of our crop diversification model.

The crop diversification indicator is defined as the ratio between the sown area of commercial crops and that of grain crops, $\alpha/(1-\alpha)$ ; since $\alpha < 1/2$ , an increase of this indicator means a greater crop diversification level.

*Relative price*, which reflects the relative return between the two crops, is measured as the ratio of the retail price index of commercial crop products[4] over the retail price index of grain. Regarding institutional factors, the *market development index* is defined as the ratio between the transaction values realized in free markets and the total retail sale value. It should reflect the importance of free markets in a province's commercialization system. The *opening policy index* is measured by the ratio between the international trade and the province's GDP. In addition, two dummy variables are also introduced in the model to capture the effect of reform retrenchment from 1989 to 1991 as well as the provincial governor's grain responsibility system from 1996 to 1997.

As far as the risk factors are concerned, two types of risk are considered: market risks and climatic hazards. During the transitional period, agricultural prices were very instable and unpredictable. To capture the effect of price risk on crop choice, an indicator of agricultural price instability is constructed in three stages within an anticipation model. First, the relative price ($P$) is estimated by the following function:

$$p = \alpha \cdot p_{-1} + \beta \cdot T + \gamma \cdot T^2 + \varepsilon \tag{9}$$

where $P_{-1}$ is the relative price lagged by one period, and $T$ denotes the time trend. Second, using these estimation results, the price is decomposed into two parts, the anticipated price, $\hat{p}$ (the predicted value of the price), and anticipation error, $\varepsilon$ (residue of the above equation). Finally, the indicator of price instability is calculated by the following formula:

$$I_p = \frac{|\varepsilon|}{\hat{P}} \tag{10}$$

where $|\varepsilon|$ is the absolute value of the residue.

With regard to the climatic risks, *calamities index* is the ratio between the sown area seriously hit by natural calamities—with a yield loss of no less than 30 percent compared with the yield of a normal year—and the total sown agricultural area.

To capture the joint effects of the risks and the institutional factors, two *interactive variables*—one between the market-development index and the price instability indicator, and the other between the market index and the calamity index—are also introduced into our crop diversification model. Other variables used in the empirical analysis are defined in Table 14.2 which gives the descriptive statistics of all variables.

---

[4] This index is a simple mean of price indexes of four products: vegetal oil, fresh vegetables, fresh fruits and sugar.

**Table 14.2 Descriptive statistics of the variables**

| Variables | Observation | Mean | Standard Error | Minimum | Maximum |
|---|---|---|---|---|---|
| *Commercial crop-grain crop ratio* | 660 | 0.34 | 0.15 | 0.11 | 0.91 |
| *Relative price* | 453 | 0.99 | 0.05 | 0.90 | 1.12 |
| *Price risks* | 453 | 0.07 | 0.06 | 0.00 | 0.31 |
| *Market development index* | 550 | 0.33 | 0.26 | 0.00 | 1.68 |
| *Opening policy* | 646 | 0.17 | 0.24 | 0.00 | 1.96 |
| *Calamities* | 598 | 0.21 | 0.13 | 0.00 | 0.68 |
| *Livestock* | 482 | 0.60 | 0.41 | 0.00 | 2.13 |
| *Off-farm diversification* | 567 | 0.26 | 0.15 | 0.02 | 0.83 |
| *Irrigated land ratio* | 660 | 0.34 | 0.15 | 0.07 | 0.96 |
| *Rural population share* | 660 | 0.74 | 0.16 | 0.25 | 0.91 |
| *Comparative advantage index* | 594 | 0.97 | 0.24 | 0.38 | 2.53 |
| *Multiple cropping index* | 660 | 1.50 | 0.50 | 0.65 | 2.58 |
| *Rural family size* | 484 | 4.14 | 0.57 | 2.83 | 5.64 |

*Notes*: Definition of variables

1. The institutional and risk variables are defined in the text. The other variables are defined as follows. *Livestock* is the number of draught animals per household in rural area; *Off-farm diversification* is measured as the share of rural enterprises' employment in total rural employment; *Irrigated land ratio* is measured as the share of irrigated land in total sown area; *Rural population share* is defined as the ratio of rural population over total population; *Comparative advantage index* of commercial crops compared with grain crops in each province is measured as a ratio between the simple mean of yield indexes (yield per hectare of a crop divided by its national average yield) of all commercial crops cultivated in a province and that of grain crops; *Multiple cropping index* is calculated by dividing sown area by cultivated area; And *Rural family size* is the average number of family members of rural households.

## 5 Econometric Results and Interpretation

The panel data estimation method allows us to control for unobservable and time-invariant factors for each province. The Breusch–Pagan test confirms the significant individual effect of provinces. In addition, the Hausman-specification test indicates that the fixed-effect model is to be preferred to the random-effect model. In the estimated specifications, all explanatory variables are lagged by one period under the hypothesis that the crop-diversification decision is made at the beginning of the year, given the information set available at the end of the preceding year. This treatment does have the advantage of reducing the endogeneity problem but at the cost of a one-year observation loss. Hence, our data set effectively runs from 1986 to 2001, a period of 16 years.

**Table 14.3 Estimation results of the crop diversification model**

| Dependent Variable: the commercial crop-grain crop ratio | | |
|---|---|---|
| Variables | Regression 1 | Regression 2 |
| *Anticipated relative price* | 0.46 (5.46[1])*** | 0.18 (1.91)* |
| *Opening policy* | 0.18 (5.77)*** | 0.004 (0.20) |
| *Price risks* | 0.11 (2.00)** | 0.08 (1.37) |
| *Calamities index* | 0.13 (3.97)*** | 0.17 (3.91)*** |
| *Livestock* | -0.05 (-1.66)* | 0.01 (0.63) |
| *Off-farm diversification* | - 0.11 (-1.92)* | -0.03 (-0.61) |
| *Irrigation ratio* | -0.72 (-6.34)*** | -0.60 (-5.41)*** |
| *Rural population share* | -0.42 (-4.26)*** | -0.11 (-1.49) |
| *Comparative advantage index* | 0.04 (2.21)** | 0.02 (1.72)* |
| *MCI* | 0.07 (3.02)*** | 0.02 (1.18) |
| *Rural family size* | 0.10 (3.56)*** | 0.02 (0.82) |
| *Trend* | 0.02 (10.51)*** | 0.02 (7.26)*** |
| *Dummy 89-91* | 0.004 (0.49) | -0.02 (-3.53)*** |
| *Dummy 96-97* | -0.02 (-2.45)** | -0.01 (-1.18) |
| *Market development index* | | 0.04 (1.31) |
| *Market index × calamities* | | -0.45 (-4.22)*** |
| *Market index × price risk* | | -0.26 (-1.91)* |
| *Observations* | 452 | 355 |
| *$R^2$ within* | 0.59 | 0.53 |
| *Method* | Fixed effect | Fixed effect |

*Notes*: 1. The T-Student values are between brackets; ***significant at 1%, **significant at 5%, *significant at 10%.

The estimation results are presented in Table 14.3. The model explains more than half of the crop diversification's variations. Most variables are significant at the usual threshold of 5 percent with the expected sign. Regression 1 gives basic results of the model. The role of market development[5] and its interactive terms with price and climatic risks are highlighted in Regression 2.

In Regression 1, the significant and positive sign of the relative price variable suggests that the crop choice is determined by the relative return of the two crops. When the anticipated prices of commercial crop products increase compared to grain price, more land will be allocated to commercial crops at the expense of

[5] Since data on market transactions are not available after 1999, the data set for Regression 2 covers the period 1986-1999 instead of 1986-2001.

grain crops. It seems that with price reforms and the market liberalization during the period, decision-makers of crop choice became more sensitive to price evolution.

The opening-up of the country to foreign trade encourages diversification from grain crops to commercial crops: the international market integration pushed the Chinese provinces to readjust their cropping structure in line with their comparative advantages determined by factorial endowments. In addition, this readjustment is confirmed by a positive and significant sign of the comparative advantage index, which suggests that provinces with more favorable agronomic conditions for commercial crops compared with grain production tend to increase the share of commercial crops in the total sown area over time.

Despite an up-going trend, the downbeat effect of the provincial governor's grain responsibility system on the crop diversification is confirmed by a negative sign associated with the dummy variable for 1996 and 1997. Likewise, the political retrenchment between 1989 and 1991 is proved to have a negative effect on crop diversification (Regression 2). During this period, the state compulsory system of grain procurement and the government's control over sown area were both strengthened in order to increase grain production.

As far as risk variables are concerned, the results show that the risks are taken into account in crop-choice decisions. In the face of the important price risks, rural households tend to diversify their cropping system. Similarly, the positive and very significant coefficient for the natural calamities index is consistent with the hypothesis that an increment of risk induces a greater diversification in order to protect against crop failures. However, the existence of other risk-protection mechanisms is associated with a low agricultural diversification level. The livestock variable has a negative and marginally significant sign. The livestock, as an *ex post* insurance mechanism in rural areas, can reduce the risk-protection need by crop diversification. Similarly, off-farm diversification is found to be a substitute for on-farm diversification, since stable incomes from non-agricultural activities, especially from the rural industry, can make rural households less averse to risk. As expected, the irrigated-land ratio decreases the agricultural diversification level by reducing the vulnerability of agricultural production to climatic risks.

Regression 2 provides some insight into the role of institutional factors related to market developments. Market development has a positive but not very significant effect on the diversification from grain crops to commercial crops. Grain market development as well as intra- and inter-provincial market integration release local grain self-sufficiency constraint and push each province to adjust the cropping structure according to its comparative advantage. The interactive variable between the price risk and the market development indicator is associated with a negative and significant sign. This result supports the hypothesis that the market development reduces the price risks and thus makes the crop diversification less necessary. Likewise, the negative and significant sign of the market-calamities interactive variable shows a risk-reducing effect of market development since in a well-developed and integrated market system, climatic risks are well-pooled. Nevertheless, in this regression, the opening policy index is no longer significant, which suggests that domestic market development and integration have a more important impact on the crop diversification than international market integration.

Finally, most structural variables are significant with the expected sign. The rural population share reduces the diversification toward commercial crops. This factor captures changes in the demand structure of agricultural products induced by demographic changes. A higher rural population share is associated with a lower demand for commercial crop products, such as vegetables and fruits, more frequently consumed by urban residents. On the contrary, a larger family size and a higher multiple-cropping index facilitate the crop diversification by a greater availability of labor and land.

## 6 Conclusions

Since 1949—and more importantly since the reform period—the Chinese cropping structure has been characterized by a diversification trend from grain to commercial crops. Using panel data of twenty-nine provinces from 1986 to 2001, we found that reform factors have important effects on crop-choice decisions. Since these decisions became more sensitive to market conditions, it is necessary to further deepen the market development and international opening process for an efficient allocation of limited agricultural resources, like land so that the crop choice is more determined by relative price changes and the comparative advantage of each province rather than by administrative measures.

The entry of China into the WTO will force the country as well as its provinces to abandon their grain self-sufficiency policy and adjust the production structure toward more labor-intensive crops, such as vegetables and fruits. In order to facilitate this adjustment, all levels of government can play an active role in providing market information and financial support to this structural change, which involves a non-negligible adjustment cost from the beginning.

Due to their severe occurrence on agricultural production, risks are important determinants of crop diversification. First, the market system should be further improved so as to reduce price risks. Second, in order to avoid crop failures, other more efficient risk-protection mechanisms should also be made available in rural China. Three solutions are put forward: (1) establish a national or regional insurance system against crop failure (Wu, 2000); (2) the collective risk-sharing role of agricultural production cooperatives, which developed rapidly in rural area during the 1990s; and (3) the strengthening of the irrigation system in order to make agricultural production more resistant to climatic hazards.

Finally, on-farm diversification from grain toward commercial crops occurs within a more general framework of rural, economic structural changes. It has an important impact on not only rural employment and income, but also the rural environment since this multi-crop farming can be a remedy to environmental degradation from a long period of mono-crop practices, such as fertility depletion of land. Therefore, on-farm diversification constitutes an important component of the sustainable development strategy in rural China.

## References


CCP (Chinese Communist Party Central Committee), 'Regulations on the Work of Rural People's Commune(Draught)', *Compilation of Important Economic Regulations* (Beijing: State Planning Committee, Office of Regulation and Law, China Statistics Press, 1978, in Chinese).

Chavas, J. and Holt, M., 'Acreage Decisions under Risks: The Case of Corn and Soybeans', *American Journal of Agricultural Economics*, 72(3) (August, 1990): 529-538.

Cook, S., Yao, S. and Zhuang, J., *Chinese Economy under Transition*, Macmillan Press, 2000.

Davis, J. and Wang, L., 'The Economic Behavior of China's Grain Producers in Transition', in S. Cook, S. Yao and J. Zhuang, (eds), *Chinese Economy under Transition* (Macmillan Press, 2000), pp.198-217.

DDZGLSGZ, *Grain works in the Contempory China* (Beijing: Chinese Social Science Press, 1988, in Chinese).

Deaton, A., 'Saving and Liquidity Constraints,' *Econometrica*, 59(5) (September, 1991): 1221-1248.

Dercon, S., 'Risk, Crop Choice, and Savings: Evidence from Tanzania', *Economic Development and Cultural Change*, 44(3) (April, 1996): 485-513.

Dixit, A., 'Scale Economics, Technological Change, and Diversification', in K. Hoff, A. Braverman and J. Stiglitz (eds), *The Economics of Rural Organization: Theory, Practice, and Policy* (Oxford University Press, 1993), pp.500-518.

Fafchamps, M., 'Cash Crop Production, Food Price Volatility, and Rural Market Integration in the Third World', *American Journal of Agricultural Economics*, 74(1) (February, 1992): 147-174.

Fleisher, B. and Liu, Y., 'Economics of Scale, Plot Size, Human Capital and Productivity in Chinese Agriculture', *Quarterly Review of Economics and Finance*, 32(3) (Autumn, 1992): 112-123.

Ke, B., *China's Grain Market and Policy* (Beijing: China's Agricultural Press, 1995, in Chinese).

Kurosaki, T., 'Risk and Insurance in a Household Economy: Role of Livestock in Mixed Farming', *The Developing Economies*, 33(4) (December, 1995): 464-485.

———, 'Production Risk and Advantages of Mixed Farming in the Pakistan Punjab', *The Developing Economies*, 35(1) (March, 1997): 28-47.

Lin, J., 'Rural Reforms and Agricultural Growth in China', *American Economic Review*, 82(1) (1992): 34-51.

———, 'Collectivization and China's Agricultural Crisis in 1959-1961', *The Economics of Famine*, (1999): 386-410.

Newbery, D. and Stiglitz, J., *The Theory of Commodity Price Stabilization: A Study in the Economics of Risk* (Oxford: Clarendon Press, 1981).

Reardon, T., Matlon, P. and Delgado, C., 'Coping with Household Level Food Insecurity in Drought-Affected Areas of Burkina Faso,' *World Development*, 16 (1988): 1065-1074.

———, 'Determinants and Effects of Income Diversification Amongst Farm Households in Burkina Faso,' *The Journal of Development Studies*, 28(2) (January, 1992): 264-296.

Reardon, T. and Taylor, J., 'Agroclimatic Shock, Income Inequality, and Poverty: Evidence from Burkina Faso', *World Development*, 24(5) (May, 1996): 901-914.

Rosenzweig, M. and Binswanger, H., 'Wealth, Weather Risk and the Composition and Profitability of Agricultural Investment', *The Economic Journal*, 103 (January, 1993): 56-78.

Rozelle, S. et al., 'Liberalization and Rural Market Integration in China,' *American Journal of Agricultural Economics*, 79(2) (May, 1997): 621-627.

SSB (State Statistics Bureau of China), *China Statistics Yearbook* (Beijing: China State Statistics Press, 1981-2002).

Townsend, R., 'Risk and Insurance in Village India', *Econometrica*, 62(3) (May, 1994): 539-591.

Udry, C., 'Risk and Saving in Northern Nigeria,' *American Economic Review*, 85(5) (December, 1995): 1287-1300.

Wu, L., *Studies on the Integration of Agricultural Product Markets* (Agricultural Publishing House of China, 2000, in Chinese).

Yang, H., 'Grain Production in China: Productivity Changes and Provincial Disparities 1978-90' (PhD dissertation, University of Adelaide, 1994).

ZGSYNJ, *Zhongguo Shangye Nianjian (China commercial yearbook)* (Beijing: Ministry of Domestic Trade Press, 1990-94).

Zhang, B. and Carter, C., 'Reforms, the Weather, and Productivity Growth in China's Grain Sector', *American Journal of Agricultural Economics*, 79(4) (November, 1997): 1266-1277.

Chapter 15

# An Empirical Analysis on Farmers' Demand of Alternative Types of Insurance in China

Holly H. Wang
Guangwen He

## 1 Introduction

The insurance industry has been quickly developing in China since the 1990s when China People's Insurance Company was restructured. The need for health insurance and life insurance becomes increasingly important as unemployment, benefit restructuring in state-owned enterprises, and a rising education cost are faced by many urban residents in the economic transition. Property insurance is also getting popular as the wealthier of urban residents are starting to own real estate and automobiles. On the other hand, the improved income and living standards in rural areas, lack of health benefits from the government, increased healthcare costs, and reduced family size with fewer children have all contributed to the newly emerged need of insurance in rural areas for health, life, and retirement. The highly risky nature of agricultural business imposes another need for production insurance (for example, crop yield, livestock, aquiculture, and so on), and such insurance products are not widely available in China yet. Sporadic experiments have been conducted in the past, and systematic programs have been available only in Shanghai and Xinjiang.

However, the increased gap between urban and rural incomes in recent years raises a serious question on whether the insurance products in the markets are affordable to rural residents and whether they are willing to pay. Qualitative studies and discussions have been published widely on popular presses, internet as well as academic journals (Tuo, et al., 2003; Xie, et al., 2003), and these studies have been focused on the supply aspects of production insurance, such as government policy, insurance administration, and risk pooling. Case studies are also available reporting the existing experience (Zhang, et al.□2004).

Rigorous economics studies on the demand of rural insurance products in China are few. Liu, et al. (2003) investigated the health insurance demand of rural residents. No such analysis is found on production or other types of insurance, and although a vast amount of literature is available on health and agricultural insurance demands, the former usually does not separate rural from urban demands, which are quite different in China (Dushi and Honig, 2003; Vanness, 2003), since the latter is mostly focused on production insurance in developed countries (Sherrick, et al.; 2003; Serra, et al.; 2003). The need for a quantitative analysis on the Chinese rural demands on health, life, production and other types of insurance is important.

The goal of this chapter is to examine the factors that affect the need and demand of insurance products in the rural areas of China. Specific objectives include: (1) to develop a socioeconomic model on the need and demand of alternative insurance; (2) to identify the major influential factors on the demand; (3) to identify the major factors that prevent a need from becoming an effective demand; and (4) to derive policy implications on the development of rural insurance in China.

## 2 Model

Based on survey data, in which we only have farmers' insurance participation indicator and their perception of their insurance need instead of a quantitative measure of coverage selection. A Logisitc (Logit) model is chosen to estimate the demand equations. We separate the need equation from the actual participation equation first, and then a joint Logit model is estimated.

### *2.1 Univariate Logit Model*

The dependent variable $Y$, an indicator of insurance need, is a binomial random variable, taking values of zero and one only. Its probability of taking one is:

$$P(Y=1)=\frac{e^{X\beta}}{1+e^{X\beta}} \tag{1}$$

In the content of this study, $Y = 1$ if the farmer agrees that insurance is necessary; and if otherwise, then $Y = 0$. $X$ is a vector of all explanatory variables, and $\beta$ is a vector of the parameters to be estimated. A positive element of $\beta$ means the larger the corresponding explanatory variable, and the more possible it is for the dependent variable to be one. More specifically, one more unit of a particular variable $X_i$ will help increase the log ratio of the probability that $Y$ takes the value of 1 to the probability $Y$ takes value 0 by the corresponding $\beta_i$ level.

Given Equation (1), the other distributional characters of the binomial variable such as means and variance are all available. The Maximum Likelihood Estimation (MLE) is the common way to estimate Equation (1).

The same Logit model as in (1) is used when evaluating actual insurance participation. The dependent variable, $Y$, is then the indicator of insurance participation. It equals one if the farmer purchases any insurance products—and zero if otherwise. Alternative versions of Equation (1) are estimated by the geographic location and type of insurance of the survey respondents.

*2.2 Joint Endogeneity*

Due to the existence of the separation of need and participation—for example, actual demand, a simultaneous equation system approach developed by Schmidt and Strauss (1975) is adopted. Because the decision on insurance participation should be strongly affected by the perception of need, the need variable is included in the participation equation in the following way:

$$\ln\left[\frac{P(Y^P=1|Y^N)}{P(Y^P=0|Y^N)}\right]=X\beta^P+\alpha Y^N \tag{2}$$

where the superscripts *P* and *N* denote participation and need, respectively, and α is the coefficient for the need variable in the participation probability equation. The need and participation variables are actually jointly determined in the economic decision process of a decision maker. Schmidt and Strauss showed that a symmetric condition exists for the probability of need conditional on the participation:

$$\ln\left[\frac{P(Y^N=1|Y^P)}{P(Y^N=0|Y^P)}\right]=X\beta^N+\alpha Y^P \tag{3}$$

Similarly, one more unit of a particular variable $X_i$ will help increase the log ratio of the probability that $Y^j$ takes the value 1 to the probability $Y^j$ takes value 0 conditional on the other dependent variable by the corresponding $\beta^j_i$ level, $j = P$ or $N$.

MLE is the natural way to estimate equation systems (2) and (3), based on the following Logit probabilities:

$$\begin{aligned}
P(Y^P=0,Y^N=0)&=\frac{1}{1+e^{X\beta^P}+e^{X\beta^N}+e^{X(\beta^P+\beta^N)+\alpha}}\\
P(Y^P=0,Y^N=1)&=\frac{e^{X\beta^N}}{1+e^{X\beta^P}+e^{X\beta^N}+e^{X(\beta^P+\beta^N)+\alpha}}\\
P(Y^P=1,Y^N=0)&=\frac{e^{X\beta^P}}{1+e^{X\beta^P}+e^{X\beta^N}+e^{X(\beta^P+\beta^N)+\alpha}}\\
P(Y^P=1,Y^N=1)&=\frac{e^{X(\beta^P+\beta^P)+\alpha}}{1+e^{X\beta^P}+e^{X\beta^N}+e^{X(\beta^P+\beta^N)+\alpha}}
\end{aligned} \tag{4}$$

## 3 Data

A survey has been conducted by the China Agricultural University during the summer of 2003 on rural households in Ningxia Autonomous Region and Zhejiang Province. They represent one western region in a less-developed area with relatively low incomes and one eastern region in a more-developed area with relatively high incomes. There are 291 observations in the survey, obtained through personal interviews.

The survey collected information on rural residents' assessment of the need of insurance, their actual insurance participation, and the types of insurance. Therefore, the need and actual demand for the insurance can be separated. The respondents are asked to identify the type of insurance that they feel needed with multiple selections allowed. Without providing any insurance premium information, the respondents evaluate the necessity of each type of insurance only by the risk protection feature of that insurance.

Ninety-five households, or 32.6 percent, did not think insurance was necessary in 2003 and did not buy any insurance either (Figure 15.1). Nine households actually bought the insurance but thought it was unnecessary. This is partly caused by some posterior short-term experience that insurance did not pay as they expected and partly by the mandate nature of the insurance. For example, property insurance can be mandated for vehicles and other farm machinery, and health and life insurance can be mandated by some schools for the school children. Ninety-four households, or 32.3 percent, thought that insurance was necessary but did not buy any, which may be due to the high cost. Eighty-seven households, or 29.9 percent, actually bought some insurance and thought it was necessary. The remaining six households, which were excluded from the analysis, did not buy any insurance while they were not sure whether or not it was necessary to buy.

For those who think insurance is necessary, their assessment of the necessity for each type of insurance is recorded. There were 181 respondents who indicated that insurance is needed, while 171 of them listed at least one of the three types of insurance as what they needed most. The three types of insurance include: (1) property; (2) health and retirement, also including life; [1] and (3) production, including crops, forest products and fruits, livestock and poultry, aquaculture, nursery, as well as special plant/animal farming.[2] The remaining 10 respondents

---

[1] The retirement plan is referred to as insurance in China because the payment scheme is pay-as-you-go instead of personal account. The senior farmer is facing a risk of living long but having exhausted personal financial resource, so that the retirement plan is a risk reducing instrument.

[2] The most popular insurance that farmers participate are life and property insurance. Production insurance especially livestock insurance is also used. The livestock insurance is like property insurance that it pays farmers the cost of the animals if a death or other severs condition occurs.

either listed other types of insurance or simply omitted the question, and their records were eliminated from this type-specific analysis. Overall, about 21 percent of the survey respondents thought that property insurance is needed, while almost 81 percent thought that health and retirement insurance is needed. Awareness of a production insurance need is very low—only 14 percent.

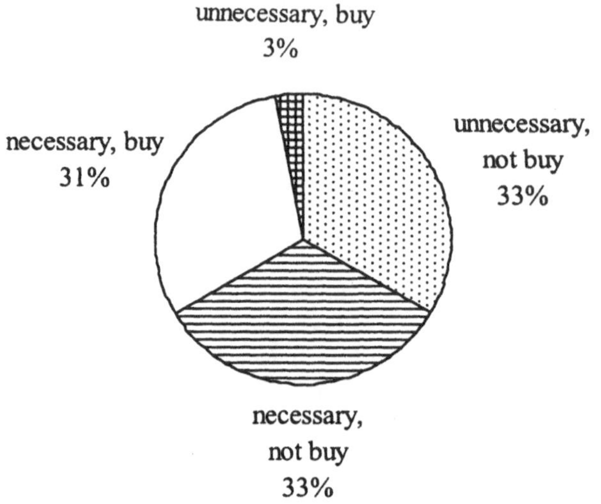


**Figure 15.1 The share of insurance participation and attitude**

Because we are building a demand model for insurance, the explanatory variables in an insurance demand function should ideally include: the income of farmers, their risk preference measures, the distributional parameters of risky variables, and the insurance premium levels. Because some variables, such as risk preference and distribution, are very difficult to obtain directly from a survey, other variables are used as proxies. The survey included the financial situation of rural households, the income and employment situation, a location fumy variable, and other demographic variables, such as family size, education, and so on. The descriptive statistics of relevant variables used in this analysis are reported in Table 15.1.

The financial variables include the relative wealth level of each household compared to the average level of their village (*Wealth*) and the investment activities in recent years (*Investment*). *Wealth* can partially represent risk preference as decreasing absolute risk aversion is the most popular type of preference. The higher wealth a farmer has, the less risk averse he tends to be. *Investment* can partially represent risk distribution because those with a major investment are facing higher financial risks. *Wealth* takes the value of one if the household considers themselves at a high level, two if at a medium level, and three if at a low level. The sample average is 1.79, indicating that respondents slightly underestimated their level of wealth. *Investment* is equal to one if they had any investment activities recently. Otherwise, it equals zero. The average value overall was 0.16, with Ningxia slightly higher than Zhejiang.

**Table 15.1 Descriptive statistics of variables**

| Variables | Definition | Unit | Mean | St. Dev. | Max. | Min. |
|---|---|---|---|---|---|---|
| Dependent Variables | | | | | | |
| Need | Need=1, otherwise = 0 | | 0.636 | 0.482 | 1 | 0 |
| Insurance | Buy = 1, otherwise = 0 | | 0.336 | 0.473 | 1 | 0 |
| Property | Important =1, otherwise = 0 | | 0.211 | 0.409 | 1 | 0 |
| HealRet | Important =1, otherwise = 0 | | 0.807 | 0.396 | 1 | 0 |
| Production | Important =1, otherwise = 0 | | 0.140 | 0.348 | 1 | 0 |
| Independent Variables | | | | | | |
| Location | Zhejiang = 0, Ningxia = 1 | | 0.576 | 0.496 | 1 | 0 |
| Age | Age of family head | Years | 43.6 | 11.3 | 73 | 20 |
| Labor | Number of adults >16 years | Number | 2.49 | 1.16 | 7 | 0 |
| Education | Years of education of family head | Years | 5.73 | 3.32 | 13 | 0 |
| Child | Number of children | Number | 0.78 | 0.84 | 5 | 0 |
| OffFarm | Total months working off farm in 2002 by all labors | Months | 4.00 | 8.00 | 48 | 0 |
| IncNonFarm | Income is primarily from non-farm salary and business =1, otherwise=0 | | 0.36 | 0.48 | 1 | 0 |
| IncBoth | Income is from both crop and off-farm income = 1, otherwise = 0 | | 0.35 | 0.48 | 1 | 0 |
| Wealth | Wealth relative to neighbors High =1, medium =2, low=3 | | 1.78 | 0.61 | 3 | 1 |
| Investment | Investment in recent years Yes = 1, no =0 | | 0.17 | 0.37 | 1 | 0 |

The income and employment variables include *Income*, the relative level of income compared to others in the same village, *OffFarm*, the time spent in off-farm, or non-farm, employment, and two additional dummy variables to represent the major sources of income: *IncNonFarm* and *IncBoth*.

*Income* takes the same values and categories as *Wealth*. However, because it is highly correlated with *Wealth*—with a correlation coefficient of 0.85—it is excluded from the regressions to avoid the multi-colinearity problem. *OffFarm* represents the aggregated months in a year that any family members work off-farm—ranging from zero to 48—with an average of about 4 months. *IncNonFarm* and *IncBoth* take a value equal to one if the major source of income for the household is primarily from off-farm employment salaries (teachers, administrators, and other professionals, for example) and non-farm business income, and both farm production and other off-farm sources, respectively. Otherwise, the value is zero. The default would be those households whose income is primarily from farm, crop, or animal production, such as livestock, poultry, aquiculture, and more. The share of each listed category is 35.8 percent and 35.4 percent, respectively, leaving the default category accounting for 28.8 percent. The *IncBoth* variable can also represent the risk distributions of income because those with two major sources of income tend to run less of a risk than those whose income comes primarily from a single source.

The *location* dummy variable takes the value of one if the observation is from Ningxia—otherwise, Zhejiang. Because our samples are from the two distinct areas, the location variable can represent several factors: the income difference between the two locations as Ningxia has a lot lower average income level; or the insurance premium level difference because Zhejiang is closer to major cities and thereby may have easier access to services as well as more competitive prices. About 58 percent of the survey respondents were from Ningxia.

Demographic variables include the age of the family head (*Age*), the number of adults in the family who are at least 16 years old (*Labor*), the family head's education level measured by years in school (*Education*), and the number of children (*Child*). The overall average *Age* is 43.6 and ranges from 20 to 73. In Ningxia, the average age is 41.5, much younger than the average in Zhejing, which is 46.5. This may be caused by the relatively greater number of opportunities for young people to seek off-farm employment and migrate to nearby cities in Zhejiang.

The average number of adults, *Labor*, is 2.52 per family. The average amount of *Education* overall is 5.76 years. However, the education level is a lot higher in Zhejiang—which is 6.38 years—than in Ningxia—which is 5.28 years. The overall average *Child* is 0.78 per family, which is very similar in both villages.

Demographic variables describe the individual characteristics of the surveyed farmers, and they affect the risk preferences of farmers. For example, those with more children may be more risk averse than those with less, or none, because parents are more cautious for the sake of their children. The same can hold true for education because more-educated people may understand the effect of risks—unforeseen events—better.

## 4 Results

The MLE results estimated in GAUSS are reported in Table 15.2. We use Akaike's Information Criteria and Log Likelihood Ratio Statistics to identify the best specification of each model. The independent variables not included in any particular model means that they are highly insignificant in general. All of the models have a Log Likelihood ratio that is highly significant at the 1 or 5 percent level. This means the dependent variables are explained well by the chosen set of independent variables.

For the overall assessment of the need of any type of insurance, the significant contributions are positive from *Child* and negative from *OffFarm*, *Wealth* and *IncBoth*. This suggests that households with more children seem to be more interested in insurance, which is consistent to the conventional wisdom that parents want to protect their children—even more than themselves—from any and all possible risks. More specifically, families with one more child will have a higher probability of needing insurance to the extent that the log ratio is increased by 0.3.

The relatively poorer families (remember the larger value of *wealth* means to be poorer) think insurance is less important because their concern is focused more on their day-to-day, basic life-sustaining consumption than property, health, and production risks. Insurance is a luxury good to them. This is consistent to the increasing risk aversion premise in that the higher the level of wealth, the more averse to risk and in need of insurance a household is. Because wealth also represents income—as they are highly correlated—this is also consistent to the income effect that lower income will cause a reduction in the demand of any non-inferior good. More specifically, families' poverty moving one category up will result in lower probabilities of needing insurance to the extent that the log ratio (of the probability they feel the need to the probability they don't) decreases by 0.33.

Households spending more time in off-farm, or non-farm, jobs also feel less need for insurance. Although the correlation between *OffFarm* and *Wealth* is close to zero in our data set—indicating that working off-farm does not lead to relatively higher income in the village—more time spent on off-farm work means that the household depends less on farm production, needing less production insurance, and may have fewer fixed properties to protect. The households with income coming equally from both farm and non-farm sources do not need insurance as much as those whose incomes are primarily from one source only—whether that be farm or off-farm. This is consistent to the diversification effect, especially for the production type of insurance because they can self-insure their income risks.

**Table 15.2 Logistic regression results**

| Variables | Need | Partici-pation | Simultaneous Logit | | Participation | | Need by Type | | |
|---|---|---|---|---|---|---|---|---|---|
| | | | Need | Participat. | Zhejiang | Ningxia | Property | HealRet | Production |
| Intercept | 1.14 | -0.99 | 0.59 | -3.06$^{***}$ | -1.59$^{*}$ | -0.14 | -3.67$^{**}$ | 1.16 | -3.08$^{***}$ |
| | (0.77) | (0.85) | (0.79) | (0.99) | (0.95) | (0.77) | (1.53) | (1.62) | (1.19) |
| Labor | 0.14 | 0.15 | 0.10 | 0.11 | 0.21 | 0.017 | -0.13 | 0.15 | 0.35$^{*}$ |
| | (0.13) | (0.15) | (0.14) | (0.16) | (0.20) | (0.15) | (0.17) | (0.18) | (0.21) |
| Education | 0.050 | 0.089$^{*}$ | 0.022 | 0.079 | 0.13$^{**}$ | 0.016 | -0.013 | 0.21$^{***}$ | -0.035 |
| | (0.041) | (0.048) | (0.045) | (0.052) | (0.062) | (0.066) | (0.067) | (0.074) | (0.076) |
| Child | 0.30$^{*}$ | 0.72$^{***}$ | 0.060 | 0.70$^{***}$ | 0.94$^{***}$ | 0.46$^{*}$ | | | -0.22 |
| | (0.16) | (0.19) | (0.18) | (0.20) | (0.31) | (0.25) | | | (0.28) |
| OffFarm | -0.034$^{*}$ | -0.022 | -0.030 | -0.0086 | -0.029 | 0.027 | | | -0.11$^{*}$ |
| | (0.018) | (0.021) | (0.020) | (0.023) | (0.028) | (0.032) | | | (0.064) |
| Wealth | -0.53$^{**}$ | -0.36 | -0.48$^{**}$ | -0.15 | -0.054 | -1.18$^{***}$ | -0.21 | 0.35 | 0.023 |
| | (0.23) | (0.25) | (0.25) | (0.28) | (0.32) | (0.39) | (0.35) | (0.36) | (0.29) |
| Location | -0.28 | -1.78$^{***}$ | 0.46 | -1.98$^{***}$ | | | -0.011 | 0.45 | -1.25$^{**}$ |
| | (0.27) | (0.31) | (0.32) | (0.34) | | | (0.29) | (0.45) | (0.55) |
| IncNonFarm | 0.20 | 0.63 | 0.0003 | 0.62 | | | 1.52$^{***}$ | -0.80 | |
| | (0.34) | (0.38) | (0.11) | (0.39) | | | (0.59) | (0.62) | |
| IncBoth | -0.62$^{***}$ | 0.54 | -0.90$^{***}$ | 0.94$^{**}$ | | | 1.14$^{*}$ | -1.40$^{**}$ | |
| | (0.33) | (0.39) | (0.31) | (0.42) | | | (0.63) | (0.62) | |
| Age | | | | | | | 0.050$^{**}$ | -0.028 | |
| | | | | | | | (0.021) | (0.023) | |
| Investment | | | | | | | -1.20$^{*}$ | | 0.54 |
| | | | | | | | (0.68) | | (0.58) |
| A | | | | 2.45$^{***}$ | | | | | |
| | | | | (0.42) | | | | | |
| Number of Observations | 285 | 285 | | 285 | 121 | 164 | 171 | 171 | 171 |
| Log Likelihood Ratio | 24.61$^{***}$ | 68.71$^{***}$ | | 140.87$^{***}$ | 20.62$^{***}$ | 13.75$^{**}$ | 19.90$^{***}$ | 23.12$^{***}$ | 14.95$^{**}$ |

*Notes*: 1. Numbers in parentheses are standard errors. $^{*}$, $^{**}$, and $^{***}$ denote significant at 10%, 5% and 1% levels, respectively.

Although about only half of the households who expressed a need for insurance actually purchased it. Their behavior reveals a willingness to pay, which is more important information to the insurance market. The difference between a need and a demand is that the latter is what consumers allocate their income to, creating an opportunity cost to their other consumptions. However, the former potential consumers are not willing to do so, and it is difficult to measure the importance of this need when comparing many other needs in their economic decisions. Interestingly, the signs of all coefficients remain the same as the need model. The significant contributors are slightly different now for the insurance participation model.

*Location* is now very significant, indicating that residents in Zhejiang are more likely to buy insurance. The location variable represents the effect from many economic factors that are significantly different between the two areas, such as income level, crops, production technology, and insurance service. Zhejiang farmers are much wealthier than Ningxia farmers, but the previous negative effect of wealth in need equation and insignificant wealth effect in the following demand equation do not support the income as a major factor to explain the location difference. The insurance services are more available and have higher quality service in Zhejiang area which has a higher degree of urbanization. The quality and availability can be considered as part of the price effect when quality, premium, and searching costs are included. Therefore, the location variable is also a proxy for price. Although we do not have price information in this analysis, the results suggest a lower price in Zhenjing brought by better service and availability, contributing to the higher demand. The crop and production technology are also different in that Zhejiang has more higher-valued horticulture and aquiculture as opposed to the field crop production. This factor can be further investigated in the production insurance estimation results.

*Child* contributes to the insurance participation more positively and significantly than the need, indicating families with more children are more likely to buy insurance than other families, and the difference is more significant compared to the case of expressing a need. *Education* is now significantly positive, suggesting that the more educated the household head is, the more willing he or she is to buy insurance. This should not be explained as higher-educated households are exposed to a more risky environment or that they are more risk averse. Rather, they understand the mechanism of how insurance can provide protection in adverse situations better and are more willing to allocate their family budget on insurance services. It is a proxy of the knowledge about insurance. All of these results are consistent to Liu et al. (2003).

*Wealth* is still negative, though not significant. Wealthier families have a larger budget to allocate to insurance goods (the income effect). Comparing the differences between the need model and the participation model, we can conclude that convenient access to service, household head's education level, and wealth can all encourage the insurance need to become an effective demand. On the other hand, factors preventing a need from becoming an effective demand must be inconvenient access to service, limited education, and low income.

The perceived need of insurance services should be a major determining factor of insurance participation. The need variable should then be included into the demand equation. It is also reasonable to hypothesize that the need and participation variables are jointly endogenous. Results of the joint Logit model are also listed in Table 15.2.

First, we see that the coefficient of the interaction variable, α, is very significant and positive, which supports the joint-endogenous hypothesis. When a need is perceived, it will be very possible for a real purchase to occur. Second, the signs are almost identical to those in individual equations. This confirms that although a joint model is a better specification, the qualitative results from individual equations are valid. One important difference, though small, is that the *Education* coefficient in the participation equation is insignificant while the value is similar. This means, while the need is considered in the participation equation, *Education* will not make a significant difference. This is confirming our earlier point that *Education* only affects people's perception of the value of the insurance service but not their actual risk exposure.

Because the location dummy variable is not significant in the need equation but very significant in the participation model, we re-estimated the participation model for each area separately. The separate results reveal some differences for the two areas, while the signs of coefficients are basically the same to each other as well as to the overall equations. *Education* is a significant and positive contributor in Zhejiang but not in Ningxia. Interestingly, *Education* is positively correlated with *OffFarm* in Ningxia, indicating those with higher educations tend to have more opportunities in working off-farm, which decreases their insurance need. This may explain why *Education* is not a positive contributor for Ningxia. The correlation between the two variables is slightly negative for Zhejiang because off-farm employment is more accessible for rural residents in Zhejiang, not depending much on their education levels. *Child* is significant in both provinces, however, for the same reason explained in the overall need and participation models. *Wealth* is significantly negative in Ningxia but not in Zhejiang. This means the wealthier households tend to buy insurance in Ningxia, but the wealth does not make a difference in the demand for insurance in Zhejiang.

The effects of the above factors on insurance needs and demands in China are sometimes difficult to analyze when the three different types of insurance are pooled together. We then separated the insurance products into their three types: property; health and retirement; and production. The observation number of insurance participation is too low for a meaningful statistic analysis, however, so we estimated the need model only.

The significant contributors to the assessed need of each type of insurance are different, and they are also different to the overall need model. The significantly negative contributor to the property insurance need is *Investment*. Those households who made investments in recent years tend to think the property insurance is unnecessary. This is because the investments in production primarily involve assets not covered by property insurance, such as a herd of dairy cows or an aquiculture structure, and the diversified assets make the risk on insurable property less important. The significantly positive contributors include *IncNonFarm*, *IncBoth*, and *Age*. Older people tend to need property insurance because the life savings of many rural people might be in their houses that need to be protected. Both of the other two dummy variables indicate those whose income is more from off-farm activity may have more of their wealth in the form of family property, such as real estate and vehicles, needing the property insurance more than those who farm.

The only significantly positive and negative contributors to health and retirement insurance are *Education* and *IncBoth*, respectively. It seems that more-educated people care more about health insurance and retirement insurance, while their preference on the other two types of insurance is similar to that of less-educated respondents. This reveals that more-educated people have a higher expectation for their quality of life with better health care and a decent income after retirement. Interestingly, there is no significant location difference in the needs of these two types of insurance.

Different from the previous two insurance types, production insurance is significantly affected by *Location*. Zhejiang has a higher production insurance need than Ningxia, which can be explained by the higher risk of horticulture and aquaculture production in Zhejiang in comparison to field crop and livestock production in Ningxia. The adverse weather, such as typhoon and disease, has a significant influence on aquaculture production in Zhejiang, and the farmers are well aware of this. Other significant contributors include *Labor*, which is positive, and *OffFarm*, which is negative. Larger households with more adult laborers tend to need more production insurance because their production scale is larger, which makes their risk exposure larger as well. Oppositely, more labor time spent off-farm diversifies the income risk and eases the pressure from farm production insurance. Although *Investment* is not significant at 10 percent, the production need equation is the only place the variable is included and has a positive sign. Hence, we can conclude that investment in production is weakly contributing to the need of production insurance.

## 5 Summary and Conclusion

In this chapter, we analyzed survey data from the Ningxia and Zhejiang rural areas using Logit and Simultaneous Logit models to explore the insurance needs and demands of Chinese residents. We find that the needs and demands are different from each other and that the needs for different types of insurance are also different.

Important factors affecting the demand for rural insurance include: the household decision maker's education level; the number of children in the family; and location. The location effect may represent the availability and convenience of insurance services. These results are consistent to existing literature. Our Simultaneous Logit model results revealed that the perceived need has a significant impact on the actual demand. However, the big difference between the need and demand—with the latter only accounting for about one half of the former—must be caused by either the price being too high (although no price information was available for this analysis) or the service not being available or convenient.

The subjective perception of the need for insurance has a different pattern to the actual insurance demand. First, it is not much different across regions. Rural residents in the two regions equally express their need for insurance services. This implies that the information of insurance has been delivered to both regions. Second, one's education level does not affect need but rather participation. Third, off-farm work reduces the perceived need but does not reduce the actual demand. Fourth, income will increase both the perceived need as well as the demand for insurance.

These differences between the need and the demand for insurance suggest that: (1) improving insurance services may increase the actual rural demand; (2) although the number of children will not increase, the insurance industry can pay more attention to families with more children; (3) improving overall education will increase the insurance demand; and (4) the increase in rural income will increase the demand for insurance.

While the majority—80 percent of the survey respondents—realized that health and retirement insurance are needed, only 14 percent thought that production insurance was necessary. Different types of insurance are also influenced by different factors. The age of the household head uniquely influences property insurance, as his or her education level does to health and retirement insurance, and as location and labor do to production insurance. While the idea of production insurance has not been perceived very well by farmers, it does have a potential to expand in horticultural, aquicultural, and special animal production—productions that carry a higher risk.

## References

Dushi, I. and Honig, M., 'Price and Spouse's Coverage in Employee Demand for Health Insurance.' *American Economic Review*, 93(2) (2003): 252-256.

Liu, G.G., Wu, X., Peng, C. and Fu, A.Z., 'Urbanization and Health Care in Rural China.' *Contemporary Economic Policy*, 21 (1) (2003): 11-24.

Schmidt, P. and Strauss, R.P., 'Estimation of Models with Jointly Dependent Qualitative Variables: A Simultaneous Logit Approach.' *Econometrica*, 43 (1975): 745-755.

Serra, T., Goodwin, B.K. and Featherstone, A.M., 'Modeling Changes in the U.S. Demand for Crop Insurance during the 1990s.' *Agricultural Finance Review*, 63(2) (2003): 109-125.

Sherrick, B.J., Barry, P.J., Schnitkey, G.D., Ellinger, P.N. and Wansink, B., 'Farmers' Prefer,ences for Crop Insurance Attributes.' *Review of Agricultural Economics*, 25(2) (2003): 415-429.

Tuo, G. and Li, J., 'The Achievements, Conflicts and Prospective of Agricultural Insurance Experiments in China.' *Finance Studies* 9 (In Chinese, 2003).

Vanness, D.J., 'A Structural Econometric Model of Family Valuation and Choice of Employer-Sponsored Health Insurance in the United States.' *Health Economics*, 12(9) (2003): 771-790.

Xie, J. and Pu, L., 'A Study of the Government Induced Agricultural Insurance Development Model.' *Finance Studies* 11 (In Chinese, 2003).

Zhang, Y., Gu, H. and Wan. H., 'An Investigation Report on Xinjiang Troup Agricultural Insurance' (Working paper, Department of Economics and Finance, Shanghai Jiaotong University, 2004).

# Chapter 16

# Price Behavior in China's Wheat Futures Market*

Wen Du
Holly H. Wang

## 1 Introduction

Wheat production, consumption and trade account for a major share of China's food system. In 2002, wheat production and consumption reached 93.87 and 108.74 million tons respectively, about 27.0 percent and 28.9 percent of all grain[1] production and consumption. Wheat exports and imports are 1.51 and 1.09 million tons respectively, about 12.6 percent and 32.9 percent of all grains exports and imports. Wheat price volatility also plays a very influential role in overall grain price volatility. The prosperity of wheat futures in world's major commodity futures markets has provided an effective channel for market participants to hedge price risks and insure profits (Yang and Leatham, 1999). If the futures market is efficient, price will move in a way to reflect its real equilibrium level in the spot market. Efficient futures prices help the formation of a rational market expectation of price in both the short run and the long run.

Agricultural commodity futures markets emerged in China in the early 1990's, when China was stepping into a higher phase of its market-oriented economic reform. One of the motives to establish futures markets was to provide a price indicator and stabilizer to reduce the volatility in agricultural spot markets in China. In this chapter, we investigate the price behavior in China's wheat futures market in an attempt to provide a tractable model for prediction.

China's first exchange market, the China Zhengzhou Commodity Exchange (CZCE) was founded in 1990. Wheat futures trading started in May 1993. CZCE is the only exchange trading wheat futures contracts in the country today. In 1999, CZCE accounted for 50 percent in total trading value and 49 percent in total trading volume of all commodity exchanges in China. Since then, the trading of

* Reprinted from China Economic Review, vol.15(2), 2004, page 215-229.

[1] The low trading in 1999 was mostly affected by the regulatory change in CZCE, which was designed to discourage the Mungbean trading then. As a result, Mung Bean trading declined sharply and disappeared in the following years.

wheat futures has experienced a stable growth.[2] In 2002, the total trading value amounted to 225.25 billion *Yuan*[3] and total trading volume was 18.27 million contracts (Figure 16.1).

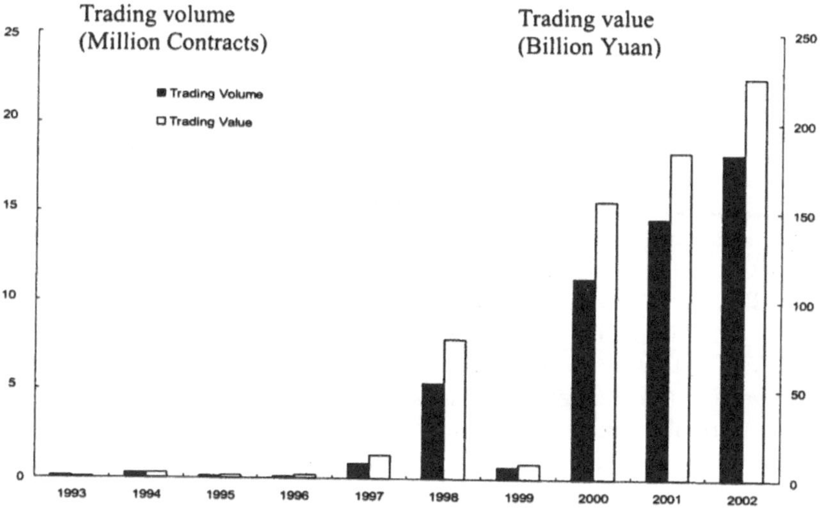


**Figure 16.1 Annual wheat futures trading in CZCE 1993-2002**
*Source:* http://www.czce.com.cn/publish/data/200107/142.asp

After about 10 years of development, the wheat futures price in CZCE is on the way to becoming an important indicator of China's wheat price. The correlation between the spot price and futures price is as high as 0.96 and a strong association is identified between the wheat futures price of CZCE and that of Chicago Board of Trade (CBOT) (CZCE Report, 2001). China's wheat futures price became more important to the world after November 2001 when China obtained full membership in the WTO. The previously over-valued domestic wheat price is facing challenges from major wheat exporters such as the USA and Canada, and is expected to undergo a downward shift. Meanwhile, the futures price in CZCE may become more volatile from the stronger linkage to the world commodity markets and the unpredictable factors in the world economy. Conversely, price may become less volatile because domestic speculators, which had a fairly strong influence on prices in the past (Durham and Si, 1999), will not be able to affect the world market price.

[2] One US dollar equals about 8.3 Yuan.
[3] Trading of the May 2002 contract started in February 2001. These prices were not included until May 2001 when the May 2001 contract expired. The old contract trading prices are chosen for this overlapping period because the old contracts are traded more actively than the new one during the period.

China is the biggest wheat production and consumption country in the world. China's successful economic reform has drawn the whole world's attention for the past twenty years. However, studies on China's agricultural commodity futures markets are limited, particularly with regard to wheat futures. Moreover, most of existing studies are only descriptive analyses on regulatory and market development issues rather than quantitative investigations of futures prices. Such studies include Tao and Lei (1998); Fan, Ding and Wang (1999); and Zhu and Zhu (2000). A historical perspective on the development of China's futures market is shown in Yao (1998), which includes a detailed structural analysis of the commodity futures markets and the government's legislative and regulatory attempts.

Some quantitative analyses have been attempted in recent years. Williams, et al. (1998) investigated mungbean trading in CZCE to test for market efficiency. Durham and Si (1999) examined the relationship between the Dalian Commodity Exchange (DCE) and the CBOT soybean futures prices. Ke and Wang (2002) investigated the information efficiency of the CZCE wheat and DCE soybeans futures markets in a market cointegration framework.

Studies explicitly investigating China's wheat futures price behavior have not been found. Careful examination of price models can lead to effective prediction, which is very important for traders in the futures market. Reliable price models will also provide a foundation for any empirical analyses involving futures price, such as a risk management analysis for growers and processors who hedge in futures market. This research represents an effort to focus on a quantitative assessment of China's wheat futures prices.

Modeling the time varying pattern of agricultural commodity futures prices has been investigated by many economists using various approaches. The moving average (MA) model, autoregressive (AR) model, or the more general, autoregressive integrated moving average (ARIMA) model, is usually fitted to identify the pattern of a time series (Box and Jenkins, 1976). More complete but complicated price models were developed in the last two decades. The autoregressive conditional heteroskedasticity (ARCH) model (Engle, 1982), and generalized autoregressive conditional heteroskedasticity (GARCH) model (Bollerslev, 1986) have enjoyed the most attention. The ARCH model succeeds in modeling the stochastic time-varying volatility and excess kurtosis of commodity price changes. ARCH allows the shocks in nearby earlier periods to affect the current volatility positively. The GARCH model generalizes the ARCH model by assuming not only previous shocks, but also previous volatilities affect current volatility. Volatility behaves like an AR process with drifts.

Once developed, these models were widely adopted to successfully fit agricultural commodity prices (Tomek and Myers, 1993; Myers, 1994). Stochastic trend or unit root was discovered as a characteristic property of many high frequency commodity price series (Ardeni, 1989; Baillie and Myers, 1991). Conditional heteroskedasticity constitutes another common characteristic of commodity futures prices (Bailie and Myers, 1991; Yang and Brorsen, 1992).

The objective of this chapter is to find the best time series model to describe the price behavior of China's wheat futures market. Specifically, this analysis will: 1) estimate ARMA and ARCH/GARCH models for China's wheat futures; 2) integrate ARMA and ARCH/GARCH models to capture the autoregressive effects on both first and second moments; and 3) compare the estimation and forecasting performances among these models.

## 2 Models

### *2.1 ARMA Model*

To fit an ARMA model to a time series process, the error terms are assumed to be a Gaussian process with mean zero and constant variance $\sigma^2$. The general form of the ARMA(p, q) model is defined as:

$$Y_t = X_t'\beta + \sum_{i=1}^{p} \phi_i Y_{t-i} + \varepsilon_t + \sum_{j=1}^{q} \theta_j \varepsilon_{t-j} \tag{1}$$

where $Y_t$ is the dependent variable; $Y_{t-i}$ for $i = 1, 2, ..., p$ are lagged dependent variables; $X_t$ denotes the explanatory variable matrix; $\varepsilon_t$ is the error term and assumed to be white noise, or

$\varepsilon_t \overset{iid}{\sim} N(0, \sigma^2)$; $\varepsilon_{t-j}, j = 1, 2, ..., q$

are lagged error terms; $t$ denotes the time period; $\beta$ (a column vector), $\phi_i$ and $\theta_j$ are parameters.

As a general form, ARMA model incorporates both AR model and MA model as special cases. It becomes AR model when the moving average part vanishes, i.e. $\phi_i$ s are set to zero, or MA model when the autoregressive part vanishes, i.e. $\theta_j$ s are set to zero.

### *2.2 Conditional Heteroskedastistic Models*

To describe data series with time-varying volatility, ARCH or GARCH models are needed. These models allow the variance of error terms to change over time. An ARCH(q) model is commonly defined as:

$$Y_t = X_t'\beta + \varepsilon_t \tag{2}$$

where $\varepsilon_t \mid \Omega_{t-1} \sim N(0, \ h_t)$

$$h_t = \omega + \sum_{i=1}^{q} \alpha_i \varepsilon_{t-i}^2$$

where $\varepsilon_t$ is the error component in the ARCH model; $h_t$ is the time-varying variance of the error; $\Omega_{t-1}$ is the information set available at $t$ -1; $\omega$, $\alpha_i$ for $i = 1, 2, ..., q$ and $\beta$ are parameters. $\varepsilon_t$ s are not serially correlated, however, their dependency lies on the second moment evolution.

A GARCH ($p$, $q$) model is defined in the same way except that

$$h_t = \omega + \sum_{i=1}^{q} \alpha_i \varepsilon_{t-i}^2 + \sum_{j=1}^{p} \gamma_j h_{t-j} \tag{3}$$

with $\gamma_j$ for $j = 1, 2, ..., p$ as additional parameters.

The basic ARCH($q$) model is a short memory process in that only the most recent $q$ residuals have an impact on the current variance. The GARCH($p$, $q$) model allows a longer memory processes, in which all the past residuals can affect the current variance either directly or indirectly through the lagged variance terms.

### 3 Data Description

Data for the study are collected from CZCE's online database at http://www.czce.com.cn/shuju. The daily settlement price series for the May wheat contracts from May 24, 2000 to April 9, 2002 are used. The prices are taken as continuous for each trading day. There are 454 observations in total. A yearly contract dummy variable, $D_t$, is introduced as part of the explanatory variable $X$, to indicate when the price series switches from the 2001 contract to the 2002 contract. The switching point is set as the last trading day of the old contract following the method as in Myers and Hanson (1993).[4] $D_t$ equals 0 from May 24, 2000 to May 23, 2001 and 1 from May 24, 2001 to April 9, 2002.

The time series plot (Figure 16.2) of the data suggests nonstationarity and a downward time trend. Because it is common that a logarithm of price is used in analysis instead of price itself, the necessity of data transformation is then examined through the BOXCOX procedure built in SAS.[5] Results indicate, however, data transformation is not necessary.[6]

Sample autocorrelation function (SACF) of the prices shows very slow exponential decay, and the sample partial autocorrelation function (SPACF) shows

---

[4] Conceptually the Box-Cox procedure identifies transformation from the family of power transformations on the data. See Box and Cox (1964) for more information. SAS incorporates this algorithm as a built-in module.

[5] The BOXCOX procedure in SAS yields 8=1.6 as a candidate transformation parameter. Since it is not significantly different from 8=1 according to transformation criteria of log likelihood, AIC (Akaike Information Criterion) and SBC (Schwartz's Baysian Criterion), the original data set is selected for analysis convenience.

[6] The SACF and SPACF also show that, the residuals for these two models behave like white noise.

a large spike in the first lag. Therefore, taking the first difference is probably needed. The augmented Dickey-Fuller unit root test yields a P value of 0.37, confirming the existence of the unit root.

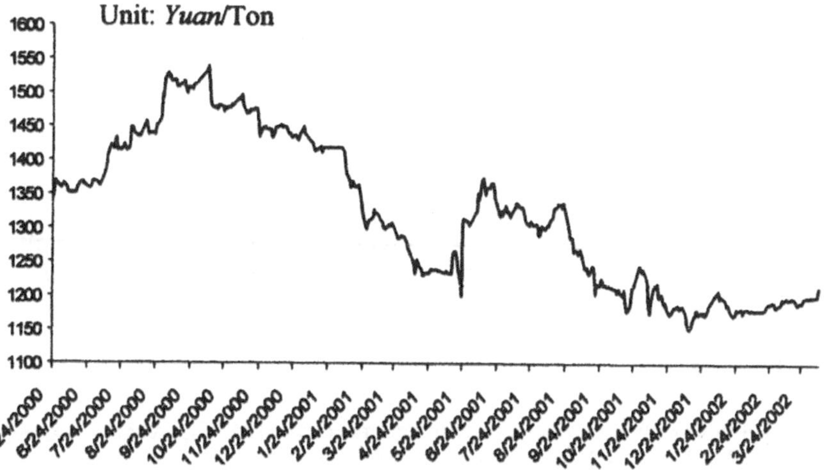


**Figure 16.2 CZCE wheat futures price for May contract**

From the time series plot (Figure 16.3) of the squared first difference data, evidence of a time-varying volatility pattern is visible. That is, big changes are often followed by other big ones and small changes followed by small ones. This pattern is consistent with the ARCH/GARCH processes.

*Note*: 1. Since the squared first difference at the switching point (5/24/2001) is way high compared to the rest, we cut off most part of the spike to fit it into the plot.

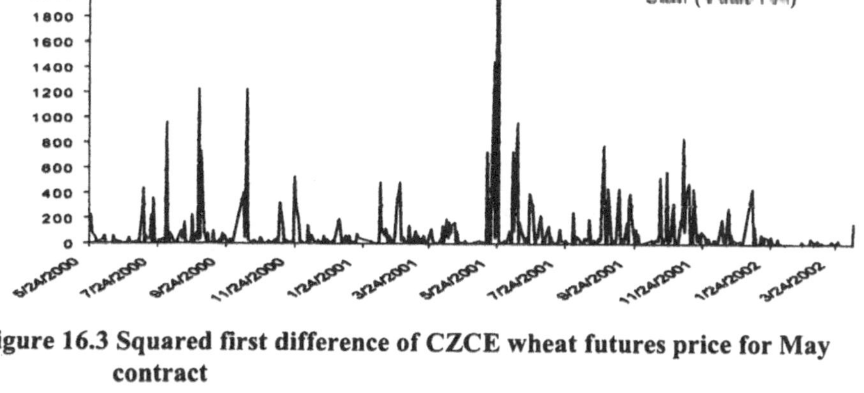


**Figure 16.3 Squared first difference of CZCE wheat futures price for May contract**

## 4 Results

For each time series model, there can be numerous specifications in terms of lags. In this section, the best specification of each class of models (ARMA, ARCH and GARCH) is determined first, based on several statistical criteria. Then, the models are estimated and compared using their best specifications. Finally, predictions are made based on the estimated models, and out-of-sample data are used to evaluate prediction performances.

### *4.1 Selection of Model Specification*

First differences of the price data are fit into alternative time series models. SAS procedures ARIMA and AUTOREG are used to estimate these models. These procedures are based on maximum likelihood estimation method.

#### *4.1.1 ARMA Model*

Three goodness-of-fit criteria, mean square error (MSE), Akaike Information Criterion (AIC), and Schwartz's Baysian Criterion (SBC), are used in a coordinate fashion to select the best model. The values of these three criteria from alternative model specifications are reported in Table 16.1. The insignificant coefficients are also reported. From Table 16.1, both AR(1) and MA(1) are appropriate since all the MSE, AIC and SBC measures are relatively small compared to other specifications, and all the coefficients are significant.[7] Although the AR(1,4) and MA(1,4) have even smaller MSE and AIC, however, the critical coefficients for the $4^{th}$ lag are insignificant, which makes them no different to the AR(1) and MA(1) models. Overall, the AR(1) model yields slightly smaller MSE, AIC and SBC. Therefore, the AR(1) model is selected to analyze, i.e. ARI(1,1) for the original price data.

#### *4.1.2 Conditional Heteroskedastic Model*

Although the AR(1) model has been chosen to describe the mean level of price movements, the constant variance assumption has not been tested. Since time-varying pattern of the data series is implied from Figure 16.2 and 16.3, testing for the presence of an ARCH effect in the data set is the next step. Both the *Portmanteau Q statistic* and the *LaGrange Multiplier statistic* provide strong evidence of ARCH effect (Table 16.2). Almost all of the P values for the two test statistics, Q and LM, for testing $H_0$, no ARCH effect, are less than 0.005 for lag two to ten and in eleven out of twelve lags the P values are less than 0.02. Such

---

[7] The SACF and SPACF also show that, the residuals for these two models behave like white noise.

strong evidence supporting an ARCH effect suggests it is appropriate to use conditional heteroskedasticity models.

**Table 16.1 Goodness-of-fit for alternative ARMA models**

| Model[1] | MSE | AIC | SBC | Insignificant Coefficients |
|---|---|---|---|---|
| AR(1) | 73.73 | 3234.68 | 3238.79 | None |
| MA(1) | 73.90 | 3235.69 | 3239.80 | None |
| AR(2) | 73.82 | 3236.19 | 3244.42 | $\phi_2$ |
| MA(2) | 73.72 | 3235.61 | 3243.84 | $\theta_2$ |
| AR(1,4) | 73.39 | 3233.60 | 3241.83 | $\phi_4$ |
| MA(1,4) | 73.54 | 3234.51 | 3242.74 | $\theta_4$ |
| ARMA(1,1) | 73.84 | 3236.39 | 3244.62 | $\phi_1, \theta_1$ |
| ARMA(2,2) | 73.66 | 3237.23 | 3253.69 | $\phi_2, \theta_2$ |

*Note*: 1. No constant term is included in the above ARMA processes, because it was estimated as insignificant in all the models.

**Table 16.2 Tests for ARCH effect in CZCE futures prices for May contract**

| Order | Q | Pr > Q | LM | Pr > LM |
|---|---|---|---|---|
| 1 | 0.86 | 0.3529 | 0.86 | 0.3529 |
| 2 | 15.36 | 0.0005 | 14.98 | 0.0006 |
| 3 | 15.54 | 0.0014 | 15.50 | 0.0014 |
| 4 | 23.22 | 0.0001 | 20.27 | 0.0004 |
| 5 | 23.86 | 0.0002 | 20.90 | 0.0008 |
| 6 | 23.99 | 0.0005 | 22.20 | 0.0011 |
| 7 | 24.61 | 0.0009 | 22.28 | 0.0023 |
| 8 | 24.90 | 0.0016 | 22.59 | 0.0039 |
| 9 | 25.39 | 0.0026 | 23.89 | 0.0045 |
| 10 | 25.40 | 0.0046 | 24.00 | 0.0076 |
| 11 | 25.73 | 0.0071 | 24.13 | 0.0122 |
| 12 | 27.16 | 0.0073 | 25.40 | 0.0130 |

The same goodness-of-fit criteria are reported in Table 16.3 for alternative specifications of ARCH and GARCH models when AR(1) is modeled in the mean equation. From Table 16.3 it is apparent different error structures impact the fitness of the model. Generally GARCH and ARCH specifications outperform AR by all criteria. Another thing noteworthy is, among all the presented candidate models, higher order in conditional skedasticity models do not necessarily improve the fitness and tend to become increasingly unstable in that normally convergent estimates are difficult to obtain.

The switching dummy coefficient, $\delta$ , becomes insignificant in ARCH and GARCH models, indicating the switching effect is probably absorbed by the specified error structures. This is because as the contract close to maturity, the prices get more volatile with larger changes. The ARCH and GARCH models take the contract switching effect as one of the random effects caused by information. The significance of AR, ARCH and GARCH parameters in the AR(1), ARCH(2) and GARCH(1,1) models indicate the actual price changes are affected by the previous price changes, and the volatility of these changes are affected by the residuals and the past volatilities. The best fit associated with GARCH(1,1) suggests current variance is influenced not only by the past shock, but also by the past variance. This result is consistent with results from the studies of commodity futures prices around the world (Yang and Brorsen, 1992; Myers and Hanson, 1993; Haigh and Holt, 2000).

**Table16.3 Goodness-of-fit for alternative conditional heteroskedastic models**

| Model[1] | MSE | AIC | SBC | Insignificant Coefficients |
|---|---|---|---|---|
| AR(1) | 73.73 | 3234.68 | 3238.79 | None |
| ARCH(1) | 73.50 | 3228.23 | 3244.68 | $\delta$ [2] |
| ARCH(2) | 73.50 | 3216.11 | 3236.68 | $\delta$ |
| ARCH(3)[3] | 73.50 | 3216.11 | 3236.68 | $\delta, \alpha_3$ |
| GARCH(1,1) | 73.62 | 3213.69 | 3234.26 | $\delta$ |
| GARCH(1,2) | 73.50 | 3216.11 | 3236.68 | $\delta$ |
| GARCH(2,1) | 73.49 | 3235.01 | 3255.58 | $\alpha_1, \gamma_1, \gamma_2$ |
| GARCH(2,2) | 73.49 | 3236.99 | 3261.67 | $\alpha_1, \alpha_2, \gamma_1, \gamma_2$ |

*Notes*:

1. No constant term is included in the above processes, because it was estimated as insignificant in all the models.
2. $\delta$ is the coefficient for the contract switching dummy in the mean equation.
3. Higher order of ARCH and GARCH models are not stable in estimation.

*4.2 Model Comparison*

Based on the model selection criteria used previously, the AR(1), ARCH(2), and GARCH(1,1) models based on the first difference price are selected for analysis. These models can be summarized as:

$$Z_t = \phi Z_{t-1} + \delta SD_t + \varepsilon_t \tag{4}$$

where $Z_t = P_t - P_{t-1}$ ,

$$SD_t = D_t - D_{t-1}$$

$$\varepsilon_t \mid \Omega_{t-1} \sim N(0, h_t) ,$$

$$h_t = \begin{cases} h, & \text{for } AR(1) \\ \omega + \alpha_1 \varepsilon_{t-1}^2 + \alpha_2 \varepsilon_{t-2}^2, & \text{for } ARCH(2) \\ \omega + \alpha_1 \varepsilon_{t-1}^2 + \gamma_1 h_{t-1}, & \text{for } GARCH(1,1) \end{cases}$$

$P_t$ denotes the price at time $t$. The expected long-run equilibrium variance for each of the model is: $h$; $\frac{\omega}{1-\alpha_1-\alpha_2}$; and $\frac{\omega}{1-\alpha_1-\gamma_1}$, respectively.

Table 16.4 gives the regression estimates from the models, with standard errors shown in parentheses. Generally, the three models yield close results in terms of signs as well as magnitudes. The positive value of about 112 for the switching dummy coefficient $\delta$ in all three models corresponds to an increase in price level when the contract switches from May 2001 to May 2002. The standard error of the estimates, however, increases substantially from AR(1) to GARCH(1,1) and ARCH(2). Thus only in AR(1) model is the switching effect significant. A possible explanation might be that the switching effect is absorbed by the specified error terms in the ARCH or GARCH model. The switching point is right in the summer, when the price is very volatile. Other large price changes occurring in close proximity to the switch make the contract switching price jump similar to one of the natural price changes (Figure 16.3).

All three models generate a positive and significant estimate around 0.15 for the AR parameter. This indicates the current change in price is positively associated with the price change in the last period. This relationship is as expected for two reasons. First, the price has a tendency to keep increasing or decreasing over a few months, which makes the daily price difference to maintain the same sign over that period (Figure 16.2). Second, the ARCH/GARCH property shows large price changes tend to be followed by other large ones and smaller changes by smaller ones. Therefore, a previous price change contributes positively in both sign and magnitude to current price change.

For the specified error structure, the AR(1) model gives the estimated constant variance of the price change as 73.73. Variance in the ARCH model is primarily due to the constant term, with less than 20 percent of the two past errors contributing to current variance. The long-run equilibrium variance of the ARCH model is 73.10. Similarly, the GARCH model also indicates the current variance is not influenced much by the past shocks but largely by the past variance. The long-run equilibrium variance for the GARCH model is 77.50. The GARCH model behaves better than ARCH because it describes the error term with more flexibility, and all estimates have consistently smaller standard errors.

Overall, the estimates of the three models are consistent, but the difference in error structure is important. The AR(1) has a nice fit because all the parameters are significant. AR(1) also has a smaller standard error associated with the parameter estimate for the switching dummy. However, AR(1) fails to capture an important characteristic of the futures price. Large (small) price changes tend to be followed by other large (small) ones. The ARCH and GARCH models outperform AR(1) in that both models capture the time-varying volatility as indicated by the significance of the conditional heteroskedastic parameters. ARCH(2) has a nice fit in terms of standard errors compared with GARCH(1,1), while the latter statistically shows the impact of the previous variance on the current variance. GARCH(1,1) also fits the data best in terms of AIC and SBC.

**Table 16.4 Regression estimates from the three selected models**

| | |
|---|---|
| AR(1) | $Z_t^1 = 0.13^{*2} Z_{t-1} + 112.54^* SD_t + \varepsilon_t$ , <br> (0.0402) (8.6289) <br> $h_t = 73.72, \ \forall t$ |
| ARCH(2): | $Z_t = 0.14^* Z_{t-1} + 112.68 SD_t + \varepsilon_t$ <br> (0.0483) (898.807) <br> $h_t = 58.48^* + 0.07^* \varepsilon_{t-1}^2 + 0.13^* \varepsilon_{t-2}^2$ <br> (2.9896) (0.0365) (0.0468) |
| GARCH(1,1): | $Z_t = 0.16^* Z_{t-1} + 112.19 SD_t + \varepsilon_t$ <br> (0.0481) (159.1601) <br> $h_t = 4.65^* + 0.085^* \varepsilon_{t-1}^2 + 0.856^{*3} h_{t-1}$ <br> (1.9455) (0.0202) (0.0391) |

*Notes*:
1. $Z_t = P_t - P_{t-1}$.
2. "*" indicates significance at 0.05.
3. Because the long-run equilibrium variance for GARCH(1,1) is sensitive to the parameters, we report three digits here.

*4.3 Forecasting*

Besides parameter estimation, the forecasting power of the models is also of interest. Because the three models have different variance structures, instead of giving the predicted value alone which is the expected value of the future price conditional con current information, we also provide information on the variability of the future price. The forecast of China's futures prices for the next ten trading days ($P_{t+1}$ to $P_{t+10}$) are obtained using the fitted models just discussed. Table 16.5 shows these short-term predicted values of the CZCE wheat futures prices. The realized true values from the CZCE are also shown for comparison purpose.

Generally all three models perform well in terms of forecasting. The predicted values behave similarly to the true values and converge. Despite the difference in model specification, the three models yield similar predicted prices, only the magnitudes increase slightly from AR(1), ARCH(2), to GARCH(1,1). This increase in magnitude is as expected due to the following:

Based on model (4) we have:

$$P_{t+s} = P_t + \sum_{i=1}^{s} Z_{t+i}, \tag{5}$$

where $Z_{t+i} = \delta \sum_{j=1}^{i} \phi^{i-j} SD_{t+j} + \phi^i Z_t + \sum_{j=1}^{i} \phi^{i-j} \varepsilon_{t+j}$

From current time $t$, predictions are for $s$ periods ahead. The switching dummy term vanishes since May 24, 2002 (the contract switching period) is not in the forecasted time periods. Because the shocks have a zero mean, taking expectation on equation (5), we have:

$$E(P_{t+s} \mid \Omega_t) = P_t + Z_t \sum_{i=1}^{s} \phi^i \tag{6}$$

This equation is same for the AR(1), ARCH(2) and GARCH(1,1) models. Providing the same information on $P_t$ and $Z_t$, the prediction difference for the alternative models is caused by the different estimated values of $\phi$.

All three models have positive estimators for $\phi$, and $Z_t$ is also positive.[8] Additionally, $\frac{\partial E(P_{t+s} \mid \Omega_t)}{\partial \phi} = Z_t \frac{\partial \sum_{i=1}^{s} \phi^i}{\partial \phi} = Z_t \sum_{i=1}^{s} i\phi^{i-1}$, which is positive. Thus, the predicted price is affected positively by $\phi$. According to the estimation results in Table 16.4, GARCH has the largest $\phi$ value, 0.16, followed by the ARCH estimate of 0.14 and the AR, 0.13. These values are consistent with the progressively higher predicted values shown in table 16.5.

As expected, the predicted prices have the same pattern for all three models, and differ only by the numerical difference in $\phi$. However, the three models have distinct implications. The volatility of the future levels conditional on current information is different for each model.

[8] Zt =13 at the end of our historical sample.

**Table 16.5 Short-term forecast of CZCE wheat futures prices for May contract**

| Date | 04/10/02 | 04/11/02 | 04/12/02 | 04/15/02 | 04/16/02 | 04/17/02 | 04/18/02 | 04/19/02 | 04/22/02 | 04/23/02 |
|---|---|---|---|---|---|---|---|---|---|---|
| True Value | 1215[1] | 1213 | 1215 | 1217 | 1217 | 1220 | 1220 | 1220 | 1221 | 1219 |
| AR(1) | 1215.65 | 1215.85 | 1215.88 | 1215.89 | 1215.89 | 1215.89 | 1215.89 | 1215.89 | 1215.89 | 1215.89 |
| 90% interval[2] | ± 14.12 | ± 20.61 | ± 25.57 | ± 29.72 | ± 33.35 | ± 36.63 | ± 39.64 | ± 42.43 | ± 45.05 | ± 47.53 |
| *SSE=98.4* | | | | | | | | | | |
| ARCH(2) | 1215.78 | 1216.02 | 1216.06 | 1216.06 | 1216.06 | 1216.06 | 1216.06 | 1216.06 | 1216.06 | 1216.06 |
| 90% interval | ± 13.80 | ± 21.11 | ± 26.09 | ± 30.25 | ± 33.86 | ± 37.11 | ± 40.09 | ± 42.86 | ± 45.47 | ± 47.93 |
| *SSE=92.2* | | | | | | | | | | |
| GARCH(1,1) | 1216.11 | 1216.45 | 1216.51 | 1216.52 | 1216.52 | 1216.52 | 1216.52 | 1216.52 | 1216.52 | 1216.52 |
| 90% interval | ± 11.60 | ± 17.19 | ± 21.56 | ± 25.29 | ± 28.63 | ± 31.68 | ± 34.52 | ± 37.20 | ± 39.74 | ± 42.17 |
| *SSE=78.5* | | | | | | | | | | |

*Notes*: 1. Unit: Yuan/Ton. 2. The value is computed by ± (1.645 × standard deviation).

$$Var(P_{t+s} \mid \Omega_t) = Var(\sum_{i=1}^{s}\sum_{j=1}^{i}\phi^{i-j}\varepsilon_{t+j})$$

$$= \begin{cases} h\sum_{i=1}^{s}\sum_{j=1}^{i}\phi^{i-j} = h\sum_{i=0}^{s-1}(s-i)\phi^{i}, & AR(1) \\ \sum_{i=1}^{s}\sum_{j=1}^{i}\phi^{i-j}h_{t+j}, & ARCH(2)/GARCH(1,1) \end{cases} \quad (7)$$

These volatilities measure how much the true price can deviate from its predicted values. The volatility keeps increasing as the predicting horizon extends in all three models, which implies the long-term prediction is less accurate than the short-term prediction. Furthermore, the AR model's volatility path follows a deterministic pattern, while ARCH and GARCH models' volatility paths are stochastic.

Because the error terms are assumed normally distributed, the 90 percent confidence intervals for each model are calculated based on the volatility predictions from (7) and reported in table 16.5. According to the 90 percent confidence intervals, all three models incorporate the realized true values in the forecasting period with 90 percent confidence, and GARCH(1,1) yields narrower ranges in all periods than ARCH(2) and AR(1), due to smaller prediction variances. This means the GARCH(1,1) model can give a more efficient prediction than the other two models at the same confidence level. Also in terms of sum of squared prediction errors, GARCH(1,1) shows better fit than ARCH(2) and AR(1). Based on these out-of-sample data, the prediction results imply that GARCH(1,1) outperforms ARCH(2) and AR(1).

## 5 Conclusions

China's agricultural commodity futures markets have been available for about a decade. The futures price can be used as a predictor for the spot market price if the market is efficient. This study has investigated the futures price movement by fitting three types of time series models to the historical prices in an attempt to identify the best model. This effort is important and meaningful to futures studies on market efficiency and price prediction, which can lead to better policy and trading decisions.

The futures prices in CZCE for the wheat contract maturing in May for 2000-2002 followed an almost pure random walk except for a jump at the contract switching point of May 24, 2001. Using first difference data, ARMA models are initially applied by assuming the error variance is constant. Results show AR(1) model is the best among all other ARMA candidates. Due to the probable time-varying volatility in the data, the conditional heteroskedasticity models are then examined. Compared to AR(1), both ARCH(2) and GARCH(1,1) models improve the goodness of fit relative to the error structures. The performance of GARCH(1,1) is similar to its ARCH(2) counterpart with a slight improvement in estimation.

The fitness of the models is further examined in terms of forecasting performances. Out-of-sample prediction evaluation indicates the three selected models, AR(1), ARCH(2) and GARCH(1,1), provide close results to the mean level of the true values. The GARCH model still performs the best, which is consistent with the evaluation in in-sample estimation.

The GARCH model based on first difference data accounts for time-varying volatility and excess kurtosis in daily prices and dominates the other models for our selected China's wheat futures price. Thus, the GARCH model is recommended as an important empirical method for future analyses of the price behavior in China's wheat futures market. GARCH effects in other commodity futures prices in China should also be tested when these prices are involved in time series analysis. Moreover, this result is consistent with results from the studies of commodity futures prices around the world, showing that futures prices in China behave in a similar way as futures prices in other countries.

## References

Ardeni, P.G., 'Does the Law of One Price Really Hold'?, *American Journal of Agricultural Economics*, 71(3) (1989): 661-669.

Baillie, R.T. Myers, R.J., 'Bivariate GARCH Estimation of the Optimal Commodity Futures Hedge', *Journal of Applied Econometrics*, 6(2) (1991): 109-124.

Bollerslev, T., 'Generalized Autoregressive Conditional Heteroskedasticity', *Journal of Econometrics*, 31(3) (1986): 307-327.

Box, G.E.P. Cox, D.R., 'An Analysis of Transformations', *Journal of the Royal Statistical Society*, Series B (1964): 211-264.

Box, G.E.P. Jenkins, D., *Time Series Analysis: Forecasting and Control*, 2nd ed (San Francisco: Holden-Day, 1984).

CZCE Report, http://www.czce.com.cn/Publish/research/200108/498.asp, April 14, 2002.

Durham, C. Si, W., 'The Dalian Commodity Exchange's Soybean Futures Contract: China's Integration with World Commodity Markets', *Chinese Agriculture and the WTO Proceedings* (Western Coordinating Committee, December 1999).

Engle, R.F., 'Autoregressive Conditional Heteroskedasicity with Estimation of the Variance of U.K. Inflation', *Econometrica*, 50(4) (1982): 987-1008.

Fan, Y., Ding, X. and Wang, H., 'Factors Affecting the Development of Agricultural Commodity Futures Markets in China', *Farm Economic Management*, 1 (1999): 35-36.

Haigh, M.S. Holt, M.T., 'Hedging Multiple Price Uncertainty in International Grain Trade', *American Journal of Agricultural Economics*, 82(4) (2000): 881-896.

Ke, B. Wang, H.H., 'Efficiency of the Chinese Agricultural Commodity Markets', *CES Annual Conference, The Integration of the Greater Chinese Economics: Causes, Consequences, and Implications* (Hong Kong, June 2002).

Myers, R.J., 'Time Series Econometrics and Commodity Price Analysis: A Review', *Review of Marketing and Agricultural Economics*, 62(2) (1994): 167-182.

Myers, R.J. Hanson, S.D., 'Pricing Commodity Options when the Underlying Futures Price Exhibits Time-Varying Volatility', *American Journal of Agricultural Economics,* 75(1) (1993): 121-130.

Tao, J. and Lei, H., 'Futures Market and the Grain Circulation Reform', *Economic Problems*, 9 (1998): 29-31.

Tomek, W.G. Myers, R.J., 'Empirical Analysis of Agricultural Commodity Prices: A Viewpoint', *Review of Agricultural Economics*, 15(1) (1993): 180-202.

Williams, J., Peck, A., Park, A. and Rozelle, S., 'The Emergence of a Futures Market: Mung Beans on the China Zhengzhou Commodity Exchange', *Journal of Futures Markets*, 18(4) (1998): 427-448.

Yao, C., *Stock Market and Futures Market in the People's Republic of China* (Oxford Express, Oxford, New York, 1998).

Yang, S.R. Brorsen, B.W., 'Nonlinear Dynamics of Daily Cash Prices', *American Journal of Agricultural Economics*, 74(3) (1992): 706-715.

Yang, J. Leatham, D.J., 'Price discovery in Wheat Futures Markets', *Journal of Agricultural and Applied Economics*, 31(2) (1999): 359-370.

Zhu, L. Zhu, J., 'Futures Market and Contract Agriculture', *Journal of Zhengzhou Grain College*, 21 (2000): 29-34.

# Index